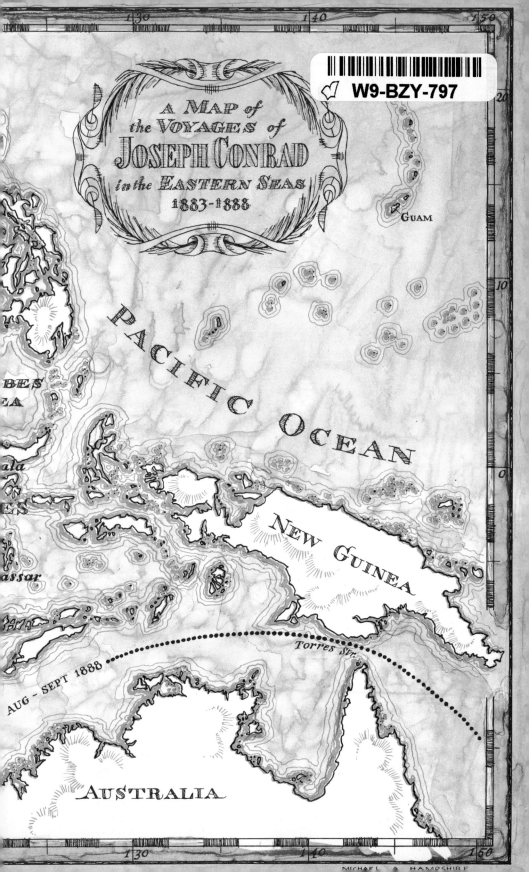

A MAP of
the VOYAGES of
JOSEPH CONRAD
in the EASTERN SEAS
1883-1888

W9-BZY-797

GUAM

PACIFIC OCEAN

NEW GUINEA

CELEBES

assar

AUG – SEPT 1888

Torres Str.

AUSTRALIA

THE SEA YEARS OF JOSEPH CONRAD

BOOKS BY JERRY ALLEN

The Sea Years of Joseph Conrad

The Thunder and the Sunshine, A BIOGRAPHY OF JOSEPH CONRAD

The Adventures of Mark Twain, A BIOGRAPHY

Hearth in the Snow

THE SEA YEARS OF
JOSEPH CONRAD

BY JERRY ALLEN

DOUBLEDAY & COMPANY, INC., GARDEN CITY, NEW YORK, 1965

Library of Congress Catalog Card Number 65-19927

Copyright © 1965 by Jerry Allen

All Rights Reserved

Printed in the United States of America

First Edition

To

Francis R. Drake

PREFACE

No one lived life more fiercely than Conrad, said one who knew him for many years, André Gide, and "no one since has subjected life to as enduring, as aware, and as wise a transmutation into art." Gide's words, after forty years, still ring true. In the new look being taken at the author fitting our day better than he did his own, the international rediscovery of Conrad now under way, he is seen both as an "ancestor" of modern fiction, literary father of authors as varied as Hemingway, Faulkner and Graham Greene, and as a valid interpreter of the uneasy world we know. One reason for the "eminent place in international letters which is his today," suggests the French scholar Raymond Las Vergnas, is that his work carries "a message having an affinity with the anxieties of our times"—this age of anxiety atomic power and two world wars have produced. The place he occupies in letters is as the English critic Walter Allen now gives it: "Conrad's best work represents a body of achievement unequaled in English fiction this century by any writer except James."

A corollary of the current Conrad revival which, says DeLancey Ferguson, "bids fair to outdistance even the Henry James and D. H. Lawrence cults," is the wish to know how much was true. If Conrad's greatness lies above all in the "absolutely convincing illusion of reality" of his stories, as Carlos Baker believes, this sense of the actual, "the very head and front of the art of fiction," has much to do in Conrad's case with actuality itself, not invention. Reticent and expansive by turn, complex always, he was by all odds the most mystifying novelist in English literature. Being to an unusual degree an autobiographical novelist, the vital connection between his experiences and his work has caused old questions to be asked again: What *was* his life and the fierce living Gide referred to?

Something of the romance of his sailing-ship era was felt by the crowds who watched as tall, square-rigged windjammers such as Conrad knew, phantoms out of the past as they were called, sailed in a fleet of twenty-three sailing ships from thirteen countries across New York harbor and up the Hudson in July, 1964. Not since the turn of the century had an American port seen a like flotilla, a gathering, said the *New York Times*, "such as may never be witnessed again." The stately, silent ships moving under full canvas in a light breeze were as beautiful as they were awesome. On square-riggers looking very much like these Conrad sailed about the world. Some he shipped on were similar in size to the American *Eagle* and the Norwegian *Christian Radich* New York saw in the 1964 "sail-past," as New York once saw his *Highland Forest* and Baltimore his *Narcissus*. It is against the background of that day when harbors were filled with wind-driven ships, when the sea was friend or foe but never neutral, that these events are told.

At sixty-six Conrad died of a heart attack, on August 3, 1924, in his rented home of Oswalds in Kent, afflicted with a crippling illness during the latter half of his life. Due to his long illness the image of him retained in the public's memory is of a man aged and worn producing his work with meticulous care in secluded country homes in England. To his contemporaries, such as Arnold Bennett who, only ten years younger, alluded to him as "that poor tired old man," he was a withdrawn, embattled recluse. But for twenty years of his young manhood he lived an adventurous life at sea, in the final days of sailing ships. The experiences of those furiously active years, woven into his novels and short stories, formed the outlook of the writer whose singular honor was to be rated an English classic in his own lifetime.

Because there were so few parts of the world he did not know, the wide geography of his fiction links him with our own globe-shrunken age in a way seeming to abolish the time between. Added to the physical one-worldness he offers are issues familiar to us: his outlook and the problems he wrote of bring home to present-day readers, as Walter Allen points out, "how essentially modern he is. . . . The world Conrad describes, the moral dilemmas facing his characters, are those we know today, that seem to us now, as someone has said, almost to have come into existence in 1940." The American critic Morton Dauwen Zabel finds this same timeliness in Conrad: "The world of his books is one whose dimensions, conflicts, and conditions have become much more familiar to most people during the past thirty or forty years than they ever were in Conrad's own lifetime. The physical globe has shrunk and become constricted through rapid travel and communication, quick-flying news and information services, international crises, and notably through the wars that have not only divided and estranged nations but thrown them into a closer intimacy of knowledge, a more intense community of action and conflict, than even the Nineteenth Century knew."

A gifted, sensitive, intellectual youth with a bent for exploration and a strong sense of daring, a roamer without home ties, Conrad came to look upon mankind not as nationals or races but as people, simply. Those he defended, if defended is the word for his compassionate but clear-eyed portraits, were the nonbelonging, outsiders as detached from the mainstream as himself. In advance of his time as a novelist, out of key with the narrow concerns of the empire-building era he lived through, he was strides ahead of that period's point of view. Where the Victorians and Edwardians of his day were content with the visible, dismissing introspection as a disease, he probed beneath the surface: long before Freud's work was translated into English or known abroad he wrote *Lord Jim.* Of this psychological novel one question has repeatedly been asked, as it is asked today by V. S. Pritchett in *The Living Novel & Later Appreciations:* "Why did he write *Lord Jim?*" In the answer to it, it has always been believed, lies a major clue to the make of mind of the author for whom, out of bafflement, has come the term used for him, the "Conrad enigma."

What experiences during his sea years molded his views, shaped him into an "original" of his time, have been largely unknown. Questions about his life, unanswered in his lifetime and in the years since 1924, have added to the mystery surrounding him. Did he, as he claimed, fight a duel in his youth? Who was the American with whom he fought it? What true sea tragedy did he develop in that universally listed masterpiece *The Nigger of the Narcissus?* What episode in the Congo led to "Heart of Darkness," the short story with insights for the Africa of today? What country in the Caribbean, what contacts with revolution there, gave him the background for "the greatest novel in English in this century," *Nostromo?* Was there an actual person behind Tom Lingard, the character with so many of the qualities Conrad admired? There is also the question of what turned him to writing. On a river in Borneo, in a settlement so long hunted for and only now finally identified, lived the people who became the scalawags and heroes of his earliest stories. Conrad's reluctance to supply details of the dramas in his life, and the impression he gave of inscrutability—even to such a devoted admirer as Hugh Walpole he was "too mysterious"—instilled a doubt that has lingered on. His almost-melodramatic episodes, it was broadly suggested, were less real than imagined.

To combat this fallacy he had planned to tell in a new book of the people he had known in the course of his world-wide roving. Only a bare start had been made on that volume of autobiography: it was the initial chapter "Legends" he was writing the day before he died. It was all to come from his memory. So little relating to his sea life was found among his papers after his death that it seemed the extraordinary history must remain as incomplete as he had left it. He had related episodes out of that past in conversation over the years and those who listened to his storytelling were, without exception, impressed with the wonder of his tales. No Boswell, however, jotted down his reminiscences; the incidents lying behind his fiction were heard and then forgotten.

One who knew much about his life was Henry James, a friend for twenty years. James marveled at the "immense treasure," the "prodigy of your past experiences" which supplied Conrad with the wealth of material he drew upon for his books. The colorful career of the author who found it difficult to invent, and had so little need to, prompted James to write Conrad on November 1, 1906:

"No one has *known*—for intellectual use—the things you know, and you have, as the artist of the whole matter, an authority that no one has approached."

Extolling the use Conrad made of his "inexhaustible adventures," James went on: "I read you as I listen to rare music—with deepest depths of surrender, and out of those depths I emerge slowly and reluctantly again to acknowledge that I return to life. . . . You knock about in the wide waters of expression like the raciest and boldest of privateers,—you have made the whole place your own . . . you stir me, in fine, to amazement and you touch me to tears, and I thank the powers who so mysteriously let you loose with such sensibilities, into such an undiscovered country."

Conrad's style, the poetry and originality of it, has continued to be as absorbing to others as it was to James. It is doubtful if any other novelist of recent times has had the form of his work, and the meaning, subjected to as many studies. In Western languages alone more than three thousand critical items had been published by 1955 and each year since has brought new additions.

Exerting as strong an appeal as the work itself has been the life the work came from. With the confusing trail of his odyssey often lost—it reached back, in time, to the "gilded age" of the Third Republic in France, while the places involved add up to a list of gazetteer proportions—very little was ever published. What did appear was largely the work of the biographer Conrad had chosen, G. Jean-Aubry. In *Joseph Conrad: Life and Letters* and *Vie de Conrad (The Sea Dreamer)* Jean-Aubry gave the results of careful research engaging him for twenty years. Basic sources for Conrad's history as they still are, they dealt only briefly with his sea years. A comprehensive account was lacking for good reasons. No one on any of Conrad's voyages wrote of him, or wrote of the events of the voyage—never was there a recorder on board such as Magellan had in Pigafetta—and of the letters Conrad wrote throughout his twenty years of seafaring a mere handful have survived. With the exception of a terse day-by-day record of his trek through the Congo he kept no diary, no journal of any kind. Two small volumes, of which one alone was wholly concerned with his sea career, constituted his autobiography.

What would have told so much were the letters he wrote while at sea to his uncle in Poland, Thaddeus Bobrowski, but there is no evidence to show they were ever saved by the disapproving relative who received them. With none of these letters of Conrad's to go by (they would have given a running account of his life between 1874 and 1894), substitute papers—the uncle's replies, scolding comments Conrad chanced to keep —have been heavily depended upon by biographers. Too heavily, it proves, for a less reliable reporter than Uncle Thaddeus would be difficult to find. Living in Poland, he knew only what his nephew for reasons of his own chose to write him; his statements conflicted, the few facts he gave were often askew, and his attitude to Conrad, as to others, was belittling and caustic: when his *Memoirs* were published in Poland in 1900, writes Zdzislaw Najder in *Conrad's Polish Background*, they "created an uproar: they are full of malicious gossip and scornful opinions about most of the people he knew." He was also "ready to sacrifice truth." His letters to Conrad and the notebook he kept of his nephew's expenses, the "Bobrowski Document,"—all handwritten in Polish—have received varying, even contradictory, English translations; for this volume the originals of these and other family papers, a total of two hundred and fifty items photocopied in Poland especially for this study, are the texts used.

When this book was begun ten years ago it was in the belief that the happenings and the people Conrad had planned to write of could, through research of preserved records, be traced down the years from 1874. The earliest findings, given in *The Thunder and the Sunshine*, were published while a full-time hunt for documents, scattered over the world, went on. In a crisscrossing of his routes of seventy to ninety years ago records written in Malay, Dutch, Spanish, Polish, French and English have been found along the trail he made and in places he never reached: Marseilles, Toulon, Genoa, Bastia, ports in Australia and Borneo, cities and villages in England, Scotland, Wales and the United

States, Spain, New Zealand, Poland, Aden, Singapore, Paris, Holland, Java, the islands and the countries of the Caribbean. In the various parts of the world Conrad knew are the readers of his novels—he is read today in almost every language—and they, enriched by him and for that reason devoted to him, have unearthed many of the sources brought into the history given here.

By his art, Conrad transmuted actual events into enduring fiction. Minor events as the great world goes, they concerned "a few individuals out of all the disregarded multitudes of the bewildered, the simple and the voiceless," those whose stories he re-created in, among others, *Lord Jim, The Nigger of the Narcissus,* "Heart of Darkness," *Almayer's Folly, An Outcast of the Islands, The Arrow of Gold, Nostromo, The Shadow Line.*

It was long after his roving years had ended that Conrad impressed friends as the lonely, backward-looking man Jean-Aubry recalled:

"Huddled into himself, giving an observer the impression he was crushed by the weight of his memories, he sometimes remained for long moments in silence. In the course of a conversation, by means of a name, of a landscape recalled, one saw him sink into a profound meditation, opaque, impenetrable, like a ship plunged out of sight, and none of us at such moments could break this silence, not only out of respect for the reverie of this great mind, but more because of a sort of physical impossibility which literally held you chained, until the moment when he emerged again like a rock the receding wave uncovers. At times these silences had for us something so profound, so anguishing, that one wished to break them at any price. Yet one could not bring oneself to do it."

Conrad turned "for sustenance to memories" for volume after volume of the many-faceted stories he produced, placing in them the people and the places he had known. In this recounting of his sea years he is again the exuberant, volatile young man making the voyages out of which those memories came.

JERRY ALLEN

CONTENTS

LIST OF ILLUSTRATIONS

1. Conrad at twenty-five.
2. St. Pierre, Martinique, in 1875. (A. D. Edwardes Collection)
3. Mount Pelée eruption. (Courtesy of The American Museum of Natural History)
4. Cartagena, Colombia. (Courtesy of The New-York Historical Society, New York City)
5. William H. Aspinwall. (Courtesy of The New-York Historical Society, New York City)
6. Vieux Port of Marseilles. (Chambre de Commerce de Marseille)
7. Paula de Somoggy. (Author's collection)
8. Don Carlos. (Courtesy of The New-York Historical Society, New York City)
9. Thaddeus Bobrowski. (Courtesy of the Jagellon Library, Cracow, Poland)
10. Page of the "Bobrowski Document." (Courtesy of the Jagellon Library, Cracow, Poland)
11. Apollo Korzeniowski. (Courtesy of the Jagellon Library, Cracow, Poland)
12. Wool clippers at Circular Quay, Sydney. (A. D. Edwardes Collection, New South Wales Government Printer)
13. Spain's Costa Brava. (Spanish National Tourist Office, New York City)
14. The *Falls of Halladale*. (A. D. Edwardes Collection)
15. The *Pero Alemquer*. (A. D. Edwardes Collection)
16. The Pool of London. (National Maritime Museum, London)
17. Sailing ships in New York. (J. Duffett)
18. *Loch Etive*. (A. D. Edwardes Collection)
19. Wrecks off the coast of England. (Courtesy of The New-York Historical Society, New York City)
20. Bangka Strait. (Standard Oil Co. of N.J.)
21. Singapore. (National Maritime Museum, London)
22. Portion of Agreement and Account of Crew of *Tilkhurst*. (General Register and Record Office of Shipping and Seamen, Cardiff)
23. Augustine Podmore Williams. (Mrs. Vallory Wise)
24. The *Narcissus*. (Dan McDonald)
25. The *Tilkhurst*. (National Maritime Museum, London)
26. Calcutta waterfront. (National Maritime Museum, London)
27. Campbell's Wharf, Sydney. (A. D. Edwardes Collection)
28. Portion of 1887 navigation chart. (Survey Department, Federation of Malaya)

PART ONE
THE SHORE

I

In all these households she could hear stories of political outrage; friends, relatives, ruined, imprisoned, killed in the battles of senseless civil wars. . . . And on all the lips she found a weary desire for peace.

Nostromo

Revolution after revolution flamed through Latin America that year. Seven countries were embroiled in civil war: Cuba, Colombia, Haiti, Santo Domingo, Mexico, Peru and Argentina. Hurricanes, "the worst in living memory," added to chaos in the Caribbean, the late summer and autumn storms of this year of 1876 inflicting losses unequaled in fifty years. From July 19 when the first of the high winds struck Jamaica until November 3 when the last reached Nicaragua—"such stormy weather never before experienced on this coast"[1]—disastrous hurricanes scourged the "American Mediterranean." Key West, Havana, Puerto Rico, from the Leeward Islands to those in Bartlett Deep, from cities and towns buried under debris poured news of casualties: the island of Vieques leveled to the ground; homes crushed, ships capsized by winds which "ignoring alike wood, wall and iron" whipped St. Thomas; 170 homes demolished on Grand Cayman, 215 on St. Martin; ships and wharves a tangled mass of wreckage in the harbors, vessels driven ashore, cattle washed into the sea; sugar cane, rice and coffee crops ruined; trade at a standstill. As civil wars circled the Caribbean the tragic news mounted: towns burned in Cuba in the bloody guerrilla fighting of the Ten Years' War; armies marshaled in Colombia where government and rebel forces in a battle lasting seven hours left "1,000 killed and over that number wounded"[2] on the field; governments overthrown in Mexico, Haiti, Santo Domingo, others on the verge of toppling.

The combined havoc of civil wars and hurricanes so much paralyzed Caribbean trade that few engaged in that commerce continued as un-scathed as the giant New York financial house of Howland & Aspinwall. A massive banking and brokerage concern with world-wide holdings, it held within its chain of control ships and railroads and mines and banks and insurance companies throughout Latin America, the East and West Indies, the Mediterranean and Pacific. A king of the financial world, pos-sessing not only the Pacific Railroad across the Isthmus of Panama—a key link between America's east and west coasts in this time before the Panama Canal was built—but the Pacific Mail Steamship Company and its fleet of ships, the firm dominated the water-rail traffic between New York and San Francisco. Holding a monopoly of the American trade with Venezuela and nearly that with Mexico, having agents in its service and ships bearing its flag in almost every port of the Caribbean, it was a house without a rival on that sea. The trade slowdown in this single segment of its vast commercial empire was of minor consequence to Howland & Aspinwall. But the small 432-ton French barque *Saint-Antoine*, coming from Marseilles to the West Indies on the lookout for cargo, sailed in ballast or, like many others, carried arms to the countries fighting.

Into this rarely peaceful but rarely so embattled part of the world, encountering revolution at first hand in Colombia and Haiti, caught at sea in the worst of the season's hurricanes, Joseph Conrad arrived on the *Saint-Antoine*. He was eighteen.

Slight, with dark brown hair and brilliant brown eyes, he was ener-getic in speech and movement, seldom still in either. "I can be deaf and blind and an idiot if that is the road to my happiness—but I'm hanged if I can be mute," he once wrote his editor Edward Garnett.[3] "Ardent and original," "exceedingly sensitive," "reserved, yet excitable," "able and eloquent"—so he appeared to his uncle, Thaddeus Bobrowski. The boy who had insisted on leaving Poland to go to sea "loves his profession . . . seems to know his job and likes it very much," Thaddeus wrote to a family friend,[4] and "is very much liked by his captains and by sea-men." Referring to an ingrained gallantry always distinguishing Conrad —"his manners are very good—as if he spends all his time in drawing-rooms"—he described his young nephew as "in appearance—quite hand-some" and "quite well-built." Neither short nor tall—"his height to be exact was 5 ft. 8½ in.," his wife told H. G. Wells[5]—he had outgrown a sickly childhood and, while never robust, was strong now in a lean way. An orphan, he had the physical and temperamental make-up of the daredevil stamp earlier sought by the Pony Express: "Wanted: young skinny wiry fellows not over eighteen. Must be . . . willing to risk death daily. Orphans preferred."

Crews on sailing ships took risks unmatched by any other calling (10,827 seamen on the sailing ships of just one nation, Britain, were lost at sea in the seven years of 1873–1880, leading the New York *Herald* to comment that "a bare recital of the facts alone must fill the mind with wonder and with dread"[6]) and this adventurous, roving life, with all its hazards, appealed to young Conrad.

At eighteen, making his third voyage in a year and a half from Marseilles to the West Indies, once as a passenger, once as an apprentice and now as an assistant to the three officers, he found everything "so fresh, so surprising" in the turbulent Caribbean. For nearly four months he sailed the sea blanketed under the general term of "Gulf of Mexico" in the French and English seamen's manuals of the time, a term Conrad ever after retained. From Martinique to the Isthmus of Panama and back again, he stopped in ports along the way. Drawing later upon his experiences then—"I had to *make* material from my own life's incidents," he wrote in an unpublished 1917 letter to A. T. Saunders,[7] a retired shipping agent in Adelaide, Australia—he created *Nostromo*, the novel emerging from the first of the dramatic incidents his sea rover's life supplied.

Nostromo is described today as "one of the most powerful, imaginative and exact political novels in our language, and one which has gathered force and cogency since 1904"[8] by V. S. Pritchett, and as "one of the few mastering visions of our historical moment . . . more solid and significant than most of our actualities"[9] by Robert Penn Warren, and that it remains so timely, sixty-one years after it first appeared, is in some part due to the accuracy of Conrad's eye. "What I claim as true are my mental and emotional reactions to life, to men, and their affairs and their passions as I have seen them," he continued in his letter to Saunders, and what he saw in the Caribbean was an end-of-empire era when the race was to the shrewd. With little beyond Cuba and Puerto Rico remaining in Spain's once great Caribbean empire, her former colonies were now young republics, tottering republics at war with themselves; reservoirs of undeveloped mineral wealth—rich in gold, silver, platinum, copper, emeralds—lands producing sugar, coffee, fruit, cattle and hides, they offered alluring prospects to foreign capital in this get-rich-quick time on the hustle for El Dorado.

While men were rushing to the ends of the earth this year to find the golden land—to Australia, where gold had been discovered at Opossum Hill, sixty miles from Melbourne; to Nevada, where the Big Bonanza of the Comstock lode ($200,000,000 in gold and silver) had been struck three years before and now was drawing thirty thousand hopeful men to Virginia City—the original, nearby El Dorado was scarcely looked at by those hurrying across the Caribbean, across the isthmus, westward.

This legend of treasure, born in Colombia, had lured Spanish conquistadors to the exploration of a continent; had been the well-believed if nebulous land, El Dorado, which early map makers uncertainly shifted here and there; had tantalized the ever searching Sir Walter Raleigh, whose obsession with it aroused the mockery of England. In 1876 men were seeking El Dorado no less than ever and Conrad, observing the power of the dream still, wove it into *Nostromo:*

"There is something in a treasure that fastens upon a man's mind. He will pray and blaspheme and still persevere, and will curse the day he ever heard of it, and will let his last hour come upon him unawares, still believing that he missed it only by a foot."[10]

For 350 years men had been pursuing El Dorado, and by the chance of a voyage he was never to repeat, Conrad saw the country where the myth began. Inland on Colombia's plateau of Bogotá, in the centuries before the white man's coming, was the empire of the Chibcha Indians. A nation under five rulers with an advanced civilization second only to that of the Incas, the empire covered an area the size of Connecticut, held 1,500,000 people; a gold-rich land, the fame of its remarkable Zipa ceremony had spread over South America.

Power and property passed by law of inheritance from uncle to nephew among the Chibchas, but before a nephew of rank could become a Zipa or king he was required to live six years in a cave, fasting, never in that time seeing daylight, never in the presence of a woman. Meeting these tests successfully, the new Zipa was inaugurated in an elaborate ceremony—carried on a platform held by twenty men to the shore of Lake Guatavita where, stripped naked, his body was smeared with resin and sprinkled with gold dust. El Dorado, the golden man, was then rowed out into the lake on a raft piled with gold and emeralds. To win the favor of the god in whose honor the ceremony was held, El Dorado spilled the treasure into the lake, his people on shore making offerings of jewels and gold to the god of waters too. Returning to shore, the Zipa washed away his golden coating and, breaking his six-year fast, celebrated the beginning of his new reign, in a manner long associated with New Years, by becoming gloriously drunk.

The Zipa ceremony was so frequently repeated over centuries of time that word of it spread widely, up through the Isthmus of Panama, down the valley of the Orinoco. Early Spaniards on the isthmus heard Indian tales of El Dorado and set off to find a country where gold was thrown away. Gonzalo Jiménez de Quesada, leading an expedition of 700 soldiers in 1536 into the interior of Colombia, reached the empire of the Chibchas at the end of seventeen months with but 160 of his men still alive. Quesada overawed rather than overpowered the Chibchas and founded Bogotá as a stronghold for Spain, a feat recalled by Santiago Pérez Triana in *Down the Orinoco in a Canoe*. The Colombian diplomat, whom Conrad came to know through their mutual friend Robert Bontine Cunninghame Graham, told in a brief sketch of his country's history how Quesada, clad in full armor and surrounded by a Chibcha crowd at the site of the present Bogotá, "plucked some grass from the ground, and, unsheathing his sword, declared that he took possession of the land for the greater glory of God as the property of his King and Master, Charles V of Spain. Then turning, with a fierce glance, to those who surrounded him, he challenged one and all to single combat should they dare to dispute his action. Naturally, no dispute arose, and so the title was acquired."

The Indians received the Spaniards in a friendly, hospitable way and gave their gold generously, wrote Pérez Triana, but the Spaniards' "cruel greed and insatiable thirst for gold" led to such barbarous treatment of their hosts that hostilities began. In 1564, to end the attraction their country held, the Indians filled in the San Sebastian de la Plata mines, the original source of El Dorado gold, so effectively they were never found again. Quesada, led on by Indian reports that the great gold source was in another direction and far away, set off for the valley of the Orinoco, adding weight to the tales taking Sir Walter Raleigh there.

During two voyages to South America Raleigh searched for El Dorado, believing the fabled land to lie in "the Large, Rich, and Beautiful Empire of Guiana." As thoroughly misled as the Spaniards before him, he showed in the report written after his first voyage how the distortion all tales receive in the telling had made a new story of the original Chibcha rite. "The empire of Guiana," he wrote in 1596, "is directly east from Peru towards the sea, and lieth under the equinoctial line, and it hath more abundance of gold than any part of Peru, and as many or more great cities than ever Peru had when it flourished most . . . as I have been assured by such of the Spaniards as have seen Manoa, the imperial city of Guiana, which the Spaniards call El Dorado, that for the greatness, for the riches, and for the excellent seat, it far exceedeth any of the world."[11]

The first to see Manoa, and give the name of El Dorado to it, was, Raleigh declared, Juan Martinez, "master of the munition" to Diego de Ordaz, explorer of the Amazon. The Guianians being "marvellous great drunkards," they celebrated their solemn feasts in riotous orgies, the Emperor carousing with his captains and governors in the fashion that Raleigh, believing the myth, reported. "All those that pledge him are first stripped naked, and their bodies anointed all over with a kind of white balsam . . . certain servants of the Emperor having prepared gold made into fine powder, blow it through hollow canes upon their naked bodies, until they be all shining from the foot to the head, and in this sort they sit drinking by twenties and hundreds. . . . Upon this sight, and for the abundance of gold which he [Martinez] saw in the city, the images of gold in their temples, the plates, armours, and shields of gold which they use in the wars, he called it El Dorado."[12]

Raleigh never found El Dorado, nor the San Thomé gold mine four hundred miles up the Orinoco, which the aging adventurer of sixty-five believed would make his monarch richer than all others. Without gold from the San Thomé mine, without proof that treasure was ever to be had there for James I, he, who had given England the vast, unmapped tract of Virginia, returned from his final voyage empty-handed, to renewed imprisonment and execution.

From Raleigh's illusory San Thomé mine, the fixed idea of treasure calcifying the mind of one of the most brilliant of Elizabethans, Conrad took the name San Tomé for the all-consuming mine in Nostromo— "hateful and immense, lording it by its vast wealth over the valour, the toil, the fidelity of the poor, over war and peace, over the labours of the town, the sea, and the campo."[13] For the setting of this novel of war and peace he chose the fictional republic of "Costaguana," adopted from the "coast of Guiana" where Raleigh had so vainly searched for his "Treasure House of the World."

II

As it always had been, the gold was still in Colombia in this year of 1876, gold and silver both, to be found together in the mountains behind the high walls of the Cordilleras. The single state of Antioquia, in these Colombian mountains, had exported $2,403,241 in gold and silver the year before. Title to a gold mine was made enticingly easy—a mine of one's own was to be had for $100 down and $6 a year—and extravagant stories circulated to lure gold-seekers on. "In my youth," the Colombian official Vicente Restrepo wrote of this time from Bogotá, "I saw negroes who brought from inaccessible localities lumps of gold many lbs. in weight. They cut them into great pieces with their knives in order to sell them when they needed clothes."[1]

But the "inaccessible localities" posed a problem. "When the railroad affords the introduction of machinery into the mines," the British vice-consul in Medellín, Mr. White, wrote in his 1876 report to London,[2] "it is expected that this state [Antioquia] will be one of the greatest gold-producing countries in South America." The adjoining gold-bearing and silver-rich state of Tolima, he added, "also cries aloud for a railway." Foreign investors in England, America, France and Germany looked hungrily at the gold and silver deposits, even thought of the needed railroads. "The State has proposed rather a novel contract for a railway from the river Magdalena to the capital, a distance of 133 miles," Mr. White urged, "the Government offering to pay $10,000 for every kilometer of rail laid down, plus giving 100,000 hectares of land on the line (land worth a million dollars when the line is opened)."

But Colombia was undergoing another civil war—"one of the natural and periodical diseases of young republics, like measles, scarlet fever, etc. in children," the Panama Star and Herald[3] said of the "diabolical war of barricades" carried on "in spite of the opinion of the majority of the people who seek only to live and let live"—and foreign capital was reluctant to invest in a fighting El Dorado. Three years before, when Colombia's foreign debt exceeded £6,500,000 and her constant civil wars made repayment of that debt unlikely, bondholders, who were largely in Britain, surrendered 60 per cent of their claim in the wan hope that the balance at least might be secured.

Investment was risky in this country of unrest where 90 per cent of the people, illiterate, were poor beyond belief; where power was held by the old feudal landholding class, descendants of early Spanish colonists, who consistently carried their contests for self-enrichment to the point of war, however much the country suffered for it. Despite that past, Colombia had a magnetic appeal for European capital, for her historically coveted Isthmus of Panama and the tempting wealth in her mountains. The greatest emerald mines in the world were here, Muzo and Coscuez, from which Europe's emeralds had come for over three hundred years. The platinum mines were equally famous, the Italian merchant señor Bonolli once shipping so much platinum from Cartagena that the world price fell. Above all there was gold and silver: £41,600,000 produced in the 1800s, most of it by men and women who, as Mr. White reported, worked "with nothing but a crowbar and a spade."

Mr. White was shortly to organize two companies in London to mine this gold and silver, while in France interest was focused on the isthmus. For three centuries trading nations had dreamed of cutting through the spine of land, thirty-five miles wide at its narrowest point, to provide a passageway for ships. Now, in 1876, an organization to build such a ship canal had been formed in France, the Société Civile Internationale du Canal Interocéanique, and Lieutenant Wyse of the French navy was to obtain a concession for it from Colombia—the Wyse Concession as it came to be known all over the world during the ups and downs of a project that was to see mismanagement and corruption on a scale never equaled, bankruptcies, ownership shifted from France to the United States, and the passage of thirty-nine years, not eight years of the original plan—before the Panama Canal was formally opened in 1915 by President Woodrow Wilson.

This ending was far ahead at the time Conrad arrived at the Tierra Firme seaboard, a time when France seemed on the eve of solving a problem that had defeated other nations since 1550. A young seaman on a French ship and with French naturalization in view, he came to the isthmus when a striking new chapter was being written to a history of which he knew so much of the old. The favorite books of his schoolboy years had been about explorers and he now found himself at the scene of earliest discovery and conquest; in the seas of treasure ships and buccaneers, the gold-finders and the gold-keepers; at the "treasure house of all the world," as Sir Francis Drake described this land to his crew. Most of all Conrad had come to the exploration ground of two of his boyhood heroes, Balboa and "the greatest of them all"—Columbus.

Founding the first gold mine in the New World, the San Tomaso mine in today's Dominican Republic, and through his voyages of discovery opening the way for the westward rush for gold, Columbus at the same time provided an early demonstration of the ironies of reward. The wealth of the untapped New World inspired clawing jealousies; caught in the mesh of them, the red-haired explorer of forty-five was returned to Spain from his second voyage to America in chains. On his fourth voyage—seeking a sea route to the Cathay of Marco Polo, the fabulous East credited in Europe to be overflowing with spices, jewels and gold—Columbus reached the isthmus in 1503, believing the Ganges River was but a ten days' sail beyond, and found quantities of gold, the everlasting prize, on the isthmus too. Ten years later Balboa, with an army of seventy men, fought his way across it to discover the Pacific;

his achievement aroused the envy of the Spanish colony's governor Pedrarias and the forty-two-year-old Balboa was beheaded here at Acla. One who attended that beheading, Francisco Pizarro, carried out Balboa's plans, sailed south on the newly found ocean to discover and conquer Peru, in his turn to be assassinated by his supporters in the land he found. And so the cycle of discovery and bitter payment began.

Peru's gold and silver flowed to Spain; portaged across the isthmus on the *camino real*, or royal road, to Porto Bello, the bullion was taken to Cartagena, Queen City of the Spanish Main, for shipment on the famous Plate Fleet. Inevitably, the treasure ships were preyed upon. In the Gulf of Panama, enclosed on the north by the Azuero Peninsula with its projecting tip of Punta Mala (Conrad, finding it "one of the calmest spots on the waters of the globe," retained the names of this Golfo Placido's landmarks in *Nostromo*), Drake captured the rich treasure ship *Cacafuego*, writing in his journal: "We found in her great riches, as jewels and precious stones, thirteen chests full of reals of plate, four score pound weight of gold, and six and twenty ton of silver."

Three centuries later a "vagrant anecdote" about a modern buccaneer, operating in the same Gulf of Panama and making off with a ship loaded with silver bullion, was told to Conrad during his voyage to the Panama coast. It had happened about 1866, according to a young Yankee sailor named Herbert Elliot Hamblen, born in Ossipee, New Hampshire, who spread the story in Aspinwall (now Colón) during the several weeks of the fall of 1873 he spent in that isthmus port. Conrad, hearing a fresh account of it there, and reminded of it in England years later through a secondhand copy of Hamblen's book—*On Many Seas: The Life and Exploits of a Yankee Sailor*, written under the pseudonym of Frederick Benton Williams and edited by William Stone Booth—developed the silver-ship incident in *Nostromo*. As told in *On Many Seas*, a book Conrad felt "gave the most accurate picture of a seaman's life"[4] in his time, the highjacking was done by a "swarthy, piratical-looking fellow" named Captain Nicolo, master and owner of the sixty-ton coasting schooner *Santa Maria*. Nicolo as a boy had landed in Panama, where the shallowness of the bay required all freight to be lightered, and for sixteen years worked for the line owned by Howland & Aspinwall, the Pacific Mail Steamship Company, becoming a captain of their lighters.

"The Isthmus in those days," Hamblen-Williams wrote of 1866, "was an exceedingly turbulent territory, and when a revolution was on, mob law prevailed, and property of all kinds was stolen or destroyed with perfect impartiality.

"During his sixteen years' service, Nicolo had gained the confidence of his superiors to such a degree that, on the breaking out of one of the usual revolutions, he was chosen to take charge of a lighter containing a large and valuable consignment of silver bullion, and his orders were to get it out of Panama as quickly as possible, and take it up the coast to a little port called Chiriqui, and deliver it to the first northbound steamer that should arrive there. He had two negroes for a crew, and left Panama that night." Nicolo killed the two men, threw their bodies overboard, "then he ran the lighter in near the beach, scuttled her, and swam ashore. He tramped back to Panama, arriving there all ragged and scratched, and reported that a big steamer had run him down and refused to stop to pick any of them up, and his crew had both drowned. He himself, being a famous swimmer, had managed to reach shore, and that was all. He returned to work for the company and stayed with them five years longer, and then, taking a holiday, he went to Malme and raised a little of the treasure, and a month afterwards bought a little old sloop, paying only part of the price down, and saying it was all that he had been able to save out of his wages.

"He sailed the old sloop for a year, occasionally visiting his cache, and then traded her off for a schooner. This, in time, he finally traded for the one we were now in, the largest and finest vessel in the coasting trade"—the *Santa Maria*.

Nicolo touched his cache prudently—"I mus git reesh slow, don you see?"—and, according to Hamblen-Williams, who heard the tale from Nicolo while serving with the crew of the *Santa Maria*, was still doing so at least as late as 1873, the year the Yankee seaman deserted that ship at the isthmus port of Esmeralda, made his way to Aspinwall and on from there to an eventual career as railroad engineer and author in New York.

This tale of the rogue Nicolo, Conrad referred to in his introductory note to *Nostromo:* "As a matter of fact, in 1875 or 1876, when very young, in the West Indies, or rather, in the Gulf of Mexico—for my contacts with the land were short, few, and fleeting—I heard the story of some man who had stolen, single-handed, a whole lighterful of silver, somewhere on the Tierra Firme seaboard during the troubles of a revolution."

Hearing it as a youth in 1876 while on a voyage to Colombia, then again in the midst of revolution, Conrad long remembered the story which so ironically illustrated how three centuries of material progress had affected this historic part of the globe. In contrast to the cutthroat, surreptitious Nicolo of the 1870s, lining his own pocket, was the bold, gentleman adventurer of the 1580s, Drake, the most famous Englishman of his day. A superb navigator—first in England to sail around the world, accomplishing in one voyage what Diaz, Vasco da Gama and Magellan, separately, had required a span of over thirty years to do—Drake sailed in the queen's service, for England's profit, not his own. He plundered Cartagena, attacked Spanish settlements in the West Indies, captured Spain's treasure ships, and, rare for any corsair in any time, acted in the manner making him the darling of England. Courteous to the treasure-ship prisoners whom he invariably released, a Robin Hood disbursing reals to the poor among them, a dandy at sea who dined "to the music of viols" off silver dishes, having aboard "all possible dainties and perfumed waters," Drake, himself a painter, carried with him on his long voyages artists and musicians, that he might live at sea with all the refinements of Elizabethan England his ship could hold.

Back at the Isthmus of Panama in 1595, to enrich his queen further at Spain's expense, he was taken ill aboard his ship off the town Columbus had founded, Nombre de Dios; there, having dressed in armor to "meet death like a soldier," he died, his body consigned to the sea where his exploits had begun.

This was the sea Conrad sailed over. At sea, he wrote in "Geography and Some Explorers," "I never felt lonely, because there I never lacked company. The company of great navigators, the first grown-up friends of my early boyhood. The unchangeable sea preserves for one the sense of its past, the memory of things accomplished by wisdom and daring among its restless waves. It was those things that commanded my profoundest loyalty."

The western coast of this sea, the Isthmus of Panama which Balboa had crossed on foot, now had a railroad, brought into existence by the 1848 discovery of gold in California. When the famous strike at Sutter's Mill sent Howland & Aspinwall's San Francisco business booming, the firm sought some means of speedier contact between its offices in California and New York. Sailing ships required from 100 to 150 days to make the passage from New York to San Francisco around Cape Horn, and to reduce this costly loss of time William H. Aspinwall organized and built the Panama Railroad in 1855. In his honor Colón for a time was renamed Aspinwall, and when he died in 1875, in his New York home at 33 University Place, the *New York Times* credited him with a resounding achievement: "Few, if any, among the many enterprising Americans who have obtained a world-wide reputation in commercial affairs can rival that gained by William H. Aspinwall . . . through his efforts with the Panama Railroad . . . the way was opened to direct communication between Asia and America and Oceanica and

Australasia, besides an immense coast line extending from Panama to Behring's Straits."[5]

Aspinwall, described as "a good man, generous if not open-handed, lenient to debtors," never sought a political position, though one of the richest men in the country. Born in New York of English descent, of a family tracing back to the earliest settlers in New England, he was the son of a New York dry goods merchant and began his own career as a clerk in the trading house owned by his uncles, G. G. and S. S. Howland. Socially he was "a modest, retiring, liberal gentleman" who, devoting himself "wholly to his business affairs," had one outside interest, the Society for the Prevention of Cruelty to Animals, of which he was a charter member. The financial house he helped to build into a world commercial power, Howland & Aspinwall, became in *Nostromo* the "house of Holroyd." The "considerable personage" Holroyd, the American financier in that novel, in essence like Aspinwall, speaking in the terms Latin America labeled Yankee imperialism, told of the sweeping intent of American business:

"We shall be giving the word for everything: industry, trade, law, journalism, art, politics, and religion, from Cape Horn clear over to Smith's Sound, and beyond too, if anything worth taking hold of turns up at the North Pole. And then we shall have the leisure to take in hand the outlying islands and continents of the earth. We shall run the world's business whether the world likes it or not. The world can't help it—and neither can we, I guess."[6]

The desire for gain had, from the beginning, been the prime motive for the exploration of this southern continent, as of other parts of the world. Conquest, a footstep behind exploration, had, also from the beginning, been closely tied with religion—with Islam, "the religion of the sword," planted over half the earth and holding sway for nearly twelve centuries; with Christianity, imported to the New World. During the Spanish Conquest soldiers marched behind the banner of the cross, shouting the battle cry of *Espíritu Santo*, erecting churches in this Indian land immediately a foothold was gained.

Conrad, who was to know an Islam world in Borneo, saw the Christian world in conflict in Colombia, where a revolution over a religious issue was under way. Arriving in Cartagena, the city whose gigantic walls thirty feet high had not been strong enough to withstand Drake, he saw how "men die and suffer for their convictions."

Forty-one years later he was reminded of how little change those years had brought. In 1917 his friend Robert Bontine Cunninghame Graham arrived in Cartagena, with a cattle-raising project in mind and to gather material for one of his many books of travel, *Cartagena and the Banks of the Sinú.* In it he wrote of the old white town where "the innumerable church bells jangle and clang," finding that "as all Colombia is a land of priests and pious laymen, or at least of outward, visible conformity, the church's bells are seldom still." He told of the "blue pellucid sea" in which Cartagena lay, the placid gulf Conrad knew —"few ports in the whole world are better sheltered or less exposed to wind." Bandits, terrorizing Colombian villages from earliest times (and a marauding peril still), left gruesome traces of their raids: "Not more than a few months before the evening that I passed at Berástegui, a troop of bandits had attacked the little frontier village of Arauca, put it to sack and pillage, killed the chief magistrate, cut off his head and then played football with it in the square." In the jungle he came to the town of Magangué, "built upon piles and looking like a Dyak village in the Straits of Singapore." He stayed at old mansions in the country near Cartagena, where the owners, all descended from early Spanish settlers, were educated men. "Most of them had been through several revolutions; but all of them saw clearly that their country wanted peace."

While in Colombia, Cunninghame Graham wrote to Conrad, then in England. Relaying the news of "Don Roberto" to a mutual friend, Conrad wrote to Mrs. Dummett on March 29, 1917: "The few lines he gives to Cartagena brought to me for a moment the feeling of my vanished youth. I saw the place for the first and last time in 1875 [1876 in fact]. It seems not to have changed a bit."

Many years before his 1876 voyage to the Caribbean, Conrad's life had been crucially affected by a revolution in the making, the early stages of an uprising in Poland, when he was four. His father, Apollo Korzeniowski, and his mother, born Evelina Bobrowska, were both Polish patriots. The two families, middle-class, well-educated landowners, were similar in wealth and social position, and old—the original Nalecz line of the Korzeniowskis traced back to 1584. Over the generations members of the two families had functioned as army officers, government officials, managers of estates.

Apollo had spent six student years at St. Petersburg University when, in his turn, he became an estate manager, an unsuccessful one, being wholly absorbed with literature and his work as a poet. On a great-uncle's estate near Berdichev in the Ukraine, Conrad, the only child Apollo and Evelina were to have, was born on December 3, 1857. Christened Józef Teodor Konrad Korzeniowski, he contracted the name during his years as a seaman to the one he became known by, Joseph

Conrad—relinquishing the tongue-twisting Korzeniowski which, rarely caught correctly, appeared in shipping documents in such wrenched forms as "Konkorzentowski" and "Korrcuiwski."

Apollo was a passionate, courtly, literary man, as his son was to be. An ardent patriot, he was, like his fellow countrymen, savagely impatient for partitioned Poland—divided for nearly a hundred years between Prussia, Russia and Austria—to become free. In Warsaw in 1861 he became one of the founders of the secret Central Committee whose purpose was to organize the uprising developing as the rebellion of 1863. The Czarist police learned of the Committee shortly after it was formed and Apollo was arrested; after seven months of confinement in Warsaw's citadel, he was sent into exile. Evelina, equally sentenced[7] for her part in the underground activities, was permitted to take her four-year-old son; at the end of a six weeks' carriage journey from Warsaw the family arrived at Vologda in June, 1862. There in Russia's arctic north they became part of the lonely, disheartened and impoverished group of twenty-one Polish exiles. Conrad was the only child.

He played by the bedside of his mother as, her health destroyed in this country of relentless cold and scanty food, she lay ill with tuberculosis. Conrad was seven when she died, in another town of exile, Chernigov, 120 miles north of Kiev. Apollo, shattered by his wife's death, became a melancholy and brooding man, turning to religion with a consuming zeal. In a despair so complete as to resign his role of father too, he referred to his son, the nervous, frequently ill child who was his sole companion, as "the little orphan." Conrad was eleven when his father, freed from exile, died of tuberculosis in Cracow.

Poland honored Apollo as a patriot, a martyr, and a poet, but the son carried a lasting scar from a childhood unrelievedly lonely and tragic. "We all like, in our audacities, to feel something solid at our backs. Such a feeling is unknown to me," Conrad wrote H. G. Wells in 1898.[8] He was then forty, well-launched as an author, the second of his two successful careers. At that time, three and a half years after making his appearance as a writer, he had published four books, seen his stories appear in eight of the leading magazines of England and America. It was a soundly impressive start, his writing from the beginning being highly praised. In a lavish use of space and cascading compliments T. P. O'Connor devoted seven and a half columns in the *Weekly Sun* to a review of Conrad's first novel, *Almayer's Folly*, named by H. G. Wells as one of the best books of the year, and of which H. L. Mencken, an immediate Conrad admirer, flatly declared: "If it is not a work of absolute genius then no work of absolute genius exists on this earth."[9]

Conrad had known an equally quick and remarkable rise in the British merchant marine where, passing from ordinary seaman to commander in ten years, he had become master of a ship at thirty. Arriving as an impoverished foreigner in England without connections, he soared rapidly in two fields opposite in their requirements, yet his own astounding performance failed to reassure him. Imbedded at the age of seven, by his father, was the concept of "orphan," of nonbelonging, which the remaining years of his boyhood did little to relieve.

Upon the death of his father, Conrad came under the guardianship of an uncle, his mother's brother, Thaddeus Bobrowski. Thaddeus was an honest, sincere man, very righteous, hard-headed and parsimonious to an unusual degree. Methodically keeping a financial checklist, tabulating each gift he made to the dependent boy from the age of twelve to manhood, Thaddeus provided in his account book—to become known as the Bobrowski Document—the family's only biographical record of its most famous member. Though the prosperous owner of a large Ukraine estate and a widower whose only child had died, his concern for his ward centered on the costs of maintaining the boy. Noting such small amounts as $25 sent to carry Conrad through five months in Sydney, though substantially aided in his support of Conrad by various family contributions, he gave in his record an indication not only of his closeness but of the bleakness of his understanding. His letters to Conrad, consistently scolding, and those written about him to a family friend, Stefan Buszczynski—"I have not deserted him" was a threatening note—offered thin endorsement to the young nephew he called "our wanderer."

Victorian uncles were not unlike Victorian fathers, both acquiring reputations as frigid parents and guardians. The relationship Conrad had with his uncle ran parallel in many respects to that between Samuel Butler and his austere Victorian father. Butler, who died in England the year Conrad's *Youth* was published, maintained a surface of filial devotion toward his father, who scoffed at every effort of his son, seeming to wish him failure. Upon the death of the elder Butler in 1886, the son added to the outward appearance of harmony by writing an extolling obituary. But in *The Way of All Flesh*, published after the deaths of both father and son, the senior Butler appeared as Theobald Pontifex, the most unpleasant father in the whole of English literature.

In his letters to Conrad, Thaddeus was consistently derisive, writing with heavy-handed sarcasm to the young voyager acutely conscious of being alone and trying to make his way in the extremely rugged and dangerous world he had chosen. Seeing him seldom, Conrad retained an expressed affection for his uncle, the one member of the family with whom he maintained a close tie. Long after Thaddeus' death, when Conrad himself was in his fifties, he wrote of his uncle as "the wisest, the firmest, the most indulgent of guardians, extending over me a paternal care and affection, a moral support which I seemed to feel always near me in the most distant parts of the earth."[10]

But in Conrad's novels and stories uncles and orphans came to figure prominently, and the uncles were far from lovable. Nostromo was "an orphan from his tenderest age . . . with no ties in Italy except an uncle, owner and master of a felucca, from whose ill-usage he had run away before he was fourteen";[11] in "Falk," the heroine, Captain Hermann's niece, was an ill-treated girl, "an orphan and very silent, I never saw attempt a smile"; in *The Arrow of Gold* the orphan Rita was as a child under the care of a harsh, parish priest uncle, a fanatically religious man. Each of the characters escaped to a larger, more welcoming world, and so it was with Conrad.

III

"The principal thing was to get away." In his autobiography, *A Personal Record*, Conrad described his boyhood efforts to leave Poland, holding so few tolerable memories for him, and go to sea. This deep desire, "cried upon as a stupid obstinacy or a fantastic caprice" by his relatives, he first told them of when he was fifteen; for more than a year he battled for it. "I don't mean to say that a whole country had been convulsed by my desire to go to sea. But for a boy between fifteen and sixteen, sensitive enough, in all conscience, the commotion of his little world had seemed a very considerable thing indeed. So considerable that, absurdly enough, the echoes of it linger to this day. I catch myself in hours of solitude and retrospect meeting arguments and finding things to say that an assailed boy could not have found, simply because of the mysteriousness of his impulses to himself."[1]

From his earliest years Conrad had been a "reading boy." The isolation of exile had barred him from the activities and friendships of a normal childhood and, having as both companion and father a literary man absorbed in his work (Apollo, writing poetry and plays, also translated Shakespeare, Dickens, Victor Hugo and Alfred de Vigny into Polish), Conrad had taken to books at a precociously early age. At eight he read his father's translations of Victor Hugo's *Toilers of the Sea* and

Shakespeare's *The Two Gentlemen of Verona*. At eleven his preferred books were the novels of Fenimore Cooper, *The Last of the Mohicans*, *The Deerslayer*, *The Prairie*, read, as he recalled, in that order. The authors he came to know as a boy—Cooper, Shakespeare, Dickens, Turgenev—remained favorites with him, but from other books he drew his heroes, "that special kind of men who devoted the best part of their lives to the exploration of land and sea."[2]

When a schoolboy in Cracow, between the ages of ten and sixteen—five and a half years of formal schooling was all he was ever to have—he read the lives of the great explorers: Columbus, Balboa, Abel Tasman, James Cook, Mungo Park, James Bruce, David Livingstone, Sir John Franklin. They were restless and daring men who explored rivers and continents and seas: the Niger, Blue Nile and Zambesi rivers in Africa; America, New Zealand, Tasmania, Australia, the Arctic and Pacific oceans. Five died in the hostile lands or seas they found, but their discoveries were followed by a tide of emigration as Europeans looked abroad for a new life better than the old.

The promise of the new place was contagious. In the year Conrad left Poland, 1874, over 313,000 moved from Europe to the United States; during the forty-five years ending in 1890 more than 7,000,000 came to New York alone. Young men especially joined the emigration, hopeful, restless, welcoming the challenge the unknown offered. But romance had a part in it too and other European boys than Conrad were affected by the story of Sir John Franklin, a legendary hero during the years he was searched for in the Arctic by more than forty expeditions.

"When I was fifteen years old, the works of Sir John Franklin, the great English explorer, fell into my hands," Roald Amundsen, the Norwegian polar explorer, a few years younger than Conrad, wrote of his life.[3] "I read them with a fervid fascination which has shaped the whole course of my life . . . Sir John's descriptions decided me upon my career. Secretly—because I would never have dared to mention the idea to my mother, who I knew would be unsympathetic—I irretrievably decided to be an Arctic explorer." At twenty-one, an orphan then, he left the university where he had been studying medicine by his mother's wish and set out on the career that, as the first explorer to reach both the North and South Poles and the only one to negotiate both the Northwest and Northeast passages, ended in the Arctic in 1928, lost during a rescue search for Umberto Nobile. Like so many explorers before him, Amundsen began as a seaman.

Young Conrad ("I could imagine myself stepping in the very footprints of geographical discovery"[4]) sought a ship too and left Poland for Marseilles. Fluent in French through early training, he arrived in this port, one he had never seen, at the end of October, 1874, at sixteen.

For two months he sailed on the pilot boats outside the Vieux Port of Marseilles as a guest of the Corporation of Pilots. Five companies, manning the clock round, conducted ships into the harbor, and Conrad, free to go with any crew, attached himself to the Third Company. On his last outing with the pilots, as he wrote in *A Personal Record*, "my hand touched, for the first time, the side of an English ship."

Rowing in the dinghy carrying the pilot to one waiting ship, he read the name of it, a big three-masted cargo steamer—"I read it letter by letter on the bow"—the *James Westoll*. "A few strokes brought us alongside, and it was then that, for the very first time in my life, I heard myself addressed in English—the speech of my secret choice, of my future, of long friendships, of the deepest affections, of hours of toil and hours of ease."

The address consisted of three words, "Look out there!" called by a deckhand tossing down a rope for Conrad to catch. With the pilot put aboard, the dinghy "danced a squashy, splashy jig in the wash of the wake; and, turning in my seat, I followed the *James Westoll* with my eyes. Before she had gone in a quarter of a mile she hoisted her flag, as the harbor regulations prescribe for arriving and departing ships. I saw it suddenly flicker and stream out on the flagstaff. The Red Ensign! . . . the symbolic, protecting, warm bit of bunting flung wide upon the seas, and destined for so many years to be the only roof over my head."[5]

The *James Westoll*, which Conrad remembered as coming into Marseilles in 1874, to furnish him then with his first contact with the British merchant marine in which he served for sixteen years—and with the language he adopted—has vanished, like so many other ships, from existing records. James Westoll, Jr., head of the James Westoll & Co. shipowning firm in Sunderland, England, has told all that is likely to be known of the ship Conrad saw. In a letter of April 20, 1951, he wrote to Dr. J. G. Reed:

"My great-grandfather had a ship which was called after him, the *James Westoll*, but this ship was not built until 1884. Moreover from our records we find that the *James Westoll* had only two masts whereas Conrad describes the ship he saw as being 'powerfully rigged with three masts.'

"These two points taken together seem fairly conclusive that the ship Conrad saw was not the *James Westoll* and the most probable solution is . . . that he transferred the name of the owner to the ship. Possibly later in his life he may have seen the real *James Westoll* and transferred the name to the ship described, knowing both were in the same ownership.

"It is hard to say what the ship might be, as our records of 80 years ago are difficult to trace. We did have a ship, the *John Adamson*, built in 1872 with three masts which might fit the bill; but I cannot say with certainty that this ship was trading to Marseilles at that time, nor, if she was, that we had not other three masted ships so trading."

After two months on the pilot boats, cruising in the Mediterranean a mile or two offshore, Conrad embarked on his first ocean voyage. On December 11, 1874, as a passenger just turned seventeen, he sailed from Marseilles for the West Indies on the *Mont-Blanc*,[6] a three-masted wood barque of 394 tons and a ship twenty-two years old. The *Mont-Blanc*, owned by C. Delestang et Fils of Marseilles, reached St. Pierre, Martinique, on February 16, 1875, and, remaining there until March 30, returned to Marseilles on May 23. Conrad's first voyage, lasting five months, was quickly followed by a second. After a month's stay on shore he sailed as an apprentice on the *Mont-Blanc* from Marseilles on June 23, 1875, arrived at St. Pierre on July 31, where he remained almost two months. Leaving St. Pierre on September 23, his ship made stops in the Caribbean—St. Thomas on September 27, Cap Haitien in Haiti on October 2—before sailing from Cap Haitien on November 1 with a cargo of logwood, coming into Le Havre on December 23 after a stormy passage.[7]

The two voyages of routine trading gave Conrad sea experience but neither was drawn upon to any extent in his later writing. Rather than sail again over the same route in the *Mont-Blanc*, an old ship that "leaked fully, generously, overflowingly, all over—like a basket," he idled away six months in Marseilles, waiting for the newer ship chartered by Delestang et Fils, the *Saint-Antoine*. This, a three-masted barque, was owned by J. M. Cairo of Nantes and from 1875 to 1880 was under charter to Delestang et Fils;[8] built in England in 1870, she was a ship six years old at the time of Conrad's voyage.

Although he did not reach New Orleans, as his Uncle Thaddeus stated (New Orleans port records show that neither the *Mont-Blanc* nor *Saint-Antoine* entered there, nor did Conrad arrive as a passenger on any other ship[9]), he did sail the full length of the Caribbean. Nineteen years would pass before the appearance of his first novel (its setting to be a river village in Borneo) but the experiences lying ahead for him on this Caribbean voyage of the *Saint-Antoine* would provide the first of the many dramatic adventures to be developed in his work.

IV

On the hot Friday of August 18, 1876, the *Saint-Antoine* sailed into the open roadstead of St. Pierre,[1] the trading town of Martinique, and anchored south of Place Bertin. Dropping anchor near shore in the circular bay where the bottom fell away steeply, the barque took her place in the line of merchantmen in port for cargoes of logwood, molasses, rum, cocoa, and sugar. Sugar plantations, forests and grass covered the hills rising behind the town, covered all but the highest hill, the barren Mount Pelée or Bald Mountain. Pelée, over four thousand feet high, a volcano, had been dormant for twenty years; in the security that it always would be, houses had been built on its lower slopes.

Leaving Marseilles on July 8, the *Saint-Antoine* had moved across the Atlantic under light winds, reaching St. Pierre at the end of a slow forty-two-day passage. Captain C. Escarras had three officers and thirteen men in his crew, and a passenger[2] picked up after the ship left Marseilles. Conrad, though listed as a steward—another steward on board filled that cabin-boy role—served as a junior officer, assisting the three officers on deck during the passage, and, in port, with loading and unloading the cargo. Two of the men on the ship he was to bring into his books: Dominic André Cervoni, the chief mate, a Corsican of forty-two, portrayed as the leading character in *Nostromo;* César Cervoni, Dominic's nephew and also from Corsica, an apprentice of eighteen, a month younger than Conrad. Dominic and César were shortly to be involved with Conrad in the Marseilles-to-Spain gunrunning venture, told in *The Mirror of the Sea.*

St. Pierre was a familiar town to Conrad. The year before he had passed a total of three months here, the first of the many foreign ports he was to see. Here were the homes of the island's great planter families, the *békés* or bosses as they were spoken of in the Creole dialect, old colonial aristocracy retaining royalist sympathies still. Britain had occupied Martinique during the French Revolution and through that hiatus in French rule this island, alone of France's possessions in the West Indies, had escaped the social turnover the Revolution had brought to France. The Bourbons were of the distant past elsewhere, but here, oblivious of time and change, the planters carried on the traditions of the *ancien régime.*

With its white houses and red-tiled roofs, its cathedral towering high above them, St. Pierre had the appearance of a southern French town transplanted to a tropical setting. Wrought-iron balconies fronted on the streets from houses with enclosed courtyards where bougainvillea bloomed, luxuriant green gardens offering some relief from the unrelenting heat. Beyond the palm-lined shore of the bay white awnings stretched over the decks of ships in the harbor to protect crews from the beating sun—"you would take them at first sight for so many white houses, whose roofs are built like a terrace," *Blunt's American Coast Pilot*[3] described them.

The town moved at the lazy pace of the tropics, coming to life when the burning sun went down. Carriages then ambled along the promenade, the fashionable drives as customary here as on the Prado in Marseilles, and the music of outdoor concerts gave the town evening entertainment. There were innumerable cafés in the narrow streets, opera in the winter season, and always elaborate suppers in the planters' homes, homes that, staffed with many Negro servants, held private libraries of leather-bound books, heirlooms of crystal and bronze, *objets d'art* dating back to Louis XIV when the first royalist families came. Sharing the pleasures of this life and, with the French, controlling its commerce, were American businessmen; almost the whole of the white population of this creole Negro town derived from France and America.

But for all the elegance and indolence life offered the wealthy families of St. Pierre, it was a hazardous seaport during the hurricane season. From July 15 to October 15, the hurricane months, ships were unable to lie with any safety in the exposed roadstead and French merchantmen were commanded by the government to leave it.

Blunt's American Coast Pilot, a navigating guide for the Caribbean (its counterpart in England being Imray's *Sailing Directions for the Gulf of Mexico* and in France the *Golfe du Mexique* advices of the *Service Hydrographique*) warned that during the hurricane season in St. Pierre "vessels surprised at the anchorage by strong winds from the open sea, or from a heavy ground-swell, find themselves in a critical situation. If they cannot tow out or beat out they are oftentimes thrown ashore by the enormous surges; if instead of attempting to go to sea they remain at anchor, their loss is almost certain . . . they drive on shore and soon go to pieces. With the intention of preventing such shipwrecks the Colonial government orders all French vessels to quit the road."[4]

Foreign brigs, barques and schooners—among them the American *Racehorse, Reindeer* and *Daylight*, and the British *Apollo, Laura Bride* and *Italia*—could, and did, remain in port. But the French-owned *Saint-Antoine* was required to leave promptly, and disappeared from the list of vessels in St. Pierre.[5] The log of her voyage written by Captain Escarras is still in the archives of the Port of Toulon in France, but is no longer complete. Among the missing parts are those detailing the ship's movements between August 18 and September 19, 1876, the only unaccounted-for period providing time enough for the voyage along the Caribbean coast to the ports Conrad named in letters to Richard Curle and Mrs. Dummett[6]—the Venezuelan ports of Puerto Cabello and La Guaira, and Cartagena in Colombia. These, with Aspinwall, were regular ports of call for all merchant ships in the southern Caribbean trade.

Conrad's voyage was a "lawless" one, as he referred to it, carrying contraband arms to the rebel side during a revolution. Colombia alone, on this coast, was undergoing revolution. Its chief port, Cartagena, was a center of rebel activity—the rebels being Conservatives fighting the central Liberal government—and was, like St. Pierre, a merchant city of royalist sympathizers. No one was more dedicated to such turn-the-clock-back causes than the charterer of the *Saint-Antoine*, Monsieur Delestang of Marseilles, the banker and shipowner Conrad declared was "such a frozen-up, mummified Royalist that he used in current conversation turns of speech contemporary, I should say, with the good Henri Quatre; and when talking of money matters, reckoned not in francs, like the common, godless herd of post-Revolutionary Frenchmen, but in obsolete and forgotten *écus—écus* of all money units in the world!—as though Louis Quatorze were still promenading in royal splendor the gardens of Versailles."[7]

Many of Colombia's aspiring Conservatives, out of office for fifteen years, had spent those years in France, seeking support for a political comeback. By the long-established custom of their country, this entailed a forceful overthrow of the existing government in Colombia; and Monsieur Delestang, a dedicated ultraconservative, had authorized his ship to carry a consignment of arms. Running guns to rebels in any of the Latin American countries involved in revolution was widely practiced and, in Colombia at least, only mildly illicit. Steamers from New York transported such arms, usually Remington rifles, without disguise, openly landing them at Aspinwall. From there, freighted by railroad across the isthmus, shipped south on the Pacific to Buenaventura, they were used on the revolutionary battlegrounds beyond Cali. The moral wrong of this trade of arming Colombia's rebels was pointed out by an American sea captain in Aspinwall in 1875 but the Panama *Star and Herald*[8] promptly took issue with him, editorially reprimanding him for an uncommercial view. Not until 1886, by an act of constitution, did

Colombia prohibit the unlicensed trade in arms which had been flagrantly carried on for half a century.

When Conrad sailed into Cartagena he saw the city that had earlier been the South American headquarters of the Spanish Inquisition (in *Nostromo* "the highest ecclesiastical court, for two viceroyalties, sat here in the olden time") and a country epitomizing the southern continent's unrest. Nowhere had revolution been more costly than in Colombia. Men were killed, or fled to the mountains to escape military service in the constant civil wars, in such numbers that for seventy years births and deaths were barely in balance. And nowhere was there so little peace, civil wars draining the nation throughout half its life as a republic.

The 1876 revolution Conrad saw, at its halfway mark, began after the election in February of the Liberal party candidate for president, Dr. Aquileo Parra, the personal choice of the retiring president, Santiago Pérez[9]—father of Santiago Pérez Triana, whom Conrad came to know in London. Before the year ended, Colombia, a nation with three million inhabitants, sustained casualties equaling the total losses of the United States in the Spanish-American War. During that year an impoverished people supported the crushing burden of seventy thousand men under arms; casualties in the two principal battles were high—one out of every seven men was killed or wounded; trade was halted; the foreign debt rose to $35,000,000.

The specific cause of the revolution was the contested issue of religious education in public schools. This, said Ricardo Pereira, first secretary of the Colombian legation in Paris, "gave the civil war the character of a religious struggle, which made one fear all the horrors of a war of partisans."[10]

Colombia, a Roman Catholic country, had enforced the separation of church and state in 1861, a position the Liberal party supported and the Conservatives sought to reverse. After country-wide balloting which began in August, 1875, and lasted six months, Dr. Parra won a close vote over Rafael Núñez, leader of the Conservative party advocating church control of education. Losing the election, the Conservatives in the rich gold and silver mining states of Antioquia and Tolima declared war on the federal government. On August 12, "under the immediate orders of the Bishops of Pasto and Popayan, as well as those of Cundinamarca, Boyaca, and Santander," Ricardo Pereira reported, the rebel army invaded the state of Cauca. President Parra replied in a manifesto issued on August 17 declaring Colombia at war.

After several weeks of skirmishes the first main battle was fought on August 31, at Los Chancos in the Cauca, the rebels attacking with

6000 men under General Joaquin Maria Córdova, the government defending with a force of 4000 under General Julian Trujillo. The battle lasted seven hours. It was, said the Panama *Star and Herald* on September 19, referring to Colombia's war of freedom from Spain sixty years before, "the most important engagement that has perhaps taken place since the War of Independence."

The battle, fought with rifles and mainly by boys, peons of mountain villages impressed into service, "must have been desperate," the newspaper concluded from the fragmentary reports brought by ship from Buenaventura. The brief dispatch told what seven hours of fighting behind the high mountain wall of the Cordillera Occidental had meant: "More than 400 prisoners have fallen in the hands of the Government forces, with over sixty mule loads of ammunition. . . . The rebels lost more than a thousand killed and wounded, while the Government forces lost 200 killed and 300 wounded."

The rebel army, routed, retreated into Antioquia. Guerrilla warfare spread up and down the valleys while both sides built up strength for the last engagement, the two-day battle of November 20–22 fought at Garrapata in Tolima, where the government forces, numbering 5000, defeated 7000 rebel troops. There the revolution ended.

The arms Conrad's ship carried were intended for General Córdova's rebel forces and may have reached him for the battle at Los Chancos. This battle in the great valley of the Cauca River, like those of the revolutions before and after, was fought several hundred miles from Cartagena, beyond the high mountains, in the southern and more heavily populated part of Colombia. In *Nostromo* the true location, with only the name of the valley altered, was given as the war ground of revolutions—"Their course ran in the more populous southern parts of the Republic, and in the great valley of Sta. Marta, which was like one great battlefield of the parties, with the possession of the Capital for a prize."[11]

Conrad's view of Colombia was limited to the cities along the Caribbean coast. Two of these his ship had to pass, Savanilla and Barranquilla, and three, Santa Marta, Cartagena, and Aspinwall (Colón) he gave evidence in his novel of knowing. Savanilla and Barranquilla were busy ports lying near the mouth of the one-thousand-mile Magdalena River, the Mississippi of Colombia, which, like the Mississippi, was traveled by steamboat—paddle-wheel steamers built in Ohio that, in this year of revolution, were armed by the government as transports.

Santa Marta, where South America's great revolutionary hero Bolívar had died in 1830, was a town of six thousand people in Conrad's time,

the capital of the state of Magdalena which the year before had attempted
to secede from the federal union Bolívar created. Built on the coast in
a dramatic setting, the centuries-old seaport lay at the base of the great
Sierra Nevada de Santa Marta mountains, the highest of the snow-capped
peaks rising nineteen thousand feet straight from the tropical shore and
visible for seventy miles at sea.

Conrad retained the name of Santa Marta in *Nostromo*, a government
seat in the novel too, and to its striking snow-covered mountain,
Cristóbal Colón, jutting above the crags of the rugged Cordillera range
and standing out as an imposing white sentinel of the coast, he gave
the name of Higuerota: "The dawn breaks high behind the towering
and serrated wall of the Cordillera, a clear-cut vision of dark peaks rear-
ing their steep slopes on a lofty pedestal of forests rising from the very
edge of the shore. Amongst them the white head of Higuerota rises
majestically."[12]

Cartagena became "Sulaco" in *Nostromo*, a name derived from Turbaco, the healthier hill section of the city where the well-to-do white
population had their homes. Cartagena, as Conrad knew it, held fourteen thousand people, a picturesque and antiquated merchants' town of
sandy streets and Moorish-style houses, so far from modernization that
water was still collected in primitive rain tanks or brought by muleback
from springs a few miles inland. "I had no notion that a place on a sea-
coast could remain so isolated from the world" was a comment in
Nostromo fitting the city which, as late as 1917, Robert Cunninghame
Graham found to be the most Old World town in all of South America.

Though a major seaport, Cartagena had no modern quays, and ships
anchored offshore in the harbor with its waters "smooth as glass," as one
voyager after another reported. As in Panama, where the gulf was
equally placid, all cargo had to be lightered. The driving winds of the
Caribbean were deflected from the deep oblong harbor by three islands
lying in a string two miles off the mainland's sandy shore. None was
inhabited—one was a barren rock—but Tierra Bomba and Baru were
long, narrow islands, green with palms and bushes.

These islands became "The Isabels" in *Nostromo*, the "Great Isabel"
being like its original in real life, Tierra Bomba, "an emerald green
wedge of land a mile long, and laid flat upon the sea." Ships, Conrad's
among them, anchored in the lee of Tierra Bomba, directly opposite the
port, and the isolation of the unused island inspired him to give it a
fictional purpose, the hiding place of Nostromo's stolen silver.

As Cunninghame Graham said of him, Conrad had a "tenacious
memory that let nothing slip that he had heard."[13] Nor did much that

he had seen vanish from his mind. Writing *Nostromo* twenty-seven years after his short stay in Cartagena, he gave to the fictional Sulaco innumerable features he remembered of the Colombian port. The islands, the placid harbor, the homes on the Turbaco hills were accurately recalled in the novel, as were Cartagena's city gates and ancient walls—walls so wide nine carriages could drive abreast upon them—the impregnable fortress Drake had captured.

" 'Just imagine our forefathers in morions and corselets drawn up outside this gate, and a band of adventurers just landed from their ships in the harbour there,' " Decoud said in the novel. " 'There used to be in the old days the sound of trumpets outside that gate. War trumpets! I'm sure they were trumpets. I have read somewhere that Drake, who was the greatest of these men, used to dine alone in his cabin on board ship to the sound of trumpets. In those days this town was full of wealth. Those men came to take it. Now the whole land is like a treasure-house, and all these people are breaking into it, whilst we are cutting each other's throats. The only thing that keeps them out is mutual jealousy. But they'll come to an agreement someday—and by the time we've settled our quarrels and become decent and honourable, there'll be nothing left for us. It has always been the same. We are a wonderful people, but it has always been our fate to be'—he did not say 'robbed,' but added, after a pause—'exploited!' "[14]

Colombia's resources had been exploited during the centuries following the Spanish Conquest and at the time of Conrad's visit foreign-held concessions were at the beginning of a steep new rise. "Never have mines been so much talked about as during the last two years," Vicente Restrepo wrote of the renewed interest abroad in Colombia's gold and silver mines. "Seldom before that were mining companies formed among foreigners; now rarely does a month pass without the announcement of some new one."[15] The announcements continued as the years passed, to reach a peak in 1965 when, according to the *Statesman's Year Book*, 60 per cent of Colombia's gold, 100 per cent of her oil, and a major part of her emeralds, railroads, fruit and coffee were owned by foreign investors. In a rich country where the people remained among the poorest in the world the imbalance continued to be much as it was in 1807 when Baron Alexander von Humboldt, the famous German naturalist-explorer, wrote of Colombia's startling contrast of wealth and hunger.

"Conrad never preaches," Cunninghame Grahame said of his friend of many years. "He only holds the mirror up to nature for men to see themselves."[16] In *Nostromo* he held the mirror up so effectively that, as he wrote Edward Garnett in 1908, "*Nostromo* has met with no end of appreciation on the seaboard where the scene is laid, and from people in the know."[17]

Identification was not difficult for Colombians, who recognized in the novel so much of their country and its history. Conrad drew its characteristic landscapes—the "rampart of mountains," the Cordilleras; the llanos or flat plains; the cold, windswept plateaus or paramos, ten thousand and more feet high, desert passes over the Cordilleras made almost impassable by fierce winds and heavy mists, where men often were, as in *Nostromo*, "frozen to death by the icy blasts of the high paramos."

He recalled Colombia's two parties, Liberals and Conservatives, so often at war; its intendencias, areas governed as territories, too sparsely populated to become states; the attempts at secession recurringly made, as in 1875 and 1876, by one or another of the loosely joined states; the historic *camino real* or old royal highway built by early Spaniards; the submarine cable at Buenaventura, Colombia's sole cable connection with the outside world and from which news of the 1876 revolution was relayed, news of the battle at Los Chancos two weeks late in being cabled to Panama when two thousand rebels laid siege to the port—becoming in *Nostromo* the port of Esmeralda with its "submarine cable connecting the Occidental provinces with the outer world," the seizure of the cables "for a whole fortnight" cutting off the country from outside contact. The government's single warship *General Trujillo*, named for the army's commander, arriving in Buenaventura with reinforcements to guard the key Pacific port from attacking rebels became in *Nostromo* the transport steamer commanded by Sotillo, also arriving at a crucial time. The two principal battles of the 1876 revolution, the daylong desperate fighting at Los Chancos and the two-day battle at Garrapata came into *Nostromo* as "a day of desperate fighting" at Rio Seco and the later "two days' battle . . . fought near Sta. Marta." Like a signature phrase, the "Treasure House of the World," as this country had been labeled by Drake, is heard as a repeated chord in Conrad's story.

Conrad was in Cartagena when the railroad between that seaport and the inland town of Calamar was under construction, a British enterprise with Italian labor, and this sight too he remembered for *Nostromo*. The departure from Colombia of ex-president Pérez, accompanied by his son, Santiago Pérez Triana, so much impressed Conrad that he referred to it three times in the novel. At the very height of the revolution ex-president Pérez left his war-torn country, arriving at Aspinwall on August 30, 1876, on his way to New York. "Señor Santiago Pérez, late President of the United States of Colombia, arrived on the Isthmus by the steamer *Ville de Paris*, from Savanilla," the Panama *Star and Herald* stated on August 31. The ship's officers, the newspaper continued, brought fragmentary news of the revolution, of "a battle in Antioquia between the Conservatives and the Liberals. The Conservatives are said to have been worsted in the engagement. The details of the fight are not yet positively made known here."

In *Nostromo*, changing the name of the steamer, Conrad wrote: "From the time the fugitive President had been got off to the ss. *Minerva*, the tide of success had turned against the mob"; and again, "That was the position yesterday, after the *Minerva* with the fugitive President had gone out of harbour, and the rioters had been driven back into the side lanes of the town"; and finally, "But the *Minerva*, carrying off the ex-president, had taken the news up north of the disturbances in Sulaco. It was possible that the next steamer down would get instructions to miss the port altogether since the town, as far as the *Minerva's* officers knew, was for the time being in the hands of the rabble."

Some of the background of the revolution Conrad undoubtedly learned from Santiago Pérez Triana, the president's son, who was living in England in 1903–1904 when the novel was being written. The Colombian diplomat and author—whose *Down the Orinoco in a Canoe*, an account of an 1897 adventure, carried an introduction by his friend Cunninghame Graham—was then representing his country as minister in London and Madrid. Conrad knew Pérez Triana (in Colombia during the first half of the 1876 revolution, he was also there for others) well enough to draw his personality in *Nostromo*, in the character of Don José Avellanos, "a statesman, a poet, a man of culture, who had represented his country at several European Courts."

Alluding to this fictional portrait, Conrad wrote to Cunninghame Graham on October 31, 1904, "I am compunctious as to the use I've made of the impression produced upon me by the Ex. Sr Don Perez Triana's personality. Do you think I have committed an unforgivable fault there? He'll never see or hear of the book probably."

Conrad also sought information about Colombia from another friend expertly qualified to give it. Cunninghame Graham, author of numerous histories of South America, a frequent traveler on the continent where he died, in Buenos Aires in 1936, came of a prominent Scottish family having old ties with Colombia, his grandfather playing a part in its history in 1831 as mediator between Bolívar and General Páez, first president of Venezuela. While at work on *Nostromo*, Conrad wrote to Cunninghame Graham on May 9, 1903, "I want to talk to you of the work I am engaged on now. I hardly dare avow my audacity—but I am placing

it in Sth America, in a Republic I call Costaguana." The Scot who knew
so much about South America not only came for the talk, to discuss the
subject of the novel, but made further visits before the book was completed on August 30, 1904.

When Conrad had been working on the story for some ten months—it
took twenty intensive months to complete it—one event of world importance occurred on the historic isthmus, and this too came into *Nostromo*. The state of Panama had made frequent attempts to secede from
Colombia and in 1903 another such crisis was reached. The United States
was in the process of negotiating a Panama canal concession with Colombia, through the Hay-Herrán treaty prescribing payment of $40,000,000
for America's perpetual control of a five-mile-wide strip of the isthmus,
when the Colombian Senate placed the canal plans in jeopardy by refusing to ratify the treaty. An uprising in Panama presented the United
States with an excuse to intervene. President Theodore Roosevelt
brusquely ordered the U.S. gunboat *Nashville* to Colón on November 3,
1903, to prevent Colombian troops, sent to quell the rebellion, from landing on the isthmus. Four days later, on November 7, the United States
recognized Panama as a sovereign state, the first nation to do so. "I took
the Canal Zone," Roosevelt declared, "and let Congress debate, and while
the debate goes on, the Canal does also."

Alluding in *Nostromo* to this "international naval demonstration,"
Conrad told through the loquacious Captain Mitchell how "the United
States cruiser, *Powhattan*, was the first to salute the Occidental flag,"
and how Don Carlos Gould, owner of the San Tomé silver mine, had
thereupon packed his bags for Washington, since "the United States, sir,
were the first great power to recognize the Occidental Republic."[18]

In a reference to his short stay in Panama, in the Central American
port of Aspinwall, Conrad wrote on July 8, 1903, to Cunninghame Graham while at work on the novel: "I am dying over that cursed *Nostromo*
thing. All my memories of Central America seem to slip away. I just had
a glimpse 25 years ago,—a short glance. That is not enough *pour bâtir
un roman dessus*." It had actually been twenty-seven years, not twenty-
five, and the ambiguity of the novel's setting was intentional—"Costaguana is meant for a S. American state in general; thence the mixture of
customs and expressions. *C'est voulu.* I remembered but little and rejected nothing."

Few writers were as self-critical as Conrad or deprecated their own
achievements so much—"he was, you see, quite modest," his wife wrote
H. G. Wells in 1934[19]—and, true to his temperament, he discounted his
knowledge of South America and the reliability of his memory. But so

well did he recall Colombia and Panama, from the voyage made there at eighteen, that he included many details in *Nostromo* only memory could have supplied. He read widely always, and believing, as he told Wells in 1907, that "the perfect novelist should be chronicler, biographer, and historian,"[20] read to insure the accuracy of the history brought into his novel. During the months of writing *Nostromo* his reading included books by Cunninghame Graham, to whom Conrad dedicated *Typhoon*. In addition to histories of the Spanish conquistadors, these were books on social reform, *Success* and the "Impenitent Thief" among them. Regarding the latter piece, Conrad wrote him in 1898:[21]

"You and your ideals of sincerity and courage and truth are strangely out of place in this epoch of material preoccupations. What does it bring? What's the profit? What do we get by it? These questions are the root of every moral, intellectual or political movement. Into the noblest cause, men manage to put something of their baseness: and sometimes when I think of you here, quietly, you seem to me tragic with your courage, with your beliefs and your hopes. Every cause is tainted: and you reject this one, espouse that other one as if one were evil and the other good, while the same evil you hate is in both, but disguised in different words. I am more in sympathy with you than words can express, yet if I had a grain of belief left in me I would believe you misguided. You are misguided by the desire of the Impossible,—and I envy you. Alas! what you want to reform are not institutions,—it is human nature. Your faith will never move that mountain. Not that I think mankind intrinsically bad. It is only silly and cowardly. Now you know that in cowardice is every evil,—especially, that cruelty so characteristic of our civilization. But, without it, mankind would vanish. No great matter truly. But will you persuade humanity to throw away sword and shield? Can you persuade even me,—who write these words in the fulness of an irresistible conviction? No, I belong to the wretched gang. We all belong to it. We are born initiated, and succeeding generations clutch the inheritance of fear and brutality without a thought, without a doubt, without compunction, in the name of God."

It was the outcry of a man who found cruelty and injustice intolerable. "I am awfully sickened by public affairs. They made me positively ill in Feb.," Conrad wrote of the Boer War on July 28, 1900, to the friend whose ideals of sincerity, courage and truth he shared. Cunninghame Graham, in his turn, found Conrad a brilliant conversationalist; "Formidable in argument, to which he brought all the resources of a mind steeped in the modern literature of Europe, especially in that of France, he yet never laid down the law."[22]

Avoiding lawgiving in *Nostromo*, he gave a many-faceted view of a country torn by revolution or, rather, not the country but the people. "As in most of my writings," he said in the Author's Note to *Typhoon*, "I insist not on the events but on their effect upon the persons in the tale." The setting was Colombia and the isthmus, Cartagena and Panama and Colón, where the search for El Dorado had begun and where the still-sought gain wore the modern prosaic name of "material interests."

"So foul a sky clears not without a storm." Taking this phrase from Shakespeare's *King John* as his motto for *Nostromo*, Conrad wove a complex story of social violence in a darkened country where ideals withered in the rancid air of corruption. "Silver is the pivot of the moral and material events, affecting the lives of everybody in the tale," he defined the theme of the novel to the Swedish professor Ernst Bendz. "That this was my deliberate purpose there can be no doubt. . . . The word 'silver' occurs almost at the very beginning of the story proper, and I took care to introduce it in the very last paragraph."[23]

The storms of civil war seldom cleared the skies for long in Latin America, as Conrad had an opportunity to see during a memorable voyage made at eighteen. The scent of tropical blooms drifting far out to sea from the West Indies carried "the luscious smell of that delicious land" to early voyagers but in the centuries since Columbus charted the way to El Dorado the violence of this Promised Land has matched the violence of the sea where hurricanes are born. Conrad's first experience of revolution in the New World was in Colombia. Within two months he would have another.

V

On the return voyage to Martinique from Colombia, Conrad sailed into two Venezuelan ports, Puerto Cabello and La Guaira. Forty-seven years later, attempting to recall his slight and only contact with Venezuela, he wrote to Richard Curle on July 22, 1923: "If I ever mentioned 12 hours it must relate to P. Cabello where I was ashore about that time. In La Guayra as I went up the hill and had a distant view of Caracas I must have been 2½ to 3 days. It's such a long time ago! And there were a few hours in a few other places on that dreary coast of Venezuela."[1]

Curle, a close friend of later years and author of *The Last Twelve Years of Joseph Conrad*, was at this time in 1923 preparing a newspaper article on the history of Conrad's books, an idea Conrad told him "does not strike me as brilliant." Wishing to "get freed from that infernal tail of ships, and that obsession with my sea life which has about as much bearing on my literary existence, on my quality as a writer, as the enumeration of drawing-rooms which Thackeray frequented could have had on his gift as a great novelist,"[2] he declined to give Curle many details about his voyages.

"After all, I may have been a seaman, but I am a writer of prose," he pointed out, attempting to direct Curle into a literary assessment of his work and away from personal history. To deflect further "that obsession with my sea life," he withheld, then and later, a full account of his travels, as Curle indicated in a letter of March 26, 1951, to a correspondent, Dr. J. G. Reed: "Conrad, by and large, had a dislike of detailed questioning about his voyages and travels, as critically unenlightening, and I rather suppose that he told me more than he told most people. And yet what a lot remains untold!"[3]

In so thoroughly submerging the episodes of his sea career, that his writing might be seen divorced from its dramatic sources ("the nature of my writing runs the risk of being obscured by the nature of my material" was the concern he expressed to Curle), Conrad unwittingly invited the judgment that much of his work and the settings for his novels were "dreamed up." His reading, not life, was erroneously credited as the inspiration for his writing, despite the fact, as he reiterated over and over in the prefaces to his novels, that it was personal experience he drew upon. The letter to Curle led to the early mistaken belief that the setting of *Nostromo* was Venezuela, whereas Conrad's clear intention in mentioning Puerto Cabello and La Guaira was to point out how very little he knew of a country he had no reason to remember. These two colorless, commercial seaports were regular ports of call in the period of Conrad's 1876 voyage along the Venezuelan coast. Severely damaged during the long years of Venezuela's war of independence, they held few buildings of historical interest after 1830 and for the many who saw and wrote of them in Conrad's time the published accounts were bleak.

One author of travel books, Frank Vincent, entered the two ports not long after Conrad and to the small and sultry town of Puerto Cabello gave infinitely less than his usual fulsome treatment of places to see. "The roadstead," he wrote of the harbor, "is of crescent shape, with a fine sandy beach, and groves of cocoa-palms in the distance. To the east of the town is an extensive and deep lagoon, into which large steamers may enter, and lie snugly at the wharves. The town reaches directly down to the water's edge."[4] On a long, low, narrow peninsula sheltering the large bay called the Golfo Triste by early Spanish navigators, Puerto Cabello was an unhealthy, malarial town. Ships did not remain long in it, often, like Conrad's, leaving within twelve hours.

Eighty miles east on the Venezuelan coast was La Guaira, or La Guayra, the seaport of Caracas, the nation's capital seven miles inland. Caracas could be seen from the heights of La Guaira, a popular climb for its spectacular view. To reach the capital, walled in by mountains, required a twenty-three-mile journey on the British-owned railroad, skirting and scaling the peaks.

Unbearably hot, its narrow and crooked streets dimly lit by oil lamps, La Guaira was the sea outlet for the coffee, cocoa and hides shipped out of the country by the English and German merchant firms of Caracas. Slightly larger than Puerto Cabello, though still a town of less than ten thousand, La Guaira was built on steep slopes, reddish-brown mountains rising sharply from the harbor. "The hills back of La Guayra are so steep that the town has the odd appearance of being built upon the sides of a precipice," Vincent wrote in *Around and About South America: Twenty Months of Quest and Query*. Homes were roughly-made cabins which, perched on the sheer hills, gave an air of jeopardy to the town, accented by the seldom-quiet waters of the harbor.

One of the most dangerous anchorages on the Caribbean coast, other ships than Conrad's were held up in the port, waiting upon the weather. "A tremendously big swell generally rolls into the roadstead of La Guayra," Vincent wrote of it, "and it is frequently so heavy that for days together no freight can be landed or embarked, and passengers have to be hoisted on board the steamers by means of chairs and ropes."

Conrad made no literary use of his passing contact with Venezuela, with the slightly possible exception of employing the father's surname of Venezuela's president, Antonio Guzmán Blanco, for the minor character Guzman Bento in *Nostromo*. Guzman Bento, a brutal tyrant in the novel, bore no resemblance to Guzmán Blanco, called by his countrymen "Illustrious American," the dominating force in Venezuelan affairs for two decades who, serving as president for three terms after 1873, ruled through figureheads when not himself in office. "As regards the development of the country, whatever there was in Venezuela in 1877 was due to the energy of President Guzmán Blanco," Vincent wrote of the "benevolent dictator" who extended public education, spent large sums on railways, roads, bridges, telegraphs and city improvements, being, said Vincent, "the only ruler of the country who has done much to develop it." A Liberal and anticlerical, he was opposed by Conservatives and aristocrats, but the country was freed from revolutions for a number of years, both before and after Conrad's short stay there. The politi-

cal "Blanco party" of aristocrats in *Nostromo* was a reference not to
Guzmán Blanco, but to the "Blancos" or "Whites," as right-wing parties
had long been called in Europe, even as the Carlists in Spain were
"Blancos" at this time.

From La Guaira to Martinique's St. Pierre was a four-day passage. The
"extremely small" 432-ton *Saint-Antoine,* though barque-rigged, was on
occasions referred to as a schooner, and during months in the Caribbean
became a dirty ship inside and out—inside from such cargoes as coal carried during her tramping; outside, her wooden hull, fouled by long weeks
in tropical waters, required the bottom-scraping she was to receive in
Haiti. Crossing the Caribbean, a sea Conrad unfailingly remembered
from early French charts as the "Gulf of Mexico" ("in the Gulf of
Mexico . . . off the Colombian coast" was such a reference in *Victory*),
the *Saint-Antoine* returned to St. Pierre from her long voyage to the
isthmus on September 16, 1876, the day St. Pierre was shaken by an
earthquake. The earthquake shock was not severe; the London *Times*
carried this delayed news on October 17. Other islands in the West Indies
were being buffeted by hurricanes, but the weather in St. Pierre was
nearly normal, showery and hot.

Conrad alluded to this part of his voyage in the Author's Note to
Victory. Identifying the originals of the characters in the novel, among
them the sinister Ricardo ("As scoundrels go he was far from being a
bore"), he wrote:

"It so happened that the very same year Ricardo—the physical Ricardo
—was a fellow passenger of mine on board an extremely small and extremely dirty little schooner, during a four days' passage between two
places in the Gulf of Mexico whose names don't matter. For the most
part he lay on deck aft as it were at my feet, and raising himself from
time to time on his elbow would talk about himself and go on talking,
not exactly to me or even at me (he would not even look up but kept
his eyes fixed on the deck) but more as if communing in a low voice
with his familiar devil."

Ricardo was the "servant or the confidant" of an aged Spanish gentleman, an acutely ill passenger who, dying on board, was buried at sea
as the *Saint-Antoine* came within sight of the mangrove-lined coast of
Martinique. At St. Pierre, Ricardo went ashore. "I would perhaps have
tracked the ways of that man of immense sincerity for a little while,"
Conrad continued, "but I had some of my own very pressing business to
attend to, which in the end got mixed up with an earthquake and so I
had no time to give to Ricardo."

Hurricanes were violently striking the West Indies and it was unsafe for the *Saint-Antoine* to remain long in St. Pierre. On September 19—the ship's log tells of the voyage—an Italian passenger, Castayune Guiann, embarked at St. Pierre, remaining on the ship for thirty-seven days, until the *Saint-Antoine* reached Port-au-Prince. On September 23 a second passenger, Gabriel Ribas, a Spaniard, came aboard at St. Pierre, destined for St. Thomas. In a hurry to leave and having secured no cargo, the *Saint-Antoine* sailed freightless on September 23 (a hurricane struck St. Pierre the following day) with a crew of fourteen. Her first stop was St. Lucia,[5] the island to the south which Sinclair Lewis, going ashore in 1923 from the steamer *Crynssen*, portrayed as the plague area of *Arrowsmith*.

From St. Lucia the *Saint-Antoine* turned north and, four days after leaving St. Pierre, arrived, still in ballast, at St. Thomas in the Danish West Indies on September 27.[6] The Danish port, then the government seat of the fifty islands the United States was to purchase from Denmark in 1917 and name the Virgin Islands, was a coaling station for steamships and the central port of the West Indies. It was normally crowded with ships but Conrad saw it in shambles, strewn with wreckage from the hurricane of two weeks before, the worst the town had known in fifty years.

The approaching cyclone gave warning one evening at sunset, said the *St. Thomas Times*, when "the sky was of a strong yellowish colour, the wind was northeast, gradually rising in strength, further on coming in puffs and terrible rain squalls."[7] On September 13 the hurricane struck St. Thomas, demolishing homes and shipping, "ignoring alike wood, wall, and iron." The wharves were nearly all destroyed; ships were capsized, dismasted, flung ashore. Captain Turner, his wife and all but three of the crew were drowned when the American barque *Idella Berry* went down in the harbor; the British brig *Veteran*, coming into port leaky on her way to Rotterdam, was sunk at her moorings; the Dutch schooners *Sarah* and *Midas* were driven onshore; the harbor became a jungle of dismasted and crippled ships—the Danish barque *Fereningen*, the Danish schooners *Petrel, Lizzie, Lotus, Adriana*, the British steamer *Ebro*, the English sloop *Ocean Bird* listed among them.[8]

From the islands around St. Thomas came reports of damage dealt by the "fearful" hurricane: on the Spanish island of Vieques everything destroyed; on Puerto Rico the coasts strewn with wrecked shipping, the season's crops of sugar cane, rice and coffee ruined; on St. Croix extreme losses of life and property, the schooner *Vigilant* sunk in the channel, the *Hugo, Thyra,* and *Dolphin* ashore; on St. Kitts the town littered with wreckage, the brig *Nellie Clifford*, the *Emeu*, the sloops *Tickler* and

Breeze and the boat *Annie Sunshine* ashore; on Antigua, Cuba, and Jamaica destruction widespread.[9]

Immediately following the hurricane of September 13–14, a second struck the West Indies on September 16–18, St. Kitts, St. Martin, and Port-au-Prince in Haiti receiving the brunt of it. The most serious storm of all was to come within a month.[10]

The *Saint-Antoine* escaped the September storms, Conrad seeing only the effects of them in the torn-up harbor of St. Thomas. It was an untidy port at any time—"that universal marine junk-shop, St. Thomas," Williams called it in *On Many Seas*, where "derelicts, wrecks, and all sorts of unseaworthy hulks seem to arrive, as though it was the gateway to the 'hereafter' of ships. Here they are condemned and sold for what they will bring, so that almost anything in the marine line can be got here at a bargain."

Human derelicts and drifters also came to this crossroads port, dropping off ships arriving from Europe, North and South America, taking passage on mail steamers bound east across the Atlantic or west for Aspinwall, alighting from tramp schooners or inter-island boats, birds of passage pausing in the conglomerate, bustling port before taking wing again. In St. Thomas, Conrad met two such men passing through, one a nameless cardsharp, the other a wandering Swede, and upon them built the characters of Mr. Jones and Axel Heyst* in *Victory*.

"Mr. Jones (or whatever his name was)" Conrad saw in a small waterfront hotel in St. Thomas when ashore with the men of the *Saint-Antoine*. "We found him one hot afternoon extended on three chairs, all alone in the loud buzzing of flies to which his immobility and his cadaverous aspect gave a most gruesome significance," Conrad recalled in the Author's Note to *Victory*. "Our invasion must have displeased him because he got off the chairs brusquely and walked out leaving with me an indelibly weird impression of his thin shanks. One of the men with me said that the fellow was the most desperate gambler he had ever come across. I said: 'A professional sharper?' and got for answer: 'He's a terror; but I must say that up to a certain point he will play fair. . . .' I wonder what the point was. I never saw him again because I believe he went straight on board a mail-boat which left within the hour for other ports of call in the direction of Aspinwall."

---

* The original Mr. Jones was possibly W. R. Jones, who spent a few hours in St. Thomas on October 4, 1876, coming from Martinique and leaving for Jamaica on the Aspinwall-bound mail steamer *Para*. Behind the character of Axel Heyst may have been A. von Asseburg, a transient "baron" during Conrad's stay in St. Thomas. Arriving from St. Croix on September 29 on the schooner *Lizzie*, he left for Puerto Rico on October 4 (*St. Thomae Tidende*, October 4, 1876).

Of Axel Heyst, the novel's hero, Conrad wrote in the same Author's Note that the "flesh and blood individual who stands behind the infinitely more familiar figure of the book I remember as a mysterious Swede right enough. Whether he was a baron, too, I am not so certain. He himself never laid a claim to that distinction. His detachment was too great to make any claims big or small on one's credulity. I will not say where I met him because I fear to give my readers a wrong impression, since a marked incongruity between a man and his surroundings is often a very misleading circumstance. . . . He was not the whole Heyst of course; he is only the physical and moral foundation of my Heyst laid on the ground of a short acquaintance. That it was short was certainly not my fault, for he had charmed me by the mere amenity of his detachment which, in this case, I cannot help thinking he had carried to excess. He went away from his rooms without leaving a trace."

Revealing where he met the supremely self-composed man so much out of place in these chaotic surroundings, Conrad wrote in a letter of June 3, 1917, that Heyst dated back to "my visual impression of the man in 1876; a couple of hours in a hotel in St. Thomas (West Indies). There was some talk of him after he left our party; but all I heard of him might have been written down on a cigarette paper. Except for these hints he's altogether 'invented.' "[11]

Conrad remained in St. Thomas for fifteen days. At eighteen, spending idle hours ashore while his ship secured a cargo, he stored up impressions from the port where, in a setting of mangled ships and splintered wharves, he met the first of the unbelonging he was to know in many parts of the world and to write of so often.

On October 12 Captain Escarras of the *Saint-Antoine* paid customs charges of $1.08 for light fees, $34.72 harbormaster fees, and $208.32 shipping fees to the Customs Office in St. Thomas and cleared his ship that day for Port-au-Prince, Haiti, with a cargo of 680 tons of coal.[12]

Port-au-Prince was an eight days' sail away but the *Saint-Antoine*, caught at sea by the "worst hurricane in living memory," spent fifteen days on the passage. From October 13–21 a series of hurricanes swept across the Caribbean and for those nine days the sailing ship was in the direct path of the winds. Among the many vessels at sea, some damaged, others lost with their crews, was the American steamship *Ossippee*, reporting to the New Orleans *Daily Picayune* that during the gales the days were as black as night, "it was hard to breathe, and all animals on board went into hiding."[13]

"A look in the eyes of a shipmate, a low murmur in the most sheltered spot where the watch on duty are huddled together, a meaning moan from one to the other with a glance at the windward sky, a sigh of weariness, a gesture of disgust passing into the keeping of the great wind, become part and parcel of the gale," Conrad wrote in *The Mirror of the Sea*. "The olive hue of hurricane clouds presents an aspect peculiarly appalling. The inky ragged wrack, flying before a nor'-west wind, makes you dizzy with its headlong speed that depicts the rush of the invisible air." On this voyage to Port-au-Prince he knew "the peculiar, terrible, and mysterious moaning that may be heard sometimes passing through the roar of a hurricane," an "unforgettable sound."

On shore the hurricanes left a trail of disaster. They swept over the island of Grand Cayman from October 13–17; 170 houses there were demolished, all cattle and crops lost, all vessels in the harbor destroyed. On St. Martin 215 houses were down, ships were stranded or sunk at their moorings. From St. Barts and Antigua to Jamaica, Havana and Key West (an unknown schooner, bottom up, among those ashore at Key West), storms scythed the islands, reaching as far as the Gulf of Mexico where ships groped through a five-day tempest. No siege of winds had been known to equal it. The *Saint-Antoine*, long overdue, limped into Port-au-Prince on October 26.

Haiti was in the midst of revolution and the inflamed port exhibited a violence matching that of the sea. General Boisrond-Canal, the newly elected president, had escaped assassination shortly before Conrad arrived in Port-au-Prince, where the rebel leader, General Saloman, had landed from exile in Jamaica to lead his troops in battle. The ups and downs of the contest for power (to end with President Boisrond-Canal exiled and General Saloman in office), coupled with sporadic fighting in the city, made trade "very much depressed," the New York *Herald*[14] declared. For six weeks in Haiti Conrad remained in a country torn apart by revolution, one of the uprisings the nation had known in an unrelenting sequence since winning independence from France in 1804.

Haiti's neighbors on both sides, Santo Domingo and Cuba, were also undergoing revolutions and Conrad was in the center, at Port-au-Prince, of battle news. In Santo Domingo (the Dominican Republic) revolution broke out in August, being in full swing as Conrad sailed on his hurricane voyage along the Dominican coast, where seesaw battles were being fought at Puerto Plata and Monte Cristi. President Espaillat conceded defeat at the end of October, and General Gonzales, ex-president and leader of the rebels, moved into the executive's chair.

In Cuba the struggle for freedom from Spain was in the eighth year of the Ten Years' War, one costing 50,000 Cuban and 208,000 Spanish lives, $300,000,000 in financial losses, innumerable homes destroyed. In

1876 it seemed, hopefully, to be ending. In this October Cubans under
General Vicento García were making strong gains in their scorched-
earth drive and Spanish troops were deserting. The encouraging news
led the New York *Herald* to report on October 3, "Cubans are greatly
elated, and believe that their independence is nigh." But an alarmed Madrid despatched General Martínez de Campos, victor of Spain's newly
ended Carlist War, sent a fleet of transports, men-of-war, 55,000 soldiers,
for a winter campaign which grew into a succession of others. Cuba's
independence, so near in 1876, was delayed twenty-two years.

Beyond Cuba, Mexico's year-long revolution reached its end during
the weeks of Conrad's stay in Haiti, the government of Lerdo de Tejada
overthrown by Porfirio Díaz. A seaman played a part in Díaz's success
that fall and the widely known incident would have appealed to Conrad, whose later short story "The Secret Sharer" centered on a similar
ship-saloon concealment. Díaz, attempting to reach Vera Cruz by sea to
lead a planned uprising, was recognized on the steamer, jumped overboard, and, while making a four-mile swim for the shore, recaptured. The
purser of the ship, claiming Díaz had jumped overboard a second time,
concealed him for days in one of the ship's saloons, afterward helping
him ashore, in disguise, at Vera Cruz. Díaz overthrew the Lerdo government at the November 16, 1876, battle at Tecoac, to begin his thirty-five
years' dominance of Mexico.

While in Haiti Conrad had an encounter with a Negro which "fixed
my conception of blind, furious, unreasoning rage, as manifested in the
human animal, to the end of my days," a man of whom he "used to
dream for years afterwards." Street fights between the partisans of
Boisrond-Canal and Saloman in the Negro republic of Haiti made ex-
hibitions of rage plentiful enough and the incident may have been one
Conrad later recalled to Edward Garnett—when, armed with nothing
but a short stick, he kept an enraged razor-wielding Negro from coming
aboard ship, driving him back down a ten-inch plank to the wharf.[15]
The character of Pedro in *Victory* was, Conrad declared, built upon
two men he met during the *Saint-Antoine* voyage, the Negro in Haiti
and another man of "terrible ire" he saw in a "hovel of sticks and mats
by the side of a path" in Martinique two months earlier.

Conrad had not heard from his Uncle Thaddeus for some months,
though he had written repeatedly to ask what was wrong. A boy "sensitive enough, in all conscience," anxious for reassurance in the hazardous
life he was leading, he received in Haiti the long-looked-for news. His
uncle's chilling letter reached Conrad when, having just survived a hur-

ricane in which other ships and men were lost, he was, for the second time on this voyage, an exposed bystander in a violent civil war.

Knowing only the untroubled routine of his estate in the Ukraine, Thaddeus was incapable of picturing the dangers of his nephew's life in the distant Caribbean. In his letter of September 27, 1876 (by the old-style Russian calendar, the date being October 9 elsewhere), he wrote Conrad, in part:

"I am in good health and you should get rid of all anxiety in that matter. I had not seen any merit in showering you with letters without having an exact address, or to write without being certain my letters would reach you. That is the whole secret of my silence; there is no anger in it at all. The question still remains whether my silence would constitute a punishment for you. From what I read in your last letters I feel it could be. But that is not what I had been thinking of, quite the contrary. I believe it my duty to lead you by way of advice and reprimand on the right path, which is the path of reason and duty. That is what I am doing and will continue to do whenever the need arises. And if I should ever turn silent from "*anger*," which would depend entirely on you, then it would probably be forever."

Harping upon Conrad's "carelessness"—the year before Conrad's trunk had been lost following the stormy voyage of the *Mont-Blanc* when the ship came into port disabled—Thaddeus went on: "Last year you lost your trunk. What else was there to think about on your journey but yourself and your belongings?" His rebukes closed with: "So here you have my reprimand for your carelessness in watching over your property. You also deserve a second one: for slovenly letter-writing, about which I have written you many times. Can't you have a supply of paper and write in an orderly manner?" Thaddeus was as far as ever from understanding the storm-made and man-made disorders his nephew was facing half the world away.

On November 25 the *Saint-Antoine* left Port-au-Prince for Miragoâne,[16] fifty miles west on the Haitian coast, where, on the careening island in the deep, cliff-enclosed Miragoâne Bay, the ship's crusted wooden hull was scraped and made ready for the long Atlantic voyage ahead. "These careening-places," *Blunt's American Coast Pilot* advised, "have been formed by nature, require no wharfs, and only a capstan to turn the keel above ground." Upon reaching the careening island at Miragoâne, Imray's *Sailing Directions for the Gulf of Mexico* instructed sea captains, "you will perceive a small town at the foot of a mountain, and some mangrove islands to the westward. . . . about a mile to the eastward of the town are some springs of good fresh water."[17]

With a clean hull for faster sailing, with a supply of fresh water and a cargo of logwood and sugar, the *Saint-Antoine* left Haiti for Marseilles where she arrived on February 15, 1877.

Turning nineteen on the way back to France, Conrad completed a voyage of seven months, acquiring during those months in the Caribbean the views of men and events he was to recapture twenty-seven years later in *Nostromo* and thirty-eight years later in *Victory*, two of the novels considered among his finest.

A few months before he began writing *Nostromo* one of the world's major tragedies occurred, and this, in the Caribbean, undoubtedly had a part in turning his mind back to the sea of his youth. Not since Pompeii, almost two thousand years before, had there been a disaster like it. When Vesuvius erupted on August 24, 79 A.D., the cities of Pompeii, Herculaneum and Stabiae were buried under volcanic ash to a depth of forty-five feet; caught and interred while sitting in the theater were many of the luxury-loving aristocrats whose gay world came to an end so abruptly. Xiphilinus in *Epitome of Dion* gave an account of the terrors of that day:

"Stones of an extraordinary Size were thrown out of the Top, attended with Fire and Smoke, so that the Air was darkened thereby, and the Sun was hidden, as in the time of an Eclipse. Night sprung from Day, and Light from Darkness, and People imagined that the Giants had rebelled, as Images of them were seen in the Smoke, and the Sound of Trumpets was heard. . . . These Things made People run out of their Houses and into the Streets, and those who were on the Streets go within Doors. Those who were on Shipboard went ashore, and those on Land went aboard, every one thinking that any Situation was better than their present one. And along with all this, there were such Quantities of Ashes as possessed all Space, Earth, Sea and Air; and wherever it happened it did hurt both to Men, the Cattle, and the Grounds, and the Fishes, and all the Birds were destroyed."

Like Pompeii and Herculaneum, St. Pierre had long sheltered under its towering and sleeping volcano. It was a gay city of aristocrats too, twice the size of Pompeii, this first town beyond Europe that Conrad knew. On the morning of May 8, 1902, it was totally destroyed by the eruption of Mount Pelée. The townspeople were caught unprepared by the burst of fire and suffocating fumes which took the lives of all but one man, a Negro murderer, Joseph Surtout, locked in a cell deep underground awaiting execution. The last day of St. Pierre, a city never to be rebuilt, was described by Assistant Purser Thompson of the

Quebec Steamship Company's vessel *Roraima*, who arrived at St. Pierre from the island of Dominica just before the eruption.

"I saw St. Pierre destroyed. It was blotted out by one great flash of fire. Nearly 40,000 persons were all killed at once. Out of eighteen vessels lying in the roads, only one, the British Steamship *Roddam*, escaped; and she, I hear, lost more than half of those on board. It was a dying crew that took her out. Our boat, the *Roraima*, arrived at St. Pierre early Thursday morning. For hours before we entered the roadstead we could see flames and smoke rising from Mount Pelée. No one on board had any idea of danger. Captain Muggah was on the bridge, and all hands got on deck to see the show. The spectacle was magnificent. As we approached St. Pierre we could distinguish the rolling and leaping of the red flames that belched from the mountain in huge volumes and gushed high into the sky. Enormous clouds of black smoke hung over the volcano. There was a constant muffled roar. It was like the biggest oil refinery in the world burning up on the mountain top. There was a tremendous explosion about 7:45, soon after we got in. The mountain was blown to pieces. There was no warning. The side of the volcano was ripped out and there was hurled straight toward us a solid wall of flame. It sounded like thousands of cannon.

"The wave of fire was on us and over us like a lightning flash. It was like a hurricane of fire. I saw it strike the cable steamship *Grappler* broadside on, and capsize her. From end to end she burst into flames and then sank. The fire rolled in mass straight down upon St. Pierre and the shipping. The town vanished before our eyes.

"The air grew stifling hot and we were in the thick of it. Wherever the mass of fire struck the sea, the water boiled and sent up vast clouds of steam. The sea was torn into huge whirlpools that careened toward the open sea. One of these horrible, hot whirlpools swung under the *Roraima* and pulled her down on her beam-ends with the suction. She careened way over to port, and then the fire hurricane from the volcano smashed her, and over she went on the opposite side. The fire wave swept off the masts and smokestacks as if they were cut with a knife. . . .

"Captain Muggah was overcome by the flames. He fell unconscious from the bridge and fell overboard. The blast of fire from the volcano lasted only a few minutes. It shriveled and set fire to everything it touched. Thousands of casks of rum were stored in St. Pierre, and these were exploded by the terrific heat. The burning rum ran in streams down every street and out into the sea. This blazing rum set fire to the *Roraima* several times.

"Before the volcano burst, the landings of St. Pierre were covered with people. After the explosion, not one living soul was seen on land."[18]

Conrad was in England, at his Pent Farm home in Kent, writing "The End of the Tether," when St. Pierre was destroyed. Seamen, sole eyewitness survivors, were the reporters, wrote the history of that holocaust. Seeing it from ships in the harbor or sailing the weird sea it caused (Captain Eric Lillienskjold of the Danish steamship *Nordby* told of the reality, more chilling than myth, of an eccentric sea of giant waves rising out of nowhere on a windless day, lightning without thunder, sea water hot to the touch and filled with fleeing sharks), these seamen with their vivid tales informed the world, through newspapers, of a city's end everywhere likened to Pompeii. The dead St. Pierre inspired stories of how it had once been, a regal port yet one of hurly-burly trade, and while these were being read a final event closed the history of the town. In December, 1902, Mount Pelée erupted with another great cloud of volcanic dust and steam, a cloud rising thirteen thousand feet in the air, falling on a deserted landscape. That month Conrad, at forty-five and "with my head full of a story," began *Nostromo*.

It was almost two years later that he completed the "tale of an imaginary (but true) seaboard." In it he recalled Colombia and the revolution there he had seen on his voyage from St. Pierre, in that early time when Mount Pelée was the still and familiar Bald Mountain landmark of seamen. The intense and exhausting work of writing what was to become known as one of the world's great novels Conrad told of in *A Personal Record*.

"All I know is that, for twenty months, neglecting the common joys of life that fall to the lot of the humblest on this earth, I had, like the prophet of old, 'wrestled with the Lord' for my creation, for the headlands of the coast, for the darkness of the Placid Gulf, the light on the snows, the clouds in the sky, and for the breath of life that had to be blown into the shapes of men and women, of Latin and Saxon, of Jew and Gentile. These are, perhaps, strong words, but it is difficult to characterize otherwise the intimacy and the strain of a creative effort in which mind and will and conscience are engaged to the full, hour after hour, day after day, away from the world, and to the exclusion of all that makes life really lovable and gentle—something for which a material parallel can only be found in the everlasting somber stress of the westward winter passage round Cape Horn. . . .

"There were pages of MS. on the table and under the table, a batch of typed copy on a chair, single leaves had fluttered away into distant corners; there were there living pages, pages scored and wounded, dead pages that would be burned at the end of the day—the litter of a cruel battle-field, of a long, long, and desperate fray. Long! I suppose I went to bed sometimes, and got up the same number of times. Yes, I suppose I slept, and ate the food put before me, and talked connectedly to my household on suitable occasions. . . . But I felt, somehow, as grimy as a Costaguana *lepero* after a day's fighting in the streets, rumpled all over and disheveled down to my very heels."[19]

In *Nostromo* Conrad created a vital world as essentially true of today, when the frequency and causes of Latin American revolutions remain much the same, as it was true of the world he knew nearly ninety years ago. Of that world Colombia stands out still as a grim example of social chaos. With a desperately poor population imbued with a frenzied passion for politics and extraordinarily isolated within its mountains, it continues to be raked by the bloody political feuding *La Violencia*. "One is born a liberal or conservative," Professor Theodore Caplow tells of the Colombian's ferocious political zeal in the Winter 1963 issue of the *Columbia University Forum*. "Whole villages and families are liberal or conservative. Good liberals do not marry conservatives, or drink with them. Political grievances stay fresh indefinitely. The policies of Santander, who became president in 1832, are still hotly debated." In Colombia, the violent schism between liberals and conservatives has existed for a hundred and thirty years. The most recent epidemic of disorder, *La Violencia*, began in 1946 when the conservatives took office, abating somewhat in 1958. "The liberals at first figured as victims," writes Professor Caplow. "They soon developed their own armed bands for revenge and plunder. With the passage of time, many of the units on both sides lost their political character sufficiently to rob and kill their friends as well as their enemies.

"The material losses were enormous. In the regions most affected, the whole institution of agriculture was liquidated, the livestock was stolen, the buildings were burned, the schools were closed, the roads were neglected until they became impassable, and all movable wealth was carried away. Some municipalities were completely emptied, and from many others, the majority of the population remains in exile to this day.

"The barbarity of the proceedings was unprecedented even in this ingenious century. . . . Whatever else it was, *La Violencia* was deserving of its name." It continues. The Violence now is "a purposeless struggle of angry, suffering individual men and women" in a country where industrialization makes progress in the cities, where wealth, by a feudal standard inherited from Spanish colonialism and entrenched by the conduct of modern business, lies in the hands of the very few.

"There is no peace and rest in the development of material interests," was Conrad's conclusion in *Nostromo*, a reflection of the views written to Cunninghame Graham in 1898 on "this epoch of material preoccupations" with its motivating questions "What does it bring? What's the profit? What do we get by it?" Through the pursuit of El Dorado Latin America emerged nearly five centuries ago; in 1965 it was still judged in terms used three years earlier: "rich in unexploited wealth, miserably poor in the living it offers to most of its 200 million inhabitants, too often presided over by governments that are feckless and corrupt."[20]

This failure at the core of modern civilization was one theme in the novel Conrad considered his largest canvas—frequently compared to that other of great range, *War and Peace*—but there were many others. "A transgression, a crime, entering a man's existence, eats it up like a malignant growth, consumes it like a fever" in *Nostromo* was his subject in *Lord Jim*, developed from an incident and a man whom, in 1876, he was yet to know. Before meeting the "Jim" of that story would come the contraband adventure Conrad shared with Dominic Cervoni, the seaman friend he drew as the Genoese character Nostromo, adopting the name from the Italian *nostromo* (boatswain) and from the old title still current in Genoa *nostromo del porto* (boss of the stevedores), giving to his character its Spanish equivalent "capataz de cargadores."

As *Nostromo* grew from Conrad's 1876 experiences in the Caribbean on the *Saint-Antoine*, so another novel, *The Arrow of Gold*, grew from an experience soon to follow. Back in Marseilles on the *Saint-Antoine* in February, 1877, he was swept into a further involvement with revolution, the unresolved closing of the Carlist War in Spain.

General Martínez de Campos, transferred to Cuba to lead Spanish troops in the civil war there, had been declared the victor of the Carlist War; but Don Carlos, the vanquished, had spent the summer of 1876 touring the United States and Mexico, soliciting support for his cause.[21] In Mexico City, he published a letter on June 22 in which he proclaimed himself the legitimate king of Spain, calling on Mexicans, for the love they bore Spain, to aid him in his campaign for the throne; on August 28 his appeal appeared in the Panama *Daily Star and Herald* as he widened the area in which he sought the help of Spanish-Americans for a reopening of the Carlist War.

Taking with him two of the men of the *Saint-Antoine*, Dominic and César Cervoni, Conrad was drawn into the Spanish conflict he was to describe as "a very straightforward adventure conducted with inconceivable stupidity and a foredoomed failure from the first."[22] There was "indeed nothing great there worthy of anybody's passionate devotion,"[23] he could say of it years later. But at nineteen, through his love for a beautiful girl, the *amie* of Don Carlos, Paula de Somoggy, he took part in a venture ending in a duel with an American whose identity, by remaining unknown for so many years, contributed to a controversy about Conrad's life.

VI

The state of being nineteen is unsteadying enough, even for a young man bulwarked by a family, and for those like Conrad, orphaned or half-orphaned in early boyhood—Washington, Andrew Jackson, Alexander Hamilton, and Tolstoy among them—the urge for self-location has more than normal force. In search of some group to belong to for the "something solid" at his back acceptance gives, Conrad, who was "lucky with people" and liked by everyone, as his uncle said of him, made friends in three sets in Marseilles, known by a different name in each. In the aristocratic Legitimist salons, where he appeared as a meticulously dressed and impeccably mannered young man with a beard (he was never to be without it the rest of his life), he was the Count-like "de Korzeniowski"; on the waterfront, as a gunrunner on cloak-and-dagger business, seamen knew him as "Monsieur Georges" ("I have more than once seen what cordial greetings were exchanged between him and sailors, who call him Monsieur Georges," Thaddeus wrote to the family friend Stefan Buszczynski after his 1878 visit to Conrad in Marseilles[1]); among the artists and poets of his Bohemian circle he was "Young Ulysses," a voyager relating his own bizarre adventures, the incomparable raconteur, "ever the great teller of a tale," John Galsworthy later knew.

Like Balzac, who, at thirty announced to the world that he was Honoré de Balzac and never dropped the assumed "de" from his name, Conrad too appropriated that defining mark of nobility as a pose in his early youth. To the French owners of his first ships, Delestang et Fils, he was "Conrad de Korzeniowski," the implied title and mannered airs earning him the nickname of "The Count" on the *Saint-Antoine*. He continued to use the "de" when signing on his first three British ships, but by twenty-two had outgrown the fantasy and was "Conrad Korzeniowski" on crew lists until 1891 when, as first mate of the *Torrens* and then thirty-three, he wrote his name on the Agreement and Account of Crew as "J. Conrad (Korzeniowski)."[2]

No one who knew him in Marseilles published a remembrance of him but later recollections told of a glowing, many-faceted personality, capable of carrying through with ease the varied roles he played in Marseilles. Of those he came to know many took him to be a Frenchman. Wearing a monocle, a tapered beard, speaking English with a foreign accent, he gestured in the French manner, hands and shoulders active as he recounted the episodes of his life, acting them out as he told them. His stories were inexhaustible, his talk "a romance, free and swift."

"Fascination was Conrad's great characteristic," John Galsworthy said of him, "the fascination of vivid expressiveness and zest, of his deeply affectionate heart, and his far-ranging subtle mind."[3] Galsworthy first met Conrad in Adelaide, Australia—Conrad then being chief mate of the British sailing ship *Torrens* on which Galsworthy booked passage—and recalled his volatile friend of thirty-one years in this first view: "Very dark he looked in the burning sunlight—tanned, with a peaked brown beard, almost black hair, and dark brown eyes, over which the lids were deeply folded. He was thin, not tall, his arms very long, his shoulders broad, his head set rather forward. He spoke to me with a strong foreign accent. He seemed to me strange on an English ship. For fifty-six days I sailed in his company."[4]

Five and a half years earlier the daughter of Captain James Craig, a child taken to meet the young chief mate of her father's steamer *Vidar* in Singapore, saw him as "tall and very fair . . . he was standing at the head of the gangway receiving us,"[5] wrote Mrs. Ivy Fairweather of the officer her father so often talked of, remembering Conrad impressionistically for those sunny qualities Edward Garnett recalled—the "brilliant charm," the "gay tenderness," the "extraordinary soft warmth of his eyes."

The youthful exuberance of Conrad's seafaring days, his "gay buoyancy of spirit," carried into the early years of his writing ("at 37 I *was* young," he wrote the English book-collector Clement Shorter in 1916[6]) and it was as a beginning author that Garnett met him, a stranger "extremely graceful in his nervous gestures" with mercurial shifts of mood. "To no one was the art of harmonizing differences so instinctive when he wished to draw near," Garnett wrote. "To no one was the desire of emphasizing them more emphatic, when he did not. . . . Conrad's courtesy was part of his being, bred in the bone, and serving him as a foil in a master's hand, ready for attack or defense."[7]

Resilient and ardent, he had an outstanding characteristic Garnett remembered: "When Conrad wished to surrender himself to anybody he did it single-heartedly in irresistible fashion."[8] With the ardor of nineteen, in single-hearted devotion to a girl, he was drawn into the lost cause of his day, embarking on the exploits of his "wild oats period," as, in his sedate sixties, he referred to this time in his youth. His clandestine adventure as "Monsieur Georges" he recalled in the "Tremolino" chapter of *The Mirror of the Sea* and in *The Arrow of Gold*, in that novel using the real names of several of the people involved, including his own of Monsieur Georges slightly altered to Monsieur George (a name Conrad apparently selected from a favored book, *Don Quixote*, the Monsieur Georges or Micer Jorge there being a Spanish caballero in the service of the Duke of Austria, as Conrad, serving a prince from Vienna on his Spanish voyages, equally was, as he called himself, a "young caballero").

The lost cause he joined in Marseilles, being introduced to it by the Delestangs, the banking-shipowning family who were among his first contacts, was that of the Legitimists or Carlists, known in France as the *Blancs d'Espagne* or *Blancos*. It had a romantic, wide attraction, this last attempt Europe was to know of a Pretender making an active fight for a crown, one with a long history dating from 1833 when Ferdinand VII of Spain died, leaving no male heir. On his deathbed, setting aside the Salic law denying succession to females, Ferdinand named his three-year-old daughter, Isabella II, to be Spain's ruler, bypassing his brother Carlos. Carlos challenged the succession of his infant niece and for six years, until 1839, fought the first and unsuccessful Carlist War. His grandson, Don Carlos, took up the challenge in 1868 when Isabella was deposed, and in 1872 began the second Carlist War against his fifteen-year-old cousin Alfonso XII, Isabella's son. Until 1898 Don Carlos was an actual or potential challenger to the government of Spain; an explosive exile in a country having claimant troubles of its own, he was repeatedly expelled from France, in the end being permanently barred from living there.

Don Carlos (Charles Maria de los Dolores Juan Isidore Joseph Francis Quirin Antony Michael Gabriel Raphael), Prince of Bourbon, Duke of Madrid, was a direct descendant of Louis XIV and on the death in 1883 of his uncle, the Count de Chambord, was, genealogically, the legitimate heir to the thrones of both France and Spain. A large Legitimist following gathered behind him in France, and in Marseilles,[9] as in all the cities of the Midi from Bayonne to Nice, Carlist committees were formed which were active during the whole length of the war and immediately afterward. Across the Channel London also had such a group. The London *Times*, receiving its news from "the London Carlist Committee," on February 5, 1876, stated that "a cargo of rifles, stores, and munitions of war was successfully landed by the Carlists on the 2nd inst. near Motrico

(Biscay)," that "twelve fresh Carlist battalions are to be at once equipped with the arms just landed" for a battle "imminent in the vicinity of Vera."

The battle proved to be the Carlist defeat at Tolosa, and Don Carlos —"the King" as Legitimists called him—crossed the frontier into France from Spain on February 27, 1876. On that day Conrad, at eighteen, was at the Marseilles salon of a wealthy hide-and-tallow merchant when "the possibility of raising Catalonia in the interest of the *Rey netto*, who had just then crossed the Pyrenees, was much discussed."[10]

"Like all Pretenders, he never gave in," the 1910 *Encyclopaedia Britannica* states in its biographical sketch of Don Carlos, "and his pretensions, haughtily reasserted, often troubled the courts and countries whose hospitality he enjoyed." Refusing to accept his 1876 defeat at Tolosa as final, Don Carlos "continued to ask his partisans to go on organizing their forces for action some day, and to push their propaganda and preparations," the *Encyclopaedia Britannica* says of the claimant who went abroad to enlist support for his cause. During the summer months of his 1876 stay in the United States and Mexico ("Don Carlos is now making a pleasure tour of the United States," having visited "a number of leading American cities," *Frank Leslie's Illustrated Newspaper* reported on August 19, 1876, as the Pretender, having spent June in Mexico, closed his tour with July and August visits in Philadelphia, Newport and New York), his partisans in Spain continued fighting. Uprisings there were planned to reach a major crisis in the fall.

On September 2, 1876, Don Carlos sailed from New York for Liverpool on the *Baltimore* and, after eight days in London, arrived in Paris on September 23 to rejoin his wife and five children in the Pavilion he had taken at 49 rue de la Pompe, a house famous in French and Spanish social circles, formerly occupied by the Dowager Queen Christina of Spain, mother of Isabella II. The Pavilion became the center of the Carlist movement, with its wide variety of followers. Of the most prominent men who gave active or tacit support to Don Carlos were the Duke of Norfolk, premier duke of England; President MacMahon of France; the Count de Chambord, Pretender to the throne of France; the Count de Paris; Pedro II, Emperor of Brazil; the Duc de Nemours; the Duc de la Rochefoucauld. Less prominent were soldiers of fortune from various countries, of which America supplied a few.

"America has not furnished very many soldiers of fortune, but they have all been marked men, and the number is increasing," the *New York Times* said on January 18, 1875. Of these "men of enterprise seeking restless adventure," the newspaper proudly pointed to several: Colonel Burr Porter of New Jersey, in Turkey's service during the Crimean War, in the U. S. Army as colonel of a Massachusetts regiment, in France's service during the Franco-Prussian War where he was killed on the battlefield; General Thomas Jordan, a West Point graduate on Beauregard's staff during the Civil War, who "at one time held command of the Cuban Army"; the American officers Ward and Burgevine, in China during the Taiping Rebellion.

One American soldier of fortune the *New York Times* did not mention was then serving with the Carlist forces in Spain. Conrad, meeting him in Marseilles, was to fight a duel with him over the extraordinary girl Don Carlos brought to France from Vienna eleven months after the defeat at Tolosa. She appeared in Conrad's life at a time when the possibility of raising Catalonia in the interests of Spain's "true king" seemed very real.

Northern Catalonia, a Carlist stronghold from the beginning, was the last area in Spain to give up fighting for the *rey netto*. When the Carlist fortress there of Seo de Urgel fell to Alfonso's General Martínez de Campos on August 27, 1875, it was a setback for the Blancos but far from a total collapse; resistance to Madrid was to continue in that area until 1882, four years after Conrad's involvement in Spain's internal quarrel. Though a shipwreck in Catalonia's Gulf of Rosas ended his gunrunning participation at the close of 1877, contraband arms were still reaching the Basque Carlists in northern Catalonia in June, 1881, for a fresh rising the London *Times* reported on June 20 of that year; not until a year later did the last Carlist fighters in Catalonia give up, the same newspaper on March 19, 1882, announcing, by that news, the end of ten years of warfare in Spain's "maquis."

Arms for the Catalonia guerrillas were shipped from Marseilles where an active Carlist committee functioned. Funds were plentiful. Don Carlos was himself wealthy and had the support of two of the richest men in Europe, his uncle the Count de Chambord, and the Duke of Norfolk; the sums collected were large enough for two bankers in France, M. Dubrocq in Burdeos and M. de Laulne in Paris, to be delegated to handle Carlist accounts.[11] As extensive as funds was the popularity of "the Cause" in southern France during Conrad's years in Marseilles. Frédéric Mistral, the Provençal poet awarded the Nobel Prize for literature in 1904 and the outstanding celebrity in the Marseilles Conrad knew, was a Carlist sympathizer. According to A. Camdessus in *Mistral, était-il Carliste?*, the famous poet had contact in Marseilles with the chief Catalans and personalities of the Carlist world in the "tormented" period of 1867-1878, a time when Carlism, drawing the support of French Legitimists involved in the related attempt to enthrone the Count de Chambord in France, was "very popular" throughout the Midi.

Among the chief personalities of the Carlist world who appeared briefly in Marseilles during those years was Don Rafael Tristany, aide of Don Carlos and a marshal in the Carlist army in Catalonia; of a family with a very famous name in Spain throughout the Carlist wars from 1833 on, he was, before his death in 1899, an outstanding personage in that special world, as were his forefathers, uncles and brothers.[12] Conrad indicated he met the Spanish grandee in Marseilles in the fall of 1877 while acting as a gunrunner for the Carlists. In an early draft[13] of *The Arrow of Gold* he wrote of Don Rafael Tristany—a name altered in the published version to Don Rafael de Villarel—describing the austere aide of Don Carlos, "a person of great political (and domestic) influence at Court" as "a frail little man with a long, yellow face and sunken fanatical eyes, an Inquisitor, an unfrocked monk." The Inquisition, not far in the past in Spain, still had its strong supporters; aligning themselves with Carlism, they were of "the clerical party of intransigeant Catholics" *Le Figaro* designated as the principal backers of the movement.

With uncle and nephew both striving for thrones—the Count de Chambord seeking to be proclaimed Henry V of France and Don Carlos to be Charles VII of Spain—the two men and their followers joined forces in France during a chaotic period when monarchist hopes were high. When those hopes died, dissolved by the strengthening of democracy in France, a large proportion of the private papers concerning the two Legitimist movements were destroyed or made inaccessible to historians. Two whose archives contained such papers were Joseph du Bourg, secretary of the Count de Chambord for many years, and Count de Melgar, secretary of Don Carlos for an even longer period of time. In the last years of his long life Joseph du Bourg burned a great many of his documents, his granddaughter remembered, but among the surviving yearbooks of his correspondence those relating to the French Pretender's 1875–1880 activities indicate his wide contact with Royalists at that time, including those in Marseilles.[14]

Count de Melgar, a Spanish aristocrat who joined the Carlist cause early in Spain and as a continuing participant migrated to Paris in March, 1876, had for more than twenty years, 1876 to 1900, a close personal association with Don Carlos; in his position as private secretary he was, in his words, "of all the people who surround Your Majesty the one who is privileged to be in closest touch with you." Drawing his information from records kept during those years, not from memory, he wrote his memoirs, *Veinte Años con don Carlos*, completing them before his death in 1926. Edited by his son, Count Francisco de Melgar, they were published in Madrid in 1940. An authoritative account of Carlism given by a man in an unequaled position to know it, his volume offers a reliable inside story of a movement that, like all political fiascos, had its share of recriminations and slanders.

To relate developments accurately was one purpose of the memoirs; another was to give an equally truthful and frank history of Paula de Somoggy, *l'amie du Roi*, the Count de Melgar writing of her to erase whatever might have been remembered of the vilifying statements once made by an aide Don Carlos had disowned.

The disowned aide, General Böet, was accused of theft by Don Carlos, in a lawsuit brought in Milan. While traveling in Italy in December, 1877, the Pretender notified the Milan police that he had been robbed of a priceless piece of jewelry, the diamond-studded collar of the Order of the Golden Fleece, which he had found missing from his luggage when he returned to his hotel. The robbery, thought to have been committed either in Venice or Milan, grew into an international scandal since the ornament was, as *Frank Leslie's Illustrated Newspaper* said on February 2, 1878, "valuable not only in the pecuniary sense, but historically, as having been made in 1430 for Philip, Duke of Burgundy, on the occasion of his founding the Order in celebration of his third marriage." Charged in the Milan lawsuit with absconding with the historic ornament, the General countered with accusations, jubilantly published by the foes of Carlism in Spain, in which he liberally smeared his former cohorts in the cause; among his victims was the young *amie* of Don Carlos, a girl General Böet had had little time or opportunity to know. Correcting the General's misstatements, the Count de Melgar devoted a chapter of his memoirs to her. Having known her well for more than thirty-five years, he told from his own knowledge, in the only firsthand account of her life ever published, of the peasant girl who became the Marquise de Trabadelo; who, at fifty-nine, died in Paris, her death and funeral reported by *Le Figaro* on November 18, 1917.[15]

For almost six years, from the first months of 1877 to the middle of 1882, she had been a striking, important figure in the Carlist world, the girl Conrad drew so exactly in the beguiling character of Doña Rita de Lastaola in *The Arrow of Gold*. An orphan raised in poverty by a parish priest uncle in a Hungarian village (the assumed name by which she was known, Baroness Paula de Somoggy, or more correctly Somogyi, being taken from her native Hungarian region of Somogy), she had extraordinary beauty and intelligence. An accomplished linguist acquiring fluency in five languages between 1876 and 1878—French being the first and always preferred of them—she acted as hostess, in her early twenties, to the social elite of Paris. Her influence on Don Carlos had been major from the start, comparable, it was said, to that exerted upon Louis I of Bavaria by Lola Montez, the Irish girl who in effect ruled Bavaria for a time, her support of Liberals leading to the struggle with Conservative and Clerical parties resulting in the Revolution of 1848. Paula de Somoggy had no such lasting effect upon history but her career as a power behind "the king" was also brought to a close by Clerical, aristocratic partisans whose opposition to the nonreligious, peasant girl forced Don Carlos to break with her in May, 1882. How she came to enter upon that career was told by the Count de Melgar in his memoirs:

"At the end of 1876 or the beginning of 1877 when Don Carlos returned from the Russo-Turkish War, during which he took sides with King Carol I of Rumania who honored him with the Military Bravery Cross for his brilliant conduct in the field of battle, he stopped in Vienna to see his relatives.

"He was accompanied by his aide, Don José de Suelves, who later became the Marquis de Tamarit. During his stay in the capital of Austria Don Carlos met a young and very beautiful Hungarian actress with whom he fell madly in love, becoming intimate with her and taking her to Paris.

"Her name was Paula de Somoggy. She was scarcely eighteen years old and a proud young miss who brought out admiration from those passing her in the street; blonde, with magnificent blue eyes, tall and with a majestic bearing, she possessed at the same time an extraordinary intelligence.

"When Don Carlos met her she spoke only Hungarian and a few words of German; after two years she could speak almost every European language: French, Spanish, Italian, German, and English, although the first of those was the language she favored until her death."

The time of their meeting in Vienna, "at the end of 1876 or the beginning of 1877," was accurately given by the Count de Melgar, the presence of Don Carlos on the eastern battle front at that end-of-year time confirmed by the London *Times* on January 27, 1877.[*]

Arriving in Paris with Don Carlos in January, 1877, Paula de Somoggy

---

[*] Further endorsement of the Count de Melgar's statements concerning Don Carlos appears in, among other newspapers, the London *Times* of 1877 in the issues of March 16, April 9, May 24, 25, 26, 29, 31, June 21, 22, and December 8; January 1, 3, 1878; January 5, August 1, 1880; June 9, 28, 1882. The efforts of the Pretender to secure the throne of Spain were of international concern in these years and were widely reported in the press of France, Spain, England and the United States.

first took up residence in the Hotel Friedland and, in the interests of her protector, soon began her frequent trips to that key center of Carlism, Marseilles ("In Paris, in our apartments in the hotel" was an allusion to the Hotel Friedland made by Conrad in *The Arrow of Gold*). Later Don Carlos established her in her own home on the rue Pauquet, where she lived until her marriage in 1887 to the well-known Spanish teacher of operatic singing, Angel de Trabadelo, upon whom the king of Spain conferred the title of Marquis. For thirty years following her marriage she had her home in Paris at 4 rue Marbeuf, the house in which she died.

It was during her early months in France, as a girl of eighteen and a year younger than himself, that Conrad met her. By his calendar as given in *The Arrow of Gold* and verified by the events he wrote of, the time was March, 1877, "this adventure which took about twelve months to develop" ending in March, 1878. How it began he told in the First Note of that novel, being sought out as "an eccentric youngster" in Marseilles "for what the legitimist sympathizers had very much at heart just then: to organize a supply of arms and ammunition to the Carlist detachments in the South."

South of Marseilles, in the Basque provinces of Spain, Carlist rebellions had been mounting. So out of hand had his unruly country become by February, 1877, that King Alfonso dissolved the Spanish Senate and called for new elections. Defiantly, the rebelling provinces announced their refusal to assimilate with the rest of the country and give up the Carlist cause, the London *Times* reported on March 16, 1877. Don Carlos praised their decision in a commendatory letter, having decided in those first months of 1877 on a new attempt at the throne, as the Count de Melgar, a journalist acting that year as press spokesman for Don Carlos in Paris, recalled in his memoirs.

The "supply by sea of arms and ammunition" to the rebelling Spanish provinces proved so effective that the Spanish consul in Marseilles, the Marquis de Gonzales, protested to French authorities in the Bouches-du-Rhône against the export of Carlist munitions from that port, Conrad's ship being a small part of the network.

The ship, as he named it in his memoirs *The Mirror of the Sea*, was the *Tremolino*, a sixty-ton balancelle "with two short masts raking forward and two curved yards, each as long as her hull; a true child of the Latin Lake, with a spread of two enormous sails resembling the pointed wings on a sea-bird's slender body, and herself, like a bird indeed, skimming rather than sailing the seas." The name *Tremolino* (the "Quiverer") may have been a fond nickname for the gunrunning vessel, posing as a fruit and corkwood trader during this affair, which Conrad remembered throughout his life with deep affection. It had, he said, been "built on the River of Savona by a famous builder of boats." The famous builder of boats in Savona of the time was Francesco Calamaro, widely known for his wooden sailing ships, and presumably the builder of Conrad's vessel.[16] The ship was possibly a felucca, similar to a balancelle, and—by the practice he followed of employing names in his books almost identical with those of real life—perhaps named not *Tremolino* but *Cremolino*, taken from the old historical palace near Genoa of that name, an outstanding landmark of that and the close-by Savona area. In *Nostromo*, the novel in which Conrad drew his Marseilles-to-Spain gunrunning partner Dominic Cervoni as the leading character, he referred, as if directed by memory of his gunrunning ship, to a "fruit-laden felucca" of sixty tons, and wrote of the Genoa he knew as "a big port, where the coasting feluccas, with their lateen sails outspread like motionless wings, enter gliding silently between the end of long moles of squared blocks that project angularly toward each other, hugging a cluster of shipping to the superb bosom of a hill covered with palaces."

A thorough search of shipping records in the official archives of Italy, France, Corsica and Monaco has failed to uncover a *Tremolino*, an unusually casual name for a ship, though no conclusion can be final: shipping records were haphazardly kept in the 1870s and of those that were kept many have been lost in the course of eighty-eight years, two world wars playing a part in that loss. The illegal nature of the ship's activity, as well as the insignificance of its size, insured a lack of mention in the press.

Existing records tell, however, something of the two men with Conrad on the Carlist gunrunning voyages, Dominic Cervoni and his young nephew César Cervoni. Dominic, born in Luri, Corsica, on May 22, 1834, had a long career as a French seaman. Beginning it at seventeen, he spent twenty-eight years of his life on ships, sailing about the world. Excluding the frequent, often long, layovers in port between voyages, the lot of every seaman, his active service included three and a half years in the French navy, twenty-three years on foreign and coastal voyages, nine months on coastal fishing boats.[17] He died at fifty-six in his home town of Luri on July 27, 1890.

Dominic was forty-three, a black-haired, rugged man with curled mustaches, when he acted as *padrone* of the *Tremolino* (to give the name as Conrad did; Dominic's detailed service record, listing such ships as that of which he was *padrone* in 1877, was held by the Inscription Maritime in Bastia until, along with other records, it was lost in the destruction of World War II[18]). Broad-chested, stronghearted, Dominic was "a Southerner of a concentrated, deliberate type," astute and fearless, a "Man of the People" with a deep scorn for upper-class conventions and laws.

"For want of more exalted adversaries," Conrad wrote in *The Mirror of the Sea*, "Dominic turned his audacity fertile in impious stratagems against the powers of the earth, as represented by the institution of Custom-houses and every mortal belonging thereto—scribes, officers, and guardacostas afloat and ashore. He was the very man for us, this modern and unlawful wanderer with his own legend of loves, dangers, and bloodshed. He told us bits of it sometimes in measured, ironic tones. He spoke Catalonian, the Italian of Corsica and the French of Provence with the same easy naturalness."

Though Conrad knew the Corsican seaman for less than two years, from 1876 to 1878, and never saw him again after the latter year when he left Marseilles, Dominic made such a lasting impression upon him that he drew him as Dominic in *The Arrow of Gold*, as Peyrol in *The Rover*, as Nostromo in *Nostromo*, as Attilio in *Suspense*, and told of him under his full name in *The Mirror of the Sea*. For more than fifteen years during his writing career Conrad built fictional characters upon the man still vivid in his memory a quarter of a century after his last contact with him. That contact, as it began, ended in Marseilles, following the shipwreck of the *Tremolino*, the craft in which Conrad "plied his fantastic trade."

For this exploit the ship was owned by a syndicate of four young men, "an international and astonishing syndicate," as he wrote of them in *The Mirror of the Sea*, who were "all ardent Royalists of the snow-white Legitimist complexion—Heaven only knows why!" Since all were living in 1906, when *The Mirror of the Sea* was published, Conrad gave them disguised names. The three others in addition to himself were "Poor J.M.K.B., *Américain, Catholique, et gentilhomme*, as he was disposed to describe himself in moments of lofty expansion"; Henry C——, an Englishman of a well-to-do London suburban family; and Roger P. de la S——, "the most Scandinavian-looking of Provençal squires, fair, and six feet high."

Conrad was the active member of the four, going to sea with the ship under Dominic's command. At nineteen he carried on his "fantastic trade" for eight months of 1877, transporting rifles, concealed under a cargo of oranges, from Marseilles to the Catalonian coast, there to be used by the Pretender's guerrilla bands in Spain. The risky exploit was one he often liked to tell of and appeared prominently in the stories recalled by such memoir-writing listeners as his wife and Ford Madox

Ford. Giving what he remembered of the story as he had heard it from Conrad some twenty years before, Ford told in *Joseph Conrad: A Personal Remembrance* how Conrad, "in company with like-minded friends," set about providing the contraband rifles.

"They purchased a small, fast sailing ship—the *Tremolino*, beautiful name. And of all the craft on which Conrad sailed this was the most beloved by him. In our early days her name was seldom off his tongue and, when he mentioned her, his face lit up. Nay, it lit up before he mentioned her, the smile coming, before the name, to his lips.

"The writer never heard, in those days, what make of ship she was. He was expected to know that: Conrad would say: 'You know how the *Tremolino* used to come round. . . .' So the writer imagined her as a felucca. . . .

"Pacing up and down Conrad would relate how they ran those rifles."

Running the rifles to Spain became increasingly hazardous as the months of 1877 went by. On May 22, 1877, Don Carlos was expelled from France, at the request of the Spanish Embassy in Paris, which saw him stirring up hopes for a renewal of the civil war in Spain—the news of that expulsion, carried in the London *Times* of May 31, 1877, appearing widely throughout the European press. Though the Basque provinces were still showing defiance as the year ended, as the London *Times* said on December 8, the Spanish government was sending *guardacostas* on a more active pursuit of smugglers. In France, too, monarchist activity was under hostile scrutiny—the French elections of October, 1877, having proved a victory for Gambetta and the republicans —and Marseilles was ceasing to be what it had once been, a port friendly to Carlists.

"The business was getting dangerous," Conrad wrote of the final days of his gunrunning in *The Arrow of Gold.* "The bands in the South were not very well organized, worked with no very definite plan, and now were beginning to be pretty closely hunted."

On the Costa Brava, the wild Catalonian coast of Spain where the sharp *tramontana* blows offshore with an unpredictable charge into the large Gulf of Rosas, Conrad's gunrunning ended. He had landed rifles often before on that steep, rocky, granite coast, the *selva* or *garrotxa* of Spain where the dwarfed pine and cork oak trees sweep down almost to the sea, long the unsettled maquis so well suited to smugglers and to the landing of arms for Carlist guerrillas fanning out from their stronghold of Seo de Urgel, ninety miles inland. A lantern signal on shore had previously given Conrad's ship the all-clear but on his last voyage a *guardacosta* gave pursuit. The sudden squalls of the *tramontana*, blotting out vision at sea, gave partial protection to his fleeing ship. But each clearing of the sky showed the coast guard vessel to be gaining and, to escape capture, Dominic chose to wreck the *Tremolino*.

"You must steer her yourself," he told Conrad, "and I shall see to it that she dies quickly, without leaving as much as a chip behind."

Off Cape Creus, twelve miles from the safety of the French border, Conrad steered the *Tremolino* toward the rocks of the weird coast obliterated by "a sort of murky whirlwind."

"No ship ran so joyously to her death before," he wrote in *The Mirror of the Sea*. "She rose and fell, as if floating in space, and darted forward, whizzing like an arrow. Dominic, stooping under the foot of the foresail, reappeared, and stood steadying himself against the mast, with a raised forefinger in an attitude of expectant attention. A second before the shock his arm fell down by his side. At that I set my teeth. And then—

"Talk of splintered planks and smashed timbers! This shipwreck lies upon my soul with the dread and horror of a homicide, with the unforgettable remorse of having crushed a living, faithful heart at a single blow."

After the shipwreck, according to Jessie Conrad in *Joseph Conrad as I Knew Him*, the smugglers—there had been seven aboard the *Tremolino*, including Conrad, Dominic, César, and four of the crew—hid for days in an underground cellar on the Catalonian coast, making their way overland to France after the Spanish authorities had given up searching for them.

In *The Mirror of the Sea* Conrad implied that one of the crew, César Cervoni, was drowned in the shipwreck, the nineteen-year-old youth knocked overboard by Dominic as the ship itself went down. It was Dominic's belief that César had betrayed them to the Spanish authorities when the *Tremolino* called at Barcelona; he had subsequently, Conrad was sure, broken into the ship's locker and stolen the money belt of gold, Carlist cash to be used for bribes on shore.

"I struck once, and the wretch went down like a stone—with the gold," Dominic said in the words Conrad recalled in *The Mirror of the Sea*. "Yes. But he had time to read in my eyes that nothing could save him while I was alive. And had I not the right—I, Dominic Cervoni, Padrone who brought him aboard your felucca—my nephew, a traitor?"

Conrad's intense dislike of the young Corsican led him to obliterate César, on paper. "Without being in any way deformed, he was the nearest approach which I have ever seen or could imagine to what is commonly understood by the word 'monster,'" was Conrad's description of him. "That the source of the effect produced was really moral I have no doubt. An utterly, hopelessly depraved nature was expressed in physical terms, that taken each separately had nothing positively startling. You imagined him clammily cold to the touch, like a snake."

But César Cervoni did not in fact drown when the *Tremolino* was wrecked. He continued at sea until 1910, when fifty-two, his sea service of thirty-eight years having begun at fourteen in 1872.[19] He was very much alive in 1906 when *The Mirror of the Sea* was published, then captain of the French coaster *Memphis*. After the loss of the *Tremolino* he spent the following five years on French ships in coastal waters; in 1883 he made the second of his foreign voyages (the first on the *Saint-Antoine* in 1876 with Conrad) when he sailed as a crew member of the *Djemah*, a passenger and mail steamer of the Messageries Maritimes line, on a voyage from Marseilles to India. In twenty-seven years he served on twenty-eight different ships, some for a few days only, giving in that unusually restless record some support for Conrad's view that he was not the most compatible of seamen.

From 1883 to 1902 César sailed on French steamers to ports in India, China, Japan, the East Indies, the Mediterranean, Africa and Australia. He and Conrad voyaged over many of the same sea lanes and in the same years. In 1884 their ships passed at sea—Conrad as second mate on the *Narcissus*, César a seaman on the French steamer *Sindh*—one leaving India as the other approached it. By the narrow margin of seven days they missed meeting in Singapore in 1885, Conrad leaving that port on the *Tilkhurst* a week before César arrived on the S.S. *Anadyr*.

By the coincidence of name though not of place, when Dominic died in Corsica on July 27, 1890, Conrad was in the Belgian Congo undergoing a thirty-six-day trek through the scorching heat, heading for the command of a small river steamer (the Congo experience he recalled in "Heart of Darkness") and César was a *matelot* of thirty-two on the ocean-going ship *Congo* in the early part of a four-months' voyage. It was after Conrad had left the sea that César, at thirty-seven, secured command of his first ship, the coaster *Sidor* in 1895. From 1900 to 1910 he was master of eight seagoing and coastal ships, the last six years in command of coasters only.

Born in Luri, Corsica, on January 18, 1858, César returned to his home waters in the later years of his life. On his last ship, the *Madonna* —he was captain of it—a coastal voyage of forty-five days ended on June 18, 1910; on that day closed the last record of his life.

After the wreck of the *Tremolino* César and Dominic found berths on other ships. But Conrad, back in Marseilles, entered the tempestuous time involving two others, the girl for whose sake he had undertaken the gunrunning and the American soldier of fortune who had been instrumental in his meeting her. Both men, "like two hundred others, or two thousand, all around," were in love with her. Their rivalry ended in the manner then observed in France by men of fashion.

Dueling had originated in France (American cowboys and German university students being the last in the world to practice it) and had taken the lives of twenty thousand Frenchmen during the twenty-one-year reign of Henry IV. To stamp out the "social institution" strict laws had been passed in France, yet so ineffectively were they enforced that in the fifteen years between 1869 and 1884 as many as 545 publicly known duels were fought, with an unknown number of others taking place in secret.[20] So widespread had the vogue become by 1882 that in December of that year Theodore Child, writing from Paris, described it as a "mania" in the New York *Sun:*

"Opinion has sanctioned duelling and, in spite of the edicts of Henry IV, of Richelieu, of Louis XIV, in spite of the eloquent protestations of Jean Jacques Rousseau, and of the philosophers of the eighteenth century, it continues to be, in France, an important social institution. Just now there is a kind of epidemic of duels in France. Every day in the week there are meetings in the woods in the environs of Paris."

The frequency of the encounters, Child went on, "has had the effect of causing a large part of the population of France to frequent the fencing-rooms." In Paris such training rooms were "counted by the score," the sweeping craze demanding that "every man who respects himself—every young fellow who pretends to be stylish—must pass an hour or two every day in the fencing-rooms under the orders of his trainer. The fencing-room is fashionable; and public opinion—or, rather, the opinion of Society under the Third Republic—is that the duel preserves honor, reputation, and dignity."

The fashionable weapon in 1882, Child declared, was no longer the pistol but the rapier or the saber. "Under the direction of Saint Michael [the patron saint of fencers], Don Quixote, and Master Vigéant [then the most celebrated fencing master in Paris], the present duelling and fencing mania is as likely as not to lead to a renaissance of chivalry. The French under the Third Republic will have their tournaments and courts of arms, their knights and nobles of the sword."

Four years earlier, Conrad, a young man of fashion living up to his name of "the Count," took his direction from the figure who was always to entrance him, Don Quixote, and sent a challenge.

VII

With the greatest deliberation he reached with his left hand for his pistol and taking careful aim shot Monsieur George through the left side of his breast.

The Arrow of Gold

Abiding by the code of *un homme d'honneur* of his Legitimist set where that code functioned austerely, Conrad, twenty, strode off counted paces in a walled garden outside Marseilles on March 1, 1878, and turned to fight a pistol duel with his American partner in the *Tremolino* escapade, a man of twenty-nine with "most distinguished connections." French law defined dueling as a crime in that year of 1878—the victor of a mortal combat could be charged with murder—and this meeting *sur le terrain*, one of many in the epidemic of duels then sweeping France, was guarded from the police. For forty-one years (nine years after his opponent's death in 1910) Conrad maintained a public silence about his duel. But upon the death of the girl who had indirectly been the cause of it—Paula de Somoggy, the Marquise de Trabadelo, who died in Paris in November, 1917—he felt released to tell the story uppermost in his mind "through all the years of my writing life." Since the five people who had been involved with him in that long-ago drama were, in 1917, "all at rest" and a recounting of it could no longer trouble anyone, he wrote of his love affair and its duel ending in *The Arrow of Gold*, the autobiographical novel published in 1919 he defined as "the product of my private garden."[1]

"I never tried to conceal the origins of the subject matter of this book which I have hesitated so long to write,"[2] he said of it. A story from his own life, as so many of his novels were, it was intended to have "the quality of initiation (through an ordeal which required some resolution to face) into the life of passion."[3] He was sixty when he began it. Two years later, as he wrote Mme. Alvar in 1919, his youthful romance was a painful memory for him still.

"The 'Divine Madness' was so strong that I would have walked into a precipice, deliberately, with my eyes open, for its sake. And now it seems incredible; and yet it is the same old heart—for even at that distance of time I can't smile at it."[4]

While correcting the proofs of *The Arrow of Gold* he told another friend, Sir Sidney Colvin, of what troubling memories the book had stirred. "The fact is, between you and me (and Lady Colvin of course), that I have never been able to read *these* proofs in cold blood. Ridiculous! My dear (as D. Rita would have said) there are some of these 42-year-old episodes of which I cannot think now without a slight tightness of the chest—*un petit serrement de coeur*. What a confession!"[5]

In an unqualified statement affirming that his duel and the circumstances of it as told in the story were true, he wrote in the copy of the book he presented to Richard Curle: "All the personages are authentic and the facts are as stated."[6] Curle, who from the earliest years of knowing Conrad had had a writer's interest in his friend's adventurous life, emphasized the factual background of the novel—which had been dedicated to him—in a letter of June 7, 1951, to Dr. J. G. Reed: "Yes, the autobiographical element in *The Arrow of Gold* is very strong."[7]

Though relatives of the "personages" Conrad portrayed so truthfully in the novel recognized the people in it; though Conrad maintained he had not attempted to conceal the origins of the story (and to an astonishing degree he did not); though he wrote so explicitly of the episode marking a turning point in his life, and of facts that were verifiable, an air of mystery grew about it. The long distance back to the time of its setting made for disbelief—to a modern world the field of honor was of the cobwebbed past, a trapping of the Gilded Age which, like the "heiresses" of that day, was too frivolously romantic for readers conditioned by the hard realities of world wars. With the first grim battles of 1914 the era of the *boulevardier* ended with finality in France. The "elegants of this amusing and happy epoch, making an assault on gayety," as Paul d'Ariste wrote of them in *La Vie et le Monde du Boulevard*, vanished as suddenly as the "sparkling and ready-witted spirit" of the giddier day. London almost as much as Paris had performed to the masquerade beat of the foppish times, as an American writing from London told of them in *Frank Leslie's Illustrated Newspaper* of January 26, 1878: "The man who would here attempt to get into a cab or out of one, or eat dinner, or drink ale, or make a speech, or shovel coal, without first adjusting his eye-glass, would be looked upon as eccentric." In the sterner Europe emerging from World War I there was little tolerance for the dandies and the *lionnes*, those figures dominating the France of Conrad's youth.

But records recently discovered of Conrad's hitherto unknown American opponent in the Marseilles duel of eighty-seven years ago underline the exceptional honesty with which he related this story of his early life. "To be dishonest is a dangerous luxury for most of us, I fancy, and I am sure it is so for me," he told H. G. Wells in 1898.[8] In a characteristic attitude of frankness and after several unsatisfying starts, he completed *The Arrow of Gold*, the story which intrigued critics ("Next thing to a 'sensation'," Conrad said of it when it came out in England) and also mystified them.

Mystery there was from the beginning, forty-six years ago when the novel first appeared. The questioning attitude of critics soon led Conrad to make an "explicit statement" of the origins of his story.

"The subject of this book," he wrote in 1920, "I have been carrying about with me for many years, not so much a possession of my memory as an inherent part of myself. It was ever present to my mind and ready to my hand, but I was loth to touch it from a feeling of what I imagined to be mere shyness but which in reality was a very comprehensible mistrust of myself.

"In plucking the fruit of memory one runs the risk of spoiling its bloom, especially if it has got to be carried into the market-place. This being the product of my private garden my reluctance can be easily understood. . . .

"I venture this explicit statement because, amidst much sympathetic appreciation, I have detected here and there a note, as it were, of suspicion. Suspicion of facts concealed, of explanations held back, of inadequate motives. But what is lacking in the facts is simply what I did not know, and what is not explained is what I did not understand myself, and what seems inadequate is the fault of my imperfect insight. And all that I could not help. In the case of this book I was unable to supplement these deficiencies by the exercise of my inventive faculty. It was never very strong; and on this occasion its use would have seemed exceptionally dishonest."[9]

So honest was Conrad in writing *The Arrow of Gold* that he employed the actual names and characteristics of four of the six main characters in the story. To the American whose dueling shot went close to his heart, nearly ending his life—he bore the chest scar ever after—Conrad gave, in the book, the name of Captain John M. K. Blunt. He was, in fact, Captain John Young Mason Key Blunt, grandson of Francis Scott Key, author of *The Star-Spangled Banner*. Blunt's distinguished connections, the "distinguished relations" Conrad repeatedly emphasized in the novel, included in addition to his famous grandfather a number of other prominent names: of Blunt's nine uncles one was George Hunt Pendleton, Senator from Ohio, Democratic candidate for Vice-President in 1864, United States Minister to Germany from 1885 to 1889; another was Daniel Turner, a member of Congress from North Carolina; another was Philip Barton Key, U. S. District Attorney for the District of Columbia, shot and killed on a street corner near the White House in Washington, D.C., in 1859 by the New York Congressman, and later General, Daniel Edgar Sickles, a *crime passionnel* resulting from Key's affair with Sickles' young Italian wife. Among Blunt's most notable connections was his great-uncle Roger Brooke Taney, Chief Justice of the U. S. Supreme Court from 1836 to 1864, long remembered for handing down the decision in the Dred Scott Case and for writing the majority opinion in which he, a Southern slaveowner, held that the Negro "had no rights which the white man was bound to respect"—words which the abolitionist leader, Senator Charles Sumner, declared would cause his name to be "hooted down the page of history." A prominent statesman of pre-Civil War years was the Virginia family friend for whom Blunt was named, John Young Mason, who served as Secretary of the Navy under Presidents Tyler and Polk and as United States Minister to France from 1853 to 1859, a term during which he became famous for his part in the Ostend Manifesto, the abortive 1854 proposal either to purchase or to take Cuba by force from Spain.

Blunt was not by any means the first to find a distinguished family background hard to live up to and he became, even as Conrad told of his adventures in *The Arrow of Gold* and *The Mirror of the Sea*, a soldier of fortune, a man proclaiming "I live by my sword." The early steps of a career ending as a captain in the United States Army were taken largely through the influence of his mother, the second of the real-life people Conrad brought into his novel.

Giving her there her own name of Mrs. Blunt, Conrad later and more explicitly identified her to his biographer G. Jean-Aubry as Mme. Key Blunt, an American widow living in Paris in the 1860s with dependent children to care for, who sought and won the aid of Théophile Gautier for her one appearance as a Shakespearean actress in Paris.

Fourteen years later, when Mrs. Blunt was fifty-six and Conrad nineteen, he met her in Marseilles a few months before he fought a duel with her son. Picturing her in that year of 1877, he described her in *The Arrow of Gold* as an "exquisite, aristocratic old woman" with Royalist sympathies; a former Southern belle who, ruined financially by the Civil War, "lived by her wits"; a perfectly preserved, expensively dressed, haughty, black-eyed woman who gazed through her lorgnette at lesser mortals; a voluntary American exile in France with "distinguished relations" who had "the hands of a queen—or an abbess" and "the assured as if royal—yes, royal—even flow of the voice"; a "slave-owning woman who had never worked," who talked of "the distinction that letters and art" gave to life and of the "nobility and consolations" to be found in aesthetics; a mother whose chief concern was for the son she admired "exceedingly" for "his distinction, his fastidiousness, the earnest warmth of his heart."

Briefly recounting her life and her "personal contact with a good many" of the Bourbons in France during the Second Empire, Conrad wrote in *The Arrow of Gold:*

"I looked at her from time to time thinking: She has seen slavery, she has seen the Commune, she knows two continents, she has seen a civil war, the glory of the Second Empire, the horrors of two sieges; she has been in contact with marked personalities, with great events, she has lived on her wealth, on her personality, and there she is, with her plumage unruffled, as glossy as ever, unable to get old:—a sort of Phoenix free from the slightest signs of ashes and dust."[10]

Mrs. Blunt did in fact live the life Conrad summarized, and was extremely devoted to her son. She was also the romantic, imperious *grande dame* who so much believed in "the distinction that letters and art" gave to life that she once wrote an overly romantic novel of her own, a disjointed story concerning the princely household of the younger son of an earl. Her accent on aristocrats, in the book as in her life, stemmed from her own early years.

The ninth of the eleven children of Francis Scott Key, Mrs. Ellen Lloyd Key Blunt was born in the Key mansion on M Street in what is now the Georgetown section of Washington, D.C., on August 16, 1821.[11] Her father was then a well-known lawyer of forty-two who had written *The Star-Spangled Banner* seven years before, the popularly adopted song which, by an Act of Congress, was made the national anthem in 1931.

Francis Scott Key was a devoted father, an Episcopalian and strong churchman, a lawyer-poet with an ardent, generous nature and democratic outlook. Of a prominent and wealthy family, he had grown up at Terra Rubra, the Maryland plantation where his father, a popular country squire and associate judge, maintained open house during the thirty years following Washington's inauguration.

Informal and friendly, Key was in sharp contrast to his wife, Mary Tayloe Lloyd Key, a reserved and regal woman five years younger than himself. The daughter of a colonel and granddaughter of Edward Lloyd, British Royal Governor of the colony of Maryland from 1709 to 1714, she also came of an old family and a wealthy one. Her marriage in 1802—she a bride of seventeen and Key twenty-two—was the most fashionable social event of the year in Annapolis, joining as it did two of the outstanding families of Maryland. But at the time of her marriage she had, and never lost, the stiff consciousness of being well-born.

"She was almost haughty," wrote Victor Weybright in *Spangled Banner*, "at least, she was considered extraordinarily proud. She was a product of the old Annapolis society, once Tory, then Federalist, that had seldom mingled with the democrats, no matter how well born, from the uplands." Bearing eleven children in the course of twenty-four years, she yet "never lost her dignity, her distinction, her air of patrician beauty. . . . There were plenty of servants to manage the household details, to attend to the children, to drive the carriage and convey messages, and it required no sacrifice for Mrs. Key to entertain a constant procession of guests."

It was Mrs. Key's manner and point of view, rather than her husband's, that governed her daughter Ellen. Ellen was also influenced, in outlook and in her later adopted religion, by her uncle, Roger Brooke Taney, a Roman Catholic born of wealthy planters in Calvert County, Maryland.

The Taneys with their six daughters, the Keys and their many children, spent summer and winter vacations together on the three-thousand-acre Key plantation of Terra Rubra in Frederick County, Maryland, where Francis Scott Key had been born. There Ellen, a remarkably beautiful girl, passed the holidays of her childhood and adolescence. Life was a gay whirl on the vast estate where the Key and Taney families could number more than thirty adults and children on any summer day (Ellen's son, in his time, was to have seventy-five first cousins).

By her seventeenth year Ellen was an acknowledged belle of the countryside. Her father's close contact with the White House, his friendships with Presidents Jackson and Van Buren, with members of their cabinets, the Supreme Court and the diplomatic corps, ensured a constant procession of guests to the estate where, nearing sixty, he was then planning to retire. Friends of Chief Justice Taney and his family, coming up from Baltimore and Washington, added to the never-ending flood of guests who showered attentions on the attractive, spirited daughter Ellen. How much she especially, of all his children, cared for that flattering notice Francis Scott Key indicated in a December 3, 1842, letter to his wife. Delayed in Washington by a law case he was to plead in the Supreme Court, he wrote to his family, isolated at Terra Rubra by an early blizzard and its heavy fall of snow:

"Tell the girls and boys I suppose they are delighted to see the snow. Ellen may perhaps be frightened by the fear it will keep her longer there & keep everybody away—but if I can manage to get away from the Court I shall not mind the snow. I must be in Court on Monday next, but I think in a day or two after that I can get away for 3 or 4 days, perhaps for a week.

"Do make them write to me—all who choose to let me see how they like the Country now—& that they have brightness enough, in & among themselves, to cheer the gloom of a deep snow in the Country."[12]

With dinner parties and balls, horseback rides and sleigh rides, musical evenings and festivals providing a flow of entertainment in the mansion buzzing with the two large Key and Taney families and their guests, Ellen retained such a vital memory of her Southern belle years that, of all the letters she received during the rest of her life, only those of her girlhood did she save and pass on to her grandson.[13] She "never got over her seventeenth year, and the manner of the spoilt beauty of at least three counties," Conrad said of her in *The Arrow of Gold*, during those pre-abolition days "when she was seventeen and wore snowy muslin dresses on the family plantation."

Yet Ellen, perhaps reluctant to leave such a setting, did not marry early. Three years after the death of her father she was married in the family home in Georgetown on January 27, 1846, to Lieutenant Simon Fraser Blunt of the U. S. Navy.[14] Ellen was then twenty-four, her husband a Virginian of thirty. Although she later told Théophile Gautier in Paris, according to Judith Gautier in *Le Second Rang du Collier*, that her husband had been "a President of the United States," Simon Fraser Blunt never rose above the rank of naval lieutenant. He was, however, something of a hero in pre-Civil War Virginia, due to his part in breaking up the Nat Turner slave rebellion in Virginia's Southampton County during the four-day terror of August 21–25, 1831.[15]

The instigator of the uprising was Nat Turner, a slave of thirty-one and a vision-inspired Baptist preacher, who believed divine orders directed him to lead his fellow slaves to freedom by eliminating their white masters. On Sunday, August 21, 1831, when many of the white adults were away from home attending a religious camp meeting, he, with seven followers, entered the home of his master, Joseph Travis, murdering everyone found there. Other homes were similarly visited— the slave band in the end numbering sixty—and before the uprising was brought to a halt fifty-five whites—13 men, 18 women and 24 children —were massacred in their homes.

When the insurrection was at its height Nat Turner led his raiders to the plantation home, Belmont, of Dr. Simon Blunt. Dr. Blunt had given the Negroes on his plantation the choice of staying to defend the family or of joining Nat Turner; they had elected to stay and had armed themselves with pitchforks and hoes. Six guns made up the arsenal of the house, with two men and three boys to use them. On horseback, as were others in his large band, Nat Turner rode into Blunt's yard just before daybreak on August 23 and fired his gun to test the defenses of the home. Young Simon Blunt, a boy of fifteen, sent the first shot back, seriously wounding the mounted second-in-command, Hark Travis. In the ensuing predawn battle one raider was killed, several were wounded and captured; the rest fled. With three thousand troops hurried into the county, the blood bath was brought to an end two days later.

Commodore Elliott of the U.S. steamer *Natchez* led part of the forces sent to quell the slaves' rebellion and, impressed with the bravery of young Blunt, related the story to President Jackson. Jackson, in recognition of the boy's valor, immediately commissioned him a midshipman in the United States Navy, which he entered—at fifteen, one of the youngest in the service—on September 7, 1831, under Elliott's command.

Fifteen years later, having risen to the rank of lieutenant and stationed in Washington, he met and married Ellen Key. During the eight years of their marriage three children were born, in Washington, D.C.: Alice Key Blunt, who died at eighty, unmarried, in Baltimore, Maryland, on May 13, 1927; John Young Mason Key Blunt, born on January 22, 1849, and living to the age of sixty-one; Mary Lloyd Blunt, born in 1852, becoming a nun in Paris at eighteen and dying in 1939, at eighty-seven, in the Sacred Heart Convent at Montreal, Canada, where she had been a nun for many years. Their father, Lieutenant Blunt, was a young man of thirty-eight when he died in Baltimore on April 27, 1854—his grave adjoins that of Francis Scott Key in the Key lot in Mount Olivet Cemetery, Frederick, Maryland.[16]

Ellen Key Blunt, left a widow at thirty-two with three small children —her son then five and her youngest child two—never married again. She continued to live with her children for several years in Washington and there, in the fall of 1856, when thirty-five, published her novel *Bread*.

It was not the Civil War that depleted Mrs. Blunt's fortune, as she wished Conrad to believe. Her husband, with a naval lieutenant's income, had left her with no great means, and the modest fortune of her father, Francis Scott Key, had been left at his death on January 11, 1843, to his widow, whose seven surviving children and many grandchildren shared the remaining estate upon her death in 1859. It was with reference to her financial need in 1856 that Mrs. Blunt titled her novel *Bread: To My Children*. Emphasizing the same note, she devoted her opening page to a quotation from an old song:

> O! weel may the boatie row,
> And better may she speed;
> And weel may the boatie row
> That wins the bairns' bread.

Although Ellen Key Blunt had been brought up a Protestant by her father, a devout Episcopalian, she became a convert to Catholicism and raised her children in that faith. (Her son, meeting Conrad years later in Marseilles, introduced himself as "*Je suis Américain, catholique et gentilhomme.*") Mrs. Blunt's novel *Bread* had, along with its romance of a titled family, the main purpose of offering a plea for religious tolerance, specifically for Catholics in Maryland. It was also laced throughout with verses of her own making, bearing out Conrad's comment upon her in *The Arrow of Gold* as given in the words of her son: "My mother has been writing verse since she was a girl of fifteen. She's still writing verse. She's still fifteen—a spoiled girl of genius."

Less than five years after her book was published the Civil War began and, immediately following the outbreak of the war in 1861, Mrs. Blunt left Washington with her children for Paris. John Y. M. K. Blunt was then twelve, his sisters fourteen and nine.

As evidenced by her novel, Mrs. Blunt had a strong liking for Shakespeare. Doing no further writing, she turned her attention to the stage, believing she had a gift for acting. Perhaps, with the fascination lineage had for her, she was drawn to Shakespeare because the old English family of Blunts, many of whom lived in Stratford-on-Avon, were related to him. One member of the family has a role in *Henry IV*, Part I; a loyal supporter of the king and killed in his defense, he is introduced by the rebel Hotspur:

> Welcome, Sir Walter Blunt; and would to God
> You were of our determination!
> Some of us love you well.

Another, Sir James Blunt, appears as a character in *Richard III*. Another, Edward Blunt, was the printer of "Mr. William Shakespears Comedies, Histories and Tragedies; Published according to the true Originall Copies," the First Folio of Shakespeare.

Waiting out the Civil War in France—and, in fact, never returning to America to live—Mrs. Blunt arrived in Paris at the beginning of a decade when Shakespeare was very much in vogue. Paris audiences in the 1860s saw Shakespeare in almost every conceivable form: *Hamlet* in Italian; *Hamlet* as portrayed by a young French comedienne, Mlle. Judith, in a translation by Alexandre Dumas; *Hamlet* as an opera; *Macbeth* as an opera, with music by Verdi; *Othello, Richard III, The Merry Wives of Windsor* also appeared on Paris stages. Reviewing them, and reiterating his appeal for a permanent Shakespeare theater to be established in Paris, was the drama critic Théophile Gautier.

It was Gautier whom Mrs. Blunt approached in 1863 with the proposal that he help her to appear in Paris in a Shakespearean tragedy. With this project in mind she was "particularly tenacious and pestered us for a long time," Judith Gautier wrote of her. Her husband had recently died, she told the Gautiers, and "had left her with children and without resources: but she had a love and, she believed, a talent for the theater which she felt would help her to restore her fortunes."[17]

A young widow then of forty-two, whose husband had died nine years before, she "was always draped in mourning crepe: 'My husband is always dead,' she would reply to those who pointed out to her that the period for mourning had passed."[18] Gautier, as his daughter said, had a marked predilection for the society of women and was touched by the "exotic unfortunate" with three underage children, the beautiful and determined widow who maintained that "in justice to her talent and in order to obtain fame in America" she must be heard in Paris. After first trying to dissuade her from acting a Shakespearean drama in English before a Parisian audience, Gautier finally succumbed and secured the help of Paul Félix Taillade, an outstanding French actor of thirty-seven, for the project. Judith Gautier, who was seventeen at the time, obviously disliked the persistent American and wrote of Mrs. Blunt in unflattering terms:

"In the end my father gave up trying to convince her and, thinking that it was the only way to get rid of her, he considered means of furthering her plan, while reducing it to as modest dimensions as possible.

"Taillade, whom Théophile Gautier helped considerably and admired immensely, consented to back the project. It came down to playing one act from 'Macbeth' in English, the act of Duncan's murder. Taillade knew very little English but this seemed no drawback to Madame Key Blunt, who undertook to teach the French artist as one teaches a parrot to talk.

"The Vaudeville obligingly lent its premises and after innumerable and laborious rehearsals that performance took place, but as had been suspected, it turned out that Madame Key Blunt had exceedingly little talent and that Taillade, even though he was acting in English, had a great deal. He was able to make himself understood by the Parisian public, much bewildered as they were by the unknown words, and he carried away all the laurels himself.

"My father, in his criticism, tried to leave a share of glory to the American actress, but it is obvious that he is much more sincere when praising Taillade. . . .[19]

"Taillade in fact was superb. Among other things, leaving the stage to return to the room of the crime, he backed into an armchair and his startled leap made the whole audience shiver.

"But I believe Madame Key Blunt never forgave my father for Taillade's success."[20]

It may have been out of gallantry, as the *chevalier français* he admitted himself to be where women were concerned, but far from skimping on Mrs. Blunt's performance or appearing to notice any animosity on her part, Gautier in his review gave exceptional prominence to her acting in *Macbeth* and, some four months later, extended to her—an inexperienced, amateur actress—unusual notice when she appeared before a Paris audience again.

Mrs. Blunt made the stage debut referred to by Judith Gautier on Tuesday evening, September 22, 1863. In its notice in *Le Moniteur Universel* the Vaudeville Theater announced the event on September 21: "This theater is preparing an extraordinary spectacle for tomorrow, Tuesday. To the continuing performances of *Un Homme de rien* and the *Exploits de César* will be added, for tomorrow only, the two acts of *Macbeth*, played by M. Taillade and Mme. Key Blunt." The following day the Vaudeville's effusive announcement, wrongly describing her as English, read: "Today, extraordinary performance, 2nd act of *Macbeth*, played by M. Taillade and Mme. Key Blunt. This act, the most thrilling in Shakespeare, will be interpreted by the French artist and the celebrated English tragedienne."

When Gautier's review appeared, in *Le Moniteur Universel* of September 28, 1863, he, omitting Taillade, singled out the American actress in the heading at the top of his column: "VAUDEVILLE: *Macbeth* (en anglais), la répresentation de Mme. Key Blunt."

Gautier devoted the major part of his theater criticism that day to a laudatory essay on Alfred de Vigny ("When one thinks of de Vigny one somehow sees him as a swan, with an arched neck and wings fluffed up by the breeze, swimming on one of those transparent and sparkling ponds in English parks") and a review of *la Mère confidente*, a comedy by Marivaux. The rest of his space he used for a long analysis of Mrs.

Blunt's *Macbeth*. Always a kindly critic, he there gave more favorable attention to her untrained acting than it seems likely to have merited. Profoundly romantic and a courtly gentleman of the old school, he, then fifty-two, was perhaps swayed by Mrs. Blunt's extreme good looks as much as by his love of Shakespeare when he extolled the performance of the "beautiful American tragedienne" whom he found making Shakespeare's thought "stand out admirably." His review gives a picture of the woman who was to figure in Conrad's life fifteen years later.

"Tall, slender, delicate, elegant, aristocratic, blonde, wearing neither eyebrow blacking nor the livid facial make-up of a villainess as one has come to expect in the theater," Gautier described Mrs. Blunt, "she was a true lady indeed, who makes of this weak Thane, violent and superstitious, the puppet of her ambition; a soul, untouched by the terrors of this world or the next, with a resolution so tranquilly implacable that it could permit her to crush the body of a cherished child under her feet in order to achieve her ends, such a soul animates this frail body who can only know reason in sleep, since, awake, Lady Macbeth is impervious to remorse. Her courage, the abstract courage of women who do not soil themselves with the red cuisine of murder, makes her consider her victims only as obstacles overcome. Mme. Key Blunt has portrayed this character very well. . . .

"Mme. Key Blunt has a natural and profoundly moving diction which achieves the effect without violence, without wild gestures. She makes Shakespeare's thought stand out admirably. Her success has been very great. . . .

"After the curtain fell Mme. Key Blunt and Taillade were recalled with great acclaim. It is a pity that such a beautiful spectacle cannot be continued. Special thanks are offered to M. de Beaufort for having given his hospitality, if only for one evening, to the great William Shakespeare."

More than four months after her appearance as Lady Macbeth, Mrs. Blunt, on February 4, 1864, acted before a Parisian audience for a second, and last, time. Gautier, announcing the forthcoming event in his column in *Le Moniteur Universel* of February 1, gave her—though a dozen prominent actors, actresses and musicians were to take part in the evening's presentation—the billing of a star. Referring to the evening as the "Concert of Mme. Key-Blunt," he wrote:

"A musical and dramatic soirée will be given next Thursday at the Hôtel du Louvre. Mme. Key-Blunt will recite a fragment of *Evangeline* by Longfellow and the monologue of *Macbeth*. Rouvière will give Hamlet's *To be or not to be*, a role he offers in a manner profoundly English and Shakespearean; M. Samson will read literary fragments;

Mme. Ernesta Grisi will sing *la Santa Lucia* and *Nel dolce incanto,* and M. Favilli will play a brilliant fantasia on the violin. *Pour être aimé,* the new comedy by Mme. Berton, will be played by MM Saint-Germain, Paër, Théodule, Mmes. Armand, Baretta; *Un tour de clef,* with M. Barnold, Théodule and Mme. Chaudes-Aigues as interpreters, will complete this charming soirée."

Anyone who shared his love of Shakespeare became endeared to Gautier. A supremely gentle man—in his forty-two years as a poet, novelist and critic he was always fondly referred to as Théo—he was unfailingly courteous to women. Although Mrs. Blunt won his support, she was an impetuous woman whose interests spurted and died, and appears to have passed out of Gautier's view rapidly, as was evidenced two months after the soirée. When the anniversary of Shakespeare's birth was celebrated in Paris in April, 1864, an event in which Gautier had a strong hand, Mrs. Blunt was not among those taking part.

Giving up the stage as she had previously given up writing, Mrs. Blunt, with her "elegance and air of good breeding," turned her attention toward the social life of Paris. By Conrad's account she had a "precarious connection with the very highest spheres"[21] of French society during the Second Empire. Precarious it may have been, but connections she did have. She knew George Bancroft, the American historian and statesman appointed in 1867 as U. S. Minister to Berlin, well enough to send him an inscribed copy of her novel. Her family connections, at a time when American sympathizers of the Confederate cause enjoyed popularity in France, guaranteed her admission to the *haut monde.*

One of many American diplomats Mrs. Blunt knew—a neighbor and close family friend of her husband, in Southampton County, Virginia— was John Young Mason, ending a six-year term as U. S. Minister to France upon his death in Paris in 1859, shortly before Mrs. Blunt arrived there. Another was George Hunt Pendleton, her brother-in-law. Pendleton, who concluded a long political career as U. S. Minister to Germany, ran against Lincoln and Andrew Johnson in 1864 as the Vice-Presidential candidate on the Democratic ticket headed by General George B. McClellan. Pendleton had married Mrs. Blunt's favorite sister, Mary Alicia Lloyd Nevins Key, and the two sisters, with their children, spent much of their time together in Paris after the Civil War. The Pendletons' daughter, Jane Frances, remembered her girlhood days in Paris with her Blunt cousins and Aunt Ellen and, before her death in 1950, told many stories of her quixotic relatives to her son, Arthur T. Brice.

In *The Arrow of Gold* Conrad accurately portrayed the personalities of Mrs. Blunt and Captain Blunt, so the family felt.[22] The Aunt Ellen who lived with such flair in Paris was vividly recalled as a free-wheeling, high-wide-and-handsome *grande dame* of her times ("delightful," Captain Blunt describes his mother in *The Arrow of Gold*, "but as irresponsible as one of those crazy princesses that shock their Royal families"[23]). Always out of money and dramatically extravagant—one family gift of $700 was splurged on earrings for her girls—her "goings-on" and those of her son aroused the disapproval of her younger daughter to such an extent that Mary Lloyd Blunt, at eighteen, became a nun,[24] entering the Order of Ladies of the Sacred Heart in Paris in 1870.

Of Captain John Blunt's life as related in *The Arrow of Gold* much was true. There the captain's history was summarized:

"Educated in the most aristocratic college in Paris . . . at eighteen . . . call of duty . . . with General Lee to the very last cruel minute . . . after that catastrophe—end of the world—return to France—to old friendships, infinite kindness—but a life hollow, without occupation. . . . Then 1870—and chivalrous response to adopted country's call and again emptiness, the chafing of a proud spirit without aim and handicapped not exactly by poverty but by lack of fortune. And she, the mother, having to look on at this wasting of a most accomplished man, of a most chivalrous nature that practically had no future before it."[25]

John Blunt was educated in a private school in Paris in the 1860s, becoming fluent in French, German and Spanish, but he did not serve under General Lee or take part in the Civil War. In 1864, when in Paris and fifteen, he received the offer of a minor rank in the Confederate navy through Admiral Raphael Semmes,[26] commander of the *Alabama*. A Confederate privateersman built in England in 1862 and manned chiefly by British subjects, the *Alabama* destroyed some sixty Northern vessels in a two-year career before being sunk in a naval battle off Cherbourg by the *Kearsarge* on June 19, 1864. Less than a year later, before young Blunt could make any further effort to join his cousins in fighting for the South, the Civil War ended.

While still in his teens, however, he embarked on his "I live by my sword" military career, a soldier of fortune serving a variety of causes, in various countries, until he died, a retired U.S. army officer, in Manila. He first enlisted in the French army, becoming a member of the Red Cross Corps. From that service he transferred to the Papal Zouaves,[27] organized by the Papal States to resist their inclusion in the new kingdom of Italy, and at twenty-one was, according to his friend John R. Volz, "among the last to surrender when the victorious Italians carried Rome"[28]—the final military action of August 20, 1870, from which a unified Italy emerged. In Italy he served under General de Charrette, "the personification of militant and ultramontane Legitimacy," who later became an advisor to Don Carlos in Paris.

Returning to France with a French unit of the Papal Zouaves, Blunt fought in the Franco-Prussian War. He was with that unit, serving his adopted country of France, when German troops entered Paris on January 28, 1871, and the corps was officially disbanded. Officially it may have been but, by the 1871 account of A. Rastoul in *L'Église de Paris sous la Commune*, the Papal Zouaves fought against the revolutionists during the Paris Commune.

Nearly two hundred Americans lived in Paris throughout the period of the Commune, Mrs. Ellen Blunt and her son among them. Not only did Mrs. Blunt live through the two sieges in Paris—the first, lasting 132 days of the Franco-Prussian War, when German troops sealed off the city and Parisians knew starvation; and the second, during the 1871 Commune when French troops fought "red republicans" in the streets, leaving twenty thousand dead—but, according to her grandson, she took an active part against the Communards as a member of a Catholic group.

Shortly after the end of the Commune, Blunt volunteered to fight for another cause, in another country. He went to Spain where he joined the forces of the Pretender, Don Carlos, in the Carlist War begun in 1872. As he was to write later in *An Army Officer's Philippine Studies*, he felt Spain had been weakened by "the various and violent changes introduced by the more or less 'liberal' governments in that country since 1868," and it was as an opponent of any liberal change that he sided with the Carlists.

When Don Carlos made his first sortie into Spain, on May 21, 1872, by way of Vera, an opposing general, Morionas, "surprised and very nearly captured the Pretender at Oroquista, sending him a fugitive to France in headlong flight with a few followers," the *Encyclopaedia Britannica* states in its history of the campaign. "For more than a year he loitered about in the French Pyrenees, the guest of old noble houses who showed him much sympathy, while the French authorities winked at the fact that he was fomenting civil war in Spain, where his guerrilla bands, many of them led by priests, committed atrocities, burning, pillaging, shooting prisoners of war, and not unfrequently ill-using even foreign residents and destroying their property."

After his near-capture by Morionas, the Pretender remained in France and did not enter Spain again until July 15, 1873. Early in the war Blunt was met near Vera by Sir John Furley, in ambulance work then and later to become head of the British Red Cross. Sir John, in his 1876 memoirs *Among the Carlists*, wrote of his encounter with Blunt.

"Soon after passing Vera we met Mr. Blunt (an American gentleman, who holds a commission in the army of Don Carlos, and whom I constantly met at St. Jean de Luz). He was with a Spaniard; and he told me he was on his way, via Hernani, to headquarters to fetch some papers he had left there. Having convinced them that they were going in an entirely wrong direction, I invited them to take places in our carriage, and I put them into the right path, just outside the Republican lines."

Blunt ended the Carlist War as a captain of cavalry—he was always to prefer the cavalry in his military service—and for some years afterward in France served, as John R. Volz wrote, as "a trusted member of Don Carlos' imperial guard,"[29] only ending that connection "when there were no further prospects for his patron." Blunt in fact remained in the service of Don Carlos until 1880, a liaison officer attached to Paris headquarters, and was in Marseilles, family records show, off and on during 1877 and 1878.[30] An active Carlist committee was functioning there and in that connection he met Conrad. The four others of the cast of *The Arrow of Gold*, in addition to Captain Blunt and his mother, were also then in Marseilles.

VIII

"There will be something of Paris in it, and something of the sea, but the actual milieu of the story is the town of Marseilles," Conrad described the manuscript he was working on, the novel to appear as *The Arrow of Gold*, to his New York publishers, Doubleday, Page & Co., in a letter of February 18, 1918.[1] "The colouring is Southern. However, all the interest is in the personages. Of these, two women and four men play an active part, the others being only mentioned in the narrative, which, I want to tell you, is dealing with facts."

The four people whose actual names he used in the story "dealing with facts" were Captain Blunt, Mrs. Blunt, Dominic Cervoni, and Monsieur Georges, Conrad's waterfront name in Marseilles. To two of the six main characters in the story he gave fictitious names. One, an Englishman he called Mills, was partially based on an English friend in Marseilles, a young man named Grand (the "Henry C——" of the *Tremolino* syndicate). In a March 24, 1879, letter to Stefan Buszczynski, written a year after his visit with Conrad in Marseilles, Thaddeus Bobrowski mentioned two of his nephew's friends in that port, Richard

Fecht, a German from Württemberg, and "a second friend, an Englishman, whose name was Grand."

The leading figure in the novel, the *amie du Roi* or mistress of "the King"—the royal title his supporters gave Don Carlos—Conrad called Doña Rita de Lastaola; in real life Baroness Paula de Somoggy. The year of their meeting, 1877, was a time of "heiresses" in France and—often with relevance to them—a time of duels. Harking back to that day while mulling over possible titles for his new novel, Conrad wrote his publishers in the same 1918 letter: "If it had been a book in French I believe I would have called it *L'Amie du Roi*, but as in English (The Friend of the King) the gender is not indicated by the termination, I can't very well do that. People would think perhaps of a friend with a great beard and that would be a great mistake. . . . *The Heiress*, which is closest to the facts, would be the most misleading of all."[2]

"Heiress" in its 1918 meaning did not then define, as it earlier had, the particular wealthy girl of the France of the 1870s, the setting of Conrad's story. In the earlier, flamboyant era of "La Belle Époque" it applied to the *grandes cocottes* of the Second Empire and the years that followed. Across the Channel—where the high-living son of Queen Victoria, Albert Edward, Prince of Wales, set the pace—"Professional Beauties" or "P.B.'s" were equally the fashion.

"Beauty had always been a desirable asset and an object of public worship, but perhaps never so much as in the late 1870's and early 1880's, when the cult of the professional beauty raged in London," wrote Pierre Sichel in *The Jersey Lily*. The star of the London cult was Lily Langtry, her place assured by the pleasure-loving man who lived for sixty years as Prince of Wales before reigning as Edward VII. So much was Lily Langtry a symbol of the 1870s that when Cleopatra's Needle was erected on London's Victoria Embankment in 1878 "the Jersey Lily was properly time-capsuled for posterity." Into the foundation of the tall pink granite obelisk—originally erected by Thothmes III at Heliopolis some three thousand years before its final move from Egypt to London—an iron box was placed, "containing photographs of Mrs. Langtry, current coins, and other trifles of the times."

Henry James met Mrs. Langtry at a ball in Scotland in 1878, when a guest at the Aberdeen home of the retired diplomat Sir John Clark, and in a letter to his sister Alice of September 15 of that year described the "London divinity" being feted by the social elite of England.

"The ball was given by a certain old Mr. Cunliffe Brooks, a great proprietor hereabouts and possessor of a shooting-lodge with a ballroom; a fact which sufficiently illustrates the luxury of these Anglo-Scotch arrangements. At the ball was the famous beauty Mrs. Langtry, who was staying in the house and who is probably for the moment the most celebrated woman in England. She is in sooth divinely handsome and it was 'extremely odd' to see her dancing a Highland reel (which she had been practising for three days) with young Lord Huntley, who is a very handsome fellow and who in his kilt and tartan, leaping, hooting and romping, opposite to this London divinity, offered a vivid reminder of ancient Caledonian barbarism and of the roughness which lurks in all British amusements and only wants a pretext to explode."[3]

Before meeting Lily Langtry, James had spent much of 1876 in France writing *The American*. Basing that novel on the social life of the times, James told in it of the young idle aristocrat, Count Valentin de Belle-garde, who, like Blunt, had served in the Pontifical Zouaves ("I couldn't go into business . . . because I was a Bellegarde. I couldn't go into politics because I was a Bellegarde . . . I couldn't go into literature. . . . The only thing I could do was to go and fight for the Pope."[4]) Bellegarde, who fought a duel over a *cocotte*, defended the French practice of dueling to the disapproving American, Newman: "It's our only resource at given moments, and I hold it a good thing. Quite apart from the merit of the cause in which a meeting may take place, it strikes a romantic note. . . . It's a way of more decently testifying."[5] (This realistic picture of the life of a French *gentilhomme* at the time of Conrad's duel was the first of James' long novels Conrad read, in 1891; rereading it again in 1908, he told James that in the "beautiful and touching" ending of the story, he found a perfection of tone "which calmed me";[6] the "calming" close of the story being the hero's resignation to the loss of the woman he loved.)

As Lily Langtry was "the most celebrated woman in England" in 1878, so were there famous beauties in France who had similar careers. Throughout a long, lighthearted epoch in "the land where dalliance is so passionately understood," as Arnold Bennett said of France, there had been many stars. Outstanding among them were Adèle Courtois, the self-styled Baronne de Sternberg who lived, rich always, until 1904; the languid and handsome Anna Deslion; the Roman girl Julia Barucci, the "Bibirucci" the Prince of Wales admired, who died of consumption in her house on the Champs Elysées where years later James Gordon Bennett lived; Léonide Leblanc, *amie* of the Duc d'Aumale, whose horses and carriages were the talk of Paris, and who died, wealthy still, in old age in 1894; the Comtesse de Loynes, a Reims factory girl who acquired the de Loynes fortune and, her taste guided by such admirers as Flaubert and Gautier, conducted one of the most distinguished salons in Paris until her death in 1908; Clara Blum and Marguerite Bellenger, favorites of Napoleon III; Rosalie Léon, who married the millionaire Prince Wittgenstein; Esther Guimond, in whose house Alexandre Dumas wrote *La Dame aux Camélias;* Blanche d'Antigny, original of Zola's *Nana;* Caroline Letessier, whose canary-colored carriage was one of several in which, accompanied by liveried footmen, she rode about Paris; Mme. Arnould-Plessy, a celebrated actress and mistress of Jérôme, Prince Napoleon; Cora Pearl, the assumed name of Emma Elizabeth Crouch, daughter of the composer of the song *Kathleen Mavourneen,* who received her house in Paris at 101 rue de Chaillet from Prince Jérôme, remained his favorite until 1874 and died at forty-four in Paris in 1886, poor and forgotten. Banished from Paris in 1872, Cora Pearl moved to London; returning to Paris on a special police permit in February, 1873, she sold her house to Blanche d'Antigny and her vast collection of expensive gifts at a public sale on March 4, 1873; and that, says her biographer Baroness von Hutten zum Stolzenberg, "in a great measure, was the last of Cora Pearl."[7]

The millionaires who endowed the "heiresses" formed a roster of the leading names in France: Napoleon III; his half-brother the Duc de Morny; Prince Jérôme, nephew of Napoleon I and cousin of Napoleon III; the Duc d'Aumale, son of Louis Philippe; the Prince of Orange; Prince Lubomirsky; Prince Galitzine; Prince Soltikoff, who married an "heiress"; Prince Wittgenstein, who did the same; the incredibly wealthy Turk, Khalil-Bey; the Spanish Aguado brothers; the Duc d'Orléans, one-time Pretender to the throne of France; Don Carlos, Pretender to the throne of Spain.

Rivaling each other in the munificence of their gifts, the millionaires lavished fortunes on the girls they favored. Each was given a house in Paris, provided with expensive horses and carriages, coachmen and footmen, jewels, silver services, gold plate, antique furniture, tapestries, paintings, mirrors, ormolu clocks, servants, country homes, vast sums of money. They were taught to ride horseback and, with the fashionable, rode in the Bois de Boulogne; they traveled like royalty, to London or to the spas fashion dictated, surrounded by courts of admirers; their portraits were painted—Lily Langtry by Millais and Burne-Jones—by the famous artists of the times; their clothes were made by such couturiers as Worth; as hostesses they entertained with splendor—their chefs the best to be found, flowers and fruit brought by courier from southern France for the dinners that were unrivaled for luxury in Paris. They received, and spent, imposing fortunes: a single dinner given by Cora Pearl for twenty men friends cost £500; during a fortnight when her house was crowded with guests her outlay for food alone was 30,000 francs, the equivalent then of $6000. The normal budget of an acknowledged leader of the demimonde was declared to be 300,000 francs ($60,000) a year, wrote Horace Wyndham in *Feminine Frailty*.

Some received newspaper notice where their full names were given; this was true of "Mme Cora Pearl." Others, less well known or protected from publicity, made rare appearances in print in the disguise of "Mlle X." Some, like Lily Langtry and Mme. Arnould-Plessy, were married; others became the wives of princes, counts and barons.

It was an equally garish time in America, where Mark Twain, in 1877, collaborated with Bret Harte in the comedy *Ah Sin*, four years after publishing *The Gilded Age*. The Gilded Age ever after described America's brassy, highflying years, years of such exotics as Lillian Russell, Josie Mansfield, Mrs. Chadwick, years of fortunes quickly made and quickly spent: when the Bradley Martins could toss away $369,200 on a ball at the Waldorf, the James Hazen Hydes $200,000 on an evening at Sherry's, when Mrs. Leland Stanford, decked in diamonds large as pigeon eggs, could entertain at a twelve-course luncheon with a service of solid gold; when fifty-seven American millionaires, buying antiquity with new-found riches, married their daughters to European titles.

In a private poke at the snobbery marking the *nouveau riche* times Mark Twain, in 1876, wrote his satire *1601*, taking delight in writing it, he said, for the "outraged old cupbearer's comment" on a conversation between such of the famous as Shakespeare, Ben Jonson, Francis Bacon and Sir Walter Raleigh, men the cupbearer loathed "because they were of offensively low birth, and because they hadn't a thing to recommend them except their incomparable brains."

Few of the favorites of the princes in France were as wellborn as the Comtesse d'Argenteau but, conforming to the customs of a day when a title, real or false, was the status-seekers' symbol, the *lorettes* created an aristocracy of their own; those at the top, affixing "Baroness" and the distinguishing "de" to names of fancy, were *lionnes*. In a glancing reference to this status of Paula de Somoggy, Conrad wrote of her, as Doña Rita, in *The Mirror of the Sea*—"young and full of illusions . . . with something of a lioness in the expression of her courageous face (especially when she let her hair down), and with the volatile little soul of a sparrow dressed in fine Parisian feathers, which had the trick of coming off disconcertingly at unexpected moments."[8]

She had, as he wrote in a deleted portion of *The Arrow of Gold*, "something of a grande dame in her; not because she could put on 'an air' (she was terribly natural) but because I suppose that to be on

HARBOR OF CARTAGENA.

[4] Cartagena, Colombia, in the days of sailing ships. Seaboard setting of *Nostromo*.

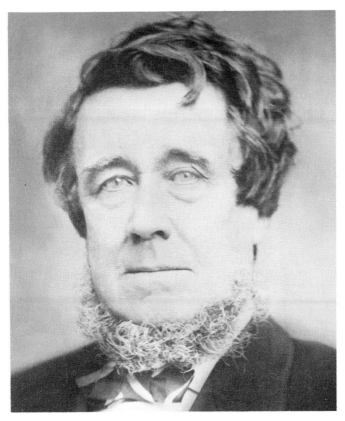

[5] William H. Aspinwall.

[6] Vieux Port of Marseilles as Conrad knew it. Vessel like *Tremolino* in fore-ground. An 1880 engraving by Lucien Gautier.

[7] Paula de Somoggy in Paris, 1880. Photograph by Nadar.

[8] *at left*, Don Carlos in New York, summer of 1876.

[9] *below*, Thaddeus Bobrowski, Conrad's uncle and guardian.

19.

Kapitał		Kapitał		
	Rue. Gr.		Rue. Gr.	Dług: Gubern:
	4000	—	9355	—
	1000	—	400	—
			1223	
			928	
	—		2408	—
Ma —			Winien —	—

top of the scale is in a sense the same sort of thing as being outside of it altogether, when one can also judge men and things with absolute independence, from a strictly personal standpoint, in utter freedom as a great lady would."[9]

Paula was impressively a *grande dame* when she appeared in the entourage of Don Carlos, as the Count de Melgar wrote, "at the theater, sea bathing, and all the other places where we used to go." But, in private, the peasant-born girl could look at the pretensions of the gilded world she had moved into and give comic imitations of it. Referring to her always under the cloaked name of Rita, Conrad recalled those carefree days in Marseilles, when she was eighteen and he nineteen—"her imitations of a Parisian personage, very highly placed indeed, as she represented him standing in the corner of a room with his face to the wall, rubbing the back of his head and moaning helplessly, 'Rita, you are the death of me!' were enough to make one (if young and free from cares) split one's sides laughing."[10]

Laughter often ran through their "unmannerly, Arcadian state of affairs." To him there was "something childlike in their relation," their "unreserved and instant sharing of all thoughts, all impressions, all sensations" having the "naïveness of a children's foolhardy adventure." But anguish more often than joy made an "intolerable weight" of his love for the girl of whom Dominic said, "and all for that Carlos . . . for that Majesty as they call him . . . one, somehow, would grudge her to a better king. She ought to be set up on a high pillar for people that walk on the ground to raise their eyes up to."[11]

Conrad was tormented by memories of her, the sound of her warm contralto voice, the touch of her hand—"The very memory of it would go through me like a wave of heat. It was over that hand that we first got into the habit of quarreling, with the irritability of sufferers from some obscure pain and yet half unconscious of their disease."[12]

"I felt tears come into my eyes at the memory of her laughter, the true memory of the senses almost more penetrating than the reality itself. It haunted me. All that appertained to her haunted me with the same awful intimacy, her whole form in the familiar pose, her very substance in its colour and texture, her eyes, her lips, the gleam of her teeth, the tawny mist of her hair, the smoothness of her forehead, the faint scent that she used, the very shape, feel, and warmth of her high-heeled slipper that would sometimes in the heat of the discussion drop on the floor with a crash, and which I would (always in the heat of the discussion) pick up and toss back on the couch without ceasing to argue. . . . I was haunted also by her waywardness, her gentleness and her flame."[13]

In the early months of her liaison with Don Carlos Paula was tutored not only in foreign languages, but in the social graces required of a companion of a royal prince. Among the skills *de rigueur* for such a role was the ability to sit well on a horse. In preparation for that day when she would ride with the Pretender at the fashionable hour in the Bois de Boulogne, she learned to ride sidesaddle in Marseilles—dressed, as horsewomen were, in a long-skirted black riding habit with a mannish silk topper as headgear—from Captain Blunt, an expert horseman and "trusted member of Don Carlos' imperial guard." Blunt early fell in love with her, and took part in the *Tremolino* venture as one of the four members of the syndicate. He was, as his friend Volz wrote of him, "ever the soul of honor, just, generous, loyal, experienced in travel above the average, a keen observer and a painstaking student, a charming personality of unusual mark, and a gentleman of high ideals worthy of the traditions of his distinguished ancestry."[14]

In that distinguished ancestry there had been one instance at least when the tradition of dueling had been observed: Blunt's uncle, Daniel Murray Key, the seventh of Francis Scott Key's children, being killed in a duel. Daniel, a midshipman of twenty in the U. S. Navy, quarreled with a fellow midshipman, a New Hampshire man named Sherburne, and sent a challenge. The two naval officers, on June 23, 1836, met on the field of honor on a farm near Bladensburg, several miles from Washington, D.C. On the second exchange of pistol shots Daniel fell with a bullet in his left side and in thirty minutes was dead. Ellen Key Blunt was fifteen at the time of her brother's death and the memory of that family tragedy may have instigated her trip down from Paris to Marseilles. There, out of concern for her son, she urged Conrad to leave France, warning him of the risk of a duel, her son's Southern blood making him "very violent sometimes."[15]

Parisians of the time found in Marseilles "*la flânerie heureuse*," the columnist Jean Lorrain of *Le Journal* wrote, and periodically fled to the exuberant, cosmopolitan, refreshing city of the south with its "*brouhaha de sons et de couleurs de la Cannebière*" to escape for a time from the wearing falseness of life in Paris. Paula's appearances in Marseilles, fleeing the ostentatious social round in Paris, were impromptu stays in the house Conrad called "the leased Villa on the Prado"[16] in *The Arrow of Gold*, a Carlist headquarters house. Coming to Marseilles on the spur of the moment, and leaving in the same fashion, her infrequent presence in that fragrant, noisy city (where Spanish balancelles unloaded oranges at the quay, said Lorrain, and the air was strong with the smell of musk and oranges) put a check on the rivalry between Conrad and Blunt. In November and December, 1877, she was out of France altogether, accompanying Don Carlos on the Italian journey referred to by Conrad as the "Venetian episode" in *The Arrow of Gold*. She had been Don Carlos' mistress for a year when, a girl with a majestic bearing "who brought out admiration from those passing her in the street," she appeared in public with him in Venice—one of the many factual episodes Conrad retained in the novel. The Pretender, though traveling incognito, was recognized, the attention of the press increasingly drawn when he alerted the Milan police, as the *New York Times* later reported, that "his collar of the Order of the Golden Fleece had been abstracted from his luggage"[17] and charged his aide General Böet with having stolen it. The dates when the journey was made which flared into public notice appear in privately held, unpublished letters in the archives of a Madrid family having a close personal tie with Don Carlos: Paula and Don Carlos were in Gratz, Austria, in the middle of November, 1877; in Vienna about November 25 or 30; in Venice until December 10, going from there to Milan and Turin and on to Paris for the Christmas holidays.

On December 30, 1877, Don Carlos dined with the Queen Mother, Isabella of Spain, at her Paris residence, Basilewski Palace. She, warmly embracing him, toasting his health, to demonstrate the completeness of their reconciliation, also published a letter in *Le Figaro* protesting his expulsion from France: "My good and cordial relations with my nephew, Don Carlos, and my niece, Doña Marguerita de Bourbon, are a secret to no one. I have never forfeited their esteem, nor have they mine; and I will not, moreover, disregard the bonds of kinship which unite us and which misfortune has cemented."[18]

The reconciliation of the two so much at odds with Spain's King Alfonso set off an explosion in Madrid which had repercussions in Paris. "As all these personages are high and mighty, descended from illustrious men and women, and bearing historical names and titles, their squabbles and scandalous doings form a part of the news of the world,"[19] the *New York Times* said of the royal quarrel. As a result of the hue and cry Don Carlos was required to quit France, for what the newspaper termed "a long voyage in other parts of the world."[20] He left Paris on December 31, going first to London to spend a few days with his father; passing part of the time in Greece, he was out of France for a year.

By announcing his proposed, prolonged absence from France, Don Carlos signaled the end of his long campaign to obtain the Spanish throne by force. (Carlist uprisings, however, continued in Catalonia throughout 1878 and 1879, precipitating a state of siege in October, 1879; the Pretender was again expelled from France for a few weeks upon his return in the fall of 1879, being warned, said the *New York Times* on November 1, "that the Government had resolved not to tolerate political manifestations, for which his stay in France recently afforded a pretext.")

The Pretender's personal withdrawal from the conflict brought home to the Legitimists in Marseilles by early 1878 that Carlism was a dead cause. As Conrad alluded to that time in *The Arrow of Gold*, "the Carlist enterprise . . . had collapsed utterly, leaving behind, as usual, a large crop of recriminations, charges of incompetency and treachery, and a certain amount of scandalous gossip."[21]

The charges of treachery were many, but one was outstanding. A distinguished-looking, tall Spaniard of forty, Fernando Guiral, posing as the "Viscount Charles Riss"[22] and a devoted Carlist of a noble family with estates in Cartagena, Spain, he attached himself to Don Carlos' party during the Pretender's tour of the United States. From July 19, 1876, when he presented himself to Don Carlos in Philadelphia, until January 21, 1877, when he ended his shadowing job in Paris, he traveled with the Pretender as an intimate friend, accompanying him to Newport, New York, London, Paris, Vienna, and learning of his plans. By an agreement with the Spanish Minister to the United States, Señor Don Antonio Mantilla de los Rios, Guiral was to secure for the Spanish government "all the information essential to counteract the plan for another uprising which Don Carlos was at that time understood to entertain."[23] The spy relayed a "trunkful" of information through a messenger, Martinez, undergoing "six months of constant peril, for had he been detected, his death was assured."[24] Guiral demanded $100,000 as payment for betraying the secrets of his friend Don Carlos and, in an attempt to collect it, brought an unsuccessful 1878 suit in America against the Spanish minister.

Of "scandalous gossip" there was little end. When Don Carlos, required to resume his travels, left on his long voyage at the beginning of January, 1878, Paula remained in France and, "to get clear of all those busybodies" in Paris, fled to Marseilles. Conrad had survived the shipwreck of the *Tremolino*, the gunrunning enterprise in which she had involved him, and the two met again for the first time in nearly three months. Both young, orphans, and with uncertain futures—"both outside the organized scheme of society," as Conrad told Sir Sidney Colvin[25]—they had much in common. Paula, as the Count de Melgar wrote

of her, "had a very fine character and a great deal of integrity," and
for the largest part of a year had sought, by time, argument, separation,
to cool the love Conrad declared "was in me just like life was in me."
But, "having once renounced her honourable scruples she took good
care that he should taste no flavour of misgivings in the cup,"[26] and
during the weeks they had together, in "their retreat in the region of the
Maritime Alps, in a small house built of dry stones and embowered with
roses," they displayed "in every phase of discovery and response, an
exact accord."[27]

Leaving this retreat for a brief trip to Marseilles at the end of February, 1878, "to get a supply of cash" from his banker Delestang, Conrad
was told by a Royalist friend that Captain Blunt, in Paris, on three public
occasions had accused Conrad of being "a young adventurer"[28] ex-
ploiting the girl both men loved. Conrad replied to the slur as the times
required, sending a challenge to Blunt through the friend who brought
the news.

The duel, as Ludovic Vaux wrote of France in 1881 in *Les Hommes
d'Épée*, "so often discussed, censured and condemned, is useful from one
incontestable point of view: most of the time it makes up for the insufficiency of legal justice." Whatever justice might come out of such a
meeting, it was considered by aristocrats and "every young fellow who
pretends to be stylish" as a way "of more decently testifying"—as it
had been in England by the Duke of Hamilton and Lord Mohun when
both were killed; by Lord Byron and Mr. Chaworth, the latter also killed;
in the combats between the Duke of York and Colonel Lennox, the
Duke of Wellington and Lord Winchelsea, William Pitt and Mr. Tierney,
Lord Castlereagh and Mr. Canning, the Earl of Cardigan and Captain
Tuckett, of Sir Walter Raleigh in two duels, and James Bruce in one. In
the United States, where Alexander Hamilton had been fatally wounded
in a duel after alluding to Aaron Burr as a "dangerous" man of whom
he could give "a still more despicable opinion," the practice of firing at
ten paces to make up for the "insufficiency of legal justice" was followed
until 1900.

Blunt, a Southerner—whose aristocratic attitudes and royalist sympathies lasted until his death thirty-two years later—accepted Conrad's
challenge and came down from Paris to Marseilles. There the two met
"in the confined, drowsy heat" of a walled garden of a private estate outside the city, with four seconds and two surgeons in attendance. If Blunt
was "utterly incapable of being carried away by love there was nothing
equivocal about his jealousy." Conrad, giving himself his harbor name
of Monsieur George, described their duel:

"What happened was this. Monsieur George fired on the word and, whether luck or skill, managed to hit Captain Blunt in the upper part of the arm which was holding the pistol. That gentleman's arm dropped powerless by his side. But he did not drop his weapon. There was nothing equivocal about his determination. With the greatest deliberation he reached with his left hand for his pistol and taking careful aim shot Monsieur George through the left side of his breast."[29]

"Je lui ai fracassé la patte," Conrad said of his duel with Blunt as he talked of it to a relative many years later.[30] Of the scar on the left side of his breast, which he was to carry for the remaining years of his life, his two sons learned from him that it resulted from the duel, a fact of their father's life upon which they insist today.

Significantly drawing upon this experience, Conrad gave to the heroes of two of his novels chest wounds identical to his own; in the novels both men, fired upon with similar weapons, from motives of jealousy and vengeance, were killed. In *An Outcast of the Islands* Willems was shot by Aïssa with a revolver "through the lung, on the left side, rather high up, and at pretty close quarters too"; in *Lord Jim* the life of Jim was ended when Doramin, taking deliberate aim with a flintlock pistol, "shot his son's friend through the chest."

Blunt's bullet entered Conrad's chest, through the lung on the left side and close to the heart. The nearly fatal wound was dangerous enough for Richard Fecht to send Conrad's uncle Thaddeus the urgent telegram: "Conrad wounded. Send money. Come."[31] Thaddeus was in the Ukraine, attending the Kiev Fair, when he received the telegram. Wiring to Marseilles for more information, he learned that Conrad was recovering and, concluding his business in Kiev in no great hurry, arrived in Marseilles on March 11, ten days after the duel.[32] By that time Conrad was on his feet and had prepared an alibi to disguise the actual cause of his injury. The severe face of Thaddeus, as photographs show him, the austere and always reproving letters he wrote to Conrad (in collections in Poland), give clear reasons why Conrad felt the need of an alibi. For a young man of twenty, dependent on his uncle for support, to have told such an uncle the truth would have precipitated the abandonment Thaddeus so frequently threatened. An ultraconservative man of fifty who took pride in never having done an incautious thing in his life, Thaddeus was a strait-laced Victorian. Having grown up in an isolated part of the country, on the family's Ukraine estate where he continued to live, he had a provincial's point of view. Little news would have reached him of the frivolous, erotic times in France, those exuberant years of elegant dandies and "Grand Horizontals" whose antics could only have nonplused and shocked the country squire. That a thousand young men in Marseilles could create a riot, as they did in 1878, over the issue of who should place whose flowers nearest the statue of Father Belsunce,[33] a kindly priest who had died a century earlier, would have been incomprehensible to Thaddeus, a display of erratic behavior as unacceptable as another which had annoyed him, Conrad's inability to write tidy letters while on a buffeted sailing ship at sea. To Thaddeus all things could be properly regulated, and should be; it was Conrad's romantic, impetuous, idealistic nature he found most fault with, as he had complained of the same unacceptable traits in Conrad's father. Errant conduct of any kind was so deplorable to him that he was not reluctant to expose it: so much so that in his memoirs, published after his death, he revealed the family scandals of his neighbors, causing "the son of one of the most horribly aspersed couples,"[34] according to Ford Madox Ford, to challenge Conrad, as his uncle's heir, to a duel to be fought in Boulogne—Ford agreeing to act as Conrad's second. The challenger—again according to Ford —"shot himself in despair over the revelations, in the railway carriage, on the journey. So we never fought."[35]

On his visit to Conrad in Marseilles, Thaddeus was in France for the first time in his life, speaking the halting French learned at school more than thirty years before. Whatever information he acquired about the cause of his nephew's wound had to come, and came, from that nephew. The first story Conrad told him was an ornately involved one—so involved that the fright of a youth covering up an unacceptable episode shows through—and ran in this tangled form: Conrad discovered he could not sail again as a seaman on a French vessel because he was an alien of twenty-one and subject at that age to military service in the Czar's army in Poland (his uncle had forgotten that he had just turned twenty, not twenty-one); that, having to stay ashore, he had engaged in some undefined smuggling on the coast of Spain and lost all his money; being penniless and in debt, he borrowed eight hundred francs from his friend Richard Fecht and went to Villefranche, intending to enter the American naval service because an American squadron was anchored there (not being an American citizen, he could not have joined the U. S. Navy; the squadron anchored in the area was French, not American, experimenting at Toulon with the new weapon, torpedoes); having been refused at Villefranche and thinking of improving his finances, he gambled and lost his eight hundred borrowed francs at Monte Carlo; returning to Marseilles, "on a fine evening" he invited Richard Fecht to his rooms for tea; while waiting for Fecht to arrive he attempted to kill himself with a revolver; and so he had acquired his wound in that way.[36]

Thaddeus remembered the desperately contrived story well enough to repeat it, once, a year later. But during the two weeks he spent with Conrad in Marseilles ("I never could invent an effective lie," Conrad later wrote Cunninghame Graham) Thaddeus discovered, though he learned nothing of Paula, that his nephew's wound had resulted from a duel. Back in the Ukraine, he listed the expenses of his Marseilles trip in a notebook where all the outlays ever made for his ward were recorded, a twenty-two-page account book kept from December 1, 1869, to February 4, 1890, which he titled "For the information of my dear nephew Konrad Korzeniowski." There, dating his entries according to the old-style Russian calendar (twelve days behind the Gregorian used in France), listing money gifts to Conrad from other relatives, writing frank remarks for Conrad alone to read, Thaddeus gave his view of his nephew's 1877–78 activities in Marseilles, the costly year of Conrad's *Tremolino* exploit and love affair. Thaddeus heard nothing precise about the gunrunning, and nothing at all of the love affair, but he disdainfully made it clear he knew about the duel, demoting that combat to the status of a gunfight, "a shooting." His anger over it bristled in his entry on page 19:

"In September, 1877 through M. Antoine Syroczynski I sent you your half-yearly allowance, from October 15, 1877 to April 15, 1878, 1000 francs—or 400 rubles. Informed by you that you are to sail with Captain Escarras on a year-and-a-half or two-year voyage around the world, I asked A.S. to send you 1000 gulden; deposited at the savings bank 1000 francs. Then, pressed by you that those 2000 francs were not enough, in December I asked to have sent to you from the same bank 1000 francs more, having planned to takes those francs out of your allowance, which would be coming due in my absence.

"In February, 1878 in Kiev I received from M. Bonnard a demand to pay your promissory note for 1000 francs and almost simultaneously news from M. Fecht that you were in a shooting. Therefore, at the end of February, straight from Kiev, I hurried to Marseilles where, having found you already on your feet, I learned this: that you could not leave with M. Escarras for reasons beyond your control, that the 2000 francs sent you through A.S. were lost through speculation, as you confirmed and which I didn't see any reason to investigate; that you had contracted debts which I paid, namely: through Al. de Toussaint (Richard Fecht) 1706 francs—M. Bonnard 1000 francs—Mme. Fogas, your landlady, 233 francs—and to the doctor 700 francs. Which equals

3009 francs or 1228 rubles. In addition to that, my traveling expenses to Marseilles, also my stay there for two weeks—328 rubles.

"Taking into consideration your needs, I have set aside for you, young man, 2400 francs a year. And so, for your first remittance covering April 15–October 15 of this year, I delivered 1200 francs to M. Fecht. Besides that I sent you 110 francs which were left over from the 1000 gulden banknote which belonged to you, and from which 2000 francs had been sent to you before. Those are now irretrievably lost and, what is worse, unproductively so. A fine state you have got yourself in! I suppose this will serve as a lesson to you but if I am mistaken, so much the worse for you!"[37]

Thaddeus could make errors (the total of the figures he gave was 3639 and not 3009 francs) but he was by no means a vengeful man and, had he been taken in by Conrad's panic story of an attempted suicide over the loss of 800 francs, his response would have been one of compassion, not the "I suppose this will serve as a lesson to you but if I am mistaken, so much the worse for you!" The round-the-world trip with Captain Escarras of the *Saint-Antoine* was patently a tale young Conrad concocted to gull his uncle into sending additional money for his harum-scarum life; Captain Escarras did not interrupt his usual voyages to the West Indies and, at the time referred to by Conrad, was bringing the *Saint-Antoine* into Marseilles from St. Thomas, having three of his family with him on board.[38]

When Thaddeus returned to Poland from seeing his convalescing nephew in Marseilles he told friends and relatives what he knew to have happened, that Conrad had been wounded in a duel. But a year later he chose to repeat Conrad's suicide alibi when answering an inquiry about Conrad and his wound from Stefan Buszczynski, a close friend of Conrad's father Apollo. Buszczynski and Apollo were extremely devout Catholics in an era when Catholicism, in its most rigid form, was a powerful force in Poland (not until 1952 was the separation of Church and State proclaimed) and it was this ascetic philosopher to whom Apollo, upon his death, entrusted the moral guidance of his orphaned son. The Church in Poland, as in other countries, held that to fight a duel was to commit not one but two major sins, attempted murder and attempted suicide. Absence of religious beliefs was held to be the cause of the "fashionable vice" of dueling (both principals and their seconds exchanged shots in the free-for-all encounters in Poland); and writers on morality, philosophers in each nation, led in efforts to stamp out a practice begun in the medieval days of chivalry—or, as some said, by David and Goliath. The moral wrong of the duel was everywhere held to be as Professor Pierre Debreyne, doctor of medicine in the Faculté de Paris, gave it in *Du Suicide considéré aux Points de Vue Philosophique, Religieux, Moral et Médical, suivi de Quelques Réflexions sur le Duel:* "He who freely and voluntarily exposes himself, without just and legitimate reason, to the danger of losing his life, is in one sense the murderer of himself. Also the duelist must be generally charged with the intention of killing his adversary; he is then a tentative murderer and if homicide does not actually take place it is only due to circumstances beyond his choice. The duel then can be considered as a kind of suicide and of homicide both, intentional or real . . . the suicide, criminal that he is, is certainly less unreasonable than the duelist, since the loss of fortune is a cause more powerful, and more capable of throwing a man into trouble or despair, than a few unpleasant words or other similarly weak motives that lie behind most duels."

The motives behind duels were often trivial—one fought in France was over the color of Hamlet's hair—and in England a lead had been taken to end the lethal sport: by 1840 it became a capital offense in England to fight a duel, punishable by hanging if a wound were inflicted, or three years' hard labor on the treadmill if only harmless shots were exchanged. Such writers on morality as Charles Moore, rector of Cuxton and vicar of Boughton-Blean in Kent, set out as early as 1790 to expose "a custom of such fashionable and honourable report, as that of 'Duelling' is esteemed to be."[39] Public opinion had not been with him then—"indeed, a moral writer, who wishes to be guided in all his researches by maxims of truth and reason alone, must be prepared to encounter neglect, if not ridicule and contempt, whilst he is opposing opinions and customs established in the circles of polite association, though militating against the principles of humanity and virtue."

Stefan Buszczynski was "a moral writer" and, in 1879, a prominent literary figure in Poland. Philosopher and critic, his study of the poetry of his friend Apollo Korzeniowski had been published in 1870, making him, to Apollo's relatives, a more imposing personage than ever. To this eminent author, whom he addressed as "Honored and Gracious Sir," Thaddeus, a provincial landowner, wrote a letter on March 24, 1879, in which he sought, by repeating Conrad's tale, to present his errant nephew in the most favorable light—a highly principled young man so overcome by remorse over the loss of a few francs that he attempted to take his life. He could with honesty offer the story—having heard it from Conrad when he first arrived in Marseilles—and a suicide attempt was infinitely less offensive to a man of Buszczynski's austere faith

than the double transgression of a duel, "a kind of suicide and of homicide both."

That Thaddeus had some compunction about presenting the false suicide version was evidenced by the confusion of his letter. Knowing his
young nephew contracted debts with ease, he was well aware Conrad
was not one to come to fatal despair by that route (only a month after
Thaddeus settled his high-spending ward's large Marseilles debts, Conrad was wiring his uncle for rescuing sums again, a habit he continued
for many years, debts always being a factor in his life); to the debt-
caused suicide-attempt story Thaddeus added a self-guarding note in his
letter to Buszczynski: "Let this detail remain between us; for I have told
everyone that he was wounded in a duel."

No doctor's report of an attempted suicide was filed with the Marseilles police, though a medical report of each such attempt was manda-
tory, and Conrad's own views on the subject of suicide he once expressed
exactly. In a December 6, 1894, letter to the relative he called "Aunt,"
Mme. Marguerite Poradowska, he wrote: "I have burnt nothing. One
talks like that and then courage fails. People talk this way of suicide!
And then something is always lacking; sometimes it is strength, sometimes perseverance, sometimes courage. The courage to succeed or the
courage to recognize one's impotence. What remains always indelible and
cruel is the fear of finality. One temporizes with fate, or tries to outwit
desire, or attempts to juggle with his life. Men are always cowards. They
are afraid of 'nevermore.' "[40]

While Conrad lived there was never any question about his duel; he
talked of it to his family and friends* and, writing of it, named his
opponent. But thirteen years after his death a controversy arose when a
writer in Poland, Maria Dynowska, published in the June 13, 1937, issue
of *Kurier Warszawski* a digest, without its background, of Thaddeus'
March 24, 1879, letter to Buszczynski, the letter (in the Polish Academy
of Science library in Cracow) retelling the suicide alibi young Conrad had prepared for him. A condensed English version of the Polish
article appeared in the out-of-town edition of the *New York Times* on
August 15, 1937, under the headline "Conrad Once Sought To Take His
Life" (the newspaper quickly suppressed the story, permitting it to appear in no other edition nor to remain in its files, retaining no record
of whose complaint instigated the brusque action). In 1940 Dr. John
Gordan in *Joseph Conrad, the Making of a Novelist* referred in a foot-

---

* ". . . as a youth he had fought a duel in Marseilles—he carried to his death the
scar of the bullet wound in his chest," wrote his close friend Richard Curle (*The
Last Twelve Years of Joseph Conrad*, p. 44).

note to the *New York Times* article but the text of Thaddeus' letter was unknown until published by Zdzislaw Najder in the October 6, 1957, issue of Cracow's *Zycie Literackie*. Two months later, in the London *Times* Literary Supplement of December 6, 1957, a partial translation was given by Jocelyn Baines who, in *Joseph Conrad: A Critical Biography*, keyed his study to the suicide alibi, contradicting Conrad about an episode in his life which, seemingly, the novelist would best have known. The contention that Conrad concocted his duel to cover up an attempt at suicide posed two critical questions: Would he, a man of extraordinary integrity—believing that "to be dishonest is a dangerous luxury for most of us, I fancy, and I am sure it is so for me"—have gone to extreme lengths to lie about an incident in his life, and maintain that lie openly for forty-six years, when there was nothing derogatory to hide? Was the better authority for what happened the man to whom it happened or one not on the scene?

Conrad was a reticent man, in public—refusing all offers to lecture, shying from press interviews, withholding details of his personal history from published accounts through a strong sense of privacy. An autobiographical novelist purposefully writing close to reality, he drew his work from the experiences and contacts of his sea life, the large world open to few in a sailing-ship era but seamen. Yet so little did he reveal of the facts of his roving years that a tendency developed to consider his work "invented." That his duel was also "invented" fell into the pattern, largely due to the extent of an odyssey without equal among modern authors (the wealth of his actual experiences, Ben Ray Redman said of him, made him "rich beyond the most avaricious dreams of desk-bound novelists with only their inventive powers to serve them"[41]).

The matter of Conrad's duel can perhaps best be left to his frank, firm statements about it and to the one friend, Sir Sidney Colvin, to whom Conrad told more than any other about his intimate affair in the exotic France both men knew in their youth. Colvin, an outstanding critic and man of letters, biographer of Keats and editor of the works of Robert Louis Stevenson, volunteered to write a review of *The Arrow of Gold* when it appeared, considering it the piece of Conrad's writing in which "his genius shows itself at its highest power," a study of "a woman's heart and mystery scarcely to be surpassed in literature." Conrad was concerned that the review might be too explicitly revealing of his personal life and wrote Colvin on August 7, 1919:

"A man of your *savoir-faire*, your sense of literary *convenances* and your *homme-du-monde* tact, is best fit to judge how the autob'al note, if struck, may affect the world—and the man.

"With all deference then I venture to suggest that the view of its being a study of a woman, *prise sur le vif* (obviously, you may say) and also the story of young, very young love told with a depth of emotion pointing to experience is what you perceive, what impresses you—which makes the 'quality' of the book. This said with your authority will amount to a confession—a sufficient confession to a not particularly delicate world."[42]

In his review in *The Living Age* of September 27, 1919, Colvin emphasized the factual history behind the novel, of the duel that determined the book's ending. Pointing out that the reader "may find himself closing the volume with some sense of disappointment or incomplete satisfaction," he declared the reason "lies in the circumstance, which discloses itself almost without disguise, that the story is not one of free and independent artistic creation, but to some extent at least of autobiographical fact and reminiscence."

"It is borne in upon us," he continued, "that not the uncontrolled choice of the artist, but the fatalities of life itself, have dictated the close of the story and the issue of that episode of youthful passion which it so enthrallingly sets forth; and if such close and such issue leave some readers feeling balked in their imaginative desires and sympathies, it is against life rather than against the artist that they must murmur."

The ending was one, he added, "which some readers long should have been different, such as an artist working in freedom might have made it and not as life determined it."

IX

The three in Marseilles whom Conrad so long remembered—Paula, Captain Blunt, and Mrs. Blunt—vanished, with the exception of Paula, out of his life altogether after the duel. Although Conrad, referring to Captain Blunt as "J.M.K.B." in *The Mirror of the Sea*, wrote that "he really did live by the sword, as far as I know. He died by it, too, later on, in a Balkanian squabble, in the cause of some Serbs or else Bulgarians,"[1] Blunt was not in fact involved in "a Balkanian squabble" nor did he die in battle; like César Cervoni, whom Conrad also despatched on paper, he lived on for many years. Returning to Paris after his duel with Conrad, he continued to serve the Pretender until Don Carlos was expelled from France at the end of July, 1880, an expulsion later made permanent when the Chamber of Deputies enacted a law forbidding the eldest representatives of families which had reigned in France to enter French territory. Don Carlos, accompanied by such followers as Captain Blunt, moved to England, his home for the next three years. With all hope gone that his patron would become Spain's king, Blunt joined the fourth of the five military forces he was to serve.

At thirty-one he entered the British army, the 1st Royal Dragoons,[2] a cavalry corps organized for police work and guerrilla warfare. While with that unit in England the death of his mother severed his principal tie abroad—Mrs. Blunt died in the health resort of Tenby, Wales, on March 30, 1884, at sixty-two[3]—and through the influence of friends in America Blunt secured a release from his British enlistment. Returning to the United States in 1884, for the first time in twenty-three years, he visited with his uncle, Senator George Hunt Pendleton of Ohio, and on February 26, 1885, enrolled in the United States Army in Maryland.[4] At thirty-six, as a second lieutenant in the 10th Infantry, he began his seventeen years' service in the American army, having spent an equal span of time as a soldier of fortune in Europe. At the U. S. Infantry and Cavalry School at Fort Leavenworth, Kansas, from which he graduated in 1887,[5] Blunt met Mary Ross, the daughter of a Louisiana cotton planter on a visit to her sister, the wife of Blunt's close friend Lieutenant Otto Louis Hein. In 1887, when thirty-eight, he married Mary Ross and a year later their only child, Colonel Wilfrid M. Blunt, was born.[6]

Blunt was not a family man. A professional soldier who married late, he continued to be wholly absorbed with military affairs as he moved from one army post to another. His promotion to first lieutenant came at forty-four, on December 11, 1893, while with the 5th Cavalry, and at fifty-two he was made captain in the 15th Cavalry, the rank at which he retired from the U. S. Army in 1902. During the Spanish-American War he served with the American forces for a time in Cuba, as assistant quartermaster of volunteers, and three years after the war's end was sent in 1901 as a cavalry officer to the Philippines, where he spent the last nine years of his life. Retiring from the army at fifty-three due to physical disability, Captain Blunt remained in Manila as a translator in the information division of the military police, the Philippines Constabulary, a position he held until, following a two weeks' illness, he died at sixty-one in the Division hospital on November 22, 1910.[7] A military funeral with a cavalry escort was held for him in Manila and he was later buried with military honors in the National Cemetery at Arlington, Virginia.

Captain Blunt appears never to have found what he wanted in life, judging by the book of personal views he left behind him. The personality running through it is that of a man as haughtily critical as Conrad portrayed him in *The Arrow of Gold*. When he was forty-five and a first lieutenant in the 5th Cavalry he published an 1894 handbook for cavalry officers, *Maxims for Training Remount Horses for Military Purposes*. A small book of practical instructions for turning recruited horses into military mounts, it was a knowledgeable analysis of horseflesh written by an austere trainer. Years later in Manila, giving his disenchanted conclusions of a world he found so much askew in *An Army Officer's Philippine Studies*, he wrote of Filipino men in terms more equine than human:

"The Filipino may be described as short, thick-set, well built, of good muscle, and very active. For his size and weight he is very powerful. He has straight black hair, thick nose and lips, high cheek bones, good teeth, large intelligent black eyes, and a well developed forehead. In color he varies from dark brown to almost white."

Writing to defend Spanish rule in the Philippines and the part played there by the Catholic Church, it was Blunt's contention that Spain lost the islands through the efforts of three groups he condemned: "Masonic agitators" bent on abolishing Catholicism; young men "educated in European universities" who were progressives and socialists; British traders who, he maintained, were hampered in their attempts to exploit the Filipinos and so helped to organize the revolution. ("In the British colonies of Hong Kong and Singapore there was a large number of adventurers who lived by their wits. For one reason or another, they had not found that royal road to fortune they had hoped to discover. Many of these had been to the Philippines, where they had failed in their undertakings.")

Displaying ultrareactionary views, opposite to those held by his liberal grandfather, Blunt regretted the end of Spanish rule of the islands and labeled America's part in freeing the Philippines a "war of conquest."

If, in Marseilles, Captain Blunt was an edgy young man of twenty-nine—"People make him wince. The things they do, the things they say,"[8] was Conrad's impression of him—he changed little in that respect throughout his life. It was a mark of the deep contrast between the two, Blunt and Conrad, that Blunt could spurn the British "adventurers who lived by their wits" in Singapore while Conrad would find in one of them the heroic figure for three of his novels, a friend, in life as in the novels, of the Malays Blunt dismissed.

That Paula immediately took herself out of Conrad's life—leaving Marseilles for Paris after nursing him to recovery from his dueling wound—was apparently for the reason both Sir Sidney Colvin and Conrad indicated, plus the determining fact that Conrad's Uncle Thaddeus was on his way to Marseilles. "In her own honesty of heart and consciousness of soilure," Sir Sidney wrote of the girl's sudden departure from Marseilles in *The Arrow of Gold*, "she holds herself no fit mate for his life."[9] Conrad gave the same reason in a May 9, 1922, letter to C. J. Fehbuts: "A connection of that kind would have spelt ruin for a young fellow of 19 without fortune or position, or any young fellow for the matter of that . . . Rita is what she is; but whatever she is, she is honest as the day. By going away beyond his reach she gives him the supreme proof of her love, stronger than mere passion, stronger than the fear of her own and of his suffering."[10]

Paula resumed her life with Don Carlos, who was "welcomed with adulation everywhere," said the *New York Times* of his return to France in 1879. In 1880, two years after Conrad parted from her, she was photographed in Paris, by the well-known society photographer Nadar in his studio at 51 rue d'Anjou, wearing the jeweled arrow-of-gold pin, a gift of Don Carlos and the "philistinish ornament" providing Conrad with the title for his novel about her, *The Arrow of Gold*. It was an indication of Paula's prominence, and of her beauty, that she was photographed by the celebrated Nadar, pseudonym of Lyon-born Félix Tournachon, close friend of Baudelaire, early admirer of Renoir, and one of the most brilliant wits of his day. A highly talented man in an epoch rich in originals, Nadar was in turn artist, journalist, balloonist, designer, political agitator, and above all famous for the photographs in which he recorded the celebrities of France during and after the Second Empire. Always closely allied with painting and ahead of his time in that and other fields, he made his former studio on the Boulevard des Capucines available to the avant garde group—Pissarro, Cézanne, Renoir, Degas, Monet—whose 1874 exhibition, denounced by the critics, won them the name of "Impressionists." Conrad wrote of "Rita" as posing for a famous Parisian painter, appearing in such portraits as "Girl in the Hat," and it is highly probable that Paula inspired the reference by sitting for one of the Impressionists. Renoir, in Nadar's circle of friends, especially favored models with her reddish blonde hair and full figure and possibly, among the unidentified girls who sat for him, she is still to be seen on a Renoir canvas.

For five and a half years Paula lived a glamorous, luxurious life as *l'amie du Roi*. Then, at twenty-three, it was over. The drop from the world of royalty to ordinary existence was for her, as it was for the Rita of Conrad's novel, "like falling out of a balcony into the street." The dramatic change in her fortunes came in 1882, the spring of that year bringing one crisis after another to the Carlist cause which, once so popular that "scarcely a painter in France failed to solicit the honor of painting" the Pretender, according to the *New York Times*,[11] was to dissolve ignominiously, in disharmony. The final military action in Spain was announced on March 19, 1882,[12] when the last Carlist groups in Catalonia disbanded. Four days later, on March 23, the efforts of disgruntled partisans to oust Don Carlos brought from him a denial that he would renounce his claims to the Spanish throne in favor of his twelve-year-old son Don Jaime. The communion of Don Jaime—a ceremony held in England on June 8 at the College of the Jesuit Fathers at Beaumont, Old Windsor—was chosen as the occasion for peacemaking among the warring Carlist factions and, to take part in it, essential if he was to retain his role as leader, Don Carlos was required to break with the girl for whom his wife, among many others, manifested a liking. Faced with a hard choice, Don Carlos "suffered a great conflict of conscience," wrote the Count de Melgar, as the Pretender and his friends in London sought "a way around the impasse." "He would be unable to receive absolution unless he formally promised to break the illicit ties with his mistress, and his absence at this solemn ceremony would produce as much scandal as suffering for his son, his father, his wife, and for the whole Carlist movement. . . .

"We had then been deliberating until midnight when Don Carlos, making a superhuman effort, decided to write to Señorita de Somoggy, who was also in London, telling her that having given the matter much serious thought he was forced to separate from her, that he would always be her best friend and that he would give her a settlement for life, a very generous one that would protect her from every need until the end of her days, but that it was essential that all intimate relations between the two of them should cease.

"The girl, who had a very fine character and a great deal of integrity, and who had been brought up in the Christian faith by her uncle, a brother of her mother, a parish priest in a Hungarian village, accepted with resignation, and in order to avoid temptation left immediately for Paris, from which Don Carlos had been banished."[13]

Five years later, in Paris, a marriage was arranged for her by the Count de Melgar and several aides of Don Carlos. In the spring of

1887, at twenty-eight, Paula, "a beautiful, distinguished, and good woman" as the Count de Melgar admiringly wrote of her, was married to the Spanish singer Angel de Trabadelo, two years older than herself, taking to that marriage a dowry of 15,000 to 20,000 francs a year provided by Don Carlos. Four Spanish aristocrats, two for the bride and two for the groom, acted as best men at the wedding.[14]

"That marriage lasted thirty years, until the year 1917 when she died, and was a very happy one," the Count de Melgar concluded his account. Paula's husband, soon to be the Marquis de Trabadelo, "earned a great deal of money and lived in true luxury. He was always very good to his wife, and very proud of her past."[15] As a gifted operatic singer Trabadelo gave concerts in New York, London, Paris, Berlin, St. Petersburg, Milan, Venice, Naples. Among those who later studied with him, a prominent teacher of singing in Paris, were Caruso, Melba, Geraldine Farrar and Mary Garden. Trabadelo died in San Sebastián, Spain, on February 24, 1939, at eighty-two.[16] Well known as he was in the musical world, his pride in his wife was such that he asked to be introduced to leading Spaniards in New York not primarily as a singer but as the husband of Paula.

Conrad gave evidence in The Arrow of Gold that he saw Paula after their parting in Marseilles. Opportunities for their meeting were many, in London and Paris, and the accurate details of the later years of her life he could only have learned from her. Immediately upon her death in 1917 he began The Arrow of Gold, "a study of a woman prise sur le vif" he had had in his mind "through all the years of my writing life," one first attempted as an uncompleted fragment, The Sisters, in 1895. So permanently did Paula remain in Conrad's memory that he gave to his heroines names similar in sound—Nina, Rita, Lena, Flora, Freya— to Paula. In the next-to-last novel he was to write, The Rescue, the hero Tom Lingard said of the unattainable woman he loved, "as long as I live you will never die"; Conrad in his own life held as constant a remembrance of the girl he loved in Marseilles. As he wrote in The Arrow of Gold, "if he had been more romantic he would never have looked at any other woman. But on the contrary. No face worthy of attention escaped him," each reminding him of her "either by some profound resemblance or by the startling force of contrast." He was sixty-two when he told J. C. Squire that "all those figures" of his youth in Marseilles whom he had been "moved to go and seek in that deep shadow" of memory when writing The Arrow of Gold would "from now on . . . rest undisturbed."[17] Yet five years later at the time of his

death he was working on an unfinished novel, *Suspense,* and the fictional
counterparts were there again of Paula, himself and Dominic.

Quite a little of "the Count" always remained in Conrad—the monocle
being a feature of his dress during the years of his writing life in
England, while his manners as *un homme galant* never changed—and the
youthful daredevil characteristics of "Monsieur Georges" long remained
a part of him too. But after leaving Marseilles it was most of all as
"Young Ulysses" that he lived, his years of wandering shaped into
stories of the world he came to know. But, much as he "longed for the
beginning of my own obscure Odyssey,"[18] Marseilles was, seemingly,
a difficult place for him to leave.

Ever a high-spirited town, it was lively with celebrations in the early
months of 1878, more than ever so then when France, having so long
been without one, acquired a national anthem, the "Marseillaise." The
year that began with the carnival of Twelfth Night soon offered
Marseilles another excuse to celebrate when Henry Stanley, at thirty-
seven, arrived fresh from the Congo where he had discovered and
named Stanley Pool and Stanley Falls, places new to the world in
1878 where, twelve years later, Conrad was to be. The enthusiastic welcome given the explorer revived talk of Dr. Livingstone, "the most
venerated" of Conrad's boyhood heroes, whose work of exploration
Stanley had carried on. Stanley came into Marseilles on January 14, 1878,
from the heart of Africa; in Conrad's schoolboy atlas the heart of that
continent had been an unmapped white space and he had promised himself: "When I grow up I shall go *there.*"[19]

Although his Uncle Thaddeus left Marseilles to return to his home in
the Ukraine on March 25, young Conrad stayed on in the port for
another month, unsure of what to do. The lure of travel, always strong
in the East-West crossroads of Marseilles, induced twenty-two young
student passengers to sail out of the harbor on the specially-built
two-masted steamer *Junon* for a 320-day voyage around the world, the
first such organized voyage for students, which had been two years in
the planning. Talk of travel, of exploration, was in the air. Ships, as many
as 2400 at a time in the two harbors, came into port from the farthest
parts of the world, landing cargoes of copra, wild rubber, coffee, pepper,
rice. Arriving from Java, India, New Caledonia, China, their Eastern
crews drifted ashore and a medley of Asian tongues was heard along
the quays.

It had been a wish of Conrad's to see the East and when he did break
away from Marseilles it was in that direction. Through his friend
Richard Fecht, employed in the commodity brokerage firm of Albert de

Toussaint, he secured a seaman's berth on the British 764-ton steamer *Mavis*, carrying a cargo of coal, and on April 24, 1878, he sailed out of the Vieux Port bound for Constantinople. Loading linseed at Yeisk on the Sea of Azov, the *Mavis* returned to Lowestoft on the east coast of England, where Conrad arrived on June 18 at the end of an eight weeks' voyage.[20] A quarrel with Captain Munnings caused him to leave the London-owned ship at Lowestoft. Two years later, on November 24, 1880, the *Mavis* was lost, taking the lives of two of the crew when she struck a submerged rock off the French coast on a voyage from Cardiff to Bordeaux.[21]

After a month ashore at Lowestoft Conrad signed on as ordinary seaman on a coasting schooner of 215 tons, the *Skimmer of the Sea*, a coal-hauling ship twenty-three years old owned by Joseph Saul of Lowestoft. For ten weeks, from July 11 to September 23, 1878, he served on the coaster[22] for wages of a shilling (twenty-five cents) a month, making three round trips between Lowestoft and Newcastle. The small ship was operated by seven men, all English with the exception of Conrad, who was, aside from the cabin boy, the youngest on board. The captain, William Cook, was a Lowestoft man of forty-two. Learning from him and the others at various times in the crew—Arthur Chandler, Henry Boon, William Munnings, Alfred Goldspink, Alfred Barnham, Earnest Sturgeon[23]—Conrad increased his knowledge of English, the language he was to make his own. Having first acquired some halting use of it from his friend Grand in Marseilles, he improved his English during eight weeks on the *Mavis* and was speaking the tongue foreign to him with reasonable fluency by the time he left the *Skimmer of the Sea*. Writing it was another matter. His first written English was a letter answering an advertisement appearing in the London *Times* of September 25, 1878: "SEA.—WANTED, respectable YOUTHS, for voyage or term in two splendid ships for Australia, and others for India, etc.— W. Sutherland, 11 Fenchurch-buildings, Fenchurch-street, near rail. Established 1851."

Traveling to London for an interview, Conrad learned from Mr. Sutherland that one of the "splendid ships" was the wool clipper *Duke of Sutherland*, a full-rigged sailing ship of 1047 tons built in Scotland in 1865 and owned by a Scot, Daniel Louttit of Wick. Captain John McKay, forty-two, from Aberdeen, would be making his first voyage in command of the ship, which would carry twenty-six officers and crew on her voyage to Australia. Conrad joined the *Duke of Sutherland* in London on October 12, 1878,[24] as an ordinary seaman of twenty, his shilling-a-month wages being the same pay twelve others of the crew received. One was a Negro of twenty-six, George White, from Barbados.[25] Answering the roll call at the signing-on for the voyage at Gravesend, he spoke his name White in the clipped English accent of Barbados as "Wait" and so suggested to Conrad the name "James Wait" he was to use nineteen years later for the central character of *The Nigger of the Narcissus*. Knowing English only by its sound in those early days, Conrad still remembered the name as Wait when, forty years after the voyage, he talked of the novel's origins with Jean-Aubry. White, like the fictional Wait who wrote his name "all a smudge" on the ship's roster, was signed on the *Duke of Sutherland* under "X his mark" and wrote an illegible scrawling signature when he left the ship at Sydney.[26]

"I was inspired with the first scene in the book," said Conrad of *The Nigger of the Narcissus*, "by an episode in the embarkation of the crew at Gravesend on board the same *Duke of Sutherland*."[27] Two other men of the ship were also drawn upon for the novel, the chief mate A. G. Baker, a Norfolk man of thirty-six, whose name was given to the chief mate Baker of the story, and a London seaman of thirty named Richard Knowles, original of "Dirty Knowles." Conrad recalled Baker in *The Mirror of the Sea* as the "Mr. B——" who gave up drink too late and the second mate, H. J. Bastard, forty-four and from Halifax, as the gray-whiskered second mate who believed wool clippers "knew the road to the Antipodes better than their own skippers."

Sailing from London on October 15, 1878, the *Duke of Sutherland* rounded the Cape of Good Hope and reached Sydney on January 31, 1879, after a voyage of 109 days. It was a rough, slow passage, Conrad's first to Australia. The Sydney *Morning Herald* of February 1, 1879, gave a concise account of it:

"The ship *Duke of Sutherland* left London on October 15th and passed through the Downs on the 17th, and was off Ushant on the 27th in a very heavy westerly gale. She had no NE trades, and the equator was crossed on the 30th November. The SE trades also proved light and unfavourable. The meridian of the Cape was passed on December 26th, and on making her easting only fine weather was experienced. The southwest cape of Tasmania was rounded on January 20th and NE winds have prevailed ever since. In Lat. 40 N and Long. 20 W a horned owl and some starlings were captured, together with several larks which flew on board."

It had been a hard voyage and sixteen of the crew quit the ship in

Sydney. Badly fed, their daily rations for a twelve-hour workday consisted of a pound of bread, three quarts of water, two ounces of sugar, weak tea and coffee, slightly more than a pound of salt beef or pork, pea soup and rice. To sail the ship back to London a crew of eighteen new men had to be hired in Sydney.[28] Conrad, very nearly the youngest, stayed on while the old hands left. His only funds being the £5 ($25) he had asked his uncle to send, and having to stretch that sum over five months, all he had an opportunity to know of Australia was the Sydney harbor. While the ship waited month after month for her load of wool Conrad held the night watchman's job, hearing from the deck of the clipper the sounds of Sydney he recalled in *The Mirror of the Sea.*

"The tinkle of more or less untuned cottage pianos floated out of open stern-ports till the gas lamps began to twinkle in the streets, and the ship's night-watchman, coming sleepily on duty after his unsatisfactory day slumbers, hauled down the flags and fastened a lighted lantern at the break of the gangway. The night closed rapidly upon the silent ships with their crews on shore. Up a short, steep ascent by the King's Head pub, patronized by the cooks and stewards of the fleet, the voice of a man crying 'Hot saveloys!' at the end of George Street, where the cheap eating-houses (sixpence a meal) were kept by Chinamen (Sun-kum-on's was not bad) is heard at regular intervals. I have listened for hours to this most pertinacious pedlar (I wonder whether he is dead or has made a fortune) while sitting on the rail of the old *Duke of S——.* . . .

"The night humours of the town descended from the street to the waterside in the still watches of the night: larrikins rushing down in bands to settle some quarrel by a stand-up fight, away from the police, in an indistinct ring half hidden by piles of cargo, with the sounds of blows, a groan now and then, the stamping of feet, and the cry of 'Time!' rising suddenly above the sinister and excited murmurs; night-prowlers, pursued or pursuing, with a stifled shriek followed by a profound silence, or slinking stealthily alongside like ghosts, and addressing me from the quay below in mysterious tones with incomprehensible propositions."

Conrad's recollections of the voyage of the *Duke of Sutherland* were mellowed by time but as a young seaman feeling somewhat tricked by the "burly apostle" Mr. Sutherland ("the first to give you a helping hand in London," Thaddeus reminded him[29]), his reactions were less tolerant. His first round-the-world voyage, producing incidents and characters for his novels, was described by his Uncle Thaddeus in two letters to Stefan Buszczynski. In the closing pages of his letter of

March 24, 1879—written when Conrad was on the *Duke of Sutherland* moored at the Circular Quay in Sydney—Thaddeus (erroneously believing Conrad paid a £20 premium for the privilege of serving on the clipper) recounted his nephew's adventures after leaving Marseilles.

"Finally, it turns out that he [Conrad] is going into the British merchant marine, which hasn't all the formalities the French demand. After I left Marseilles his friend Fecht (a Würtemberger) got him off to England in the first days of May, to Lowestoft. On that steamer he learned to handle the ship and perfected his English, which was very rough (he had a second friend, an Englishman, whose name was Grand) and then got into an English firm in London. There he had to give a premium of 20 pounds and agree to slave three years—the first year he was to pay, the second year nothing was to be paid by either side, and the third year he was to receive some small wage, after which he was required to pass an examination and become naturalized. He went to Australia, to Sydney, and is supposed to return in August—but I haven't heard anything since he left, although I have written to him and have even sent him a little money. He doesn't write to anyone because not long ago I had a letter from M. Fecht who asked me if I had any news of Conrad. I also wrote to Lowestoft, but they had no news about him or the ship. I am beginning to be worried and will write again to Lowestoft—and if I hear anything I will let you know.

"It seems to me that I am going into too many details about the Odyssey of Conrad. I'm sorry about that but I want you, Honored Sir, to know that I have not deserted, nor will desert him, unless he does something drastic, which I do not expect. I thank you very much, Honored Sir, for remembering me. Everything goes along in the usual way except that I have become much older, as they tell me and as I feel myself. I have made my will and have left Conrad 15,000 rubles, and now I'm waiting peacefully 'to get to Heaven.' Perhaps before that time comes God will allow me to see you, Honored Sir, so I can assure you personally of my respect and give you my best wishes."[30]

In his letter to Buszczynski of May 30, 1879 (Conrad still being in Sydney on the *Duke of Sutherland*, a ship with a skeleton crew, having difficulty securing a cargo), Thaddeus told how Conrad came very near to making his home in Australia and of following a trader's life in the East. Addressing Buszczynski as "Honored Sir," Thaddeus wrote:

"Although aware of your friendly concern about Conrad, I was unable to give you any news about him at the time I received your letter. But now I can tell you that I have recently had two letters from him, of

February 4 and 16 from Sydney. The letters took two months and six days to reach England, and another seven days from England. It takes two and a half months to communicate with him, and that is the secret of his silence. He is in good health, though he complains of the discomforts on board his English ship, where no one thinks of comfort for the seamen. All the men share it, but they were aware it would be like that, while Conrad counted on something better, thinking conditions would be like those on French ships. He did not anticipate so hard a life and suffered through 109 days of it, the time it took them to reach Sydney. And on top of that, poor boy, he didn't find, after getting there, the money he had asked me to send to him at Sydney—although ten days later it did arrive. Despite that, his letters show him to be content. He likes his work and he hopes for a better future. In September he will be back in England and, losing no time, will sail again to Australia. But this time he will stay out there a few years, two years at least, in order to devote himself to studying trade with the East Indies—a place of which he writes with great enthusiasm for its beauty and riches.

"In Sydney he met a captain who is famous for knowing all the trading conditions on the Javanese archipelago, a man well known in the geographic and commercial worlds. That captain is the owner of a ship and, liking Conrad very much, offered him a paying job starting at five pounds a month. That means 60 pounds a year in addition to his living, and, as I would be giving Conrad 2400 francs—which is more or less 100 pounds—he would have 150 pounds for his living expenses. Which isn't so bad. Then he also has the prospect of becoming naturalized in England. By what Conrad says, this job would be of benefit to him for what it would teach him about commerce—and who knows but what he might try his luck in that field in time?

"Of course, not having anything on which to base an opinion on the matter, I can't be against this project. The only objection I would have to it is that he would be so far away. But as it is I don't see him often, so it doesn't matter if he is in London or Sydney. If he thinks he sees his future there, let him look for it. In addition I will say that, though it is no special credit to him, he is gifted with languages. The letters he writes are in such beautiful Polish that they are like those of someone who had never left Poland—although, since he left Cracow (1874) he has spoken Polish only once, with me in Marseilles.

"That's all I can tell you right now of Conrad, Honored Sir. I'm convinced that you are interested in my nephew's fate and from time to time I will let you know what happens to him—and maybe some day I will have the opportunity to speak and tell you about our wanderer. With my great personal respect I am, Honored Sir, yours, with sincere good wishes.

T. Bobrowski."[31]

Conrad's gift with languages, contributing to the speed with which he mastered English and the richness of his style, was already a pronounced trait in his youth. His strong interest in the East Indies also dated back to that early time. At twenty-one he was looking forward to a career as a trader in the Indies, "a place of which he writes with great enthusiasm for its beauty and riches," islands to become the setting of his first novels. Though he was to continue to dream of leading a trader's life, even after his marriage, he was never to achieve it. Eight years after he first expressed a wish for that life, in Sydney, he would meet a Dutch trader in Borneo, Olmeyer, who caused Conrad to turn to writing.

In Sydney Conrad met the French sailor without hands whose physical appearance he used for the villainous Man Without Hands in "Because of the Dollars," the 1912 story about the heroism of a prostitute Conrad in 1920 made into the play *Laughing Anne*. The Frenchman, Conrad said, "kept a small tobacco shop in George Street, not very far from the Circular Quay. Both his hands were gone. He was then 75 if a day, and didn't look like a man who would live long. He used to spin long, Melanesian yarns, but he was not very interesting—except for the pent up store of energy one was aware of in that maimed body."[32]

Conrad gave an exact description of how the Man Without Hands should appear in *Laughing Anne*. "Need not be actually tall and stout but must give the impression of a *big* man. Large face, with rather long black hair brushed up from a high forehead. Black eyes. Moves ponderously. Dress: white trousers cut very broad at hip, very narrow at ankle, held up at waist by a faded sash. He has no shirt, but only a thin singlet, over which he wears open a roomy linen jacket with side pockets. White shoes. Overbearing manner. Deep voice."[33]

Although the *Duke of Sutherland* was advertised in Sydney newspapers as a "fine vessel, having all deadweights on board, and large engagements" which "will have prompt despatch," she waited on and on for cargo. In the hope of enticing passengers (five had traveled out on the ship from England) the fare to London was offered at the low rate of $80. A mixed cargo of wheat and wool was finally secured, Conrad later recalling the heavy work of stowage: "I have carried bags of wheat on my back, bent almost double under a ship's deck-beams, from six in the morning till six in the evening (with an hour and a half off for meals)."[34] With only two passengers boarding—one a Mrs. McKay and presumably the captain's wife—the clipper left Sydney on July 6, 1879,[35] arriving in London 106 days later, on October 19, 1879.[36]

The homeward passage was via Cape Horn, "where the storms dwell thickly." Though the ship's tall spars "seemed to reach up to the very stars,"[37] Conrad was proud of his nimbleness in running aloft, a frightening and hazardous undertaking in a gale. During the "endless, deep, humming roar" of a gale off the Horn, seeking company, he talked with the boatswain, a Liverpool man of thirty-three, James Brooks. The long-remembered gale was one he wrote of in *The Mirror of the Sea*.

"The ship, brought-to and bowing to enormous flashing seas, glistened wet from deck to trucks; her one set sail stood out a coal-black shape upon the gloomy blueness of the air. I was a youngster then, and suffering from weariness, cold, and imperfect oilskins which let water in at every seam. I craved human companionship, and, coming off the poop, took my place by the side of the boatswain (a man whom I did not like) in a comparatively dry spot where at worst we had water only up to our knees. Above our heads the explosive booming gusts of wind passed continuously, justifying the sailor's saying 'It blows great guns.' And just from that need of human companionship, being very close to the man, I said, or rather shouted:

" 'Blows very hard, boatswain.'

"His answer was:

" 'Ay, and if it blows only a little harder things will begin to go. I don't mind as long as everything holds, but when things begin to go it's bad.' "[38]

The *Duke of Sutherland* survived the gale but three years later, on May 3, 1882, was wrecked in heavy seas off Timaru, New Zealand.[39] Lying at anchor with one thousand sacks of wheat on board and ready to sail for England, she bumped on the bottom, started her timbers, and filled with water. The seventeen-year-old "splendid ship" that had made so many safe passages between England and Australia was sold, a total wreck, for £84. The crew were taken off in boats by the nearby sailing ship *Benvenue;* eleven days later the *Benvenue* herself was lost in the same anchorage.

Conrad, ending a voyage of just over a year, left the *Duke of Sutherland* in London immediately upon her arrival, along with the rest of the crew. For twelve months of hard work he had earned three dollars, spent before he reached London. He went ashore without funds, a stranger in the city. Life on the *Duke* had been too austere—he did not exaggerate the hardships—and he was unwilling to undergo that ordeal again. What a seaman had to endure on such a voyage as his was related by J. H. C. Brooking in "Around the World Under Sail in the Eighties," the memoir of an electrical engineer who, like Conrad, served on an English sailing ship on the London-Sydney run.

"We had no baths, basins or heating. Latrines for crew and apprentices were under the forecastle-head, and there was no privacy. Everything was rationed, including water, except the unbiteable ships' biscuits. Salt beef or pork were served four days a week, pea-soup on two days, potatoes one day. . . .

"Our working hours were normally twelve per day, but we were liable to be on duty at any time when all hands were required for emergencies, which often happened when not in 'the trades.' There were no conveniences; none for drying clothes, oilskins, boots; not even when a big wave washed over the high doorstep and flooded up to the lower bunks. We often had to go to rest wet through, in oilskins and sea boots and all, in a bunk that had been swamped. . . .

"I believe that there is no hazard to equal the reefing of a topsail under the severe weather conditions which make this operation necessary. In most cases the men are already tired, cold and wet through . . . they are standing on a swaying footrope about fifty feet up, and are for safety bent double over the yard, while on a dark night their utmost two-handed efforts are required to find the reef points and lash them up with the ship rolling and plunging under them. I do not know of any shore work that compares with this, with the almost certain penalty of death for a slip at sea, balanced against the quickness of ambulance and hospital treatment on shore. We lost one man on this operation while I was on board."[40]

Conrad wanted to go, not back to Australia where "a paying job starting at five pounds a month" might or might not be waiting for him on an East Indian trader, but to the Mediterranean, the sea which always held for him "the fascination of youthful romance." He had been away from Marseilles for twenty months when, on December 12, 1879,[41] he sailed from London as an ordinary seaman on the 676-ton British steamer *Europa*, bound for Mediterranean ports. He was twenty-two and had written his uncle of a craving to be in the Mediterranean again. He was regularly in touch with Richard Fecht, who acted as his banker and was still in Marseilles, where Dominic was apt to be. Paula, very likely spending November with Don Carlos in London, where the Pretender had first gone in a new banishment from Paris, should have arrived on the

Riviera for the winter season. The *Europa* traded between London and Genoa, touching at whatever ports her cargo called for; one could be Marseilles. But the ship failed to enter the Vieux Port and Conrad had no glimpse of his friends of *Tremolino* days. After passing through Deal on December 14,[42] the London Steamship Company vessel called at Genoa and from there put in only at Italian, Greek and Sicilian ports— Leghorn, Naples, Patras, the Greek island of Cephalonia near Patras, Messina and Palermo in Sicily. Disappointed, ill with fever, Conrad quarreled with Captain Monroe and when the *Europa* reached Gravesend on January 29, 1880, from Palermo[43] he was glad enough to leave it. The next day in London he signed off, completing an unhappy seven weeks' voyage.

He was undecided about what career to follow, what his next move should be, where to go. He had thought of returning to the French marine, where life was easier, and secured a certificate from Delestang et Fils verifying his service on their ships—a certificate officially stamped on April 26, 1880, by Alexandre Escarras,[44] a ship broker in Marseilles and perhaps a relative of Captain C. Escarras of the *Saint-Antoine*. He thought of returning to Australia, of trading in the East Indies. American naturalization had been in his mind, according to his uncle's letter of August 22, 1877. French, American and British citizenship each appealed to him in turn. Then it was Canada. In London in the spring of 1880 he dallied with the offer of a secretarial post with a Canadian businessman, Mr. Lascalle, interested in railroads and politics.[45] (The Midland Railway Company of Canada, Great Western Railway Company of Canada, and Grand Trunk Railway Company of Canada were all holding their half-yearly meetings in London. With earnings up 19 per cent, due in part to the immigrant rush, Canadian railway stocks were in great demand and Canada, to many, was the El Dorado of the day.)

At twenty-two Conrad had no clear choice of occupation, or of the country where he would follow it. An "outsider" on the British ships where he had undergone unexpected hardships, he considered, for a time, giving up the sea. To some degree he had brought trouble upon himself. Still signing "de Korzeniowski," he offered to shipmates a pretentious name unlikely to be welcomed by the plain Kings, Browns, Shaws, Palmers and Rittersens who shared the forecastle with him. In crews aligned into nationality cliques he was always the only Pole. Among men of whom many were illiterate ("X his mark" was a common signature of seamen registering on Conrad's ships) he spent his free time reading books he brought on board. A nondrinking, pensive member of a roistering crew (four on the homeward passage of the *Duke of Suther-*

land forfeited their wages for drunkenness), he was a bystander of the rough-and-tumble conviviality which was to have such tragic results at a later time. Hot-tempered, with an adamantly independent turn of mind, he also took issue with such officers as the captains of the *Mavis* and *Europa*. Though able, fearless, and loving the sea, he had a youth's usual resistance to authority and unabashedly felt free to challenge it.

Dangerous and hard as the life was, there were always more seamen than ships could use. Able-bodied seamen, a.b.'s older and more experienced than Conrad, were desperate enough to ship for the shilling-a-month pay. If he were to follow the sea, the urgent dream of his boyhood, his hope for a future lay in becoming an officer. On June 1, 1880, less than two years after enrolling on his first English ship, Conrad passed his examination as second mate in the British merchant marine. A three-hour grilling on London's Tower Hill by a white-haired man with "an air of benign intelligence," Captain Rankin, left him "limply flat, like a squeezed lemon," but he came away with his certificate walking on air.[46]

"I found myself downstairs without being aware of the steps as if I had floated down the staircase," Conrad gave to young Powell in *Chance* his own feelings on that examination day. "The finest day in my life . . . Yes, the finest day of one's life, no doubt, but then it is just a day and no more. What comes after is about the most unpleasant time for a youngster, the trying to get an officer's berth with nothing much to show but a brand-new certificate."[47]

For nearly three months he looked for a ship. Living in a furnished room at 6 Dynevor Road, Stoke Newington, he grew increasingly dejected as he "went the round of all the shipowners' offices in the city where some junior clerk would furnish him with printed forms of application which he took home to fill up in the evening." Though he would "run out just before midnight to post them in the nearest pillar box," he continued the remembrance in *Chance*, "that was all that ever came of it."

His uncle was sending him an allowance of $480 a year, in two installments, a sum hopelessly inadequate for clothes and living costs on shore. The $240 for the first half of 1880 melted away in the six months that Conrad, studying for his examination and industriously hunting a ship, spent in London. Even so, Thaddeus did not propose to increase it. Friends would have lightened Conrad's depressing daily round but he was a transient and without them. "I, in my utter loneliness," he recalled his first years in England to Edward Garnett, "was never faced by the problem of 'friends.' You were the only land one. . . ."[48]

By some such stroke of luck as he gave to Powell in *Chance* (who was helped by a sympathetic Port of London shipping master to his first officer's berth, made suddenly vacant by a shore accident), Conrad secured a ship. Having "nothing much to show but a brand-new certificate," he was signed on the *Loch Etive* in London on August 21, 1880,[49] the day the clipper, one of a famous line and with a noted captain, slipped her moorings and, passing through Deal on August 22,[50] sailed for Australia. A third mate of twenty-two, he was the youngest officer, the last to join. His wages were £3.10 ($17.50) a month,[51] his first earnings of any size in the five years he had been a seaman.

Few great authors have had experiences to equal Conrad's in those five years. By twenty-two he had made three sailing-ship voyages to the West Indies and the Caribbean, one involving the transport of contraband arms to revolutionaries in Colombia; smuggled munitions from Marseilles to rebel groups in Spain, an operation culminating in his own near escape during the shipwreck of the *Tremolino;* experienced a passionate, forever-remembered love affair with the girl he would call "the woman of all time," Paula de Somoggy; fought an almost-fatal duel; made two voyages to Mediterranean and Black Sea ports; circled the world on a wool clipper.

From these years of 1874 to 1879, the voyages and the land stays in between, Conrad drew the basic material for *Nostromo, The Arrow of Gold,* some of the characters and incidents for *Victory* and *The Nigger of the Narcissus,* the Toulon background for *The Rover,* several episodes recalled in *The Mirror of the Sea.* In 1880, assuming an officer's responsibilities for the first time, his viewpoint changed. Until then he had followed the sea in the mood of a wanderer, his involvements having been with life on shore. But his experience of such land tempests as those of revolution and of love impelled him more strongly than ever toward the sea with its "untempted life presenting no disquieting problems."

The peace of that life also proved an illusion, for on the *Loch Etive* he became acutely aware of how the sea itself could break the men who made their living by it, as unmerciful in its way as anything the passions of mankind could devise.

"To see! to see!—this is the craving of the sailor, as of the rest of blind humanity," he wrote of the black skies placing ships in jeopardy. As an author defining what his own or any work of art should be, he fastened again upon that primary need of vision: "My task which I am trying to achieve is, by the power of the written word to make you hear, to make you feel—it is, before all, to make you *see.* That—and no more, and it is everything. If I succeed, you shall find there according to your deserts: encouragement, consolation, fear, charm—all you demand—and, perhaps, also that glimpse of truth for which you have forgotten to ask."[52]

A sea calamity of 1880 brought home to Conrad how much of the truth a quick-to-judge world forgot to ask. It contributed in large degree to his later absorption as an author with those whom society for one reason or another rejected, the alienated he consistently sheltered in his novels. From his mariner's experiences of the 1880–87 years he would draw stories reflecting "that hint of loneliness, that soul of the sea,"[53] a loneliness mirrored on the land.

PART TWO
THE SEA

X

> . . . those events of the sea that show in the light of day the inner worth of a man . . . the secret truth of his pretences, not only to others but also to himself.
>
> *Lord Jim*

It was one of shipping's worst years, 1880, a year of record storms. "We do not know that it has ever been our lot to record such a list of maritime disasters as have resulted from the violence of the late gales," the London *Shipping and Mercantile Gazette* reported on November 3. "Our impression of Tuesday [November 2] contained upwards of 300 casualties, the details, although necessarily brief in each instance, extending over no less than six columns—a terrific list to contemplate. At Lloyd's as many as 130 losses [of ships] were posted in one day."

Ships of every size and vintage—an English vessel lost in the October gales was ninety-five years old—went down in a year that saw 1209 seamen lost at sea in British ships alone.[1] The London *Times* repeatedly carried disaster news and on November 1 gave one telling piece of it: "There were 186 British and foreign wrecks reported during the past week. This number is almost unprecedented for one week. Of this total 161 were lost on the British coasts."

Conrad, making his first voyage as an officer ("with us merchant sailors the first voyage as officer is the real start in life") soon came to know "the true sea—the sea that plays with men till their hearts are broken, and wears stout ships to death."[2] One stout ship lost that year was the steamer *Mavis*. Another a few months later was a Danish brig, whose crew he helped to rescue.

The shipwreck tragedies of a year of record storms had Conrad disenchantedly looking "with other eyes upon the sea," while two sea crimes of 1880 made a strong imprint upon him, a third mate undergoing his own first testing. The sensational abandonment of the crippled Singapore steamer *Jeddah* near the Gulf of Aden on August 8—the event upon which he was to base *Lord Jim*—was the talk of London for the ten days previous to Conrad's sailing on the *Loch Etive*. The other long-remembered sea crime of that year, one he credited with being the origin of "The Secret Sharer," took place aboard the *Cutty Sark* in September, 1880, when the famous clipper lay in the Javanese roadstead of Anjer. During an argument on board, her chief mate, Sidney Smith, killed a Negro member of the crew, John Francis. Captain Wallace, out of compassion, allowed Smith to make his escape by jumping overboard and swimming to the nearby American ship *Colorado*. Remorse for his action, and the uproar over it created by his mutinous crew, caused Wallace, a ship commander for less than a year, to step over the stern four days later, committing suicide. The clipper, carrying Welsh coal for delivery to the American fleet off Japan, was taken by her second mate to Singapore where a new captain named Bruce, sent down from Shanghai, took command. Bruce became convinced the ship was haunted by the ghost of Captain Wallace and, as one misfortune followed another, dissolved his days in drinking bouts until relieved of his command when the *Cutty Sark* reached New York. Later the clipper broke all records for fast passages under a less melancholy commander and sailed until 1922,[3] when fifty-three years old, eventually becoming what she is today, a museum ship in permanent drydock in London.

Haunted ships sailed over other seas, Conrad's experience in the Gulf of Siam with the ghost-seeing mate of the *Otago* forming the basis of *The Shadow Line*. From the *Cutty Sark* incident he developed one of his greatest short stories, "The Secret Sharer."

"The swimmer himself was suggested to me," Conrad wrote in a June 14, 1917, letter to A. T. Saunders, "by a young fellow who was 2nd mate (in the '60s) of the *Cutty Sark* clipper and had the misfortune to kill a man on deck. But his skipper had the decency to let him swim ashore on the Java coast as the ship was passing through Anjer Strait. The story was well remembered in the Merchant Service even in my time." In fact both the *Jeddah* and *Cutty Sark* dramas, occurring in 1880, were recent events and absorbing topics in Sydney when Conrad arrived there on the *Loch Etive*.

His own voyage, if less dramatic, was lively. The *Loch Etive*, a new full-rigged sailing ship built in Glasgow in 1877, was making her third voyage, to Australia again, under the same master. Of 1287 tons, she was

one of a fleet of clippers owned by the General Shipping Company of
Glasgow, under the management of Aitken, Lilburn & Co., a firm still in
Glasgow today. "Her first Master was Captain William Stuart, who remained Master of the vessel until he died in the early part of 1896, on the
vessel's Eighteenth Voyage out from Glasgow to Australia," the chairman of the board of directors of Aitken, Lilburn & Co., T. M. Lawrie,
writes of the Loch Etive's history.[4]

Captain Stuart, who taught Conrad how to carry sail on a ship ("And
I have carried on myself upon the tall spars of that Clyde shipbuilder's
masterpiece as I have never carried on in a ship before or since"), was a
Scot of forty-eight from Peterhead, full-bearded, sturdily built, "with
no nerves to speak of," but a man with a peppery temper. Going to sea
at fourteen, a shipmaster at twenty, he commanded The Tweed for
fourteen years and in that time of record-making crossings earned a
great name as a sail-carrier. Celebrated as he was for speed—making one
England-to-Melbourne run in seventy-two days—when Captain Stuart
died on board the Loch Etive at sixty-five he had commanded ships for
forty-five years without having lost a man or a mast overboard.[5]

Under Captain Stuart as chief mate was William Purdu of Glasgow.[6]
Though only twenty-seven, he was almost deaf. Conrad recalled the
vague rows between the two men, both bent on speed, in The Mirror of
the Sea. "If P— carried on 'like the very devil' because he was too deaf
to know how much wind there was, Captain S— (who, as I have said,
seemed constitutionally incapable of ordering one of his officers to
shorten sail) resented the necessity forced upon him by Mr. P—'s desperate goings on. It was in Captain S—'s tradition rather to reprove his
officers for not carrying on quite enough—in his phrase 'for not taking
every ounce of advantage of a fair wind.'"[7]

The second mate of the Loch Etive, James W. Allestan, was twenty-
nine and, like the captain, from Peterhead. So were the carpenter, John
Cumming, thirty-one, and the twenty-year-old sailmaker, Peter Nicol
—Captain Stuart, by custom, reserving those two berths for men from
his native town in Scotland. When Allestan fell ill during the passage
Conrad was promoted to officer of the watch "alone in charge of the
deck," where the "immense leverage of the ship's tall masts became a
matter very near my own heart." Allestan, the Peterhead second mate,
may have suggested the name for Captain Allistoun, the Scot in The
Nigger of the Narcissus who in his youth had "attained the rank of
harpooner in Peterhead whalers."

It was a young ship's company on the outward passage to Australia—
eighteen of the twenty-eight on board being in their twenties—and pri-

marily British. Nineteen were from the British Isles, ten of those from Scotland. Conrad was the only Pole in an international crew which included two from Sweden, three from Germany, one from each of three countries, India, Norway, Canada. He signed "Conrad Korzeniowski" on the *Loch Etive*, for the first time dropping the "de" from his name, and agreed to serve for an extensive voyage:

"London to Sydney and any Port or Ports in Australia, New Zealand, India, China, Pacific and/or Atlantic Oceans, West Indies, and/or America, and voyaging to and from as legal freight may offer, thence to a Port for orders and to the continent of Europe (if required) and back to a final Port of Discharge in the United Kingdom. Voyage not to exceed two years." But the ship called only at Sydney and Melbourne and the voyage was one of eight months.

Purdu—who signed on in a firm, Spencerian hand—was, said Conrad, "wonderfully clever at concealing his deafness," and possibly suggested the plight of Captain Whalley in "The End of the Tether," who successfully concealed his growing blindness while in command of an Eastern freighter. Purdu had been chief mate of the ship before the voyage Conrad made on the *Loch Etive* but he was never to secure a command. A few years later he was lost at sea, washed off the deck of a ship between New Zealand and Cape Horn.

Much as Captain Stuart might try for a new record, or to equal an old one, the weather on the outward passage was against him and the *Loch Etive* took a disappointing ninety-four days to reach Sydney, three weeks more than his best runs with the same ship. With two passengers and four stowaways on board, the clipper sailed under light winds from England to Madeira, sighted on August 31, and from there completed an eventless voyage to Sydney, reached on November 24, 1880.

"The beautiful iron clipper ship *Loch Etive* arrived yesterday," the Sydney *Morning Herald* reported on November 25, "it being the third visit to this port since she was launched from Inglis & Co.'s yards, Glasgow, about three years ago. The vessel is a high class one, and being in command of Captain Stuart, who gained a comprehensive knowledge of the Australian trade whilst commander of *The Tweed*, *Loch Etive* is apparently destined for a successful career. She has the appearance of being a thoroughly staunch ship, and has come into port in capital order. The winds experienced during the voyage were not of the kind to make a remarkable passage, the best day's performance, however, being 293 miles."

In Sydney again, Conrad was in a far more enviable position than a year and a half earlier when on the *Duke of Sutherland*, a penniless night watchman then patrolling a vessel shippers ignored. Now an officer with respectable earnings to spend, his ship was one of the most popular of the wool clippers whose tall masts could be seen from the heart of the city as they lay at Circular Quay, "the integral part of one of the finest, most beautiful, vast, and safe bays the sun ever shone upon."[8] He passed his twenty-third birthday in Sydney, his ship remaining in Australia for seven weeks. Shore life drew away some of the crew—five deserted and two were left in the Sydney jail—but Conrad, as he had Marlow say in *Chance*, liked sea life "because upon the whole it is favourable to reflection," offering "the inestimable advantages of solitude and silence."

The *Loch Etive* left Sydney on January 11, 1881,[9] her cargo mostly wool, and arrived in London at the end of a storm-slowed voyage of 103 days (Captain Stuart was later to take his clipper from Melbourne to Antwerp in eighty-seven days). Passing through Deal on April 23, 1881,[10] she reached London the next day. On April 24 Conrad signed off the ship.[11]

Two of the experiences on the homeward passage of the *Loch Etive* Conrad wrote of. In "Christmas Day at Sea," published in the London *Daily Mail* on December 24, 1923, he told of a Christmas gift dropped over the side of the *Loch Etive* for "the first whaler I had ever seen." The year was not 1879 nor the day Christmas, as he remembered it forty-two years later (on Christmas day, 1879, Conrad was in the Mediterranean on the S.S. *Europa*), but January 29, 1881, eighteen days after leaving Sydney.[12] For the American whaler *Alaska*, "two years out from New York—east from Honolulu—two hundred and fifteen days on the cruising-ground,"[13] the end of January was still near enough to Christmas for men living "beyond the confines of mankind's life." In the vast empty space of the South Pacific, between New Zealand and Cape Horn, the whaler was sighted by the *Loch Etive*. Messages between the two ships in that day before radio were exchanged by means of signal flags. For the only time in his twenty years of wandering "over the restless waters of the globe," Conrad saw a Christmas present given and received. The gift, a wooden keg filled with a bundle of old Sydney newspapers and "two boxes of figs in honour of the day," was flung overboard by the London-bound clipper and gratefully retrieved by furcapped whalermen who for seven months had been out of touch with the world.

The second experience, one of the most beautiful and moving pieces in Conrad's work, he told of in *The Mirror of the Sea*. It concerned the rescue in mid-Atlantic of nine men of an unnamed Danish brig, homeward bound from the West Indies. The Danish ship has never been identified (over the years dedicated searchers, outstanding among them being Captain P. A. McDonald, master of the sailing ships *Moshulu* and *William Dollar*, have engaged in an international hunt for the brig) and perhaps can never be known. The ship's logbook of the *Loch Etive* voyage, which would have contained an account of the rescue, has disappeared; newspapers, with an overwhelming number of sea disasters to report, tersely announced "crew saved" and rarely gave the name of a rescuing ship or details of those manifold events. Shipwrecked crews picked up at sea were often transferred to a passing ship or dropped off at some port along the way, many taking months to reach home. The fate of a missing ship might then be made known, but no published record of Conrad's brig has been found.

Conrad wrote the story during October-November, 1905, in the "Initiation" chapter of *The Mirror of the Sea*, vaguely dating the episode as one of twenty-five years before, or as happening during the 1880–81 voyage of the *Loch Etive*, when he was "an inexperienced junior." The "Sunday, the 22nd" day of his story was probably taken from a day when he was writing it, Sunday, October 22, 1905, no "Sunday, the 22nd" occurring while he was in mid-Atlantic.[14] Since the outward passage of the *Loch Etive* was reported in Sydney as having been without incident, the rescue would have taken place in early April, 1881, when the clipper, bound for England, sailed through the Atlantic storms which wrecked so many ships. (Among those lost in the Atlantic during the heavy weather of that time, their crews saved under circumstances similar to the rescue in which Conrad had a hand, were the British brig *Katie*, wrecked by a hurricane on April 17, her crew rescued by the Swedish ship *Ida;* the Swedish brig *Helios*, abandoned dismasted and on fire west of the Bay of Biscay on April 23, her crew taken on board by the British ship *Nelson;* the Danish schooner *Johanne*, grounded in a storm off the coast of Morocco on April 18, her crew taken off by an unnamed vessel. So numerous were shipwrecks that marine disaster items fill 341 books in the marine library of the Atlantic Mutual Insurance Company in New York, one of the world's largest collections, begun in 1824. It is incomplete, even so, no one of Conrad's ships being associated with a sea rescue.)

"The most amazing wonder of the deep is its unfathomable cruelty," Conrad introduced the brig story. "I felt its dread for the first time in mid-Atlantic one day, many years ago, when we took off the crew of a Danish brig homeward bound from the West Indies. A thin, silvery mist softened the calm and majestic splendour of light without shadows— seemed to render the sky less remote and the ocean less immense. It was one of those days, when the might of the sea appears indeed lovable, like the nature of a strong man in moments of quiet intimacy. At sunrise we had made out a black speck to the westward. . . ."

His ship, "which had the well-earned name of being without a rival for speed in light winds," moved so slowly toward the sinking brig that the captain dispatched two boats, Conrad in charge of one of them. "It was a race of two ship's boats matched against Death for a prize of nine men's lives, and Death had a long start. We saw the crew of the brig from afar working at the pumps . . . which spouted two clear streams of water upon their bare feet. Their brown skins showed through the rents of their shirts; and the two small bunches of half-naked, tattered men went on bowing from the waist to each other in their back-breaking labour, up and down, absorbed, with no time for a glance over the shoulder at the help that was coming to them."

The rescued men tumbled into the two ship's boats and their captain told Conrad their story. "They had lost their masts and sprung a leak in a hurricane; drifted for weeks, always at the pumps, met more bad weather; the ships they sighted failed to make them out, the leak gained upon them slowly, and the seas had left them nothing to make a raft of. It was very hard to see ship after ship pass by at a distance, 'as if everybody had agreed that we must be left to drown.' "

While the boats, with the brig's exhausted crew safe in them, were being rowed back to their waiting ship, Conrad watched the brig die. "As if at a given signal, the run of the smooth undulations seemed checked suddenly around the brig. By a strange optical delusion the whole sea appeared to rise upon her in one overwhelming heave of its silky surface, where in one spot a smother of foam broke out ferociously. And then the effort subsided. It was all over, and the smooth swell ran on as before from the horizon in uninterrupted cadence of motion, passing under us with a slight friendly toss of our boat. Far away, where the brig had been, an angry white stain undulating on the surface of steely-grey waters, shot with gleams of green, diminished swiftly, without a hiss, like a patch of pure snow melting in the sun."

Approaching England, the *Loch Etive* ran into extremely heavy weather, seeing "no sun, moon, or stars for something like seven days." Captain Stuart—"it was the pride of his life that he had never wasted a chance, no matter how boisterous, threatening, and dangerous, of a fair wind"—drove his ship hard through the blackness, testy with the inability to see. When the sky did clear the clipper proved to be close to a headland where a tremendous sea was breaking upon the coast.

"Without knowing it in the least, we had run up alongside the Isle of Wight," Conrad wrote of that near miss.[15]

The voyage had taught him much about the "brooding bitterness" of the sea (not long before, five steamships had sailed from American ports to disappear without leaving a trace), and two days after his arrival in London newspapers gave a chilling account of how men, in another way, could be broken by the sea. The German barque *Tiger*, under Captain Kruger, en route to America, had been repeatedly held up during her crossing by contrary winds. Spending 124 days on the Atlantic, she had been unable to reach any land. With all food gone, the captain had killed his dog to feed the starving crew and had offered to shoot himself, that the men might eat him. The chief mate persuaded him to wait one more day. The British steamer *Nebo* came upon the skeleton men of the *Tiger*, two hundred miles off the coast of Maryland, in time to prevent the cannibalism[16] that, a reality of the sea, was to be a factor in Conrad's story "Falk."

"Open to all and faithful to none," he wrote of the sea, "it exercises its fascination for the undoing of the best."[17] Winds too violent or too calm determined what ships, which crews, should survive to make a landfall. Hurricane winds could demolish the Danish brig he saw go down, gales could drive the *Loch Etive* dangerously near an unsuspected coast, dead air could dehumanize men through slow starvation. The contagious terror of a maddened sea could undo others not unlike himself. It was one of these whose story inspired *Lord Jim*, a novel listed today among ten of the most important books ever written.

XI

The southwest monsoon would blow with its usual gale force at that time of year, punishing ships in that lane of the sea, yet Augustine Podmore Williams, the boyishly self-confident chief officer of the S.S. *Jeddah*, trouble-triggered as he soon proved to be, had no premonition of the unprecedented disaster the high winds would bring when, having seen to the loading of the cargo—six hundred tons of sugar, garron-wood and general merchandise—his ship sailed out of Singapore on July 17, 1880, for Penang,[1] there to pick up her passengers, pilgrims bound for the Holy Land. A likable young Englishman of twenty-eight, imaginative and romantic, he was to be tricked during that voyage by his own excitement and, in panic, to perform what the London *Times* branded a "scarcely credible" act. Seeing Williams in Singapore when the famous *Jeddah* case was still the talk of the port, Conrad remembered his part in it for twenty years, building *Lord Jim* from that foundation.

Williams was forty-eight and in Singapore in 1900 when *Lord Jim* appeared; a man with many children, so well liked as to be known by the popular nickname "Daddy," he had come to be as loved and trusted as the Jim for whom he partially served as model. The character of Jim in the two-part novel Conrad created from two men he had known, Williams and James Lingard, the latter an Englishman who, at thirty-eight, was a trader in the Borneo settlement of Berau in 1900. Both men lived for a number of years after the book's appearance, both had sons in Singapore. There, where the novel often given as Conrad's masterpiece was as well known as in the rest of the world, two unrelated local seamen each bore the distinction of being "the son of Lord Jim." But it was the chief mate of the *Jeddah* whose history had prompted the story, a history beginning on a stormy night when Williams moved upon the "wild and violent sea" of *Macbeth:*

> But cruel are the times, when we are traitors,
> And do not know ourselves; when we hold rumour
> From what we fear, yet know not what we fear,
> But float upon a wild and violent sea
> Each way and move.

In the 1880 summer of his last sailing, Williams, young for a chief officer and bursting with confidence as only the untried can be, was cockily sure of his ship, his captain, and most of all of himself ("officious"[2] the court termed the tall, powerfully built, deep-voiced seaman whose manner, as reflected in Conrad's version, "displayed a kind of dogged self-assertion which had nothing aggressive in it. It seemed a necessity, and it was directed apparently as much at himself as at anybody else."[3]). Williams had solid reasons to expect the screw steamer's routine three weeks' voyage across the Indian Ocean to the Arabian port of Jedda to be a safe one. The 993-ton British steamship *Jeddah*, built in Scotland eight years before,[4] was comparatively new; in drydock in Singapore she received a thorough overhaul, and by Lloyd's rating of 100 A 1—the spotless figure assigned by Lloyd's surveyor, Mr. Fittock, in Singapore prior to her sailing—the *Jeddah* was declared to be in top condition. Henry Ellis, Master Attendant of the port of Singapore, endorsed the soundness of the ship, declaring that on her departure he considered the *Jeddah* "a first class Hadji passenger steamer in every respect."[5]

For four years the *Jeddah* had successfully served in Australian waters before being bought by James Guthrie and registered in Singapore on November 7, 1876.[6] On numerous voyages, including a recent transportation of 960 British soldiers from Suez to Bombay, the *Jeddah* had proved capable of carrying heavy loads of passengers.

Captain Joseph Lucas Clark, a Singapore resident, was the *Jeddah's* able English commander. Captain Clark had not only been master of the ship for three years, on the same pilgrim run, but was, moreover, her co-owner. The ship was staffed with a crew of fifty[7] and Williams had proved, in his fast promotion over older men, superior qualities as a seaman. Born in the vicarage of Porthleven, Cornwall, on May 22, 1852, the son of the Rev. Thomas Lockyer Williams,[8] he had come to Singapore in 1879 as a twenty-seven-year-old officer in the British merchant marine. Ambitious, with a gift for languages and an equal gift for leadership, genuinely liked, young, rugged, an eager enthusiast of the sea, holding at his early age a Master Mariner's certificate, he had every prospect of an outstanding career in the hardy seafaring world so foreign to the scholarly bent of his family. One of fifteen children, Williams came of generations of clergymen and lawyers; his great-grandfather Samuel Smith had served as a member of Parliament. Named for St. Augustine by a devout father raised in a vicarage, Williams had as his godfather Richard Podmore who, like Williams' father, was a priest in the Church of England.[9] Through abiding by the principles acquired in the strict discipline of his home and adhering as firmly to the rules for a gentleman's conduct, Williams was to bring upon himself the personal disaster stirring Conrad to write *Lord Jim.*

The crisis waiting for him just ahead, over what began as a placid sea, was to prove him a "gifted poor devil with the faculty of swift and forestalling vision"[10] and one equally incapable of bargaining with truth; it was to be due not so much to the storm or the ship or the captain but to qualities of his own—an easily excited imagination, a knight-in-armor sense of chivalry, and inflexible honesty—that the *Jeddah's* chief officer was, after that voyage, to become a seaman exiled from the sea. Williams' anxious concern for the safety of the captain's wife, the only European woman on board,[11] set off the events of the sea case which long held the headlines in both East and West, a case so enduring in ceaseless argument over the years that Conrad alluded to it as having "an extraordinary power of defying the shortness of memories and the length of time: it seemed to live, with a sort of uncanny vitality, in the minds of men, on the tips of their tongues."[12] Tragic as the affair was in itself, Williams' compulsion to volunteer self-damaging statements in a court of law led Conrad to portray him as the remorse-driven hero of *Lord Jim*.

The *Jeddah* case, with its undying query of why, its search for excuse, was so singular a one that Major G. R. Goodfellow, British Resident in Aden and Sessions Judge who handed down the first verdict, described it as "the most extraordinary instance known to the Court of the abandonment of a disabled and leaking ship at sea by the master and Europeans, and almost all the crew, with close on 1,000 souls on board when no immediate danger existed of her foundering."[13]

In a more favorable light it set a precedent as a remarkable sea rescue—the saving of nearly one thousand passengers and their ship, when a few short hours would have brought the loss of all—a heroic performance emphasized by Chief Justice Sir Thomas Sidgreaves after the second and final hearing, in Singapore.[14]

"There can be no doubt, I think," Sir Thomas stated, "that the *Jeddah* was in imminent danger when she was sighted by the *Antenor*, and that but for the service rendered her by the *Antenor* she would in all probability have foundered or been dashed to pieces, with the loss of every life on board. Taking into consideration the number of the lives thus rescued from the probability of impending death, this is I believe a case of life-salvage of a totally unprecedented character."[15]

The abandonment of the *Jeddah* with so many passengers on board, and their chance rescue, provoked strong comments in newspapers around the globe.

For the *Times* in London it was the subject of an indignant editorial on August 12, 1880: "To the honour of sailors, nothing is more rare than that, in a disaster at sea, the captain and the principal officers of the vessel should be the chief or sole survivors. Nothing can be more admirable than the manner in which, as a rule, the commanders of vessels stay by them to the end, and insist on being the last rather than the first to be saved. . . . It would have been terrible that more than nine hundred helpless pilgrims should have perished at sea. But that they should have been abandoned by the officers of the ship to which they had intrusted themselves, and saved by the accidental services rendered them by another vessel, is scarcely credible."

Vibrating with an outrage it made no attempt to conceal, the *Times* asked: "Was the vessel, with this vast number of passengers on board, actually abandoned by the master and some of his chief officers? If she was towed into Aden she could not have been in a condition which would justify her officers in leaving her at all; and the abandonment of duty which would be involved in such conduct is so disgraceful that we must regard the whole matter as a mystery until further particulars are furnished. . . . It will consequently be a duty to make the most stringent inquiry into the circumstances of this alleged disaster, and into the conduct of those who were in charge of the vessel."

Not one, but two, stringent inquiries were made. The court hearings in Aden and Singapore, during the first of which Williams gave his remarkable testimony, posed the gray question of courage developed by Conrad in *Lord Jim*. Jim, chief mate of the *Patna* who, alone of her officers, faced the court to tell the full story of their crime, was Conrad's version of Williams, chief mate of the *Jeddah* whose hardy honesty induced him to make admissions so devastating that Judge Goodfellow noted in his verdict: "Had there been any evidence, except the first mate's own statement, on this point, the Court would have felt constrained to have put him on his trial also."[16]

Williams was never put on trial, not the less-punishing trial of a courtroom at any rate, though high officials and various branches of the British government—including the Earl of Kimberley, Colonial Secretary in Gladstone's cabinet (and for whom the Kimberley diamond mine and city of Kimberley in South Africa were named)—repeatedly sought to bring criminal actions against both Clark and Williams. Feeling ran so high that Sir Cecil Clementi Smith, Colonial Secretary and later Governor of the Straits Settlements, told the Singapore Legislative Council on September 14, 1880: "The case has created excitement not only in our own minds, but of course has affected the whole character of English seamanship throughout the world. I do not think that any one could read the account without the blood mounting to his cheeks with shame."[17]

Still unforgotten seventy years later, it was termed a "cowardly disregard of the traditions of the sea" by the *Straits Times* of Singapore on December 2, 1950, in a column written by the editor G. L. Peet ("Cecil Street"), who recalled the "tremendous sensation in Singapore" it had caused.

So touchy a subject did it remain, long after the death of all the principals involved, that the 1921 history *One Hundred Years of Singapore* avoided any mention of the most famous of all cases ever connected with that port. Kept alive by harbor talk, the *Jeddah* story over the years grew into a sailor's legend, built by court proceedings, newspaper accounts, endless waterfront debate—and the acute presence of Williams, who, no less than Jim, was "bound to fight this thing down" and to that end worked among seamen in the harbor of Singapore for thirty-four years. Years of layered myth fogged and warped the affair Sir

Frederick Aloysius Weld, Governor of the Straits Settlements at the time, sternly called "most eminently disgraceful to our Mercantile flag and marine";[18] after almost a century of cooling time, it is possible now to learn—from long-forgotten documents in London, Singapore and Aden—the answer to the "why" of one of the greatest sea riddles of all time.

From those records comes the story of the *Jeddah's* voyage, standing out as it does both as a unique sea calamity with a ship-ghost ending and—the theme Conrad drew from it—as the moving, personal account of a man's "acute consciousness of lost honour."

When it was all over Williams was to hear—and with what irony—"There is no evidence before the Court to show that the life of the captain's wife was in danger."[19] In that statement lay the crux of the disaster awaiting the *Jeddah* at latitude 11°55′ north and longitude 51°55′ east.[20]

When the *Jeddah* sailed from Singapore she *seemed* to be in top condition. She had had mishaps in her short career—having been scuttled, to put out a fire, six years before in Twofold Bay, east of Australia—but subsequent examiners had found her free of defects. Leaving Singapore, the steamer called at Penang, on this run carrying Moslem pilgrims from Malaya and the Dutch East Indies to the fifteenth-century Arabian port of Jedda, waiting there while they, on foot or on camelback, crossed fifty miles of desert to Mecca and back again, the *Jeddah* then returning those who survived to their homes in the East. (Times have somewhat changed: today the 150,000 Moslems who, coming from all parts of the Arab world, annually dock at Jedda—the Arabic word for "grandmother" given to the town where Eve is said to be buried—travel the last lap of their once-in-a-lifetime pilgrimage to Mecca in buses along a hard-surfaced road.)

Although the official complement of the steamer upon leaving Penang was given as 953 adult passengers, the Court of Inquiry in Aden pointed out that when the *Jeddah* was towed into that port she carried 992 passengers, "778 men, 147 women, and children 67, not counting infants in arms." The ship of 993 tons, with 992 passengers and fifty members of the crew, was so seriously overloaded that Judge Goodfellow felt called upon to enclose a reprimand in his findings: "The Court consider it is not out of place to remark that in their estimation nearly 1,000 souls on board a vessel of the tonnage of the *Jeddah* was a greater number than should be allowed by any regulation, especially for a long sea voyage, as taken by the *Jeddah*, and at a season when bad weather might naturally have been expected."[21]

Of those on board only six were Europeans: Captain Clark, his wife, the first mate Williams, the second mate, the second and third engineers. One of the six officers, the chief engineer, was an Oriental. A wealthy Arab of Singapore, Syed Mohamed bin Ahmed Alsagoff[22]—a descendant of Malay rajahs, who had inherited one of the oldest and richest Arab merchant and shipowning firms in Singapore, dating back to Singapore's founding in 1819 and one in existence there still—shared ownership of the *Jeddah* with Captain Clark. The ship was operated under the name of the Singapore Steamship Company and sailed under British colors. In a Singapore with a population of 97,111—of whom some 1500 were Europeans—the two owners of the *Jeddah* were outstandingly prominent and had old ties with the colony.

Pilgrim ships in those years were worse than slave ships, according to Captain Henry Carter,[23] who had served as a master of them. For the eighteen or twenty days of the voyage to Jedda a thousand pilgrims were cramped together, with little room to move and little or no fresh air. They slept on the bare decks and, stretching hoarded savings to cover a pilgrimage to the Holy Land, subsisted on whatever food they had been foresighted enough, or affluent enough, to bring with them.

"There is something pathetic in the passionate devotion with which these Malay Mussulmans face danger and trials of almost every kind in order to prostrate themselves at the shrine of the Prophet," the *Manchester Guardian* declared in an editorial on August 13, 1880. "Probably the great bulk of the *Jeddah*'s passengers were people advanced in life. There is no sacrifice to which these poor people will not submit in order to realise the dream of their lives. If need be their last dollar is forthcoming to provide the passage money, and they cheerfully undergo hardships on board ship which would kill an Irish emigrant. In the case of younger people it not infrequently happens that their labour is pledged for two years or more in order to obtain the means for making the pilgrimage. A man will go to his employer, ask for the advance of a sufficient sum, and then on his return liquidate the debt by hard work. This is but one way in which Mahometans of the poorer class obtain what is necessary for a journey to Mecca. The pilgrimage is one of the highest acts of Mussulman devotion and as death on the way is believed to give perfect assurance of immediate admission into Paradise, one can understand the stolid indifference with which the pilgrim risks the perils and privations of such a voyage as that from Singapore to Jeddah."

Gathered at Penang from the backwaters of Malaya to undertake the journey, the "dream of their lives," the 992 pilgrims flowed aboard the *Jeddah* in a daylong procession. In *Lord Jim* Conrad caught, with photographic realism, the movement of such a pilgrim-loading:

"They streamed aboard over three gangways, they streamed in urged by faith and the hope of paradise, they streamed in with a continuous tramp and shuffle of bare feet, without a word, a murmur, or a look back; and when clear of confining rails spread on all sides over the deck, flowed forward and aft, overflowed down the yawning hatchways, filled the inner recesses of the ship—like water filling a cistern, like water flowing into crevices and crannies, like water rising silently even with the rim. . . . they had collected there, coming from north and south and from the outskirts of the East, after treading the jungle paths, descending the rivers, coasting in praus along the shallows, crossing in small canoes from island to island, passing through suffering, meeting strange sights, beset by strange fears, upheld by one desire. They came from solitary huts in the wilderness, from populous campongs, from villages by the sea. At the call of an idea they had left their forests, their clearings, the protection of their rulers, their prosperity, their poverty, the surroundings of their youth and the graves of their fathers. They came covered with dust, with sweat, with grime, with rags—the strong men at the head of family parties, the lean old men pressing forward without hope of return; young boys with fearless eyes glancing curiously, shy little girls with tumbled long hair; the timid women muffled up and clasping to their breasts, wrapped in loose ends of soiled head-cloths, their sleeping babies, the unconscious pilgrims of an exacting belief."[24]

So great were the hazards of the long sea voyage to and from Jedda, and the burning desert walk to Mecca, that each pilgrim equipped himself for the journey with a winding sheet in which to be buried, should he succumb on the way. No pilgrim ship being staffed with a doctor or medically trained man, the homeward voyage could be as stark as that made by the *King Arthur* in the same year the *Jeddah* came to grief. Sailing from Aden to Calcutta, a passage of twenty-seven days, the *King Arthur* carried 1200 returning pilgrims, of whom hundreds lay ill throughout the voyage and forty-six died on shipboard, some from smallpox and some—destitute or unprepared for so long a crossing —of starvation. Running short of coal, the ship's woodwork was burned for fuel; storms tossed the ship remorselessly; during one a baby was born, and died. "Seven hundred of the pilgrims live down between decks; the other five hundred live on deck in the open air, rain or no rain," the chief officer of the *King Arthur* described the monsoon-harassed and pestilence-stricken voyage in a letter published by the London *Times* on August 17, 1880.

Leaving Penang on July 20, the *Jeddah* crossed Malacca Strait and, in the blazing sun and heat of the equator, steamed westward over the Indian Ocean. For the next eighteen days she was to be treated to all the vagaries of monsoon weather—five days of broiling sunshine on a placid sea, three days of heavy squalls of wind and rain, five days of fiery sun when only the smoke of the steamer marked the sky, five days of punishing gales through which the ship fought to gain 150 miles in a day, and that, in the end, broke the overstrained mechanism of the ship.

Captain Clark, in his protest made on November 26, 1880, and filed with the Vice Admiralty Court in Singapore for the second of the *Jeddah* trials, described the ordeal his ship went through:

"During the twenty-fifth, twenty-sixth, and twenty-seventh, the vessel encountered heavy squalls of wind and rain at intervals with very heavy Northwest swell, causing her to roll and labour very severely, breaking everything about the decks and filling the cabins with water. All hands were constantly employed baling out water during the twenty-seventh, and on that day some of the water-closet pipes started, causing a quantity of water to come into the saloon."[25]

Five days of fine weather, though of stifling heat, gave the passengers and crew of the *Jeddah* time to clear the damage and to relax in the deceptive peace of the sea. Then the contrary winds of the monsoon season found the ship again.

"At noon on the second August," Captain Clark's statement went on, "there was a moderate gale and rising sea, causing the engines to race and the vessel to pitch badly and shipping much water forward. . . . At 7.0 P.M. the foretopmast staysail was blown away, and the water from the broken closet pipes continued to come into the fore and after cabins, as the leaks could not be got at. During the third August the wind blew a very strong gale and a fearful sea was running, washing the decks clear fore and aft of two native water-closets and all moveables, and causing a heavy strain on the engines and boilers."[26]

So briefly stated by Captain Clark more than three months after the storm, the wind, in fact, on August 3 increased to hurricane force and high seas crashed over the *Jeddah's* decks. On that day—the final act of the tragedy was beginning—the two boilers, huge masses weighing thirty tons each when filled with water, broke adrift.[27] The rolling of the ship in the mountainous seas put too great a strain upon what proved to be defective fastenings; working free, the boilers slid backwards and forwards as much as two inches. During the next three days, with no abatement in the storm, the jerking of the boilers broke the connecting pipes, the resulting leak increased rapidly, putting out the fires, and the wrecked engine room became untenable. The *Jeddah*, meanwhile, was shipping vast quantities of water.

Of the final day of chaos on board Captain Clark gave a graphic picture:

"At 7 A.M. on the same day, the seventh August, it was still blowing a tremendous gale, and the water in the vessel rose above the fire grates, the boilers started adrift from their seatings, and the stokehole and engine-room plates and bearers dashed about with every roll of the vessel. It now seemed that the vessel had sprung a heavy leak, and as nothing more could be done in the engine room or stokehole and the water was rising so rapidly, every deck pump was set to work and the firemen and passengers employed day and night at the pumps and baling water with buckets. Sails were also passed under the bottom of the vessel, but the water still increased a foot in twelve hours. An attempt was now made to disconnect the propeller, but the water was rising so rapidly, and was already at such a dangerous height, it was found impossible to do so."[28]

Captain Clark closed his protest hastily, brushing aside the crime of his desertion, the true disaster of the *Jeddah* case.

"At midnight on the seventh to eighth the passengers refused to pump any more, and the vessel settled down by the stern with a heavy list to starboard, and at 2 A.M. this appearer left the vessel in one of the ship's boats and arrived at Aden on the tenth of August."[29]

Behind that chary ending lay a story of panic, of a fear so overpowering as to make the master of the *Jeddah* and his chief officer see, in the very real menace of the gale, perils that were not there.

"With the rolling of the ship," Judge Goodfellow summed up their imagined plight, "the quantity of water in the stokehole appeared greater than it actually was, and from the engine and donkey-engine being useless, the vessel having water also in the after-hold through the sluice, the actual condition of affairs was thought more serious than was the case; the ship having a leak, and being in a heavy sea."[30]

As Conrad wrote in *Lord Jim*, it is not often that a seaman glimpses "the earnestness in the anger of the sea," when he is made to test himself "by those events of the sea that show in the light of day the inner worth of a man, the edge of his temper, and the fibre of his stuff; that reveal the quality of his resistance and the secret truth of his pretences, not only to others, but also to himself." It was this testing Captain Clark and his chief officer Williams were subjected to on their last day aboard the *Jeddah*.

On that day, the engines proving useless, sails were set; these, quickly blown away in the gale, were replaced by others when the wind slacked off. Pumping and baling went on without letup, the passengers taking a willing part until midnight on August 7, when Captain Clark ordered the bulk of the crew to man the boats, boats which had been swung out, in open admission of defeat, since early in the day. This act changed the temper of the pilgrims, for, even if the boats were to be successfully launched in the high seas, not more than a quarter of the thousand people on board could crowd into them. Moreover, land, as Captain Clark knew from the noon reading, was less than thirty-five miles off, due west, on the ship's course.

"Had more energetic measures been taken at the outset," Judge Goodfellow wrote of that last day, "it appears just probable to the Court that subsequent events might have been averted. When steam power was no longer available on board the *Jeddah*, it appears to the Court that no regular system of reducing the leak was organized by the master. He appears to have come to the conclusion early on the 7th August that the boats would probably be required, and they were prepared and swung out, and the crew engaged in attending to them rather than to the vessel's condition. The firemen, however, appear to have been steadily engaged in working the ash buckets up to midnight of the 7th August.

"The master does not appear to have taken his passengers into his confidence or to have endeavoured in the least degree to raise their hopes in any way. On the contrary, it seems he informed them that if they would not pump the vessel would founder, thereby giving no hope. On this point, situated as he was, the Court consider he was wanting in simple judgment, for he had much in his favour to dispel fear and raise the hopes and energies of his passengers, who appeared ready and willing to assist. . . .

"The Court consider that in this the master showed a want of judgment and tact to a most serious extent, and that he caused disorganization and discontent, not to say despair, at a time when none of these feelings should have been engendered."[31]

Captain Clark, the judges believed, would have acted differently had it not been for Williams. In the midnight darkness, with the hurricane howling and water sloshing ominously in the bottom of the ship, Williams' vigorous imagination bolted. Magnifying the menace of the leak, he believed the steamer to be sinking, that nothing could save her, that the end was but moments away. He saw the dark, troubled faces of the pilgrims, acutely aware of how few of them the boats could save, and interpreted their despairing words as threats. He saw, or thought he saw, them arm themselves with knives. Reacting with raw nerves to the storm, the floundering ship, the rumble of alarm spreading among the passengers, the visualized nightmare rush for the boats, Williams panicked. He was less concerned for his own life in the stampede he foresaw than for the wife of the captain. With the impulse of a Don Quixote he appointed himself the protector of Mrs. Clark—her limp, undeciding husband submitting that charge, as all others, to his direction—and in the clear, fine light of chivalry set the course which was to bring dishonor to them all. Whether or not Mrs. Clark was as young and fair as Dulcinea, it was for her, solely because of her, that the two men offered the sacrifice of the lives of a thousand others. Mrs. Clark's indirect but major part in the disaster was marked by W. K. Thynne, Assessor and Port Officer of Aden, one of the two judges at the Aden hearing, in his appended verdict:

"The first mate of the *Jeddah*, according to his own statement, is greatly to blame in doing what he could to demoralize the master, by advising him to leave the ship, telling him his life was in danger, also his wife's life; that he, the master, was sure to be killed if he remained on board; and that he, the first mate, did thrust the master into the boat. The mate worked on the fears of the master for the safety of his wife, and by so doing hurried the master into leaving the ship."[32]

Williams not only persuaded Captain Clark to abandon ship but, to avoid provoking the riot he believed such an action would surely cause, to do so stealthily. He warned the captain to be careful how he went about the decks, saying the passengers might kill him, and reported that some had been heard to say "they would not allow anyone to leave the ship, and would prevent them to the extent of violence if necessary."[33] The captain was not interfered with in any way, yet, his fears fed by Williams to the point where he believed his own and his wife's life would be attempted if he remained on board, he decided to place Mrs. Clark in the starboard lifeboat and to remain in it with her, to hang astern of the ship until daylight. "What the master's intentions were after daylight does not appear," the court laconically observed.

Even though the passengers all that afternoon and evening of August 7 had their frightened eyes focused on the lifeboats, provisioned, armed and swung out, ready to leave—the tantalizing evidence of an escape to be denied them—they offered no violence, made no show of force, to anyone on board.

"The Court consider that the action of the pilgrims tends to prove that they never intended to harm the master and his officers had they remained in the *Jeddah*," Judge Goodfellow declared.

The second engineer went to bed at midnight, not having seen a single man armed, and the sole source in addition to Williams warning the captain of the black mood of the pilgrims was the jittery Lezed Omar, a trembling man "much frightened for his own safety."[34]

Without checking on the statements of the overwrought Lezed Omar and Williams, and, as Judge Goodfellow pointed out, "in place of resorting to measures to restore confidence or to organize any system of defence in case of need, for the protection of the lives of himself and the Europeans on board, which he could easily have done by keeping the bridge with the arms on board," Captain Clark chose escape. The distance from his cabin to the starboard lifeboat was a short forty feet, yet the escape maneuver—and Williams took "a prominent part in this proceeding"—had the elements of a cloak-and-dagger scene.

At 2:30 A.M. on August 8, in total darkness, Mrs. Clark was passed through one of the windows of the captain's cabin, then "either walked along or was carried" to the lifeboat, which, an anticlimax to the melodramatic staging, she reached in complete safety, no attempt having been made to molest her. The captain, the chief engineer, the third engineer, and sixteen Malay members of the crew joined her in the boat, Williams standing on the rails, officiating at its lowering.

Seeing their captain, his officers and crew actually leaving them, the pilgrims became frantic. Unable to prevent the lowering of the boat, they attempted to swamp it, throwing "boxes, pots and pans, and anything they could lay hands on" down upon it.

"Their demeanour is accounted for," the judges concluded, "by the evidence that they had made up their minds that they should not be deserted by the only persons capable of protecting and helping them in the circumstances in which they were placed, and consequently they would prevent to the utmost the master or his officers leaving the ship. It is in the Court's opinion more than probable that the master was misled in regard to the real intentions of the pilgrims, but he has himself to blame for not making more certain of these intentions, or waiting for some more clear proof of these intentions than took place."

In the escape plans Williams had been assigned to command a port side lifeboat, to take off in it with the second engineer and others of the crew, but as he stood directing the departure of his captain the maddened pilgrims pushed him off the rails, flinging him overboard. Rescued from the water, he was hauled into the boat that, with four officers aboard, was the only one to get away. When the passengers continued to hurl down objects at the escapees, Williams fired two pistol shots in their direction. Captain Clark's boat then cast off, getting clear of the ship. At that time land—Cape Guardafui, the tip of Africa at the entrance to the Gulf of Aden—was but ten miles away.

Three lifeboats all told, into which only three passengers managed to secure places, were manned for the secret getaway, the captain, in spite of the crowd of passengers and the availability of additional boats, having made no plans for any others.

On board, meanwhile, the pilgrims dealt summarily with the two boats still within their reach. They saw the port side lifeboat, which Williams was to have commanded, already manned, with the second engineer at the helm. Climbing into it, they "threw all the men back from her into the ship, and would not allow them to leave." The third lifeboat, in charge of the second officer, a European, was ready for lowering. It was less than half full, containing eleven men—the second officer, seven of the crew, three pilgrims. When these, ordered to come out of the boat and return to the ship, refused, the pilgrims cut the boat's falls. It plunged to the water bow first. The eleven men, spilled into the sea, were drowned. The boat disappeared in the darkness, nothing being seen of it again.

Left on board the captainless *Jeddah* was a single officer, the second engineer. Of the ship's six officers one had been drowned and four had fled; of the original fifty crew members only eighteen remained with the ship—three sailors, one topman, the serang, eleven firemen, one clerk, one fireman working his passage. With the engines useless and the *Jeddah* compelled to rely on sail, they were far from being a competent ship's company. How little they, largely engine-room men, knew about the topside of a ship was pointedly shown when the London *Times* on August 28 revealed in a dispatch from Aden that of them "not a soul understood anything about navigation, or, in fact, could steer."

The pilgrims, resigned to what seemed an inevitable end, left the decks for a time, to reappear in their winding sheets, more than nine hundred white-clothed figures waiting in the black night for the ship to carry them down. Some, more hopeful, resumed pumping and baling; others joined them and, operating the pumps and buckets without pause, soon gained on the leak. By daybreak, sail having been set all night, they found themselves in smooth water, with land in sight.

During the night Captain Clark's boat had been held with her head to the wind and the sea, close by the listing *Jeddah*, for "about a couple of hours." Awaiting the two boatloads of officers and crew he had directed to join him, Captain Clark was near enough to his ship to know of the second officer's drowning—a death he reported as murder. In too much fear of the passengers to risk a return to the *Jeddah*, he and his officers (with the exception of Williams, whose frank testimony varied from theirs) contrived a story of the disaster during the hours their boat, allowed to drive and partially sail before the wind, took them toward the Suez Canal shipping lane where rescue could be expected. Captain Clark's story, that he concluded the *Jeddah* had gone down three hours after he left her since he had been "unable to see her at daylight," was open to challenge: by remaining near the ship until 4:30 A.M. as he claimed, he could not have failed to see her at that very near hour of sunrise. ("What did I care what story they agreed to make up?" Jim said of the boatload of deserters planning their alibi in *Lord Jim.*)

At 10 A.M., less than seven hours after abandoning his ship, Captain Clark's boat was sighted by the Liverpool steamship *Scindia*, bound for Port Said from the Burma port of Akyab. All twenty-one in the boat, including the captain, his wife, and Williams, were safely taken aboard the steamer. Captain Clark made no request for a search to be made for the *Jeddah*—which, afloat, with sails set, was but twenty-two miles away —and the *Scindia* carried the self-styled sole survivors of a tragic shipwreck to Aden.

Arriving at Aden on August 10, Captain Clark, little knowing how much his ship was to haunt him, reported that the *Jeddah*, with 953 Moslem pilgrims bound for Mecca on board, had foundered off Cape Guardafui, that all on board had perished, only one boat, his own, getting away safely while the vessel was going down. He added that the second officer and second engineer had been murdered by the pilgrims, who had also "tried to kill the other Europeans by hurling heavy articles on them in their boat." Cables bearing the news of this "terrible shipwreck" and "calamitous pilgrimage" were flashed around the world.[35]

At the time the cables were sent the very-much-alive second engineer was close on the heels of his captain. No more courageous than the others, he had attempted to leave the ship but, thrown back on deck by the pilgrims, had helped them save the vessel.

Barely out of sight over the ocean at the moment Captain Clark and his fleeing crew were being picked up by the *Scindia*, the pilgrims, with distress signals flying—flags proclaiming "We are sinking!" on one mast and "Send immediate assistance"[36] on another—were attempting to sail the *Jeddah* toward shore, having in mind to beach her under the 1300-foot-high bluffs near Ras Felook, on the coast of Africa. At 3 P.M., when only seven miles from land, the wind, by great good fortune, died away. A pounding surf in which no boats could live was breaking on the coast ahead; the sun, setting at 6 P.M., would bring darkness within three hours. The derelict, waterlogged *Jeddah* which, with so much water in her hold, could not be steered, even had anyone known how, was being helplessly driven ashore, where she would break up during the night. In their desperate hope but nautical innocence, the passengers were unwittingly aiding in their own destruction by offering to the dying wind what canvas the ship retained—fore-topsail jib, fore- and main-topsails.

"If I had been on board as a passenger I should have considered her case as a very hopeless one," Captain Charles Powell, master of the four-thousand-ton *Lusitania*, who had taken his ship past Cape Guardafui a few hours before the *Jeddah's* struggles in the same waters, testified at the Singapore hearing. "I think she would have gone ashore before daylight."[37]

The *Jeddah*, under canvas, was moving slowly, at three to four knots an hour, when, at 4:30 P.M.—six hours after the captain's boatload had found safety aboard the *Scindia*—the 1644-ton British steamer *Antenor*, bound on a voyage from Shanghai to London with 680 passengers, saw the distress signals of the *Jeddah* and bore down on her. Captain John T. Bragg of the *Antenor* sent his first mate, Randolph Campbell, the boatswain, and four of the crew in a boat to investigate the trouble aboard the *Jeddah*, then wallowing in the trough of the sea. What Campbell found he reported to the court in Singapore:

"The Engines were totally disabled, and the Engine fires put out; there were 7 or 8 feet of water in the vessel, and everything on board was in confusion, and all persons on board were panic stricken. . . . The boilers on board were adrift and had broken from their fastenings, and all the pipe connections with the boilers were broken, and no steam power on board could be used."

Campbell believed the *Jeddah* to be sinking and that "without great exertion in baling and pumping she must sink." He returned to the *Antenor* to confer with Captain Bragg, where the two officers faced a hard choice: to jeopardize the lives of their 680 passengers, their £84,000 cargo, and £30,000 ship in a hazardous nightfall rescue, or of "leaving a ship abandoned by the Captain and officers, and with nearly 1,000 souls on board, to the inevitable fate that seemed to await her of foundering at sea or being dashed to pieces on the coast."[38]

The *Antenor*, already full, could not take on the *Jeddah* passengers, but the two officers believed the derelict ship might be towed into Aden if they could manage to keep her afloat. Aden, traditionally the site of the Garden of Eden and known to voyagers as early as 2000 B.C., was the nearest port. Campbell volunteered to stay alone aboard the *Jeddah*, arrangements were made to take him off in case the *Jeddah* should sink, and by ten o'clock that night, "after considerable difficulty, and with the exercise of much patience, skill, and ingenuity," the *Jeddah* and her keening passengers were in tow. For the next three days, until she was safely delivered at Aden, Campbell never left her, and for sixty-seven hours seldom left the bridge. He steered the ship himself until he succeeded in teaching that skill to two of the *Jeddah's* crew. Of the first strenuous hours, when it seemed doubtful if the logy steamer could be tugged 450 miles to Aden, Campbell gave a brief description to the Vice Admiralty Court in Singapore.

"I called the headmen amongst the pilgrims together and organized gangs amongst the pilgrims to pump and bale the vessel. This was done, the men constantly relieving one another, and by the evening of the 9th of August, we had gained 6 inches on the water, and during the following night we gained a foot on the water and continued to gain on the water thenceforward until the water was reduced to 3½ feet in the engine room and 5 feet in the after hold."[39]

Campbell gave as laconic a recital as his counterpart in fiction, the French naval lieutenant, officer of the *Victorieuse*, whom Conrad created for the role in *Lord Jim*. More vividly, Captain Bragg told how he and his second officer kept alternate watches on board the *Antenor* throughout the three anxious days of towing, maintaining constant communication with Campbell by means of a board on the bridge of their ship.

"On the 9th, as the sun went half way down from the horizon," Captain Bragg related, "the Chief Officer telegraphed 'gained 4 inches', and I called all hands aft to give him a cheer to encourage him—we were corresponding all the time. The question was, whether we could overpower the water, or the water overpower us."[40]

Such an incident, though slight in itself, showed "the hearty good will with which the salvors were conducting their operations," Chief Justice Sir Thomas Sidgreaves stated, "and how likely it would be that they would reanimate, by their coolness and determination, the failing spirits and flagging energies of the pilgrims."

At 5:15 P.M. on August 11, twenty-four hours after Captain Clark had arrived there, the *Antenor* towed the *Jeddah* into Aden. By coincidence Captain Bragg entered the British Consulate on that day to report the salving of the *Jeddah*, with all on board safe, just as Captain Clark was leaving after filing a claim on his heavily insured vessel, declaring it lost with all hands.

"The *Jeddah* having been towed into Aden harbour on the 11th instant, with the water reduced nearly two feet in the after-hold, proved there was nothing hopeless in the state of the ship when abandoned,"[41] the Port Officer at Aden, Mr. Thynne, took occasion to point out.

The conflicting news—that the *Jeddah* was lost, that the *Jeddah* was saved—confounded newspaper editors around the world for some time, the London *Times* taking the precaution of publishing both reports in the issue of August 12:

ADEN: August 10

The steamer JEDDAH of Singapore, bound for Jeddah, with 953 pilgrims on board, foundered off Cape Guardafui on the 8th inst. All on board perished, excepting the captain, his wife, the chief officer, the chief engineer, the assistant engineer, and 16 natives. The survivors were picked up by the steamer SCINDIA and landed here.

ADEN: August 11
7:50 P.M.

The JEDDAH, which was abandoned at sea with 953 pilgrims on board, did not founder, as reported by the master. She has just arrived here, all safe, in tow of the steamer ANTENOR.

The hazards of the sea were so great in those years, the losses of ships and lives mounting to staggering totals, that acts of bravery received wide attention. To commemorate heroism at sea a series of one hundred panels was later erected in Postman's Park in London, recalling the courageous self-sacrifice of ships' crews: of Stewardess Ayres, who turned back to save a child and died when the steamer *Iona* burned at sea; of Mrs. Rogers, stewardess of the *Stella*, who "resigned her lifebelt to a lady passenger and went down with the steamer." In July, 1880, Captain A. Maclean Wait, commander of the British mail steamer *American*, was the hero of a London ceremony during which he was awarded a handsome watch and commended for "his very able and gallant conduct in safely dispatching his passengers and crew in the ship's boats"[42] when his vessel foundered near the equator on April 23, 1880. The *American*, Capetown-bound from Southampton, had fifty-four passengers on board, the captain seeing them safely away in eight boats. Seven of the boats were picked up by passing ships but nothing was known of the eighth, containing five of the crew, for four months. Then word reached London that the Portuguese brig *Taranic* had landed the men at Loanda. Captain Antonio D. Oliveira of the *Taranic* was presented with a silver gilt claret jug and two beakers by the British Board of Trade on September 22, 1880, for rescuing the boatload, which had been bobbing about on the ocean in a dinghy for four days when he came upon them.

News about the *Jeddah* was still being published around the world when the *Straits Times* in Singapore reprinted on September 24 an earlier story in the London *Globe* that, to Captain Clark's discomfort, contrasted two tales of the sea, that of the *Jeddah* and the *American*:

"By telegraph from Suez we learn that the *Jeddah*, which was abandoned by the captain and officers off Cape Guardafui, arrived at Aden, as had already been reported, and will be ready to sail in six weeks. Her appearance in Port next day must have had much the same effect upon the delinquents as the ghost of Banquo had upon Hamlet. They had declared that their ship had foundered, and to confute them, she herself hove in sight freighted with the thousand souls who had been given up for a more picturesque fate. . . .

"Even a stranger reappearance is reported.

"On this day, four months ago, the steamship *American* foundered near the Equator, and with the most perfect discipline her passengers and crew took to the boats. Of these seven were picked up by passing ships and landed at Madeira. The eighth, which was the dinghy, having on board the quartermaster and four seamen, was missing, and it is only today that news has come from the Cape Verde Islands of her safety. She had been picked up by a Portuguese brig and landed at Loanda.

"The conduct of the *Americans* is in happy contrast with those of the *Jeddah*—Not even a mail bag has been sacrificed."

Although Captain Clark was the only one of the "delinquents" directly punished, it was Williams who suffered most, and through no other testimony than his own.

The Court of Inquiry at Aden gave as its opinion that Captain Clark "aided by the officious ill-advice of his chief officer, entirely forgot his first duty as a shipmaster, and proceeded to be one of the first instead of the last to leave his disabled vessel to her fate. This last act roused the pilgrims to violence in attempting to swamp his boat, and such the Court consider might naturally have been expected from any body of human beings, even Europeans, situated as the pilgrims were.

"With every consideration for the master under the trying circumstances in which he and his crew found themselves placed, the Court is reluctantly compelled to state that they consider that Captain Clark has shown a painful want of nerve as well as the most ordinary judgment, and has allowed his feelings to master the sense of duty it is the pride of every British shipmaster to vaunt, and they consider that in the instances mentioned he has been guilty of gross misconduct in being indirectly the cause of the deaths of the second mate and ten natives, seven crew and three passengers, and in abandoning his disabled ship with nearly

1,000 souls on board to their fate, when by ordinary display of firmness, combined with very little tact in dealing with natives, with whom he is no stranger, he could have ensured their co-operation and gratitude, and saved considerable loss to his owners. The Court must here also remark on the want of anxiety shown by the master for the fate of the *Jeddah*, in not doing all in his power to induce the *Scindia* to search for her, as there is little doubt but that a proper statement of facts and little persuasion would have induced the master of the *Scindia* under the circumstances to steam for an hour or so to windward, when the *Jeddah* would certainly have been sighted.

"The Court feel compelled to mark their sense of the master, Joseph Lucas Clark's, conduct by ordering, subject to the confirmation of the Bombay Government, that his certificate of competency as master be suspended for a period of three years."[43]

The Governor of Bombay, Sir James Fergusson, reluctantly accepted the court's mild sentence but added a stiff censure of his own.

"Had I been advised that any option rested with it [the Bombay government] with reference to the details," he wrote into the record, "I should have declined to confirm them, as I think the sentence inadequate to the offence committed by the master of the *Jeddah* as described by the Court.

"Assuming that his abandonment of his ship, without necessity, and with the probable loss of an enormous number of helpless people for whose safety he was responsible, was the result rather of cowardice and want of resource than of inhumanity, his subsequent conduct in not doing his utmost to procure them succour showed that latter quality. But in either point of view, he has, in my judgment, shown himself entirely unfit to be entrusted with the charge of life and property at sea."[44]

The Court of Inquiry at Aden completed its findings on August 20 after hearings lasting a week, hearings during which Williams went out of his way to condemn his own behavior. The courage which failed him on board the *Jeddah* supported him through a withering courtroom investigation where the punishment he seemed to seek was readily given.

"The Court consider it necessary to place on record their disapprobation of the conduct of the first officer of the *Jeddah*, Mr. Williams, who may be said to have more than aided and abetted the master in the abandonment of his vessel," Judge Goodfellow declared. "The Court consider it very probable that, but for Mr. Williams's officious behaviour and unseamanlike conduct, the master would (by the first mate's own showing) have probably done his duty by remaining on the ship."[45]

In words intended to bring about Williams' dismissal—which they did

—the judge added that Williams "has shown himself unfitted for his position as first mate on a crowded pilgrim vessel."

The co-judge, W. K. Thynne, was even more severe with Williams. In his conclusions Mr. Thynne pointed to the presence of Mrs. Clark, for whose sake Williams had jeopardized so many lives.

"I am of opinion," stated Mr. Thynne, "had the master's wife not been on board the master would not have deserted his ship.

"I am of opinion had the master received proper assistance and advice from his first mate, he, the master, would not have left the ship.

"I am of opinion had the master not left the *Jeddah* no lives would have been lost.

"I am further of opinion that the first mate should not be permitted to go in the ship again."[46]

Williams did not go. Upon her arrival at Aden all of the *Jeddah's* passengers were quickly landed and, since Captain Clark "refused to have anything to do with her," the "effects of the Master, Officers and crew have been handed over to them," Major Goodfellow wrote in official letters placed in the government's file.[47] "The vessel does not appear to have a very considerable leak," he added, "as the water was reduced from 7 to 4 feet during the time she was in tow of the *Antenor* and in harbour it has been further reduced by bailing only." Within five days she had been pumped dry.[48]

The *Antenor*, having lost three days by her rescue of the *Jeddah*, remained in Aden six hours, leaving the evening of August 11 to continue on to London. Five days after leaving Aden the engines of the *Antenor*, strained by the towing operation, broke down, causing her to arrive, again overdue, at the Suez Canal on August 22. In the canal she passed the S.S. *Patna* of the British India Steam Navigation Company, en route from London to Karachi and the Persian Gulf—the steamer whose name Conrad used in lieu of the *Jeddah* in *Lord Jim*, and one he saw in 1881 at the docks in London.

Disowned by her captain, the *Jeddah* lay at her moorings in the harbor of Aden for twelve days under no command. On August 23, "responsible Agents having come forward" as Major Goodfellow informed his government, she was turned over to them and three hundred of the pilgrims were dispatched in other vessels to their destination of Jedda. Captain Thomas Morgan Craig (no relation of Captain James Craig of the *Vidar* in which Conrad later served) was one of nine pilots in Singapore qualified to command a ship the size of the *Jeddah* in the Red Sea and, by newspaper reports, was sent from Singapore to take

temporary charge of her. Captain A. I. Freebody replaced Captain Clark
as permanent master, the crew being retained.

The ship's damaged cargo was sold at auction in Aden for 307 rupees
and, being repaired "to the entire satisfaction of the Engineer Surveyor
Mr. Vogwell"—rated as being "perfectly seaworthy, fairly found and
quite fit to prosecute her intended voyage"[49]—the *Jeddah* sailed from
Aden six weeks after being towed into that port. On September 29 she
left for Jedda, delivering there 269 of the pilgrims who had patiently
waited those six weeks to continue on toward Mecca. Sailing to Alexan-
dria to load a cargo for London, the *Jeddah* avoided her home port of
Singapore for more than a year.

Captain Clark, leaving his ship, returned immediately to Singapore;
the *Jeddah* case being under furious discussion there, he gave a statement
to the press upon his arrival. "Coming back here, there is published in
his name, what I believe is authentic, a statement in the papers which is
intended evidently as a sort of justification of his action," S. Gilfillan,
a member of the Legislative Council in Singapore, said of Captain Clark
at the meeting of the Council on September 14, 1880. "In this he says
that one of the reasons of his leaving the ship was that his wife's life
had been threatened by the passengers. This allegation is specially dealt
with by the Court of Inquiry, and according to their report, there is no
truth in it."[50]

Mr. Gilfillan declared that when Captain Clark, believing his ship to
be in danger of sinking, proceeded to get out the boats, it was with no
intention of caring for the passengers in his charge, "but simply to
provide for his wife—which might be natural enough if he had remembered that other people on board his sinking ship had wives as
well as himself."

Condemning Captain Clark in no uncertain terms, Mr. Gilfillan went
on: "He further states that, when he was trying to get away from the
ship and leave his passengers to their fate, things—boxes and what not—
were thrown at him. Very unaccountable to his mind! Sir, I think if
those 900 passengers had been English, he would not have been so
leniently treated. There is a rough manner of dealing with cases of this
kind, not unknown among men of our race, and if he had found himself
getting a quick run by a line to the yard-arm, I do not think any one
who has studied the circumstances would say he was harshly dealt with."

Another member, R. Campbell, told the Legislative Council: "I question whether any of us in the same situation would not have shot Captain Lucas Clark like a dog for his dastardly attempt to desert his vessel
in such dire distress. However, he manages to get away, and on the

morning of the 8th he sights the *Scindia*, and is taken on board. What does he do then? One would have thought his first impulse would be to implore the Captain of that vessel to look out for the *Jeddah*, which he must have known might have been saved. But he does not do so; he tells, as I think one may fairly assume, a deliberate falsehood, and says that the vessel had foundered; he goes on to Aden, let us hope in a happy frame of mind, and leaves his unfortunate passengers to perish like rats in a barrel! Was anything more inhuman ever heard of? At Aden he tells a tissue of falsehoods—I have no hesitation in saying so; a Court of Inquiry is held, and the result of the inquiry is that his certificate is suspended for three years. During the inquiry not one extenuating circumstance was brought forward, and not one single excuse could be shown for the Captain's conduct. He seems all through to have acted in a most inhuman and dastardly manner; and what is the result? Merely that his certificate is suspended for three years!

"Now, Sir, I hold that that is a punishment quite inadequate for the misdemeanor he has committed. Why, the man is a murderer. He was instrumental in causing the death of his Second Mate and the others who perished with him, and he put in jeopardy the lives of over 900 pilgrims, thus casting disgrace upon the British Mercantile Marine, of which he has been an unworthy member, and a slur upon the British flag."[51]

The Legislative Council at its September 14 meeting was presided over by the fifty-seven-year-old Governor of the Straits Settlements, Sir Frederick Weld, grandson of Baron Clifford of Chudleigh and a career diplomat whose twenty-six years of service had included holding office as Premier of New Zealand, Governor of Western Australia and Governor of Tasmania. A "pioneer of empire," he directed the affairs of the colony from Singapore's enormous Government House—its marble-paved front colonnade being 354 feet long—and reacted to the *Jeddah* scandal both as a stout defender of the empire and as a devoutly religious man; he was to make a pilgrimage himself to the Holy Land in 1890, one of two hundred English Catholics led by the Duke of Norfolk, the first such organized pilgrimage in three hundred years.

Reporting to Lord Kimberley on the Legislative Council meeting, Governor Weld declared that the Council expressed "strong and unanimous" feeling for a resolution proposing "it is the bounden duty of the local government to adopt all the means in its power to bring the Master —Joseph Lucas Clark—to trial for his inhuman conduct in deserting his steamer; or, at least, to secure by representations to the Board of Trade, that his Certificate shall be suspended for such a time as will render it impossible that any lives can ever again be entrusted to his care, under the British flag."⁵²

Captain Clark, having returned to Singapore from Aden on September 12, was followed three days later by Williams. No other officer or any of the crew of the *Jeddah*, and none of the pilgrims, had returned to Singapore by September 22 and it was this "want of witnesses," as Governor Weld wrote Lord Kimberley, which prevented the local government from instituting a new trial.

On June 16, 1881, the Advocate General of the government of Bombay declared it was no longer possible to institute fresh proceedings and the issue which had involved several branches of the British government for nine months was thereby dropped. The *Jeddah* case was still, however, to have a long life.

XII

During the long and ponderous intergovernmental discussion of the *Jeddah* case Williams, through his own unsparing admissions, was accepted as equally culpable with his captain. But a point long in being resolved was whether he jumped from the *Jeddah* or was thrown overboard by the pilgrims—a question reflective of his courage and one Conrad emphasized in *Lord Jim*. At the Court of Inquiry in Aden Williams maintained, in his otherwise self-destructive testimony, that he was thrown off the rails by the pilgrims; some charged him with jumping; Judge Goodfellow hedged in his verdict, saying Williams "found himself in the water"; the co-judge, Thynne, stated "I believe [the pilgrims] knocked the first mate overboard"; and Governor Weld, in his report, took an uncommitted position, writing that Williams "says that he was thrown overboard."

Captain Clark found the hostile climate of Singapore too much to bear. Charged with being "a murderer," with "gross cowardice," with "dastardly conduct," hearing of himself that "no punishment the law could impose would be too much for such a criminal," he endured the public revulsion of his home town for two months and then disappeared. Sir Frank Swettenham, in Singapore at the time as assistant colonial secretary for the Straits Settlements and in that capacity reviewing all records of the case, declared—as he wrote in a letter to the London *Times* in 1923¹—that Captain Clark "got away out of jurisdiction." Whether Clark ever commanded another ship or not is not known. Singapore shipowning firms as a rule then had branch offices in Batavia and Manila, and it may have been in some such Pacific port that Captain Clark ended his days in scandal-free peace. When Conrad drew upon the *Jeddah* case for *Lord Jim* he reflected his loyalty toward the British merchant marine, in which, as a captain, he concluded sixteen years of service, by making the dishonored master of the pilgrim ship not English —as he was—but an obese, repulsive German, "well aguaindt in Apia, in Honolulu," who fled to some Pacific haven "where there's plenty room for a man like me."[2]

Williams too sought shelter away from Singapore, but only for a time. During the year of his disappearance he may have searched for refuge in the backwaters of the East, hounding himself from one water clerk's job to another as Conrad had Lord Jim do, but, with a courage few would display, he came back to Singapore to face the accusations and live them down.

Although both Captain Clark and Williams testified at the first of the hearings on the *Jeddah* case, in Aden, neither appeared at the second— a salvage action—held in Singapore during the six days of September 12–17, 1881. Captain Clark had left Singapore by that time and presented a written protest through his lawyer Mr. Davidson. The salvage action, which kept the *Jeddah* story alive, was a claim made before the Vice Admiralty Court in Singapore by the owners of the *Antenor* "against the steamship *Jeddah*, her cargo and freight." Before those six days of hearings were over the whole history of the disaster had been retold by a flow of witnesses, pilgrims and crew who had been aboard the *Jeddah* the night her officers abandoned her, sea captains of long experience who described the risks in a nighttime salvage of a "hopeless derelict—worse than a derelict with all those people on board." So great was the excitement caused in Singapore by this reliving of the year-old sea crime that Captain Clark's lawyer, on the last day of the hearing, sought, and was denied, a change of venue.

The *Jeddah* was insured for £30,000, Chief Justice Sidgreaves stated in the judgment settling the case, published in the *Straits Times Overland Journal* of October 22, 1881. The Chief Justice estimated the value of the ship, cargo and freight at the time of the salving as £29,000. In view of the circumstances—that the captain, officers and most of the crew abandoned the *Jeddah* "under the impression that they were leaving a sinking ship," the successful salving of the vessel "by the constant exercise of nautical skill, as well as by unremitting care and perseverance on the part of those in charge of the *Antenor*," and the large value of the property—he set the sum of £6000 as salvage award.

"The principal feature in this case," he declared, "is undoubtedly the life salvage, and by the Merchant Shipping Act the preservation of human life is made a distinct ground of salvage reward, with priority over all other claims for salvage where the property is insufficient. The value of this property salved is large, and it was undoubtedly salved when in imminent peril, although fortunately without any very great risk to the lives of the salvors. The employment of the *Antenor* and her valuable cargo on board upon the operation was clearly a service of very high merit, and as such ought to be liberally rewarded. I award as salvage the sum of £6000,—£4000 to go to the Owners of the *Antenor*, this sum to cover all expenses incurred by that ship—and £2000 to the Captain, Officers, and crew of the *Antenor*. Having been asked to apportion this sum, I do so as follows. The Captain and Chief Mate £500 each. The Chief Engineer and 2nd Officer £150 each; the balance to be divided amongst the remaining officers and crew according to their respective ratings, the Boatswain and 4 of the crew who went on two occasions to the *Jeddah* on the night of 8th August taking at the rate of 2 shares each."

The salvage payment strained the finances of the owners of the *Jeddah* and, with shippers and passengers reluctant to use a steamer bearing the notorious name, the Singapore Steamship Company went out of existence four and a half years after the disaster. The one-ship company folded on February 24, 1885, when the *Jeddah* was sold to Inche Yayah bin Sheban of Johore.[3] Seeming to be a ship of ill omen, the *Jeddah* had a series of new masters—Freebody, Chalk, Geary—each of the first two remaining with her but a year. In 1886 she was sold again, to Lee Phee Yaow, a Penang firm, and, to erase a too-well-remembered past, her name was changed to the S.S. *Diamond*. As the *Diamond* she continued to work out of Singapore until the end of the century, a vessel then more than twenty years old.

Williams retained his Master's and Chief Officer's certificates to the end of his life but never went to sea again. From some temporary hideaway he came back to Singapore when the fresh *Jeddah* case was still the bitter talk of the port. Refusing both the disguise of another name and the protection of another occupation, he took employment in the most exposed position of all, in the harbor, in daily contact with his most hostile critics, seamen. In 1882 he joined the Singapore ship chandler firm of McAlister & Company as a water clerk. "I've got to get over this thing . . . I won't shirk any of it," Jim declares in *Lord Jim*; with a similar resolve to face it out, Williams remained with Mc-Alister & Company for twenty-eight years. Fluent in Malay, a *dubash* or "man of two languages" acting as interpreter between English-speaking ships' officers and Malays of the port, he rose to be chief outside superintendent in the Dubash and Shipchandlery Department of McAlister's. There, known to every sea captain and trader entering the port—and retaining his burly I-won't-stand-any-nonsense manner—he won from seamen the respectful if half-chaffing title of "the Governor of Johnston's Pier," Singapore's main wharf, now known as Clifford's Pier. Among the many who knew, and knew well, the tall commanding figure of the waterfront were the Borneo trader Jim Lingard and Captain James Craig, master of the *Vidar*. Craig and Williams were both officials in the merchant seamen organizations of Singapore, Craig being one of the first presidents of the Masters and Mates Association he helped to found. Sailing out of Singapore from 1875 to 1920, Craig was in Singapore as a young marine officer of twenty-six, two years younger than Williams, when the *Jeddah* scandal broke; from him Conrad, in 1887, learned much of its earlier history.

By 1910, when a land boom sent Singapore prices zooming, Williams had achieved enough prosperity to buy four houses and, resigning from McAlister's, set up his own ship chandlery business in the Arcade.

The unsteady market and stifled trade brought on by World War I, however, caused him to go bankrupt in October, 1914. In his public examination heard by Chief Justice Bucknill in Bankruptcy Court, Williams gave a candid report of his efforts and his debts—debts in Malay dollars of M$34,500 ($11,500). His report was summed up in the Singapore *Straits Budget* of October 22, 1914:

"The debtor, who stated that his age was 62, said that he had been in Singapore for 35 years. For 28 years he was with Messrs. McAlister and Company, leaving them at the end of 1910. He made a little money during the land boom. He bought three houses and, with his wife, a fourth. He started on his own as a shipchandler and then came the rubber boom, during which time he lost about $16,000. He was obliged to mortgage his land and now he owed $13,500, apart from secured creditors. To secured creditors he owed $21,000. These debts he had incurred since 1910, half of them being accounted for by the rubber boom and the other half by slackness in trade and depreciation in buying and selling owing to market fluctuations. He had eight children, six of whom were dependent upon him. Although living in one of his own houses he had to pay $25 a month in respect of it. With his wife and family the least he could live on was about $300 a month. He was still endeavouring to earn a living as a shipchandler."

Williams, by determinedly shouldering the burden of his unforgotten one great failure—and, equally, by refusing to permit any to taunt him with it—had won back Singapore's esteem quickly. Two and a half years after the *Jeddah* disaster, on January 22, 1883, when he was thirty-one, he married an English girl in Singapore, Elizabeth Jane Robinson of Newcastle upon Tyne, and in the course of thirty-three years of marriage raised a large family. An older son, born in 1887, was already a seaman when Williams made his statement before the Bankruptcy Court—a seaman known to his shipmates as "the son of Lord Jim"—and an older daughter, born in 1895, sent to school in Devonshire, married and settled in England. Williams' large family in the end totaled sixteen, his youngest child born in 1915 when he was sixty-three, of whom only nine survived him.

After the failure of his ship chandlery venture in 1914, Williams joined Dawood & Co. in Singapore, in the *dubash* branch of the firm. It was while at work there on March 15, 1916, that he slipped and fell down a flight of steps, fracturing his hip. Never recovering from that accident, Williams died a month later, on April 17, 1916, at sixty-four. Although thirty-six years had passed since the sensational days of the *Jeddah* case, Williams was still remembered for it. The *Singapore Free Press*, reporting his death on April 20, 1916, showed how much the respect and liking Williams had won for himself in those thirty-six years caused the newspaper to alter the facts in its story:

"The late Mr. Williams was chief officer of the Singapore Steamship Co.'s *Jeddah*, a pilgrim ship which met with an accident in the Red Sea and was abandoned with about a thousand coolies aboard. He held a Chief Officer's certificate and was for some time the Singapore representative of the Imperial Merchant Service Guild. Many wreaths were sent to the funeral having reference to his nautical career, besides many others from private friends. Archdeacon Swindell conducted the service. The deceased leaves a wife and nine children to mourn his loss."

In *Lord Jim*, published sixteen years before, Conrad had said of the fictional Jim, "The time was coming when I should see him loved, trusted, admired"—and so it was, in fact, with Williams. The popular affection Williams knew in his later years was referred to by the *Straits Budget* of April 20, 1916:

"There passed away on Monday Mr. A. P. Williams, known to his many friends and acquaintances as 'Daddy', a very familiar figure in local shipping circles. For many years he was with McAlister and Co. as their principal outside man for the dubash branch of the business and in this capacity he became widely known."

Conrad was twenty-two, an untried, brand-new officer of the British merchant marine, when, in London, he first heard of the *Jeddah* case involving the untried ship's officer only five years older than himself.

Passing his second mate's examination in June, 1880, he received the "precious slip of blue paper" confirming his rank but which also bore, as his Uncle Thaddeus reminded him, "so many terrible threats in the event of your not fulfilling your duties."[4] Two months later London papers published the first news of the *Jeddah;* the storm that followed, in newspaper editorials, questions in Parliament, letters to the editor, in public castigation, vividly illustrated the punishment for failure. The uproar in London during the ten days before he sailed on the *Loch Etive*, an officer for the first time and the youngest of them, was duplicated at the end of that voyage in Sydney. There the *Jeddah* was well known from her four years of earlier service in Australia and, newspapers reporting full details of the case, Conrad heard it endlessly debated during his seven weeks in the port. Less than three years later, spending a month in Singapore in 1883, he saw Williams for the first time. Then, eighteen months after the *Jeddah* hearing held there, Williams, at thirty-one, was McAlister's water clerk, representing his firm as he boarded ships in the harbor. For a total of ten months, in 1885, 1887 and 1888, Conrad was repeatedly in the same marine circles in Singapore as the ship chandler's agent, the most-talked-about man among seamen. That Conrad knew Williams well was evidenced by his inclusion in *Lord Jim* of personal details generally unknown—Williams coming from a large family, having a "rural dean" father, being owed the exact amount of "three weeks and five days' pay" upon being dismissed from the *Jeddah*.

In history, in temperament, Conrad had much in common with Williams. Both were romantic, imaginative, chivalrous, earnest, and, both excellent linguists, were from cultured middle-class families with traditions hostile to the knockabout world of seafaring; each had a sternly religious father; by disposition and early training each retained a marked, unyielding sense of honor, a deep respect for truth. As their nicknames indicated—Conrad "the Count" and Williams "the Governor"—they displayed to others an almost haughty pride. Both, devoted to the sea, rose rapidly in that rigorous profession, Conrad a chief officer at twenty-nine, Williams at twenty-eight, both by then having passed for master.

"It may be my sea training acting upon a natural disposition to keep good hold on the one thing really mine," Conrad wrote in *A Personal Record*, "but the fact is that I have a positive horror of losing even for one moving moment that full possession of myself which is the first condition of good service."

The psychological fabric of the *Jeddah* case, the loss of self-possession by two ship's officers in a crucial "moving moment," supplied the texture for many of his novels. A major Conradian theme, defined as he gave it in *The Rescue* as "the Point of Honour and the Point of Passion," the loss of self or "wound of life" became his literary hallmark, a subject deeply imprinted upon his mind when he was twenty-two. Irrational fear for the safety of the captain's wife, an emotion paralyzing reason, drove Captain Clark and Williams to desert the Malay passengers in their charge; their desertion violated a basic code of the sea but it heightened, too, a critical East-West conflict of that empire-building time, the failure of white men toward the dark-skinned races they had undertaken to rule.

The "infernal alloy" existing in men, regardless of race or origin, was in Conrad's view only one cause of failure; contributing to it were circumstances beyond single control, faults of responsibilities commonly shared. That conditions on pilgrim ships, so similar to slave ships, were the fault of many nations, not one, he emphasized in *Lord Jim*: the actual overloaded *Jeddah* with an English captain and English-Arab owners was turned by him into one "owned by a Chinaman, chartered by an Arab, and commanded by a sort of renegade New South Wales German."[5] Blame for the evils of the pilgrim traffic did in fact rest on profit-seeking businessmen of the British and Turkish empires, on Europeans and Arabs, Christians and Moslems alike. Turkey, exporting £250,000 from Jedda in 1880 in the form of specie collected from pilgrims during their stay in the country, exhibited as great reluctance as British colonial shipowners toward enforcing stricter rules on the pilgrim trade, wary of reducing the flow of the poor and their gold. It required the *Jeddah* scandal to expose what had been so profitable to ignore. Ship conditions for pilgrims traveling to Mecca improved as a result of it, while Turkish fears of income loss were also justified: pilgrim spending fell to as low as £25,000 in 1904.

Of any crisis the question could be asked, as Jim asked it in *Lord Jim*, "Do you know what *you* would have done? Do you?" Weaknesses being "the common inheritance of us all," self-failures mar every life to some degree, carrying with them the pitiless reminders of experience, what the French critic Albert Saugère once described as the "unfortunate contraband it is no longer possible to declare"[6] and of which Freud, a year older than Conrad, was to make the world so lastingly aware. A man innately alone, Conrad was instinctively drawn to the exile, the rebel, the victim of mischance, his work showing, says Professor Albert J. Guerard, "more than almost any other novelist's, an intensifying conflict and interplay of sympathy and judgment."[7]

Twenty years after the *Jeddah* disaster, writing with the mellowed understanding of a man of forty-two assessing the quality of courage, one his long career at sea had demonstrated hinged so much on being "ready," Conrad recalled the young, unready Williams who, fashioned by imaginative memory into Lord Jim, "was not afraid of death perhaps," but was "afraid of the emergency." Picturing "all the horrors of panic, the trampling rush, the pitiful screams, boats swamped—all the appalling incidents of a disaster at sea he had ever heard of,"[8] Williams had propelled his captain into leaving his ship, secretly, in the night. For that, and most of all for admitting it, he became the Singapore seaman locked to the shore whom Conrad remembered:

"One sunny morning in the commonplace surroundings of an Eastern roadstead, I saw his form pass by—appealing—significant—under a cloud —perfectly silent. Which is as it should be. It was for me, with all the sympathy of which I was capable, to seek fit words for his meaning. He was 'one of us.' "[9]

XIII

. . . all around I could see the circle of the sea lighted by the fire. A gigantic flame arose forward straight and clear . . . with noises like the whirr of wings, with rumbles as of thunder.

Youth

The *Jeddah* was but one of many sea calamities. In Britain, Parliament in time forced an end to the practice of sending overloaded or unfit ships on long voyages where their survival chances were slim, and British marine disasters were gradually reduced. But two and a half years after the *Jeddah* made world headlines another unfit ship involved Conrad in his second shipwreck, the experience described in "Youth," written just before *Lord Jim.*

Injuries, sustained on this and other ships, played a major part in determining the course of Conrad's life. An accumulation of accidents and illness resulted in the broken health which caused him to give up the sea at thirty-six and devote himself to writing, his life from then on increasingly one of physical pain and breakdowns, the tortured years as an author for which he is remembered. But in his youth—"O youth! The strength of it, the faith of it, the imagination of it!"[1] was his eloquent memory of those spirited years—accidents came early, and inevitably.

Choosing sailing ships, the most romantic but also the most hazardous of seagoing vessels (of the 1965 British vessels lost between January 1, 1873, and May 16, 1880, nine-tenths—1171—were sailing ships[2]), Conrad embarked on a career where the risks were abnormally high. At twenty-three he was injured in France on a sailing vessel being towed, at dusk, through a crowded harbor. At twenty-five he was injured again when one of the least seaworthy ships in the British merchant marine exploded and sank at sea. At twenty-nine a storm accident resulted in his long hospital stay in Singapore where, poor health deciding him to remain in that warm climate, he came to know an area he might otherwise never have seen, the Borneo river of *Almayer's Folly* and the settlement of Berau, his "literary birthplace."

The inevitability of sea accidents was made vividly clear in a report by Samuel Plimsoll, the English shipping reformer known as "the sailor's friend," whose name carries on in "Plimsoll's Mark," the safe-load line vessels bear on their sides today. In an 1880 Blue Book on marine disasters compiled for the British Board of Trade, Mr. Plimsoll dramatically illustrated, in his 340-page record of wrecks, the major cause of those disasters: by far the largest proportion of the British ships lost between 1873 and 1880—overloaded, understaffed, and leaky—were unseaworthy at the time of leaving port. "Dramas of the Deep: How Sailors' Lives Are Sacrificed to Mammon" the New York *Herald*[3] headlined its story of Mr. Plimsoll's harrowing account, concluding that "much of the loss of property and life was due to carelessness and crime." The British sailors' lives sacrificed totaled 10,827. Of crippling accidents, of disablements such as Conrad's, no count was given.

Almost as important a factor as injuries in affecting the shape of his life was Conrad's wish to see the East. Having sailed three times to the Caribbean, twice to Australia, twice over the Mediterranean, his urge to be in the East led him at twenty-three to join two ships, the *Annie Frost* and *Palestine*. On both he was injured. Both went down at sea, the *Palestine* while he was an officer of it.

Back in London on April 24, 1881, after his Australian voyage as third mate on the *Loch Etive*, Conrad looked for a ship. Fruitless weeks went by. Then, on June 10, he wrote his Uncle Thaddeus he had a long voyage in view, to lands and seas new to him. This was to be to China, on the 1236-ton sailing ship *Annie Frost*—also given as *Anna Frost*—a vessel built in Quebec in 1863 and owned by Frost & Co. of London. The

Annie Frost, returning from China at the end of a ten months' voyage and bound for Le Havre, anchored in the roadstead of The Downs off Deal, England, on June 5, 1881. In the highly competitive seamen's world where too many were on hand for every job, berths were often secured in The Downs, the final starting place for long voyages from London, the first home-touching for ships returning. In the anchorage of The Downs seamen boarded foreign-going vessels scheduled for quick turn-arounds, acquiring jobs in advance of the scramble for them in London. No signing-on was required until a new voyage officially began. (Six years later Conrad was to serve on the *Highland Forest* for a month before registering, while his remembered connection with the *Falconhurst*, presumably in London before his appointment to the *Highland Forest*, has been impossible to establish due to the absence of his name from that ship's crew list. "It was nothing uncommon for a mate to serve on board of a sailing ship while in port, for weeks even, without signing-on," writes Captain P. A. McDonald in the March, 1953, *Sea Breezes*, himself a sailing-ship master with a lifetime spent at sea.) In this unofficial way, in The Downs on June 5, Conrad joined the *Annie Frost* as a mate.

Leaving The Downs on June 6, the *Annie Frost* crossed to Le Havre, arriving there the same day in tow of the tug *Napoleon*.[4] After unloading a cargo brought from Cochin China, the eighteen-year-old ship prepared to leave for London. Freakish weather—warm June days suddenly turning to bitter cold, with the temperature at 41 degrees in England and snow on the high moors—increased shipping hazards. (The combination of bad weather and weak ships accounted for 919 wrecks off the British coasts in the first six and a half months of 1881, an increase of 219 over those lost in the same period the year before.[5]) As she was being towed out of Le Havre in the darkness on June 11, weaving her way through a harbor congested with transatlantic steamers, the *Annie Frost* struck a quay wall and bridge, sustaining damage to starboard quarter and rails. The *Journal du Havre*, in its issue of June 12-13, 1881, described what had happened:

"On Saturday, on the evening tide, the English ship *Annie-Frost* left the southern end of the Eure basin in tow of the English tug *Napoleon* on her way out to sea. In passing the Transatlantic lock on her course she struck her bow, on the port side, against the granite masonry, loosening several stones. One of these fell into the lock. The ship also damaged the south side of the bridge."

Conrad, who was apparently thrown overboard by the force of the collision, was injured in the nighttime accident and also lost his seaman's gear. He referred to this near-fatal plunge in *A Personal Record*, recalling the "year of hard gales," 1881, when his next ship, the *Palestine*, badly damaged by those gales, put back to Falmouth "in a sinking condition." It was that year, he wrote, "in which I came nearest to death at sea, first by water and then by fire"[6]—the escape from a burning ship being an experience soon to follow. The *Annie Frost* reached London on June 13, two days after the accident, and Conrad went to the hospital for a stay of several days.

Two months later, on August 10, he wrote his uncle asking for financial help in replacing his belongings, a loss for which he indicated he had tried, and failed, to secure compensation. Thaddeus replied on August 15. "Thank God that you survived, and that you're alive and only had a few days of illness in the hospital—a desirable refuge this time—and that you came safely through that fatal adventure! I should have preferred that you had saved your things together with your bones—but what's happened has happened. . . . it seems to me the shipowners of the *Anna Frost*, in negotiating for compensation for the ship, should have demanded some, too, for the things lost by their officers."[7] Thaddeus sent the £10 Conrad asked for, calling it a gift to a "distressed seaman" not to be deducted from his nephew's allowance, but he cannily noted that emergency gift too in his notebook.

An insurance claim, for compensation for the damage sustained by the *Annie Frost*, was filed through Lloyd's of London, where references to the 1881 incident are still to be found. It was overlooked in earlier accounts of Conrad's life and the supposition was made that the ship's accident and his injury were fictitious, a conclusion drawn from the fact that his name was not among those on the official Agreement and Account of Crew for the last two voyages of the *Annie Frost*. But his name did not appear because he made neither voyage—the 1880–81 voyage to China and return, nor that beginning in London on July 31, 1881, again to China. The latter, about which he had hopefully written his uncle just before his injury, was one he fortunately missed. The *Annie Frost* reached China safely but, returning to England, sank in the Atlantic northeast of the Azores on September 3, 1882.[8]

Apart from his unlucky eight days on the *Annie Frost*, Conrad was without work for nearly five months in 1881. To qualify for his next officer's examination, as chief mate, he needed additional months of sea service, and to put in that "time"—on a ship bound for the East—he signed on the decrepit *Palestine*, the *Judea* of "Youth."

" 'Youth' is a feat of memory," he said of the story. "It is a record of experience; but that experience, in its facts, in its inwardness and in its outward colouring, begins and ends in myself."[9] Writing it during the last days of May and early June, 1898—nearly seventeen years after his troubles on the *Palestine* began—it truly was a feat of memory. He was forty and the father of a five-month-old son, Borys, when he composed it in a few days while living at Ivy Walls Farm in the Essex village of Stanford-le-Hope in England.

Conrad varied only slightly in the story, with its brilliantly created mood of exuberant, undefeatable youth, from the adventure begun when he was twenty-three. The story's contrasts of youth and age, splendor and squalor, courage and crisis, existed in reality, a work of fiction true enough to have been written of many other ships.

"There are those voyages," he began it, "that seem ordered for the illustration of life, that might stand for a symbol of existence. You fight, work, sweat, nearly kill yourself, sometimes do kill yourself, trying to accomplish something—and you can't." Such was his do-or-die voyage on an old "coal-wagon" bound for Bangkok.

The *Palestine* was the same age as himself—twenty-three years at sea and old for a ship—when he joined her in London as second mate on September 19, 1881.[10] A wood barque of 427 tons, built in the north of England at Sunderland in 1857, she was owned by John Wilson of London and was to sail to Bangkok with a cargo of coal. "It was my first voyage to the East, and my first voyage as second mate. . . . I had come out of a crack Australian clipper, where I had been third officer," Conrad recounted his own background in "Youth." The ship, he continued the story, "was old. . . . She belonged to a man Wilmer, Wilcox—some name like that. . . . She had been laid up in Shadwell basin for ever so long. You may imagine her state. She was all rust, dust, grime—soot aloft, dirt on deck. . . . She was about 400 tons."

Retaining other features of his own voyage, Conrad used the actual names of the captain, Beard, and the first mate, Mahon, in his story. Both were older men—Captain E. Beard of Colchester, Essex, was fifty-seven, and H. Mahon of Dublin was fifty[11]—while Conrad, at twenty-three, was the strikingly young second mate. "Between those two old chaps I felt like a small boy between two grandfathers" was his comment in "Youth." Only the three officers—Conrad, Captain Beard and Mahon—remained with the ship throughout the long ordeal of a year of false starts from England for the voyage to Bangkok, a port she never reached. Twenty-eight seamen joined and left the ship during the twelve months she repeatedly tried to leave England. The final thirteen officers and crew who saw her end in flames far from home were not youngsters, the average age for those on board being thirty-three.[12]

Everything was against a safe passage. The unprecedented storms, the decayed condition of the ship, the cargo of coal—the riskiest freight a ship could carry. Omens of a luckless voyage were plentiful. Conrad's uncle considered both him and Captain Beard to be "desperate men" going out of their way to look for trouble by embarking on a ship so plainly doomed. But a second mate's berth was not easily found, Conrad needed both the job and the pay, and the ship's staggering efforts to make her last voyage appealed to his youth. He came to love "the old thing." For eighteen months, at a wage of twenty dollars a month, he was involved in what was "altogether a memorable affair." The official documents[13] covering the final voyage of the *Palestine* verify how closely he followed his own experience in writing "Youth."

The *Palestine* sailed from London on September 21, 1881, two days after Conrad joined, and immediately met with trouble. Delayed in Gravesend for a week, two of the crew, ill, left the ship. Putting out from Gravesend on September 28, the *Palestine* ran into the famous October gales of that year, taking three weeks to reach North Shields, normally a short run up the east coast of England, where the coal was to be loaded. In North Shields four of the crew deserted and one left sick. Having missed her turn at loading, the *Palestine* remained in Newcastle upon Tyne for six weeks. On November 29, with 557 tons of West Hartley coal on board, she set sail for Bangkok with a new crew, the second of many. Leaving the English Channel, the ship encountered a series of gales, lost her sails, and on December 24 sprang a leak when three hundred miles from England. The crew refused to continue and the *Palestine* put back to Falmouth. Reaching Falmouth on January 10, that crew melted away; a new one was engaged on February 3. The vessel was thoroughly repaired in dock, all but ninety tons of the coal being discharged and stored under cover. The repairs required eight months; her crew vanished again. Conrad stayed on. On September 17, 1882—exactly a year after her departure from London, never in that time having got far from shore—the *Palestine* sailed from Falmouth for Bangkok, a fresh crew taken on the day before she left.

Six months later, still trundling on her way to Bangkok but still far away, the too-often-handled coal caught fire while the ship was in Bangka Strait off Sumatra. All efforts to stifle the fire failed and on March 14, 1883, the coal gas exploded, blowing up the decks. Conrad, taking his watch on deck, was leaning against the carpenter's bench, smoking his pipe and talking with the carpenter, Joseph Hawke, a young Falmouth man of twenty-one making his first voyage, when the ship blew up. Thrown in the air by the explosion, Conrad gave an account of that moment in "Youth."

"In the twinkling of an eye, in an infinitesimal fraction of a second since the first tilt of the bench, I was sprawling full length on the cargo. I picked myself up and scrambled out. It was quick like a rebound. The deck was a wilderness of smashed timber, lying crosswise like trees in a wood after a hurricane; an immense curtain of soiled rags waved gently before me—it was the mainsail blown to strips. I thought, The masts will be toppling over directly; and to get out of the way bolted on all-fours towards the poop-ladder. The first person I saw was Mahon, with eyes like saucers, his mouth open, and the long white hair standing straight on end round his head like a silver halo. He was just about to go down when the sight of the main-deck stirring, heaving up, and changing into splinters before his eyes, petrified him on the top step. I stared at him in unbelief, and he stared at me with a queer kind of shocked curiosity. I did not know that I had no hair, no eyebrows, no eyelashes, that my young moustache was burnt off, that my face was black, one cheek laid open, my nose cut, and my chin bleeding. I had lost my cap, one of my slippers, and my shirt was torn to rags."[14]

The *Palestine* remained afloat, her hull unshattered, and late that afternoon a passing ship, the S.S. *Somerset* (the steamer *Somerville* Conrad called it in "Youth") answered distress signals and took the smoking vessel in tow. Five hours of towing fanned the blaze dangerously and the towrope was slipped. At eleven o'clock that night the *Palestine*, "a mass of fire," was abandoned. The officers and crew got off in the ship's three boats, Conrad in command of the smallest with three of the men for a crew. For twenty-three hours in a fourteen-foot boat he was on the open sea, in waters strange to him, shark waters, the nearest land, Bangka Island, a solid wall of jungle. In this setting the boats stayed near the burning ship throughout the night, Conrad recalling the eerie blaze in "Youth."

"A high, clear flame, an immense and lonely flame, ascended from the ocean, and from its summit the black smoke poured continuously at the sky. She burned furiously; mournful and imposing like a funeral pile kindled in the night, surrounded by the sea, watched over by the stars. . . . The masts fell just before daybreak, and for a moment there was a burst and turmoil of sparks that seemed to fill with flying fire the night patient and watchful, the vast night lying silent upon the sea."[15]

At 8:30 A.M. on March 15 the three boats ended their nightlong vigil beside the *Palestine*, still above water but burning fiercely, and set out to find a landing. It was fifty miles to the nearest habitation where ships would call, Muntok or Mintok on Bangka Island, a small backwater Eastern port. Through a day of searing tropical sun and part of a night Conrad and his crew of three sailed and rowed their small boat, heading for a goal he had never seen and seemingly so far that he impressionistically dramatized the backbreaking ordeal of thirteen and a half hours as "nights and days of calm, when we pulled, we pulled, and the boat seemed to stand still, as if bewitched within the circle of the sea horizon.

"I need not tell you what it is to be knocking about in an open boat," he continued the remembrance in "Youth." "I remember the heat, the deluge of rain-squalls that kept us baling for dear life (but filled our water-cask), and I remember sixteen hours on end with a mouth dry as a cinder and a steering-oar over the stern to keep my first command head on to a breaking sea. I did not know how good a man I was till then."[16]

At 10 o'clock that night Conrad steered his boat into the harbor at Muntok, followed by the boats bearing the rest of the shipwrecked crew. Waiting for a ship to take them the 250 miles to Singapore, they spent six days in Muntok. To Conrad, as he later wrote Richard Curle, Muntok was "a damned hole without any beach and without any glamour,"[17] so unromantic he refused to have it identified as his first sight of the East—"the East of the ancient navigators, so old, so mysterious, resplendent and sombre, living and unchanged, full of danger and promise."[18]

Eventually a British steamer, the *Sissie* (Conrad referred to it as the *Celestial* in "Youth" but used the name of *Sissie* for ships in *Victory* and "Because of the Dollars") came into Muntok and carried the men of the *Palestine* on to Singapore, where they arrived on March 22. For six weeks Conrad remained in Singapore, waiting for transportation back to England, and sailed early in May for Liverpool on a passenger steamer. During his Singapore stay a Marine Court of Enquiry investigated the burning of the *Palestine* in a hearing conducted by Richard Spear O'Connor, senior magistrate, and two nautical assessors, Edward Bradberry and John Blair. Their official report, made public on April 3, 1883, in Singapore,[19] bears out Conrad's story of the ship's mishaps as he told of them in "Youth."

"The *Palestine* was built of wood, at Sunderland, in 1857, and registered 427 tons," the report states. "On the 29th November 1881 she sailed from Newcastle-upon-Tyne with a cargo of 557 tons of West Hartley coal, bound to Bang Kok, and a crew of 13 hands all told. Arriving in the chops of the English Channel, the vessel encountered a succession of heavy gales, losing sails and springing a leak on the 24th

of December 1881, the crew refusing to proceed, the vessel put into
Falmouth. The coal was there discharged and stored under cover, with
the exception of about 90 tons, and the vessel thoroughly repaired in
dock. On the 17th September 1882 the *Palestine* sailed from Falmouth
with a complement of 13 hands all told, and proceeded on her voyage
to Bang Kok. The passage was tedious owing to persistent light winds,
but nothing unusual occurred until noon of the 11th March, when a
strong smell resembling paraffin oil was perceived; at this time the vessel's
position was lat. 2 36 S and long. 105 45 E. Banca Strait. Next day
smoke was discovered issuing from the coals on the port side of main
hatch. Water was thrown over them until the smoke abated, the boats
were lowered, water placed in them. On the 13th some coals were thrown
overboard, about 4 tons, and more water poured down the hold. On the
14th, the hatches being on but not battened down, the decks blew up
fore and aft as far as the poop. The boats were then provisioned and
the vessel headed for the Sumatra shore. About 3 P.M. the S.S. *Somerset*
came alongside in answer to signals and about 6 P.M. she took the vessel
in tow. Shortly afterwards the fire rapidly increased and the master of
the *Palestine* requested the master of the *Somerset* to tow the barque on
shore. This being refused, the tow-rope was slipped and about 11 P.M.
the vessel was a mass of fire, and all hands got into the boats, 3 in
number. The mate and 4 seamen in one boat, the 2nd mate [Conrad]
with three hands in another and the master in the long boat with 3
men. The boats remained by the vessel until 8.30 A.M. on the 15th. She
was still above water, but inside appeared a mass of fire. The boats
arrived at Mintok at 10 P.M. on the 15th, and the master reported the
casualty to the harbour master. The officers and crew came on to
Singapore in the British steamer *Sissie* arriving on the 22nd March.

"The Court, having carefully inquired into the circumstances attending the burning and abandonment of the British barque *Palestine* of
London, Official Number 12684,–

"FINDS, from the evidence adduced, that there were two ventilators
fitted in the vessel, and that the main hatch was frequently taken off
during the passage, that the coal was put on board in a dry state, and
that the vessel was not provided with thermometers for testing the
temperature of the hold. After the fire broke out the officers and crew
appear to have done all in their power to subdue it, but, with the limited
means at their disposal, without success.

"The Court considers that the cause of the fire was spontaneous combustion, the passage having been unusually protracted.

"The Court is further of opinion that the vessel was not prematurely abandoned and that no blame is attached to the master, officers or crew.

"The officers' certificates are therefore returned."

In Singapore those on the *Palestine* were paid off on April 3, 1883, Conrad receiving $171.12 in Malayan currency for what was—at twenty-five, after eight years as a seaman—his longest voyage, six months without touching land.

His first view of the East he had been trying to reach for four years was the ragged port of Muntok. Dingy it might be, but the glamour was real for him and he wrote, out of memory, of his night arrival— "suddenly a puff of wind, a puff faint and tepid and laden with strange odours of blossoms, of aromatic wood, comes out of the still night—the first sigh of the East on my face. That I can never forget. It was impalpable and enslaving, like a charm, like a whispered promise of mysterious delight."[20]

The feeling of fellowship on board the *Palestine*, a time of equality and "a deal of good feeling" when "everyone took his turn, captain included"[21] during the last dangerous days, was an enduring marvel of the voyage for Conrad. This ship's company, who were "without the drilled-in habit of obedience," might have appeared to an onlooker as "a lot of profane scallywags without a redeeming point," but for him they had something "inborn and subtle and everlasting . . . solid like a principle, and masterful like an instinct." The crew of the *Palestine* at the time of the shipwreck whom he thought so highly of were a mixture of nationalities, of ages and origins. Mostly English, and one possibly a Negro from the largely Negro island of St. Kitts, their names are on record in the Agreement and Account of Crew of the *Palestine* voyage. In addition to the young carpenter Joseph Hawke, the men Conrad extolled in "Youth" were: the cook Robert Webber, twenty-two, from Falmouth; William Jennings, forty-two, from Penryn near Falmouth; Harry Page, twenty-five, from Plymouth; Henry Aishton, forty-two, from Plymouth; Peter Esman, twenty-one, from Antwerp; Charles Hughes, thirty-two, from Belfast; Anders Ellfsen, thirty-four, from Porsgrunn, Norway; Thomas Walters, twenty-eight, from St. Kitts; Henry Vodden, sixteen, from Devonport.

Men fusing in a crisis was the story Conrad told in the shining, gemlike "Youth," a positive and exhilarating view of life. But shortly after the *Palestine* went down in flames he learned through another crew how demoralization could set in on board a ship.

During his years at sea the sailor was, to an extreme, on his own. In a time before unions, unemployment insurance, social security, compensation for disabling accidents or death, the ship was a seaman's whole community. To "belong to" a ship was his proudest boast. To be without one meant more to those who followed the sea than mere unemployment, an isolation painful enough in any occupation. It was also to be without a base, without companions, and, however temporary, a home; in a sense both real and psychological it meant not to belong. In a vessel's small community, smaller than the most sparsely settled hamlet, what bound a ship's company together, or severed it, was vital on the sea. There were times, as Conrad discovered in his twenties, when the severance came abruptly, through mischance.

XIV

. . . the shadows darker than the night and more restless than the thoughts of men.

The Nigger of the Narcissus

Seven men died at sea on Conrad's ships. Two of those deaths, during his *Narcissus* voyage and the immediately following one on the *Tilkhurst* when a second mate in his mid-twenties, inspired one of his major novels, his third, *The Nigger of the Narcissus*. What prompted his memory for this, his first tale of the sea, was in part the death of a *Narcissus* Negro seaman but, equally, the suicide of a young Englishman on the *Tilkhurst*. The conscience-stricken crew of *The Nigger of the Narcissus* had their origin in fact, when the men of the *Tilkhurst*, sailing from Singapore through Malacca Strait, underwent nine painful days. They were a young crew—the average age for those on board was twenty-four—and their experience a dark one.

Seamen on sailing ships were as a rule young men, responding as impulsively to sorrow as to joy, and in two stories of the sea, *The Nigger of the Narcissus* and "Youth," Conrad reflected both moods, as tragedy caused them. The larking spirit of "Youth" derived from a group knit together by disaster, the officers and crew of the *Palestine*, half of whom were, in fact, over thirty. Two and a half years after that ship's end in Bangka Strait a personal tragedy occurred, the one unnatural death at sea in Conrad's career, the only suicide, and the morale of a truly young crew was fractured by it.

During those two and a half years, following the loss of the *Palestine*, Conrad traveled widely, on voyages from Singapore to Liverpool by way of the Suez Canal, from London to Madras, from Bombay to Dunkirk, from Hull back to Singapore again. He also visited with his Uncle Thaddeus, for the first time in five years.

In twenty years Conrad saw his uncle but four times: in Marseilles in 1878 when on the mend from his dueling wound; in 1883 when the two arranged a meeting, spending a summer month together, from late July to late August, at the Bohemian spas of Marienbad and Teplitz; in 1890 when Conrad, at thirty-two, passed two of the early months of that year on his uncle's Ukraine estate; in 1893, Conrad again in the Ukraine for a month in the fall, on the estate where Thaddeus died on February 10, 1894, at sixty-six. Opposite in temperament and interests as they were (Thaddeus' wish for Conrad was a sedentary life in Galician Poland, a naturalized Austrian following some such career as he esteemed, in government or law), the two were not only a generation apart in age but of generations so contrasting that in outlook the gulf between them was enormous. Through the chance that Thaddeus' letters were the only part of their correspondence to be preserved, the view of Conrad as a youth has, somewhat inevitably, been blurred by his uncle's negative comments.

According to Thaddeus Conrad "always lacked endurance and steadfastness," a criticism among the milder disparagements in his letters, but Conrad's record, both as seaman and author, vigorously demonstrated the reverse. What his own feelings were about being a seaman he gave in the earliest of his letters to survive. On August 14, 1883, writing in Polish and signing himself Konrad N. Korzeniowski, he told his father's friend Stefan Buszczynski: "In the last few years, since the time of my first examination, I have not been too lucky in my voyages. I was in a sinking and in a fire. Outside of that I am in good health, I have hope, a willingness to work, and am attached to my profession."[1] He was then twenty-five, writing from Teplitz while visiting with his Uncle Thaddeus. There, and in Marienbad—where Conrad's photograph was taken, showing him a handsome young man with a trimmed beard and serious, thoughtful eyes—he had accompanied his uncle who, on the advice of his doctor, was taking the mineral water treatment of the fashionable spas. Conrad's sinking-and-fire reference was to the *Palestine*, the shipwreck of five months before having failed to diminish his enthusiasm for the sea.

Leaving Teplitz toward the end of August, 1883, Conrad returned to London where he very quickly found a ship, the *Riversdale*. A sailing ship of 1490 tons, the *Riversdale* was eighteen years old. Built in 1865 by Andrews of Liverpool, she belonged to the Liverpool shipowner

L. H. McIntyre. Conrad signed on as second mate at wages of £5 5s. a month on September 10, 1883,[2] three days before sailing from London for Madras, India. His captain, L. B. McDonald, was forty-two, from Aberdeen. The first mate, also forty-two, was A. Johnson from the Shetland Islands. Conrad was three months short of twenty-six but claimed that age. Again, as on the *Palestine*, he was much the youngest of the officers. The *Riversdale* had a predominantly Scandinavian crew, with more than half of the twenty-three on board of or under Conrad's age. They contracted for a voyage of global range: "London to Algoa Bay & any ports & places in the Cape, Australian & New Zealand Colonies, India, China, Japanese & Red Seas & Straits and Persian Gulf, North and South Pacific & Atlantic Oceans, United States of America between Portland & Galveston inclusive, West Coast of America and islands adjacent, West Indies and Mediterranean Sea to and fro for any period not exceeding three years and back to the port of final discharge in the United Kingdom or Continent of Europe between the Elbe & Brest."[3]

For Conrad it meant a seven months' voyage from London to Madras. For Captain McDonald it meant the end of his command; for the ship, severe damage and a long pause in her working life.

Sailing with a general cargo from London by way of the Cape of Good Hope, the *Riversdale* reached South Africa's Port Elizabeth on December 7, 1883, spent two months there and, on February 9, 1884, sailed for Guam.[4] On April 8 she arrived at Madras. Madras, with a population of 400,000, was the Indian port next to Bombay and Calcutta in importance. Ships were forced to lie outside the forbidding line of surf, "which breaks with a mighty wave, rising several feet in height, at a considerable distance from the beach," said the *Illustrated London News*,[5] but a breakwater was under construction which would make the port "tolerably safe."

While anchored at Madras Conrad had a dispute with his captain and on April 17 left the ship, collecting 234 rupees (£24)[6] in wages, his expenditures during this passage, as was true of all he made, being slight. On his certificate of discharge Captain McDonald, apparently due to the quarrel, declined to comment on Conrad's "Character for conduct"— the only unfavorable mark in Conrad's sea records—but as to his "Character for ability" approvingly wrote "Very good."[7] There could have been a solid seaman's cause for the dispute. Six weeks after it Captain McDonald, an experienced master who had been in charge of the *Riversdale* on her previous voyage, was relieved of his command, through stranding his vessel at Masulipatam, two hundred miles up the

Indian coast from Madras. The chief mate, Johnson, took charge of the ship on May 31. The vessel was badly damaged and all the crew discharged in Madras on June 5.[8] It was not, however, the end of the *Riversdale*. Refloated, she was bought by M. C. Malik of Calcutta and underwent repairs in 1885. Two years later she was sold to C. E. De Wolf of Calcutta. Not a lucky ship, she was stranded again in February, 1891, at New Caledonia;[9] taken to Australia for repairs, she was sold to a Mr. Brown of Newcastle, Australia, who owned her until 1917, the year she was broken up.[10] Her last years were spent as a coal hulk in Sydney but, in spite of her many accidents, the *Riversdale* had a long life of fifty-two years at sea.

According to Conrad, his *Riversdale* voyage was described in portions of *The Mirror of the Sea* and reflected in the fictional *Ferndale* voyages of the novel to bring him his first large public, *Chance* ("a performance of great technical intricacy and brilliant virtuosity," Thomas Mann said of this novel). What the love story owed to Conrad's seven months on the *Riversdale* was perhaps no more than the atmosphere of a long voyage with the master's family on board. "I had never been in a ship where the captain had his wife with him," Conrad had Powell say in *Chance*. "I'd heard fellows say that captains' wives could work a lot of mischief on board ship if they happened to take a dislike to anyone; especially the new wives if young and pretty. The old and experienced wives on the other hand fancied they knew more about the ship than the skipper himself and had an eye like a hawk's for what went on. . . . In the general opinion a skipper with his wife on board was more difficult to please; but whether to show off his authority before an admiring female or from loving anxiety for her safety or simply from irritation at her presence—nobody I ever heard on the subject could tell for certain."[11]

The *Riversdale* left London bound first for Port Elizabeth, a passage Conrad ascribed to the *Ferndale* in the novel. On the actual voyage Captain McDonald had his twelve-year-old son with him and, if the novel can be taken as a guide, also his wife. Though too young at twelve to be a ship's boy, the Liverpool youngster was enrolled on September 13 as second boy, with wages of a shilling a month.[12]

The heroine of *Chance* had her origin in a girl Conrad knew long before the *Riversdale* voyage. Flora de Barral, "de Barral" being a name she assumed, traced back in essence to one of similar age, equally "unbelonging," Paula de Somoggy, whose "de Somoggy" was also assumed. In Captain Anthony's love for Flora, Conrad appears to have portrayed himself to some extent in Anthony, recalling his own romance in Mar-

seilles when, like the hero and heroine or "knight" and "damsel" of his
novel, he and Paula had been drawn together as two young outsiders in
a Victorian time.

After leaving the *Riversdale* in Madras, Conrad crossed over to Bombay, where ships were more easily found. His wait proved to be a short
one. Eleven days after his *Riversdale* discharge he signed on the *Narcissus*, on April 28, 1884,[13] as second mate, his wages to be almost as before,
£5 a month. The ship had come without a second officer,[14] the one
engaged in Penarth, Wales, at the start of her voyage having failed to
appear, and Conrad's application on the day she arrived at Bombay was
immediately accepted. He spotted the ship as she entered the harbor,
a graceful vessel sailing by as he sat with other officers on the veranda
of the Sailors' Home.

The *Narcissus*, the only one of his ships Conrad named in a novel's
title, was at sea for many of the years of the novel's fame. Under another name, her association with the story long forgotten, she was an
aged, much-changed vessel once hauled up out of the sea when she
ended a half-century of seagoing, in Brazil.

A full-rigged iron sailing ship of 1336 tons, the *Narcissus* had been
built in 1876 by R. Duncan & Co. at Port Glasgow and, when Conrad
knew her, was owned by Robert R. Paterson & Co. of Greenock.[15] A
fairly new ship as Conrad first saw her, eight years old, she may have
appeared to him to have "all the graces of a yacht" but she arrived in
Bombay at the end of a troubled voyage. She had left Penarth on November 2, 1883, two months after Conrad's own departure from London
on the *Riversdale*, and had a fractious crew on the passage to Capetown.
At Capetown, reached on January 18, 1884, after two and a half months
at sea, two Scandinavian seamen deserted and the steward quit the ship.
Five new seamen were taken on during the ship's ten days' stay in Capetown, while one of the hands, Charles Dutton of St. Ellens, was left
behind in prison. For the three months of her January 28–April 28 passage from Capetown to Bombay the friction increased enough for the
chief officer Thomas Williams and six seamen to throw up their berths
in Bombay.

For thirty-six days the *Narcissus* remained in Bombay, Conrad on
board during that time, and when she sailed for Dunkirk on June 3,
1884,[16] nearly half of her officers and crew were new. He, at twenty-
six, was again the youngest officer. The captain, Archibald Duncan, was
a Scot of forty from Campbeltown, Argyllshire. (On thirteen of his nineteen ships Conrad served under commanders who were either Scots or

English; "English and Scots seamen," he wrote in *A Personal Record*, "had the last say in the formation of my character.")

The first mate of the *Narcissus*, Hamilton Hart, forty-two, was from Hull. Among those who joined the ship in Bombay, in addition to Hart and Conrad, was an able seaman of thirty-five, Joseph Barron. He was a Negro, and apparently an American. Being illiterate, as many seamen of the time were, he spoke the place of his birth to the registering officer as Charlton, the only place of that name with a Negro population being Charlton County, Georgia, the Okefenokee Swamp area near Jacksonville, Florida. Barron, who gave his previous ship as the *Count of Dumfries*, came aboard the *Narcissus* on May 10, 1884. Four and a half months later, on September 24, he died at sea, the ship then in the North Atlantic, three weeks away from the French port of Dunkirk for which she was bound.

Barron's death, one of the two Conrad drew upon for *The Nigger of the Narcissus*, he described to Jean-Aubry two months before his own death in 1924. "I remember, as if it had occurred but yesterday, the last occasion I saw the Nigger. That morning I was quarter officer, and about five o'clock I entered the double-bedded cabin where he was lying full length. On the lower bunk, ropes, fids and pieces of cloth had been deposited, so as not to have to take them down into the sail-room if they should be wanted at once. I asked him how he felt, but he hardly made me any answer. A little later a man brought him some coffee in a cup provided with a hook to suspend it on the edge of the bunk. At about six o'clock the officer-in-charge came to tell me that he was dead."[17]

Conrad's sources for his novel were as complex as the novel itself. Its conclusion, he continued to Jean-Aubry, was "taken from other voyages which I made under similar circumstances." Being a work of fiction, not history, he emphasized, he chose what was most suitable "in regard to characters and particulars to help me in the general impression I wish to produce. Most of the personages I have portrayed actually belonged to the crew of the real *Narcissus*, including the admirable Singleton (whose real name was Sullivan), Archie, Belfast, and Donkin. I got the two Scandinavians from associations with another ship. All this is old now, but it was quite present before my mind when I wrote this book."[18]

Though the book was old then—it had been written twenty-eight years before—Conrad in 1924 recalled with impressive accuracy men he had known on a voyage made forty years in his past. Some features of the "admirable Singleton" were probably taken from the oldest man on board the *Narcissus*, the Australian sailmaker W. G. Allen. Born in Sydney and fifty-four, he was with the *Narcissus* for the year of her Penarth-Bombay-Dunkirk voyage.[19] The source for Singleton which Conrad remembered, there being no Sullivan on the *Narcissus*, was Daniel Sullivan, an Irishman of fifty-four from county Kerry, who served as an able seaman on the *Tilkhurst* and spent six months at sea with Conrad.[20] Two seamen of the *Narcissus* voyage were Arch McLean, a Scot of twenty-three, the Archie of the novel, and Belfast-born James Craig, twenty-one, the "Belfast" Conrad named. The Cockney character Donkin stemmed from a seaman with that nickname—earned by his Cockney pronunciation of the captain's name of Duncan, perhaps—and was probably John Wild, a Londoner of thirty-eight who, like the others Conrad recalled, Archie and Belfast, joined the ship in Bombay.[21] On the *Narcissus* the cook was Alfred Harvey, an Englishman of twenty-nine from Gosport, assisted by the cook-steward John Youlton, a Woolwich man of forty-six; upon these two Conrad based the evangelistic cook of the novel, Podmore, undoubtedly taking that unusual name from Augustine Podmore Williams of the *Jeddah*.

James Wait, the "Nigger" of the *Narcissus* in the story, was made up of many men, white and Negro. His name of Wait came from a Negro seaman on the *Duke of Sutherland*, George White of Barbados; the particulars of Wait's death and the crew's reaction to it had their origins in the deaths of a Negro and a white man, Joseph Barron and William Cumming; the quality of Wait's isolation grew from Conrad's lifetime of contacts with men and women, black, brown and white, who failed to receive, or failed to ask for, the acceptance nod of being "one of us."

Conrad's fiction, says Dr. Carlos Baker, "crystallizes, under immense imaginative pressure, from direct personal experience,"[22] and in no work was this more true than in *The Nigger of the Narcissus*. It was the book, Conrad declared, "by which, not as a novelist perhaps, but as an artist striving for the utmost sincerity of expression, I am willing to stand or fall." The intangibles in this and other books brought from Christopher Morley an early comment on the inadequacy of descriptive labels applied to the author of them. "If you had to label Conrad as anything, there is only one word great enough for him, the word *poet*, which simply means *creator*. He had, as highly as any man of our times perhaps, the genuinely poetic mind which dreams about its experience in life, and by its magic faculty of seeing secret resemblances and analogies, builds a fable which mirrors ourselves."[23]

Endlessly interpreted, with infinite variety, *The Nigger of the Narcissus* has been called both foreboding and shimmering, a statement of courage, of brotherhood, of struggle, a contest told of men against the sea and of men against each other. "In my opinion the very finest and strongest picture of the sea and sea-life that our language possesses," Henry James said of it. Reflecting life, it flashes a succession of con-trasts. Through it runs what Morley called "those strange troubles of the spirit that happen as often in any business office as on the decks of ships."[24] That the novel has offered limitless scope for views upon it rests as much in its truth as in the art of the novelist able to distill into his stories "my mental and emotional reactions to life, to men and their affairs and their passions as I have seen them." "It is not what actually happened," Conrad wrote in his June 14, 1917, letter to A. T. Saunders, "but the manner of presenting it that settles the literary and even the moral value of my work. My little vol. of autobiography [A Personal Record] of course is absolutely genuine. The rest is more or less close approximation to facts and suggestions."

Of The Nigger of the Narcissus he told Jean-Aubry, "the voyage of the Narcissus was performed from Bombay to London in the manner I have described."[25]

The voyage of the Narcissus, actually from Bombay to Dunkirk, was one of four and a half months, from June 3 to October 16, 1884.[26] There were twenty-four officers and crew on board, more than half in their twenties, from ten countries: England, Norway, Sweden, Canada, Aus-tralia, United States, Wales, Ireland, Scotland, Poland. They were sail-ing-ship seamen. Differing from the less adventurous seamen manning the modern steamship, they were, in Conrad's writing years, a nearly vanished breed. In the words of old Singleton in The Nigger of the Narcissus he paid tribute to all he had known.

"They had been strong, as those are strong who know neither doubts nor hopes. They had been patient and enduring, turbulent and devoted, unruly and faithful. . . . they had been men who knew toil, privation, violence, debauchery—but knew not fear, and had no desire of spite in their hearts. Men hard to manage, but easy to inspire; voiceless men. . . . They were the everlasting children of the mysterious sea."

With such a crew the Narcissus sailed out of Bombay. In the novel Conrad recalled the ship's departure.

"Flakes of foam swept past her sides; the water struck her with flashing blows; the land glided away slowly fading; a few birds screamed on motionless wings over the swaying mastheads. But soon the land disappeared, the birds went away; and to the west the pointed sail of an Arab dhow running for Bombay rose triangular and upright above the sharp edge of the horizon, lingered and vanished like an illusion.

Then the ship's wake, long and straight, stretched itself out through a day of immense solitude."

Off the Cape of Good Hope—"the Cape of Storms of its Portuguese discoverer"—the *Narcissus* ran into the gales always to be found there. The long passage of 136 days from Bombay to Dunkirk showed how often the wind-driven *Narcissus* was braked by storms. "No two gales stamp themselves in the same way upon your emotions," Conrad wrote in *The Mirror of the Sea*. There were those "like ghouls bent upon sucking your strength away," of which one came into his novel.

"No one slept in the forecastle. The tin oil-lamp suspended on a long string, smoking, described wide circles; wet clothing made dark heaps on the glistening floor; a thin layer of water rushed to and fro. In the bed-places men lay booted, resting on elbows and with open eyes. Hung-up suits of oilskin swung out and in, lively and disquieting like reckless ghosts of decapitated seamen dancing in a tempest. No one spoke and all listened. Outside the night moaned and sobbed to the accompaniment of a continuous loud tremor as of innumerable drums beating far off. Shrieks passed through the air. Tremendous dull blows made the ship tremble while she rolled under the weight of the seas toppling on her deck. At times she soared up swiftly as if to leave this earth for ever, then during interminable moments fell through a void with all the hearts on board of her standing still."

Conrad associated the gale off the Cape of Good Hope, in his novel, with the death of Jimmy Wait. A similar storm, in the season for them, may have struck the actual *Narcissus* in the North Atlantic at the time of Joseph Barron's death on September 24. Barron, in appearance convincingly strong when Captain Duncan signed him on in Bombay, had been in failing health when he joined the ship. Where jobs were at stake the need to seem robustly able led to other deceptions Conrad compassionately wrote of: the chief mate Baker of the *Duke of Sutherland* hiding his deafness; Captain Whalley in "The End of the Tether" concealing his blindness; the chief mate Bunter in "The Black Mate" dyeing his gray hair black to appear younger. Barron's determination to sail, with the inevitable prospect of dying at sea, would have stirred Conrad as much as another factor of the seaman's life. Born in Georgia in 1849, Barron had been born a slave. The strength of Conrad's feelings about slavery, which he saw at first hand not only in the Congo but among Malays in Borneo, came out in his impassioned indictment "Heart of Darkness." Burdens of conscience accumulate for all men, for all but the unthinking Singletons of the world, was Conrad's philosophy as it appears in his work, but life, forcefully demanding, shelves those burdens, if only for a time. The deeply sober, complex novel, *The Nigger of the Narcissus*—"my beloved *Nigger*" Conrad called it when, at thirty-eight, he was writing the early pages of it—carries "the stress and passion within the core of each convincing moment" of the purpose stated in his preface and ends, resonantly, with the *Narcissus* arriving safely home.

"The coast to welcome her stepped out of space into the sunshine. The lofty headlands trod masterfully into the sea; the wide bays smiled in the light; the shadows of homeless clouds ran along the sunny plains, leaped over valleys, without a check darted up the hills; rolled down the slopes; and the sunshine pursued them with patches of running light."

The actual *Narcissus* reached home, Dunkirk, on October 16, 1884. Conrad, with the other officers and all the crew, signed off the next day.[27] The ship, taken out of trade to be overhauled, passed through the hands of a succession of owners and in the end outlived Conrad by a year.[28] For her first twenty-three years she was owned in Scotland, and late in those years, in November, 1896, called at Portland, Oregon, to load a cargo of wheat. In November, 1899, she was purchased by Captain Vittorio Bertolotto of Camogli, Italy, and registered in Genoa. Converted to a barque, she traded to Australian and Pacific ports until 1907 when, condemned, she was hulked in Genoa. After seventeen years under the Italian flag she was sold, in 1916, to P. Passos of Rio de Janeiro and refitted as a sailing barque. Renamed the *Isis* when she took to the sea as a Brazilian ship, she made her last call at a United States port in 1921. From Baltimore on October 6, 1921, she sailed to Rio de Janeiro, arriving after sixty-seven days, on December 12. A month later, on January 14, 1922, she was sunk in a collision at Rio. Refloated in August of that year, she was sold to E. G. Fontes & Co. of Rio de Janeiro, her owner during her last three years. The handsome *Narcissus*, appearing on moonlight nights to Conrad to be "pure like a vision of ideal beauty," was at sea for forty-nine years, closing her career as a hulk. A hard-working ship, serving in the merchant marine of three nations as she crossed and recrossed the oceans, immortalized by a novel, known as the Brazilian *Isis* during her last nine years, she disappeared from shipping registers in 1925. In that year—her Brazilian owner had lost the final records—she was scrapped.[29]

Also broken up, and in almost the same year, was Conrad's next ship, the *Tilkhurst*, a full-rigged iron sailing ship like the *Narcissus*, of almost the exact age and size. His voyage on the London-owned vessel was to begin six months after leaving the *Narcissus* in Dunkirk.

In Dunkirk Captain Duncan approvingly wrote on Conrad's certificate of discharge: "This is to certify that Conrad Korzeniowski has served with me on board the ship Narcissus as second officer from 28/4/84 to 16/10/84 on a voyage from Bombay to Dunkerque for which I can recommend him to any Ship Master requiring his services as being a good and sober officer and should take him as Chief Officer if he should succeed in passing."[30]

Going to London from Dunkirk, Conrad studied for his chief officer's examination, passing it on December 3, 1884, his twenty-seventh birthday. His examiner, Captain Rankin, who had "a sallow, strong, unamiable face," put him through forty minutes of questioning in a room "with the now familiar paraphernalia of models of ships and tackle, a board for signals on the wall, a big, long table covered with official forms and having an unrigged mast fixed to the edge."[31] Conrad was given the problem of handling an imaginary ship on a homeward passage, "the sort of passage I would not wish to my bitterest enemy. That imaginary ship seemed to labor under a most comprehensive curse."[32] His examination was an unusually short one—his first, for second officer, had taken three hours—and of its end he wrote in *A Personal Record*: "I escaped from the room thankfully—passed! Forty minutes! And again I walked on air along Tower Hill."[33]

For some four months he looked for a ship. Unable to secure a chief officer's berth, he joined the *Tilkhurst* in Hull as second officer on April 24, 1885,[34] his pay to be £5 a month. The *Tilkhurst*, a sailing ship of 1527 tons, was owned by W. R. Price & Co. of London. She had been built by A. MacMillan & Son at Dumbarton in 1877 and, at the time of Conrad's voyage, was eight years old. His captain was an Englishman of forty-seven, Edwin John Blake of Plymouth. The chief mate, Alexander Samuel, was a Scot, thirty-nine, from Peterhead.

The *Tilkhurst* was to make an Eastern voyage, calling first at Wales for cargo. Sailing from Hull on April 27, 1885, the ship reached Cardiff seventeen days later, on May 14.[35] There, to save wages during the wait for loading, the crew of nineteen, largely Scandinavian, were laid off. Conrad, signing off on May 31 in Cardiff and on again on June 5 in the adjacent docks of Penarth, was ashore for five days. The cargo was coal, as on the *Palestine*. Like that ill-fated voyage, this of the *Tilkhurst* was to have a disastrous ending, not, however, because of a cargo rated the most dangerous of all to carry (2779 seamen lost their lives on British coal-carrying ships between 1873 and 1880 when 534 vessels transporting that combustible freight were wrecked at sea, a fifth of all disasters being linked with coal[36]).

With twenty-six all told on board, three-fourths of whom were from the British Isles and most of them English, the *Tilkhurst* sailed from Penarth on June 10, 1885, for Singapore. One American was in the crew, twenty-six-year-old Michael Sheehan of New York, and a Canadian, James McDonald, twenty-nine, from Georgetown, Prince Edward Island. All but three of this ship's company could write their names, a better-than-average rate for literacy, with only the two teen-age boys being new to the sea. In charge of the ship was the much-admired commander Conrad wrote of in *The Mirror of the Sea*, Captain Blake.

"Well over fifty years of age when I knew him, short, stout, dignified, perhaps a little pompous, he was a man of a singularly well-informed mind, the least sailor-like in outward aspect, but certainly one of the best seamen whom it has been my good luck to serve under. He was a Plymouth man, I think, the son of a country doctor, and both his elder boys were studying medicine. He commanded a big London ship, fairly well known in her day. I thought no end of him, and that is why I remember with a peculiar satisfaction the last words he spoke to me on board his ship in the dock in Dundee, where we had brought a full cargo of jute from Calcutta. We had been paid off that morning, and I had come on board to take my sea-chest away and to say goodbye. In his slightly lofty but courteous way he inquired what were my plans. I replied that I intended leaving for London by the afternoon train, and thought of going up for examination to get my master's certificate. I had just enough service for that. He commended me for not wasting my time, with such an evident interest in my case that I was quite surprised; then, rising from his chair, he said:

" 'Have you a ship in view after you have passed?'

"I answered that I had nothing whatever in view.

"He shook hands with me, and pronounced the memorable words:

" 'If you happen to be in want of employment, remember that as long as I have a ship you have a ship, too.' "

Captain Blake, who had served in the Swansea-Chile copper ore trade and risen to the rank of shipmaster at a very early age, was a seasoned commander. For this voyage he had a hardy, experienced crew as well as a staunch ship. The voyage out was an eventless one, the *Tilkhurst* making the long sail of three and a half months from Penarth to Singapore without incident, arriving at Singapore on September 22, 1885. There the crew demonstrated their satisfaction with the ship and her captain, and their own sense of comradeship, by a performance rare for restless seamen. Having spent close to four months in each other's company, all day and every day, in the confines of a ship where frictions were easily generated, only one of the crew, an Austrian, chose to quit the ship in Singapore, the East's largest port where berths were easy to find.

But discharging the coal in Singapore was a slow, tedious process. Small native boats lightered it from the ship, anchored in the roadstead, to the docks. All hand labor, each shovelful was lifted by a man, each bagful toted on a man's back, the backs of the scantily paid coolies of Singapore. Day after day for the best part of a month the cargo was nibbled down, the *Tilkhurst* lying all the while in the East's most humid, enervating port. With little to do as the unloading came to an end, and with wages to spend, the *Tilkhurst* crew went ashore for a fling before sailing again. When the fuddled group returned to their ship a drunken quarrel broke out, ending in a scuffle. In the course of it one of the seamen, a Bristol youth of twenty-three, William Cumming, received a hard blow on the head. He was treated for it and, as the later official report stated, "seemed none the worse of the injury." Another member of the crew, a Scot of twenty-two, James Black, was imprisoned in Singapore, perhaps because of the scuffle, and the *Tilkhurst* sailed on October 19, bound for Calcutta.

Like Wait in *The Nigger of the Narcissus*, whose cough was the only outward sign of his illness, Cumming appeared well enough, though he complained of headaches. As the ship moved up Malacca Strait under a searing sun Cumming "gradually became worse, and at last gave indications of delirium arising from the injury to his head, or from exposure to the sun," the Dundee Merchant Marine Office report of June 18, 1886,[37] continues. "He seems to have been kindly treated, asked to do no work and keep below, and a watch was kept over him with a view to his personal safety. He was difficult to manage, and one morning when placed in his berth he got out, and in the darkness eluded observation and went overboard. All reasonable care was taken of this man both for his safety and recovery, but on the morning in question he succeeded in terminating his life as stated, though the act was not witnessed by anyone."

Cumming was officially listed as having died at sea by drowning on October 28, 1885,[38] nine days after the *Tilkhurst* left Singapore, when twenty-four days from Calcutta. His shipmates, responsible for the injury resulting in his suicide, had looked after him solicitously, keeping a watch over him. In the still, hot air of the Strait where the ship moved slowly in the light winds the men were idled by the weather, with nothing to distract their minds from Cumming. For nine days and nights, taking turns at guarding him, they watched a tragedy develop of their own making. Into *The Nigger of the Narcissus* Conrad wove a similar tension, the crew focused on their disabled shipmate to the overstrained point of cracking, saved from a mutinous outbreak when a change in the weather provided a concrete force to cope with, the storm.

Cumming disappeared overboard, a suicide no one saw in the darkness, as the *Tilkhurst* emerged from Malacca Strait and picked up the stronger winds of the Andaman Sea. In seamen's lore ships were bewitched by such a death as suicide, haunted by it, strangled by it. As if endorsing that eerie myth, the *Tilkhurst* spent thirty-three days reaching Calcutta, crawling an average fifty-seven miles in a day.

Daniel Sullivan, who Conrad drew upon for the steadfast old child of the sea, Singleton, was a man whose world was simple; in the whole of his long life he had never learned to write, even his name. Perhaps it was Cumming's death, and the ill omen of it to his untaught Irish mind, that caused him to quit the *Tilkhurst* in Calcutta. A new berth would have been difficult for a man of fifty-four to find, yet when the ship reached Calcutta on November 21, 1885, and anchored in the river Hooghly, it was Sullivan alone[39] of all the crew who asked to leave.

The *Tilkhurst* remained in Calcutta for seven weeks, sailing with a cargo of jute on January 8, 1886, for Dundee, Scotland. "At last we are going to make a start for home!" Conrad wrote to a Polish acquaintance in Cardiff, Spiridion Kliszczewski, two days before sailing.[40] "I am glad of it, being rather tired of the voyage and the ship—although very comfortable in all respects." He asked to have letters addressed to him as "Mr. J. Conrad, 2nd Mate, Ship *Tilkhurst*," having, at twenty-seven, already dropped for nonofficial use his family name of Korzeniowski, ten years before signing Joseph Conrad to a novel. That he was an avid reader during the *Tilkhurst* voyage was remembered by one of the ship's boys, S. P. G. Evans, a youngster of fifteen from Newtown, Wales. Evans made the first voyage of his life on the *Tilkhurst*, embarking at Penarth and landing at Dundee, knowing Conrad as an officer during those twelve months. In 1927, a seaman then of long experience, Evans told a shipmate, J. S. Roe (later Captain Roe) that on the ship Conrad was a first-class sailor but a "queer feller" for books.[41]

The homeward voyage of the *Tilkhurst* was the last time Captain Blake went to sea. Taken ill in the South Atlantic as the ship passed St. Helena, he was laid up for a time when off the Azores, "but got out of bed to make his Landfall," Conrad wrote in *The Mirror of the Sea*. "He managed to keep up on deck as far as the Downs, where, giving his orders in an exhausted voice, he anchored for a few hours to send a wire to his wife and take aboard a North Sea pilot to help him sail the ship up the east coast. He had not felt equal to the task by himself, for it is the sort of thing that keeps a deep-water man on his feet pretty well night and day. When we arrived in Dundee, Mrs. B—— was already there, waiting to take him home."

The ship arrived at Dundee on June 17, 1886, ending a voyage of 160 days from Calcutta, and Conrad signed off that day. He had spent fourteen months on board the *Tilkhurst* and had accrued enough sea service to sit for his master's examination. He went by train to London with Captain and Mrs. Blake, and five months later, in London, visited his invalid commander in his home, "the only one of my captains I have ever visited in that way." Captain Blake talked of his early days at sea and of ships, one a particularly villainous ship Conrad had also seen in Sydney ("the crew of that ship were, if anything, rather proud of her evil fame. . . . We, belonging to other vessels moored all about the Circular Quay in Sydney, used to shake our heads at her with a great sense of the unblemished virtue of our own well-loved ships"[42]), the homicidal vessel of his short story "The Brute." Written many years later, in the first weeks of 1906, "The Brute" told of the *Apse Family*, a vessel known far and wide for killing someone on every voyage she made. She belonged to the great shipowning firm of Apse & Sons, who named their craft after members of the family: the *Lucy Apse, Harold Apse, Anne Apse, John Apse,* among many others. None had the viciousness of the *Apse Family* which, finally, was smashed on the rocks off Port Adelaide, Australia, the chief mate being too much absorbed with a passenger, a governess, to watch the ship's direction. A breezy vignette of life at sea, "The Brute" was published in a book of Conrad's short stories, *A Set of Six.* In his preface to the volume Conrad wrote that "Captain Blake was, of all my commanders, the one I remember with the greatest affection. . . . In his young days he had a personal experience of the brute. The existence of the brute was a fact. The end of the brute as related in the story is also a fact, well known at the time though it really happened to another ship, of great beauty of form and of blameless character, which certainly deserved a better fate."

The fate of the *Tilkhurst* was similar to that of the *Narcissus.* Owned in England for sixteen years, from 1877 to 1893, the *Tilkhurst* was sold in 1893 to the French shipowning firm, A. D. Bordes et Fils, and renamed *Blanche* after Mme. Prom, the eldest daughter of A. D. Bordes, for whom two other ships in the Bordes fleet were named. In 1901, a nitrate carrier, she was damaged when caught by the sudden hard winds of a pampero; and in 1903, concluding ten years of French ownership, was sold to Italy, to G. Mortola of Genoa. For twenty years she sailed under the Italian flag, first trading to Australia and Chile. In

World War I she was equipped with an engine and her last years were spent in the Atlantic. She was broken up in Genoa in 1923,[43] a ship forty-six years old. In 1906, when Conrad was writing "The Brute," three of the ships on which he had sailed, *Narcissus*, *Tilkhurst* and *Torrens*, were owned in Genoa.

In 1886, leaving the *Tilkhurst* in Dundee, the two things uppermost in his mind were to establish his nationality and to become a master mariner. On August 19, 1886, he became a naturalized British subject, at twenty-eight. Though a Pole, his home province had long been occupied by Russia; and technically, as his British naturalization certificate read, he had been a "subject of the Russian Empire," a condition his uncle had for years been urging him to end.

Three months later, on November 11, 1886, he passed as master. He had risen from ordinary seaman to captain in the eight and a half years he had spent in the British merchant marine, reaching its highest rank before his twenty-ninth birthday.

"It was a fact, I said to myself, that I was now a British master mariner beyond a doubt," Conrad told of his final examination, conducted by Captain Sterry, in *A Personal Record*. "That fact, satisfactory and obscure in itself, had for me a certain ideal significance. It was an answer to certain outspoken scepticism and even to some not very kind aspersions. I had vindicated myself from what had been cried upon as a stupid obstinacy or a fantastic caprice."

His uncle's opposition to his boyhood choice of the sea, a career decried by other Polish relatives, still rankled in Conrad when he wrote of it in *A Personal Record*, at fifty-one. Twenty-two years earlier he had "shown them" and, as far as was known, became then the only Polish captain in the British merchant marine.

During the last six months of 1886, Conrad, in addition to becoming a British subject and a British master mariner, also wrote his first short story, "The Black Mate." He entered it in a prize competition conducted by *Tit-Bits* magazine. Rejected then, he rewrote what he called "an extraneous phenomenon" of his writing career—he had forgotten its existence—into the story as it was published in the April, 1908, issue of *London Magazine*.

Writing "The Black Mate" was a time killer for him in 1886, not a serious attempt to change careers. He was anxious to be back at sea, in command of a ship. He had thought, in Calcutta, of buying his own ship, a whaler, securing the capital through a bank loan. "Believe me, it is not the desire of getting much money that prompts me," he wrote of his whaling plan to Spiridion Kliszczewski on November 25, 1885. "It is simply the wish to work for myself. I am sick and tired of sailing about for little money and less consideration. But I love the sea: and if I could just clear my bare living . . . I should be comparatively happy."⁴⁴

The whaling idea vanished from his mind as quickly as his earlier fleeting thought of becoming a businessman's secretary in Canada. His next step up, to serve as chief mate, soon came in an offer from Glasgow. The voyage would be to the East, to Java. He had seen the East Indies only once, briefly, at Muntok. Because of this voyage, and an injury, he would come to know those islands well.

XV

The *Highland Forest* was moored that winter in Amsterdam. A three-year-old barque of 1040 tons, Scotland-built and Scotland-owned, she was scheduled for a run to Samarang. At twenty-nine, Conrad was appointed to the next-in-command position for the first time and crossed over from London to Amsterdam to take charge of the captainless ship. During a month of record cold weather, January, 1887, managing on £7,¹ a month's wages paid in advance and the highest he had known, he lived alone on the *Highland Forest*, never forgetting "the fact of my elevation for five consecutive minutes. I fancy it kept me warm, even in my slumbers, better than the high pile of blankets, which positively crackled with frost as I threw them off in the morning."²

From the deck of his unstaffed ship he looked out at snow-covered Amsterdam, at the frozen canal with its line of ships, "their frosty mooring-ropes hanging slack and their decks idle and deserted." Like the *Highland Forest*, they waited for cargoes, Dutch goods piled on barges and schuits inland, stuck fast in the frozen canals. Running parallel with the line of ships, he saw in the distance "a line of brown, warm-toned houses that seemed bowed under snow-laden roofs. From afar at the end of Tsar Peter Straat, issued in the frosty air the tinkle of bells of the horse tramcars, appearing and disappearing in the opening between the buildings, like little toy carriages harnessed with toy horses and played with by people that appeared no bigger than children.

"I was, as the French say, biting my fists with impatience for that cargo frozen up-country; with rage at that canal set fast, at the wintry and deserted aspect of all those ships that seemed to decay in grim depression for want of the open water. I was chief mate, and very much alone."[3]

The fire in his cabin stove failed to keep the ink from freezing and, for warmth and companionship, he traveled by horsecar to the center of town. There, in the noisy crowd of a fine café, "an immense place, lofty and gilt, upholstered in red plush, full of electric lights, and so thoroughly warmed that even the marble tables felt tepid to the touch,"[4] he wrote his evening letter to the ship's owner, John Scott Colvil in Glasgow. Each letter carried his dejected news: there was no cargo "and no prospect of any coming till late spring apparently." Return mail from Glasgow directed him "to go to the charterers and clamour for the ship's cargo," and Conrad approached the charterer, Mr. Hudig, "a big, swarthy Netherlander, with black moustaches and a bold glance." In *Almayer's Folly* and *An Outcast of the Islands* Conrad gave the name of Hudig to the rich and powerful trader in Macassar, "old Hudig—the Master—" who roared friendly greetings to shipowners coming to his "lofty and cool warehouses" for cargo. Of the original Hudig in Amsterdam Conrad recalled that his office "was so warm, his fire so bright, his sides shook so heartily with laughter, that I experienced always a great difficulty in making up my mind to reach for my hat."[5]

Eventually the cargo arrived, first in dribbles, "and then fast, in a multitude of barges, with a great rush of unbound waters," and Conrad, directing his first stowage operation, distributed the weight in a ship whose peculiarities he did not know. The loading completed, the new captain arrived to take over. On February 16, 1887,[6] Conrad officially registered as chief mate of the ship, the same day as his young captain. Captain John McWhir[7] (in portraying him in "Typhoon," Conrad spelled his name as MacWhirr and made him an older man) was an Irishman of thirty-four, from county Down, who had been chief mate of the *Highland Forest* for her two previous voyages; almost on the eve of sailing he had been promoted to the command. Conrad first saw Captain McWhir, an agile and friendly man less than five years older than himself, when he appeared on the quay, "a complete stranger to me, obviously not a Hollander, in a black bowler and a short drab overcoat."

Two days later, on February 18, the *Highland Forest* sailed for Samarang,[8] carrying general merchandise to Java. Of the twenty-two on board, their average age thirty, half were from Holland. A scattering of countries—the British Isles, Sweden, Russia, Germany, Poland, South Africa and India—were represented by the others. Serving on the ship were two boys and four apprentices; one of the latter, Ernest William

G. Twentyman,[9] a youth of eighteen from Capetown, Conrad remembered in *The Mirror of the Sea*, applying his name to the apprentice of another ship he had seen in Sydney.

A married commander grieving for the family and home in Ireland he would not see again for more than a year, Captain McWhir secluded himself in his cabin immediately the ship was under way. Conrad felt flattered at seeming to be in charge and "went blithely about my duties, myself a commander for all practical purposes. Still, whatever the greatness of my illusion, the fact remained that the real commander was there, backing up my self-confidence, though invisible to my eyes behind a maplewood veneered cabin-door with a white china handle. . . .

"The good MacW—— would not even come out to his meals, and fed solitarily in his holy of holies from a tray covered with a white napkin. . . . We, his officers, could hear him moving about in his berth, or lightly snoring, or fetching deep sighs, or splashing and blowing in his bath-room; and we made our reports to him through the keyhole, as it were. It was the crowning achievement of his amiable character that the answers we got were given in a quite mild and friendly tone."[10]

The voyage started off well. "Nowhere else than upon the sea do the days, weeks, and months fall away quicker into the past," Conrad wrote of ship life on such a voyage as the *Highland Forest*. "They seem to be left astern as easily as the light air-bubbles in the swirls of the ship's wake, and vanish into a great silence in which your ship moves on with a sort of magical effect. They pass away, the days, the weeks, the months. Nothing but a gale can disturb the orderly life of the ship."[11]

The *Highland Forest* was to encounter a series of gales and, when only three weeks away from Holland, a first tragedy struck the ship. On March 11, 1887, a Dutch seaman of forty-six, Jan Hulskemper, died at sea.[12] For Conrad it was his third voyage in succession when one of the crew died, isolated by the sea itself, beyond the reach of medical help. The *Highland Forest* was to lose another of her crew in Surabaya, a young Hollander of Conrad's age, Cornelius Hendricks,[13] and to break up on the rocks herself finally, a comparatively young ship still.

On her four months' voyage to Java the ship encountered storm after storm, taking them hard. The barque was made rigid through Conrad's inexperienced distribution of the cargo, and provided a lively passage. "Never before nor since have I felt a ship roll so abruptly, so violently, so heavily," he told of the voyage in *The Mirror of the Sea*. "Once she began, you felt that she would never stop, and this hopeless sensation, characterizing the motion of ships whose centre of gravity is brought

down too low in loading, made everyone on board weary of keeping
on his feet. . . .

"Down south, running before the gales of high latitudes, she made our
life a burden to us. There were days when nothing would keep even
on the swing-tables, when there was no position where you could fix
yourself so as not to feel a constant strain upon all the muscles of your
body. She rolled and rolled with an awful dislodging jerk and that
dizzily fast sweep of her masts on every swing. It was a wonder that
the men sent aloft were not flung off the yards, the yards not flung off
the masts, the masts not flung overboard."[14]

The violence of the weather, the ceaseless lurching of the ship, were
reflected in "Typhoon," a story Conrad completed in January, 1901.
"Typhoon," as he wrote in the copy he gave to Richard Curle, "was
meant to be a pendant to the storm in the *Nigger*, the ship in this case
being a steamship."[15] A story spiced with humor and related to "Youth"
in crispness of atmosphere, "Typhoon" was developed from an incident
in the China Sea occurring on an actual steamship, the *John P. Best*,[16]
appearing in his story as the *Nan-Shan*. The story he heard seamen talking of in the East—"I never met anybody personnally concerned in this
affair," he wrote in the Author's Note to *Typhoon*—was the passage
through a typhoon of the *John P. Best* when carrying a number of
passengers, Chinese coolies homeward bound. Not so much the storm,
but the reaction of men to it, was the essence of the story, his "first
attempt at treating a subject jocularly," as he wrote his literary agent,
J. B. Pinker. As a "pendant" to the tragic *The Nigger of the Narcissus*,
Conrad offered a reverse view of men in a crisis. Tragedy, in *The Nigger
of the Narcissus*, centered upon Wait's death, the death itself and the
contagious fear of that finality; comedy, in "Typhoon," centered on a
scramble for silver dollars rolling about the ship. Traits being common
to all men, in positions high or low, Conrad portrayed Captain MacWhirr
as a ship's commander with a treadmill, unimaginative mind, the counterpart of the simple man of the forecastle, Singleton, in *The Nigger of the
Narcissus*.

More often than any other novelist, Conrad, during his twenty years
of seafaring, had opportunities to see and to share the reactions of men
whose lives were in danger. "One seems to have known gales as
enemies . . . adversaries whose wiles you must defeat, whose violence
you must resist, and yet with whom you must live in the intimacies of
nights and days," he looked back on his tempest-filled years.

Sailing ships, the most vulnerable of all craft in a gale, followed the
routes where the hardest winds blew. Twelve times Conrad rounded the

Cape of Good Hope on those slight craft; twice he rounded Cape Horn[17]–the two stormiest areas of the globe. Transfixing each man's mind in a gale off either cape–there was no remote possibility of rescue–was anxiety over the ship's ability to survive ("Coming on deck to take charge of my watch I received the instantaneous impression that the ship could not live for another hour in such a raging sea," was Conrad's memory of a Cape of Good Hope gale lashing the *Highland Forest*).

Many ships went "missing" around the capes. Others were driven far off their charted courses. The *Highland Forest*, blown so far out of her way as to approach Kerguelen Island in that near-Antarctic region, met a hazard new to Conrad which he wrote of in *The Mirror of the Sea*.

"It was on a grey afternoon in the lull of a three days' gale that had left the Southern Ocean tumbling heavily upon our ship under a sky hung with rags of clouds that seemed to have been cut and hacked by the keen edge of a sou'-west gale.

"Our craft, a Clyde-built barque of 1,000 tons, rolled so heavily that something aloft had carried away. No matter what the damage was, but it was serious enough to induce me to go aloft myself with a couple of hands and the carpenter [C. Baas, a Hollander of thirty-one][18] to see the temporary repairs properly done.

"Sometimes we had to drop everything and cling with both hands to the swaying spars, holding our breath in fear of a terribly heavy roll. And, wallowing as if she meant to turn over with us, the barque, her decks full of water, her gear flying in bights, ran at some ten knots an hour. We had been driven far south–much farther that way than we had meant to go; and suddenly, up there in the slings of the foreyard, in the midst of our work, I felt my shoulder gripped with such force in the carpenter's powerful paw that I positively yelled with unexpected pain. The man's eyes stared close in my face, and he shouted, 'Look, sir! look! What's this?' pointing ahead with his other hand.

"At first I saw nothing. The sea was one empty wilderness of black and white hills. Suddenly, half-concealed in the tumult of the foaming rollers I made out awash, something enormous, rising and falling–something spread out like a burst of foam, but with a more bluish, more solid look.

"It was a piece of an ice-floe melted down to a fragment, but still big enough to sink a ship, and floating lower than any raft, right in our way, as if ambushed among the waves with murderous intent. There was no time to get down on deck. I shouted from aloft till my head was ready to split. I was heard aft, and we managed to clear the sunken flow which had come all the way from the Southern ice-cap to have a try at our unsuspecting lives. Had it been an hour later, nothing could have saved the ship, for no eye could have made out in the dusk that pale piece of ice swept over by the white-crested waves.

"And as we stood near the taffrail side by side, my captain and I, looking at it, hardly discernible already, but still quite close-to on our quarter, he remarked in a meditative tone:

" 'But for the turn of that wheel just in time, there would have been another case of a "missing" ship.' "[19]

That year produced memorably violent weather. In China the Hwang Ho River flooded, 900,000 perishing in the greatest nature-caused loss of life ever recorded. In London, newspapers carried daily lists of ships "missing" or "overdue" as the *Highland Forest* battled through the storms of the southern Indian Ocean. Following much the same track as the *Palestine*, the *Highland Forest* reached Sunda Strait, the waterway dividing Java and Sumatra, through which the old vessel had passed a few days before exploding in nearby Bangka Strait. During the intervening four years a major landmark for seamen in Sunda Strait had all but disappeared in the most tremendous volcanic explosion of modern times.

When Conrad sailed through the Strait on the *Palestine*, guided by the high peak of Krakatao, the island holding that volcano was uninhabited, a place where the Javanese complacently searched for wild fruits. Having been inactive for two hundred years, the volcano was accepted as extinct. It was, however, preparing an outburst to affect the entire world. Shortly after Conrad sailed by it, the volcano began to play, continuing in a minor degree for fourteen weeks. Then, on August 27, 1883, Krakatao erupted. The roar was heard three thousand miles away, "the mightiest noise," wrote the English authority Sir Robert Ball in 1902, "that, so far as we can ascertain, has ever been heard on this globe." Krakatao's volcanic ash soared to a height of seventeen miles, layered vessels near the island with dust eighteen inches deep; clouds of the dust, driven by the hurricane winds of the stratosphere—the outer space in which manned capsules now orbit but, until Krakatao, was only guessed at—encircled the earth, coloring the sunsets of distant London for two years afterward. Sea and air waves of an intensity never surpassed in the history of volcanic action were produced by Krakatao, affecting the barometer in every part of the world. The strange red sunsets were recorded in places as distant as Australia, the Cape of Good Hope, California, London. Two-thirds of the island of Krakatao disappeared in the explosion; towns and villages on adjoining islands were swept away by tidal waves and whirlwinds, with an estimated loss of

36,000 lives; enormous waves, carrying ships far inland, raised the water level of harbors by as much as 115 feet; an internal convulsion spread through the mountain ranges, starting a third of Java's forty-five craters into action.

Though Krakatao was giving early signs of unrest when Conrad passed it on the *Palestine*, he, in London seeing the astonishing sunsets, missed the eruption in Sunda Strait in which "all records of previous explosions on this earth were completely broken." When he came into Sunda Strait again, on the *Highland Forest*, he bore a mark of the Indian Ocean gales, the leg injury which kept him in the East.

"It was only poetic justice that the chief mate who had made a mistake—perhaps a half-excusable one—about the distribution of his ship's cargo should pay the penalty," he wrote of the end of the *Highland Forest* voyage and the gale-inflicted damage to the ship. "A piece of one of the minor spars that did carry away flew against the chief mate's back, and sent him sliding on his face for quite a considerable distance along the main deck. Thereupon followed various and unpleasant consequences of a physical order—'queer symptoms,' as the captain, who treated them, used to say; inexplicable periods of powerlessness, sudden accesses of mysterious pain; and the patient agreed fully with the regretful mutters of his very attentive captain wishing that it had been a straightforward broken leg. Even the Dutch doctor who took the case up in Samarang offered no scientific explanation. All he said was: 'Ah, friend, you are young yet; it may be very serious for your whole life. You must leave your ship; you must quite silent be for three months—quite silent.' "[20]

The *Highland Forest* reached Samarang on June 20, 1887, and on July 1 Conrad signed off the ship, collecting £16 in wages.[21] He went to Singapore and entered the hospital where "lying on my back, I had plenty of leisure to remember the dreadful cold and snow of Amsterdam, while looking at the fronds of the palm trees tossing and rustling at the height of the window."

The *Highland Forest* after Conrad left her sailed along the Java coast to Surabaya, from there returning to Scotland, to Greenock.[22] Shortly after her arrival she was sold, in 1888, to J. R. Cuthbertson & Co. of Glasgow. New York was the last port she was ever to see. Loading a cargo for Australia, she left New York on January 27, 1901.[23] When within twenty-five miles of her destination, Fremantle, she was totally wrecked on Murray Reef near Mandurah, West Australia, on April 29, 1901. Captain Alex Chapman was penalized by the Court of Inquiry, his certificate suspended for twelve months. He was charged with lack of caution upon seeing land, of failing to take adequate measures when the coast loomed up suddenly after three storm-blinding days. A ship seventeen years old, the *Highland Forest* was one of seven of Conrad's ships to be lost at sea.[24] His ship to follow the *Highland Forest*, the steamship *Vidar*, survived well into the 1920s, gradually falling to pieces in Penang,[25] a ship approaching sixty.

His long-waited-for chance to live a trader's life in the East influenced Conrad to accept a berth on the *Vidar;* the short voyages of the steamer to and from Singapore also enabled him to reach a hospital for treatment of the nerve injury which, slow to heal, caused him to limp for several years.

For six weeks of the summer of 1887 Conrad remained in Singapore's General Hospital. Costly and usually crowded, with a capacity of fifty beds, it was far from modern. With the feeling that "I must leave the place at once or die there,"[26] another patient, John Dill Ross, Jr., described his hasty departure from it. The European ward where Conrad was treated was set aside for the Europeans and Americans who made up 3000 of Singapore's 150,000 people (the fifth largest port in the world, today it has 1,700,000). His hospital stay was recalled by Conrad in *Lord Jim.*

"There were only two other patients in the white men's ward: the purser of a gunboat, who had broken his leg falling down a hatchway; and a kind of railway contractor from a neighbouring province afflicted by some mysterious tropical disease, who held the doctor for an ass, and indulged in secret debaucheries of patent medicine which his Tamil servant used to smuggle in with unwearied devotion. They told each other the story of their lives, played cards a little, or, yawning and in pyjamas, lounged through the day in easy-chairs without saying a word. The hospital stood on a hill, and a gentle breeze entering through the windows, always flung wide open, brought into the bare room the softness of the sky, the languor of the earth, the bewitching breath of the Eastern waters. There were perfumes in it, suggestions of infinite repose, the gift of endless dreams."[27]

When Conrad was able to walk he went to the center of town, to engage a room at the Officers' Sailors' Home where he could live while locating a ship. On the site now occupied by the Capitol Cinema, the Sailors' Home "was a large bungalow with a wide verandah and a curiously suburban-looking little garden of bushes and a few trees between it and the street," Conrad, in *The Shadow Line*, described the building which had something "of the character of a residential club." In addition to being a hostel, it was the depot for navigation charts sought by steamer captains. Word of ships on the lookout for officers was passed around and there apparently Conrad heard of the *Vidar*. On August 22, 1887,[28] he signed on as chief mate.

A schooner-rigged iron screw steamer of 304 gross tons, the *Vidar* sailed under the British flag,[29] trading to ports in Celebes and Borneo. She had been built in England in 1871, by Wigham Richardson & Co. of Newcastle, and registered in Singapore in 1872.[30] When Conrad joined her the ship was sixteen years old. Her owner, Syed Mohsin bin S. Al Jaffree,[31] was one of the most influential, and had been one of the richest, of the 836 Arabs in Singapore. Along with several trading schooners, he owned the steamers *Vidar* and the twenty-ton *Emily I*.[32] Syed Mohsin had arrived in Singapore as a young man with the nakhoda or master of an Arab vessel, had saved money from his voyages, opened a small shop on Arab Street, and gradually became wealthy. Toward the end of his life—he was in his early seventies when Conrad met him—his business fell off and he became nearly blind. At eighty, he died in Singapore in May, 1894. "He was very well known and liked in Singapore by many of the European community," Charles Burton Buckley closed a summary of his life in *An Anecdotal History of Old Times in Singapore*.[33]

"I myself saw him but once," Conrad wrote in *The Shadow Line*, "quite accidentally on a wharf—an old, dark little man blind in one eye, in a snowy robe and yellow slippers. He was having his hand severely kissed by a crowd of Malay pilgrims to whom he had done some favour, in the way of food and money. His alms-giving, I have heard, was most extensive, covering almost the whole Archipelago."[34]

A part-owner of the *Vidar* was her master, Captain James Craig, an Englishman of thirty-three. Born in 1854, going to sea at twenty, he had arrived in Singapore in 1875, when twenty-one, and for twelve years had been sailing in Malayan waters when Conrad met him. Captain Craig was married, his older daughter Ivy a small child (after her marriage Mrs. F. A. Fairweather named her house in England "Vidar" for her father's ship). Captain Craig spent fifty years in the East and was well known in Singapore, Borneo, and ports all the way to Australia.[35] He sailed the *Vidar* to Borneo until 1892 when she was sold to a Dutch subject and her registry transferred to Penang.[36] Captain Craig left the sea when sixty-six, retiring in 1920 to England. He made his last visit to Singapore in 1928, leaving it on September 11 of that year. On December 10, 1929, at the age of seventy-five, Captain Craig died at his son's home in England, in East Sheen.[37]

Conrad sailed under Captain Craig for nineteen weeks in 1887–88 and won his commander's high approval. Captain F. C. Hendry, in *From the*

Log-Book of Memory written under the pseudonym of "Shalimar," told
how his friend, Captain Craig, held up Conrad "as an example to be followed, the most conscientious chief officer he ever had—a man who was
heavily bearded because he had never shaved in his life, and who had
learned to speak Malay fluently, though with a peculiar guttural accent,
in an incredibly short time."

The *Vidar* during Conrad's voyages carried, besides himself as chief
mate and Captain Craig, a chief engineer, James Allen, a second engineer,
John C. Niven, a Chinese engineer, a serang or boatswain, eleven Malays
in the crew, and eighty-two Chinese for loading and unloading the cargo
in the ports where the ship would call. Everything about the *Vidar*
pleased Conrad, as he wrote in *The Shadow Line*.

"Excellent (and picturesque) Arab owner, about whom one needed
not to trouble one's head, a most excellent Scottish ship—for she was
that from the keel up—excellent sea-boat, easy to keep clean, most handy
in every way, and if it had not been for her internal propulsion, worthy
of any man's love, I cherish to this day a profound respect for her memory. As to the kind of trade she was engaged in and the character of my
shipmates, I could not have been happier if I had had the life and the
men made to my order by a benevolent Enchanter."[38]

The kind of trade the *Vidar* was engaged in—carrying out from Singapore such general merchandise as crockeryware, bringing back gutta-
percha, rattan, beeswax, and two delicacies used in Chinese soups, birds'
nests and trepang, the sea cucumbers or *bêche-de-mer* which made a
fragrant cargo—took Conrad on a long, huckstering round. Sailing
through the Java Sea, Macassar Strait, the Celebes Sea, he passed landmarks of which some seventy were to be recalled in his fiction—among
them the Tuju or Seven Isles north of Bangka Island of "Freya of the
Seven Isles," Round Island in that group adopted as a name in *Victory;*
Cape Malatajur on the southern coast of Borneo, its name used in "The
Planter of Malata"; Cape Selatan, on the south coast of Borneo, remembered in "Because of the Dollars"; Pedra Branca, the small rocky islet
near Singapore that wrecked so many ships before the Horsburgh light-
house was built there, recalled in *The Rescue;* Tandjung Batu, the point
of land on the eastern coast of Borneo, coming into *Almayer's Folly.*

Above all, the *Vidar* took Conrad to a river in Borneo. Its main settlement was to appear in his fiction under a variety of names—"Patusan,"
"Sambir," "Samburan," "Darat-es-Salam." There Conrad knew the Dutch
trader William Charles Olmeyer, whose name, pronounced Almayer, was
retained by Conrad in that English spelling for *Almayer's Folly.* "If I
had not got to know Almayer pretty well," he wrote in *A Personal*

Record, "it is almost certain there would never have been a line of mine in print."[39]

The river on which Olmeyer lived, Conrad's geographical starting point as an author, was a well-hidden jungle stream in an unfrequented part of the East. It is a little-known river still.

PART THREE
THE RIVER

XVI

From the low point of land where he stood he could see both branches of the river. The main branch of the Pantai was lost in complete darkness . . . but up the Sambir reach his eye could follow the long line of Malay houses crowding the bank, with here and there a dim light twinkling through bamboo walls. . . .

Almayer's Folly

The river is one of the five great streams on the east coast of Borneo, a wilderness waterway with only a few small settlements along it. Rising in the hot equatorial heart of Borneo, twisting mile after mile through thick jungle where crocodiles sun on its banks and exotic, giant butterflies color the air, it breaks from Borneo's green coast into the Celebes Sea, spilling through a delta studded with islands—Sodang Besar, Lalawan, Guntung, Lunsuran Naga, Tempurung and Badak Badak among them.

The coast here, two degrees above the equator, is low and swampy, tangled with mangroves, a solid wall of dark green against the blue sea. The stifling heat and torrential, daily downpours—during the full east monsoon rain falls above five inches in a day—spur vegetation to a rage of growth and an impenetrable shield of foliage conceals the river entrance. Inland, in the mornings, heavy fog covers the river, the steam of a saturated land of perpetual July where nights are only slightly less oppressive than the days. A tidal river with numerous outlets to the sea, its estuary is a maze of reefs, mud flats, yellow sandbanks, the slightly higher ground of red cliffs matted with mangroves like the shore. It is a shallow river, its channels constantly changing. Offshoot ribbons of feeding streams merge with it, dead-end streams to follow. Peppered with islets and sand bars along its muddy flow, roiled into flood by heavy rains, carving new islands in its rush to the sea, presenting a daunting barrier of laced bushes and creepers on each bank throughout its looping jungle course, it is a hazardous river to enter. This river, Conrad's river, is the Berau. In the 1880s it was known as the Pantai and in the 1600s as the Sangkalaki.

For more than twenty years of the last century traders in Singapore and Macassar knew of it vaguely as "Lingard's river," the mysterious stream where Captain William Lingard had his campong, a source of his trader's wealth. Lingard's Crossing, a passage indicated as *Baken van Lingard*, appears still on local maps, on the Maura Pantai or Pantai mouth of the river. A tide gauge marked in feet, standing near a house with a zinc roof at Sokkan village, gives the depth in the Lingard Crossing. Lingard's way upstream is now seldom followed, another along the Maura Guntung providing better depth for steamships. Steamers are not frequent on the river, most being bound for the coal mines of Teluk Bajur. On the upper reaches of the river coal ledges come to the surface and a primitive form of mining—coal chipped out of the banks and carried away on Malay praus—began here before 1850. By 1887, when Conrad knew the village, coal mining was an old, and still primitive, industry. ("There was a coal-mine there, with an outcrop in the hillside less than five hundred yards from the rickety wharf," he referred to this setting in *Victory*.)

Occasional rice clearings break up the otherwise unrelieved green mass of the forest as you go up the river today. Palm trees rise from the clearings, cocoanuts and nipa palms, and behind them tower the giant jungle trees—ironwood, camphor, ebony, sandalwood—reaching a height of 220 feet. Against the solid wash of forest, landmarks are relied on to navigate the river—a memorably odd tree, a particular kink in the stream, a distant hill—the distant hills of the Batu Tampanung Mountains to the south, peaks of 2000 to 3000 feet, the nearest mark on the skyline 1100-foot Padai. Highest of any rise to be seen from the river are the 4500-foot Njapa Mountains, remnants of ancient volcanoes, standing south of the settlement Tanah Merah ("Red Cliffs").

Rivers provide the means of travel in this part of Borneo and villages huddle on the banks of streams. Wrapped around them is the vast stretch of jungle in which move slow and sluggish boa constrictors, twenty feet long, and the much more dangerous cobras; high up on the tops of tall trees are fabulous wild orchids, brought down by Dyak climbers for an ever demanding market. Valued as parent stock for hybridizing, the wild plants have been industriously hunted and rare varieties are disappearing. With orchid fanciers willing to pay as much as three thousand dollars for a plant, the naturalist prospector has come to Borneo in increasing numbers over the years. Another Borneo native, the orang-utan or Malayan mias, a protected animal now whose tree nests have too often been raided for zoos, is also growing rare. Also becoming less plentiful are the much-hunted, skin-valued crocodiles which, lying motionless on the banks, give the convincing appearance of logs. "Crocs" in the river grow to eighteen feet and are old and dangerous at that size, a menace to Malay children and fishermen.

The river is alive with fish; the jungle surrounding it, noisy with monkeys, is rich in timber and spices; along the stream and its many tributaries are alluvial gold, diamonds and coal. But it was the river's great asset, seclusion, that drew the first known settlers to it, its difficult entrance making a natural guard protecting those living above. Discovering its safe haven, Sulu pirates in the eighteenth century found a refuge here and built a hideout thirty-three miles up the river, taking their captives and their booty to an almost impregnable retreat. Between it and the sea, at a wide bend in the river, a sentinel hill, Upos—named for the Upos tree whose juice poisons the arrows of Dyak blowpipes—rises sharply from the water's edge, affording a lookout for pursuit. Here an outpost settlement grew, Samburakat, "the high place from which you can see all around."

Five miles upstream from Samburakat the river forks and, losing its name, becomes two rivers, the Kelai and the Segah. At this junction is the village of Tandjung Redeb, or Berau as it is usually called, even as the district is called Berau. The village, like the river, is split in two, the sultanate of Gunung Tabur on the Segah, that of Sambaliung on the Kelai. Split also is the landmark hill or twin hills on the Kelai where Captain Lingard built his first campong in 1860, naming it "Patusan," from the Malay *putus*, meaning split or broken off.

The split nature of the river, of the village, of the hill—of the very history of this throbbing part of Borneo with its conflicts between rival sultans, English and Dutch traders, white men and Malays, Moslems and Christians—was captured in the name Patusan. Conrad, retaining that name, drew the village accurately in *Lord Jim*. Anyone coming up the river now catches sight of the two hills at Berau, at the last bend of the river, just as he wrote of them:

"Patusan is a remote district of a native-ruled state, and the chief settlement bears the same name. At a point on the river about forty miles from the sea, where the first houses come into view, there can be seen rising above the level of the forests the summits of two steep hills very close together, and separated by what looks like a deep fissure, the cleavage of some mighty stroke. As a matter of fact, the valley be- tween is nothing but a narrow ravine; the appearance from the settle- ment is of one irregularly conical hill split in two, and with the two halves leaning slightly apart."[1]

From Samburakat, the river-edge settlement he passed on the *Vidar*, Conrad fashioned the name "Sambir" for the village in *Almayer's Folly* and *An Outcast of the Islands*, there retaining the river's early name, the Pantai. From Samburakat also came "Samburan," the name Conrad gave the settlement in *Victory*.

What made the river memorable for Conrad was the trader in Berau, Olmeyer. "In your earthly life you haunted me, Almayer," he wrote in *A Personal Record*, crediting the aggrieved man in Borneo, "always complaining of being lost to the world," with being responsible—by Conrad's 1912 tally of the books he had written—"for the existence of some fourteen volumes, so far."[2]

His contact with Olmeyer began in late August, 1887, when he sailed up the river to Berau for the first time as chief mate of the *Vidar*. The *Vidar*, under Captain Craig, made a round-trip voyage every three weeks. Leaving Singapore, she sailed through Carimata Strait, called at Bandjermasin on the south coast of Borneo, cruised up Pulo Laut Strait, stopping at the coaling station of Kota Baru on the island of Pulo Laut, crossed Macassar Strait to Donggala on Celebes, recrossed the Strait to Samarinda, in the Kutai or Coti district of Borneo, rounded Point Mangkalihat as she moved along Borneo's east coast to the Berau River, steamed slowly up that unpredictable stream to the settlement of Berau —where the owner of the *Vidar* had a trading station, managed by his son Syed Abdulla—came down the river, passed Tandjung Batu on the Bornean coast as she headed north for her last outward call, the Bulungan River and its upstream settlement of Bulungan or Tandjung Selor. The return to Singapore was over the same route, though the ship's calls, depending on her cargo, varied on her tramp steamer round.[3] Berau, however, was her principal destination and at times she sailed directly there from Singapore.[4] The length of the *Vidar's* stay in the settlement was determined by how quickly gutta-percha and rattan, brought from the interior in native dugout canoes, arrived for loading, the layover lasting two to three days.[5] During his four and a half months on the *Vidar*, Conrad spent more than three weeks altogether in Berau, acquiring the intimate knowledge of the village, its people and its his- tory he was to write of in his fiction.

Before ever embarking on the *Vidar* he knew about Olmeyer, or

Almayer as he always gave it. "I had heard of him at Singapore," he wrote in *A Personal Record*, "I had heard of him on board; I had heard of him early in the morning and late at night; I had heard of him at tiffin and at dinner; I had heard of him in a place called Pulo Laut from a half-caste gentleman there, who described himself as the manager of a coal-mine; which sounded civilized and progressive till you heard that the mine could not be worked at present because it was haunted by some particulary atrocious ghosts."[6]

When the *Vidar* called at Donggala, a little village on the spider-shaped island of Celebes, Conrad heard of Olmeyer there, largely because of a pony. Donggala was a colorful settlement of the Bugis branch of Malays lying at the foot of coral chalk hills on the deep Bay of Palos, a smooth stretch of blue water. The hilly and heavily-wooded Kingdom of Palos, with its capital, Donggala, was ruled by a rajah[7] who, in royal fashion, was accompanied everywhere by a retinue from his court—a "fat, dingy Rajah," Conrad remembered, who knew of Olmeyer too. The deck passengers of the *Vidar*, wandering traders scattered over the ship, "each man fenced round with bundles and boxes—on mats, on pillows, on quilts, on billets of wood, conversing of Island affairs," also talked of Olmeyer. "It was really impossible on board that ship to get away definitely from Almayer," Conrad continued the remembrance, "and a very small pony tied up forward and whisking its tail inside the galley, to the great embarrassment of our Chinaman cook, was destined for Almayer."[8]

Shortly after leaving Donggala Conrad had his first glimpse, in Berau, of the much-discussed trader, who imported a pony to his jungle village, though a quarter-of-a-mile path was the sole open area where he could ride it. In *A Personal Record* Conrad described Olmeyer as he saw him coming to the jetty where the *Vidar* was moored.

"The forests above and below and on the opposite bank looked black and dank; wet dripped from the rigging upon the tightly stretched deck awnings, and it was in the middle of a shuddering yawn that I caught sight of Almayer. He was moving across a patch of burned grass, a blurred, shadowy shape with the blurred bulk of a house behind him, a low house of mats, bamboos, and palm-leaves, with a high-pitched roof of grass.

"He stepped upon the jetty. He was clad simply in flapping pajamas of cretonne pattern (enormous flowers with yellow petals on a disagreeable blue ground) and a thin cotton singlet with short sleeves. His arms, bare to the elbow, were crossed on his chest. His black hair looked as if it had not been cut for a very long time, and a curly wisp of it strayed across his forehead."[9]

Though the man Conrad saw on this wet morning supplied him with the leading character of his first novel, published in 1895, *Almayer's Folly, A Story of an Eastern River,* Conrad never disclosed which "Eastern River" he referred to. Amply as he described in *A Personal Record* his first meeting with Olmeyer, whose name "was the common property of the winds," he avoided giving Olmeyer's full or actual name. Holding the belief that explicitness was "fatal to the glamour of all artistic work, robbing it of all suggestiveness, destroying all illusion," he did not throughout his life reveal the whereabouts of his Eastern River or the Malay village on it. The unsolved mystery exerted a magnetic pull, leading sea captains, traders and scholars alike to speculate where it might be—or if it ever was.

A river is not an easy thing to lose and yet it has taken more than a half-century to locate with certainty this turbulent, tropical stream of Conrad's. From its main settlement he created a fictional world as Mark Twain created such a world out of Hannibal, Missouri, on the Mississippi. Both knew their rivers as navigators on them, piloting their ships by remembered landmarks—as the twisting, tidal river Conrad knew must be navigated still.

Writers examining Conrad's work for his sources placed the original sites of his fiction in areas of Sumatra, the Philippines, the Tiger Islands, Sarawak—places Conrad never knew. With the river located conclusively and the life stories of the people Conrad knew there learned recently through research and interviews, it proves to be the setting of *Almayer's Folly,* of *An Outcast of the Islands,* of *Victory,* of *The Rescue,* of *Lord Jim.* As background it comes into "Karain," "The Lagoon," "The End of the Tether," "Freya of the Seven Isles."

The long search to find the river where "Almayer" had lived and its Malay village never seen by more than a scattering of Europeans involved many people over the years, from countries half the world away. Conrad's following, always a devoted one, takes in a wide range of professions and tongues, and it is a measure of its scope that in the end the final proof was found by a Dutch manager of a Borneo coal mine whose interest had been aroused by a stranger he was never to meet, an English surgeon in Malaya.

It was not until 1927, three years after Conrad's death, that the settlement was first linked with the novelist—in a passing reference by the Dutch author, Dr. Roelof Broersma, in his economic history of Borneo, *Handel en bedrijf in Zuid-en Oost-Borneo.* In the same year Jean-Aubry in *Joseph Conrad: Life and Letters* wrongly asserted it to be Bulungan, a village farther north and on another river. In 1936 Bruce Lockhart, the English writer on a search for Conrad's real-life sources in the East, told in *Return to Malaya* how he had failed to find them in Macassar, a town across Macassar Strait and far away. In 1937 an English business-man, F. Harold Gray, traveling about Borneo on a mission for his Philip-pine firm, accidentally happened upon the village on his way to Tarakan. He wrote of his adventure in an English journal, *Mirage*, published in the little port of Miri in Sarawak, but his casual identification in an obscure publication was generally overlooked. In 1939, Dr. John Gordan, curator of the Berg Collection of the New York Public Library and author of *Joseph Conrad, the Making of a Novelist*—the first American in the search—made a special trip to Borneo to find the upriver settle-ment and, after going mistakenly to Bulungan, learned of its correct location but failed to reach it. Dr. Gordan, interviewing a daughter and son-in-law of Olmeyer in Java, provided the first accurate facts of the "Almayer" Conrad knew.

World War II, during which Borneo was occupied by the Japanese, put a temporary halt to the search. At the war's end, an English doctor in medical practice in Malaya—Dr. J. G. Reed—began research in 1946 for what he hoped one day to publish as "A Conrad Notebook."

Dr. Reed, M.B.E., began his thirty-year career in the East in 1922, at Sarawak, remaining three years in the kingdom then under the rule of the third white rajah, Sir Charles Vyner Brooke. As a Surgeon Lieutenant Commander in the British navy during World War II, Dr. Reed was serving on the British ship *Mata Hari* when she was lost to the Japanese in March, 1942. Taken prisoner, he spent three and a half years in Japanese war prisoner camps, first at Muntok on Bangka Island—at a time when Bangka Strait was earning its name of "Bomb Alley"—later in a camp at Palembang, Sumatra. He was released in September, 1945, and died seven years later.

For six of those years, living in an isolated part of Malaya's state of Perak, Dr. Reed sent away for books about Conrad and wrote to corre-spondents around the globe. He traveled widely, to England and France and frequently to Singapore, where he located and, in 1951, interviewed Mrs. C. C. Oehlers, the only daughter of Jim Lingard, the young English trader Conrad had known in Borneo. Mrs. Oehlers described her birth-place as the Borneo settlement where the Lingards and Olmeyers had lived for many years and gave the name of the village: Berau.

In the hope of finding someone in Berau who had known Conrad's contemporaries there, Dr. Reed wrote three months later to the manager of the Dutch-owned coal mine at Teluk Bajur, six miles up the river from Berau, Mr. R. Haverschmidt. This chance letter reached the one man who could, and did, complete the search for Conrad's river and Borneo village which had involved so many before and for so long.

Well as he knew Conrad's Berau, in his sixteen years of residence, Mr. Haverschmidt had only a slight knowledge of Conrad. "The only book I ever read of Conrad's is *The Rescue* and I did not know till now that the district here plays such an important part in his writings," Mr. Haverschmidt wrote from Teluk Bajur on July 30, 1951, in answer to Dr. Reed.

Reading Conrad's novels for the first time—*Lord Jim, Almayer's Folly, An Outcast of the Islands*—in the very setting Conrad had used, Mr. Haverschmidt was awed by the interplay of fact and fiction. "Not only the impression one gets in general of the country but also several descriptions of local details prove to me that Conrad was a very good observer and painter with the pen," he wrote to Dr. Reed. "I found myself an intrigued observer sitting in Tandjung Redeb on the verandah of the district officer's house, imagining myself a spectator of the strange happenings which Conrad's master hand did evoke before my eyes." The district officer's house where Mr. Haverschmidt sat on the veranda reading novels about "Tom Lingard" had been built on the site of the original Lingard's home.

Captain William Lingard (Conrad altered his name to Tom Lingard for *Almayer's Folly, An Outcast of the Islands,* and *The Rescue*) had erected his immense house on the riverbank some eighty-five years before, a house constructed high off the ground on tall ironwood posts to guard against the river's flooding, with a vast open space beneath the house and its wide encircling veranda. When Conrad was in Berau the house was occupied by Jim Lingard, the captain's nephew and heir who sold it and the six acres around it in 1904[10] to the sultan of Gunung Tabur—the sultan paying that debt by allowing Lingard to collect an equivalent amount in taxes from the royal rattan forests. For some years the house was the sultan's palace; later it became the residence of the Dutch district officer. Pulled down in the 1930s, a new house for the district officer was erected on the same site; this was burned in a 1945 air raid when the village was bombed during the Tarakan campaign of World War II; another had replaced it, and it was there Mr. Haverschmidt sat reading.

Stirred by the novels and the opportunity to verify the local history given in them, Mr. Haverschmidt set out to learn from old residents what the village had been like when Conrad had known it. So many of his informants referred to an overgrown and obliterated graveyard, in which the originals of some of Conrad's characters had been buried, that he enlisted the help of a young Belgian named Cools to search for it. Cutting through the jungle, Mr. Haverschmidt came upon a headstone erected over the graves of two of Charles Olmeyer's infant sons. A large headstone with words chiseled by some Malay hand in inaccurate Dutch, it lay under thick layers of vegetable mold in what had once been a graveyard for Europeans and Malays converted to the Christian faith. Abandoned some thirty years earlier, the jungle had reclaimed it. He found the cemetery at Gunung Tabur ("hill of scattered stones," a name tragically apt for the roving Europeans at rest in the jungle there) halfway up the slope, overlooking the river. It contains markers dating from 1851 to the 1920s; because of the creep of the soil along the slope, the rooting of wild boars, and the erosion of time, many graves had disappeared altogether. Conrad, knowing the graveyard, wrote of it in the final pages of *An Outcast of the Islands*.

"Yes! I told you about that gravestone. Yes! Another hundred and twenty dollars thrown away. Wish I had them now. He would do it. And the inscription. Ha! ha! ha! 'Peter Willems, Delivered by the Mercy of God from his Enemy.' What enemy—unless Captain Lingard himself? . . . You haven't seen the grave? On the top of that hill, there, on the other side of the river."[11]

The original of the Willems of that story, Carel De Veer, was buried in the cemetery twenty-four years after Conrad last saw him in Berau. Charles Olmeyer's wife, Johanna, whom Conrad knew and drew as the trader's wife in *Almayer's Folly*, was also buried there, in 1892, but no marker for her grave now remains.[12] The stone over the graves of their first and third sons was found by Mr. Haverschmidt under matted growth and bears this Dutch inscription:

Hier rusten onze lievelingen

CAREL GEORGE

geb. 29 Dec. 1874 *overl.* 4 Febr. 1876

ALBERT EDUARD

geb. 2 Jul. 1878 *overl.* 28 Nov. 1878

Hun dood betreuren wij des te meer
daar wij alhier verlaten eenzaam
en zonder eenigen troost bevinden

CHARLES OLMEYER
JOHANNA MARIE CORNELIA
geb. VAN LIESHOUT[13]

The gravestone of the Olmeyer children, enduring evidence withstanding the devouring jungle which through the years has erased everything less durable than stone, told that this was the village of Olmeyer, whose elaborately large house in the wilderness, across the river from the graveyard, was known throughout the area by the chaffing name "The Folly." Rebuilt in 1910 to serve as a post office, it was destroyed in the same 1945 air raid that had razed the Lingard site. Olmeyer was a man with grandiose illusions, in life no less than fiction. As Conrad wrote of him, he had pinned his dreams on wealth and fame, rewards he would one day share with his daughter, yet only the graves of his two small sons remain as proof of his existence on the river where he dreamed.

With the finding of the graves the search for the village had ended. But the English doctor who had carried it so far never knew its end. Dr. Reed died suddenly in his distant corner of Malaya before Mr. Haverschmidt's jungle exploration was completed. Through tireless research and the appealing letters which won so many to assist him, Dr. Reed provided the final key to the place Conrad so often wrote of, where he had known the adventurers whose "wasted lives, for the few who know, have tinged with romance the region of shallow waters and forest-clad islands, that lies far east, and still mysterious between the deep waters of two oceans."[14]

In a part of Indonesian Borneo where the old name of Kalimantan ("Mango Island") has been revived, adventurers, white and brown, left traces of their lives upon a river. Conrad, fittingly, wove that history into romance.

XVII

"I am devoted to Borneo," Conrad wrote to his relative, the novelist Mme. Poradowska,[1] when, at thirty-six, he was beginning his second novel, *An Outcast of the Islands*. He was writing again of Borneo, as in *Almayer's Folly*, of an island and a people holding an absorbing fascination for him. The island was an ancient one, traces of man's existence there dating back to the Middle Paleolithic period, 50,000 to 40,000 B.C., being discovered by archaeologists in 1954. A seafaring country for more than a thousand years before Columbus set off on his first voyage, Borneo had once been a crossroads of the East, as Marseilles was of the West, and had contact with countries as distant as China and India seven hundred years before Marco Polo's journey to Peking. Settled so long ago that no one has known the origin of its people, they are believed to have come from India, China, Indochina, the Philippines, Java, Sumatra, and Celebes, and perhaps were never within a single empire. Today the island—the third largest in the world, five times the size of England and Wales—has four divisions: Kalimantan or Indonesian Borneo which takes in three-fourths of the whole, Sarawak, Brunei, and North Borneo (Sabah). The latter three northwestern states, for a century under British protection, in 1963 were amalgamated, with Malaya and Singapore, into the Federation of Malaysia.[2] Kalimantan was the only section Conrad knew, and he used it as the setting of his fiction.

Among the earliest written records pertaining to Borneo are those in China, telling of the arrival there of emissaries from Borneo in 518 A.D., followed by others in 423 A.D. and 616 A.D. Contact between Borneo and India had been established earlier, Hindu settlement of Borneo having begun during the first six centuries A.D. By the seventh century a large part of Borneo had adopted the Hindu religion; and in caves and grottos of the Bawoie Mountains, in the center of the island, are the Hindu idols and temples which constitute Borneo's best-known archaeological remains—stone figures showing traces of beaten gold, carvings in bas-relief on the walls of mountain caverns. In the interior of the Kutai district, adjacent to Berau, other archaeological finds became known in 1882 through the Scandinavian explorer and author, Carl Bock.[3] These included a twelve-pound gold figure of a Hindu goddess, found in some distant time on the banks of the Maura Kaman, and a bronze figure of the Hindu goddess Dingaugi or Gendawagie.

Chinese emigration to Borneo began in the fifteenth century, a time when the Moslem faith, the present religion of the island, was imported by Arabs. A century later the first white men came upon Borneo. In 1521, following Magellan's death in the Philippines, his companions continued on their world-circling voyage in the Spanish vessel *Vittoria*, stopping at what was then the large empire of Brunei. On board the *Vittoria* was an Italian gentleman-adventurer, Antonio Pigafetta, who, keeping a journal of the voyage, gave a colorful account of the ship's stay, from July 9 to September 27, 1521, at Brunei—a name Pigafetta wrote as Borneo.

Spices, pepper particularly, caused trade to be opened with Borneo in the 1570s, first by Portuguese and later by Spanish expeditions. The Dutch established trading posts in Borneo in 1604 and the English soon followed. The Dutch East India Company, however, showed little interest in the island. During the eighteenth century it had a single agency there, in Bandjermasin, and one product in mind, pepper. For another hundred years its ships sailed to Java, passing Borneo by.[4] Meanwhile English adventurers opened a profitable trade on Borneo's east coast and became the first white pioneers of Conrad's river.

In the Gunung Tabur graveyard, where the headstone marking the graves of Olmeyer's infant sons was found, another tells of the first white man who died in Berau, or Brow as it was earlier spelled. He was a young man of Conrad's age and Conrad very likely saw the stone. The inscription gives almost all that is known of the young Englishman.

> Sacred to the memory of
> George McKenzie Morgan
> who departed this life on the
> 22 October 1851, aged 25 years.
> He was the first European merchant
> established in Brow.
> Departed this life at an early age
> to the deep sorrow of his relations
> and regret of his heathen friends
> and neighbours whose esteem and
> confidence he has gained.
> This stone is dedicated to his
> memory by his affected uncle.
> G. P. King[5]

George Peacock King, who erected and signed the stone over the grave of the nephew he had established as a trader in Berau, had begun his own wide trading operations in the East Indies at Lombok, the island next to Bali. In 1843 he shifted his base to Samarinda, in the Kutai district 230 miles south of Berau—one of the Borneo ports where the *Vidar*, during Conrad's voyages on that ship, regularly called. The swampy settlement of Samarinda was unhealthy in the 1840s and King lived on board an old beached ship which he had fortified to withstand attacks from pirates who regularly plundered the coast.[6] Conrad very likely heard stories of King in Borneo who, living in Macassar in the 1860s, had come to Berau in 1848 to set up the trading post his nephew managed.

There were other early white men in Samarinda, before King. Among the first was a Frenchman, Charles Müller, killed by head-hunting Dyaks about 1825. Four Frenchmen, in an expedition led by Pierre Ivanoff, spent the year of 1958 living with the Dyaks of that region, learning that Müller had been killed due to the chieftain's fear of the white man's strange color and stranger ways.[7] The Dyaks collected heads as trophies, evidence of the prowess of the tribe, for much the same reason American Indians collected scalps; a practice having Dyak tribal and religious significance, it was officially banned many years ago but the Ivanoff expedition discovered during their long stay that it was still carried on, surreptitiously, on a small scale.

Following Müller and King, other attempts were made in the Samarinda area to set up trading posts. In 1844 an Englishman, Murray, equipped an expedition in Hong Kong and sailed on the schooner *Young Queen* to the eastern coast of Borneo, intending to establish a colony in the Kutai district. But Murray was killed on board during the landing operations and the others sailed away on the *Young Queen*, commanded by Captain Hart. Off the coast the schooner's crew mutinied, Captain Hart killing the leader of the mutiny, his brother.[8]

On Borneo's northwest coast, in Sarawak, a model state grew through the efforts of James Brooke, whom the reigning sultan gratefully appointed as rajah in 1841 and upon whom the British government bestowed a baronetcy in 1847. Sir James, the first of the three white rajahs who ruled the rain forest kingdom as a private state from 1841 to 1946 —with the exception of the World War II years when it was occupied by the Japanese—was an Englishman born in India who retired from the Indian army at twenty-seven. Wealthy, he bought a yacht, the *Royalist*, and sailed from Singapore to Borneo and Celebes on a number of long expeditions. Coming to know Sarawak first in 1839, he made it his goal in life to bring prosperity, education and hygiene to that jungle area, to suppress piracy, the slave trade, head-hunting. A fearless man, hating authority, generous and just, living simply in a thatched bungalow in Sarawak's capital of Kuching, he devoted the last twenty-seven years of his life to saving that part of the Malay world from plunder and decay.

"In the Archipelago the first voyagers from the West found the natives rich and powerful," he wrote in his journal, "with strong established governments, and a thriving trade with all parts of the world. The rapacious European has reduced them to their present condition. Their governments have been broken up; the old states decomposed by treachery, by bribery, and intrigue; their possessions wrested from them under flimsy pretences; their trade restricted, their vices encouraged, their virtues repressed, and their energies paralysed or rendered desperate, till there is every reason to fear the extinction of the Malay races."[9]

Conrad greatly admired Sir James Brooke and evidently read about him. Among the outstanding books concerned with Brooke and the Malay Archipelago which he may have read were *Narrative of Events in Borneo and Celebes* by Captain Rodney Mundy (London, 1848); *Borneo and the Indian Archipelago* by Frank S. Marryat (London, 1848); *A Visit to the Indian Archipelago in H.M. Ship Meander, with Portions of the Private Journal of Sir James Brooke, K.C.B.*, by Captain Henry Keppel (London, 1853); *The Indian Archipelago, Its History and Present State*, by Horace St. John (London, 1853); *The Malay Archipelago* by Alfred Russel Wallace (London, 1869); *A History of Sarawak under Its Two White Rajahs, 1839–1908*, by S. Baring-Gould and C. A. Bampfylde (London, 1909). Of these the only work Conrad specified as being in-cluded in his reading—a favorite book he reread often—was Wallace's de-tailed account of his eight years of travel through the islands. Wallace, however, did not go up the Berau River, nor did Brooke.

It was a far-from-famous man, like Brooke in many ways, who Con-rad portrayed in the heroic character of Tom Lingard. In *The Rescue*, the last of the three novels in which Tom Lingard appeared, Conrad re-ferred indirectly both to the original of his character, Captain William Lingard, and to the better-known man with similar sympathies, Sir James Brooke.

"The shallow sea that foams and murmurs on the shores of the thou-sand islands, big and little, which make up the Malay Archipelago has been for centuries the scene of adventurous undertakings. The vices and the qualities of four nations have been displayed in the conquest of that region that even to this day has not been robbed of all the mystery and romance of its past—and the race of men who had fought against the Portuguese, the Spaniards, the Dutch and the English, has not been changed by the unavoidable defeat. They have kept to this day their love of liberty, their fanatical devotion to their chiefs, their blind fidelity in friendship and hate—all their lawful and unlawful instincts. Their country of land and water—for the sea was as much their country as the earth of their islands—has fallen a prey to the western race—the reward of superior strength if not of superior virtue . . .

"Almost in our own day we have seen one of them [Brooke]—a true adventurer in his devotion to his impulse—a man of high mind and of pure heart, lay the foundation of a flourishing state [Sarawak] on the ideas of pity and justice. He recognized chivalrously the claims of the conquered; he was a disinterested adventurer, and the reward of his noble instincts is in the veneration with which a strange and faithful race cherish his memory. . . .

"But there were others," Conrad continued, alluding to William Lin-gard, "obscure adventurers who had not his [Brooke's] advantages of birth, position and intelligence; who had only his sympathy with the people of forests and sea he understood and loved so well. They can not be said to be forgotten since they have not been known at all. They were lost in the common crowd of seamen-traders of the Archipelago."[10]

Captain Lingard was so thoroughly lost "in the common crowd of seamen-traders" that only today, nearly a century later, have the exploits of his life become known to a wider world than Malaysia. Unlike Brooke, Captain Lingard won no fame as an administrator, never having ruled any part of the globe by legal compact. He could not claim to be the discoverer of a river, several Englishmen having preceded him in finding a way up the Berau. Dutch traders looked upon him, an English rival, as a buccaneer, as the Spanish had looked upon Drake. English traders in Singapore considered him a brave, convivial, loud-voiced sea captain who knew of a river they could not find. But the Malays, people of the forests and the sea whom, like Brooke, he "understood and loved so well," knew him as a protector, shielding them against an assortment of marauding pirates: the Illanuns or Lanuns who sailed down from Mindanao in the Philippines; Sulu pirates from the Sulu Archipelago; Sea Dyaks from Brunei; Bajaus or sea gypsies, a homeless tribe of raiders.

The settlement of Berau owed its existence to such pirates. Frank Marryat, a midshipman on the British surveying vessel H.M.S. *Samarang*, went up the river in 1844 and, in *Borneo and the Indian Archipelago*, gave the first English account of the broad, picturesque river studded with islands, and of the village of Berau, built then as he saw it on the left side of the stream, on two small hills—the twin hills of Conrad's *Lord Jim*. Marryat described the life to be found on such rivers as the Berau.

"Borneo abounds with rivers, some of them very fine, running inland for one or two hundred miles. Most of these rivers have been taken possession of and colonised by the various tribes indigenous to the neighbouring isles and continent, to wit, Arabs, Malays, Illanoans, Bughis, the natives of Celebes, Chinese, etc. The reason for this emigration to Borneo is the protection afforded by these rivers; for as all these tribes live entirely by piracy, they here find a safe retreat for themselves and their vessels. How long ago their settlements may have been first made, or what opposition they may have received from the Dyak aborigines, it is impossible to say; but as most of the head men in Borneo claim to be of Arab descent, it may be presumed that many years must have elapsed since the aboriginal tribes of Dyaks and Dusuns were dispossessed of the rivers and driven into the interior. . . .

"These piratical hordes generally infest the high lands upon the shores of these rivers, which are difficult of navigation; and, moreover, from their numerous branches, their resorts are not very easily discovered.

These towns are fortified with stockades, guns of various calibre, and the passage up the river defended by booms or piles of timber which admit of but one narrow passage for their prahus.

"It must be understood that these piratical hordes are not only independent of each other, but often at war, in consequence of their spoliations. Some of their chiefs have taken upon them the titles of princes; and one has assumed, as is well known, that of Sultan of Borneo, another of Sooloo—how far entitled to such a rank it would be difficult to say; but this is certain, that there must be a beginning to every dynasty; and if we trace back far into history, we shall find, both at home and abroad, that most dynasties have had their origin in freebooting on a grand scale."[11]

The earliest freebooters arrived in Berau some centuries before records in the archives of the sultan of Gunung Tabur begin in 1800. The Moslem religion had long been established, and the native, forest Dyaks had long been under the rule of Malay princes emigrating there, when a revolution broke out in 1833. The authority of the seventh sultan of Berau, Sultan Sjech Abedien, was challenged that year and a district over which he reigned, Sambaliung, declared its independence.[12] The revolution was led by Rajah Alam, the son of a Sulu prince and the grandson of the sixth sultan of Berau. Rajah Alam gave protection to Bugis pirates, coming over from Celebes, and the Dutch government, interfering on that account, exiled him to Macassar for three years. When he returned to Berau he succeeded, in 1844, in having the independent state of Sambaliung established, with himself its first sultan. The remainder of the original sultanate of Berau was created as the state of Gunung Tabur, and the two divisions of the district, facing each other across the river and sharing the main settlement of Berau, began the feuding which, with occasional lulls, continued as a civil war for fifty years. Conrad witnessed the power contest with motives, if not methods—here poisoned arrows were shot from stockades, while navies consisted of dugout canoes—in common with the revolutions he had seen in the Caribbean, with the Carlist War in Spain.

Among the various pirate groups who had found shelter in Berau were the Bajaus. A homeless, Moslem people whom the Malays refer to as Ibans, from the Kayan *Ivan* ("wanderer"), their origin is unknown. According to legend the sea gypsies came into existence in this way: Hundreds of years ago the sultan of Johore had a beautiful daughter named Dain Ayesha, or Aïssa (a name carried on by Moslems from Ayesha, the favorite wife of Mohammed), who was courted by the rulers of both Brunei and Sulu. She favored the sultan of Brunei but her father considered the sultan of Sulu a better match and sent her overseas, under strong escort, to him. The sultan of Brunei led his fleet out, captured her, and the defeated Johore escort, unable to return home, cruised about, stealing their wives from coastal villages, plundering, keeping warily on the move. On occasion, and for a time, they settled on uninhabited islands but, an outcast tribe, they lived mainly in their boats. When permitted, they joined other pirate groups in upstream retreats, became head-hunters, took part in war party raids at sea. In *An Outcast of the Islands* Conrad gave the name of Aïssa to the girl loved so passionately by the white outcast, Willems; Aïssa, daughter of a roving tribe, was an outcast too.

Today the Bajaus, known in some areas under the general term of Sea Dyaks, are found throughout Malaysia, the largest number, 280,000, in Sarawak, over 30,000 in North Borneo, a more fluid, uncounted population in Indonesian Borneo. Living peaceful lives on the rivers, fishing, hunting, growing rice, they move about restlessly in their fast canoes. Where they settle for any length of time they build longhouses, each of which may hold fifteen families. Along the Berau River the Bajaus live mainly on the islands where they fish and raise cocoanuts, pursuits they share with Bugis and Sulus.

The Sulus and Lanuns of Berau are descendants of pirates who came from the Philippines. The Lanuns, whom the early Spaniards called *los Illanos de la laguna,* had their base on Mindanao, on a large lagoonlike bay surrounded by impenetrable mangrove swamps. The boldest and most efficient of all pirates, they looked upon theirs as a noble profession and sailed on pillaging excursions that could last up to several years. A Lanun fleet included as many as two hundred galleys and praus, the oar-and-sail ships carried up to 150 men each, slaves manning the oars, and the largest galleys were one hundred tons. They cruised over a wide area—around the coasts of the Philippine Islands, Borneo, Celebes, Sumatra, Java, the Malay Peninsula, through the Moluccas to New Guinea, up the Bay of Bengal as far as Rangoon. Descending on a coast, they attacked a village, sacked and burned it, killing the defenders, carrying away men, women and children as slaves, slaughtered the cattle and ravaged the rice and cocoanut plantations.[13]

The Lanuns raided Berau in an early time and some came back to settle there. A hill in Berau still bears their name—Gunung Ilanun—and in *Almayer's Folly* Conrad referred, through Babalatchi, to those early days of the village: "The old times were best. Even I have sailed with Lanun men, and boarded in the night silent ships with white sails. That was before a white Rajah ruled in Kuching. Then we fought amongst ourselves and were happy. Now when we fight with you we can only die!"[14]

The Lanun men, now called Moros, have never given up piracy. Sixty of their pirate boats were captured off the North Borneo coast by British patrols in 1963. Still following the profession of their ancestors, they attack in fast four-engined power boats. Often operating in syndicates, they hold up small coastal trading ships—ninety-seven such attacks were made in 1961—or large freighters sailing between Singapore and Hong Kong, boarding and raiding a target ship with the aid of accomplices planted in the crew.[15] The northeast wind which blows down the coast of Borneo in August, September and October is called today the "pirate's wind," a term first applied to the steady sail-filling breeze which brought out the early raiders.

Sea battles with such pirates won for Captain Lingard his title of Rajah Laut, "King of the Sea." In the Singapore of Conrad's time he was the real, and legendary, figure of the port.

XVIII

The popular meeting place in Singapore when Conrad knew the city was Charles Emmerson's Tiffin Rooms and it was most probably there, in 1883 after the sinking of the *Palestine*, that he first met the celebrated Captain William Lingard. Lingard was trading to Borneo out of Singapore that year with a ship he owned, the *Johanna Carolina*,[1] a schooner-rigged steamer he had named for his wife. Conrad had other, later, opportunities to know the famous captain: in 1885 when, as an officer of the *Tilkhurst*, he spent a month in Singapore; there again in 1887–88, off and on for nine months, before, during, and after his *Vidar* voyages. Big, talkative, friendly Captain Lingard was not a man you could miss. The Rajah Laut had long been a notable of the town when the English naturalist, F. W. Burbidge, arriving in Singapore at the start of his Borneo travels, told of him in his 1880 journal, *The Gardens of the Sun*.

"A morning in the 'Square' gives one a tolerably clear insight into the enterprise and trade of Singapore. You hear a good deal about the price of sago or gutta and rice, or about the chartering of steamers or sailing craft, or the freight on home or export goods. You are sure to meet two or three captains of trading steamers, Captain Linguard, perhaps, after one of his trips to the Coti river away on the south-east of Borneo, and then you will hear something of the rubber-market, or of the pirates, of whom, perhaps, few men know more than this energetic 'Rajah Laut', or 'Sea King', as he is called by the natives. . . .

"One must of course look in at Emmerson's for tiffin, and a glance at the home papers and telegrams. Tiffin is much like breakfast, only nearly all the dishes are cold."[2]

Emmerson's establishment, opened in the 1860s, continued to operate under the same name after his death in 1883. There ships' officers met to exchange navigation news, learn of fresh hazards along the coasts and streams, secure shipping charts and newspapers, play billiards and talk of the sea. "Colonel" Emmerson's properties included the Clarendon Hotel, "a large compound house, Pavilion for bachelors and a Bar and Billiards," E. J. Robertson recalled in Straits Memories, and "he also had Emmerson's Tiffin Rooms next to Cavanagh Bridge, which was a very popular resort, for Tiffin and Billiards, especially on Saturday afternoons. It was here where you would find the Skippers of the Port enjoying themselves of an afternoon, such well known men as Capt. J. D. Ross, Capt. Lingard, Capts. Martin, Carpenter and others."[3]

Of the early captain-traders of Singapore Captain William Lingard and Captain John Dill Ross were the "best known and most worthy of remembrance," according to an account of that city's history, One Hundred Years of Singapore. The two were outstanding among "the venturesome trading captains of the older times who had done so much to open up the trade of the port," the tribute to the history-makers continues. "Vast profits they often made, but they had to be bold men, and too many of them lost their lives in uncharted seas, were murdered by pirates, and stricken down by fever. Their profits, too, were frequently lost by improvidence and extravagance and by misplaced trust; but they were a fine set of men, who should never be forgotten for the work they did."[4]

The two old friends, Lingard and Ross, arrived in Singapore as young men at nearly the same time, both traded to Borneo for more than thirty years, both fought pirates at sea, both became prosperous through the ships they sailed, both lived until well along in their sixties. Captain Ross died in Singapore on February 15, 1888, "a genial and kindhearted gentleman" who was "one of the oldest and best known residents of S'pore," the Singapore Free Press stated at the time of his death.[5] Captain Lingard died suddenly in England on the last of his visits home shortly before 1897.

Conrad knew the two bold, likable adventurers in Singapore as men in their late years. Captain Ross skippered his Glasgow-built steamer Paknam until two months before his death, trading to Labuan, Brunei and North Borneo[6] in the same months Conrad sailed over part of the same route on the *Vidar*. Captain Lingard was also at times master of the 360-ton *Paknam*,[7] one of the many ships he commanded or owned in more than forty years of seafaring. His daring exploits, and the fortune he was reputed to have made from his gutta-percha trade, were what impressed the English and Dutch writers who commented upon his life. Conrad's liking for him, however, had other causes. Openhanded, warm-hearted and fearless, he was as craggily independent as the other seaman Conrad admired, Dominic Cervoni, and merited "The Rescuer" title Conrad had first chosen for the novel about him. Where European traders in general, Olmeyer prominent among them, lived on dreams of riches-to-come, talked and thought of little else, Lingard's interests were more real and simple. Out of a plain man's sincere devotion, he loved his river and the people on it, appointing himself the guardian of them as James Brooke, in the same years, undertook a similar and more lasting role in Sarawak.

In his trilogy featuring William Lingard as "Tom Lingard," Conrad wrote of his life in reverse, presenting him as an old man in the early novels *Almayer's Folly* and *An Outcast of the Islands*, and as "about thirty-five, erect and supple" in his late novel, *The Rescue*.

William Lingard was about thirty-five when he found his way up the Berau River. There a new state, the Sultanate of Gunung Tabur, had recently been established, the boundaries between Gunung Tabur and Sambaliung fixed by contract with the Netherlands in 1850. Accepted in Gunung Tabur by the *patalolo*, the Bugis word for rajah, Lingard set up a trading post there in 1860.[8] Conrad gave this actual history to Tom Lingard in *An Outcast of the Islands*.

"A good many years ago—prompted by his love of adventure—he, with infinite trouble, had found out and surveyed—for his own benefit only—the entrances to that river, where, he had heard through native report, a new settlement of Malays was forming. No doubt he thought at the time mostly of personal gain; but, received with hearty friendliness by Patalolo, he soon came to like the ruler and the people, offered his counsel and his help, and—knowing nothing of Arcadia—he dreamed of Arcadian happiness for that little corner of the world which he loved to think all his own. His deep-seated and immovable conviction that only he—he, Lingard—knew what was good for them was characteristic of him, and, after all, not so very far wrong. He would make them happy whether or no, he said, and he meant it. His trade brought prosperity to the young state, and the fear of his heavy hand secured its internal peace for many years.

"He looked proudly upon his work. With every passing year he loved more the land, the people, the muddy river that, if he could help it, would carry no other craft but the *Flash* on its unclean and friendly surface. As he slowly warped his vessel up-stream he would scan with knowing looks the riverside clearings, and pronounce solemn judgment upon the prospects of the season's rice-crop. He knew every settler on the banks between the sea and Sambir; he knew their wives, their children; he knew every individual of the multi-coloured groups that, standing on the flimsy platforms of tiny reed dwellings built over the water, waved their hands and shouted shrilly: 'O! Kapal layer! Haï!' while the *Flash* swept slowly through the populated reach, to enter the lonely stretches of sparkling brown water bordered by the dense and silent forest, whose big trees nodded their outspread boughs gently in the faint, warm breeze—as if in sign of tender but melancholy welcome. He loved it all: the landscape of brown golds and brilliant emeralds under the dome of hot sapphire; the whispering big trees; the loquacious nipa-palms that rattled their leaves volubly in the night breeze, as if in haste to tell him all the secrets of the great forest behind them. He loved the heavy scents of blossoms and black earth, that breath of life and death which lingered over his brig in the damp air of tepid and peaceful nights. He loved the narrow and sombre creeks, strangers to sunshine: black, smooth, tortuous—like byways of despair. He liked even the troops of sorrowful-faced monkeys that profaned the quiet spots with capricious gambols and insane gestures of inhuman madness. He loved everything there, animated or inanimated; the very mud of the riverside; the very alligators, enormous and stolid, basking on it with impertinent unconcern. Their size was a source of pride to him."⁹

Lingard was a white-haired mariner when Conrad heard him yarn-spinning in Singapore. His booming voice as he talked of the Berau River and its people in Emmerson's hotel and billiard rooms was a portrait Conrad drew from life.

"His thunderous laughter filled the verandah, rolled over the hotel garden, overflowed into the street, paralyzing for a short moment the noiseless traffic of bare brown feet; and its loud reverberations would even startle the landlord's tame bird—a shameless mynah—into a momentary propriety of behaviour under the nearest chair. In the big billiard-room perspiring men in thin cotton singlets would stop the game, listen, cue in hand, for a while through the open windows, then nod their moist faces at each other sagaciously and whisper: 'The old fellow is talking about his river.'

"His river! The whispers of curious men, the mystery of the thing, were to Lingard a source of never-ending delight."[10]

As Conrad indicated in the same novel—"the common talk of ignorance exaggerated the profits of his queer monopoly"[11]—Captain Lingard's fortune was believed to be far greater than it was, his large house in Berau and the six acres of land around it bringing only two thousand dollars when it was sold in 1904. But if his fortune was misjudged, other features of his life and personality were remarkable enough to come into several chronicles. John Dill Ross, Jr., who grew up in Singapore and knew his father's crony, told of him in two books, the first, *Singapore and the Straits Settlements*, being completed in Singapore in February, 1897, shortly after Lingard's death.

"Another trading captain who made a great deal of money in his time," Ross went on after relating the story of his father's career, "was the late Captain Lingard, the old 'Rajah Laut.' It is related of Lingard, that finding it impossible to obtain payment of a very large sum of money due to him by a certain Bornean Sultan, he landed his crew, stormed the Sultan's palace and captured His Highness, who thereupon found it convenient to pay what he owed. The extreme danger of this new way of collecting old debts need not be pointed out, and it is marvellous that the Sultan and his people never revenged themselves upon Captain Lingard afterwards."[12]

In a second book, published fourteen years later, *Sixty Years: Life and Adventure in the Far East*, Ross wrote of Captain Lingard as "Captain Lugard" and told of one of his visits to England, late in his life. At a curry lunch in London he was described as "positively watering at the mouth, as he muttered that this was his first happy hour since he left Bolongan—which happens to be somewhere in Borneo. . . . Captain Lugard, with a sigh of relief, called for a brandy and soda, and with feverish haste commenced to light his pipe, a small, black, charred and chipped old meerschaum, which he invariably smoked upside down. Puffing clouds of smoke and scattering ashes liberally all over the place, the captain took repeated pulls at his long tumbler of grog, and was completely happy. . . . settling himself and his long brandy and soda on an iron seat, [he] soon had the lads interested in the oft-told story of how he and his sailors stormed the Sultan of Bolongan's palace."[13]

It was the sultan of Bulungan who conferred upon Captain Lingard the title of Rajah Laut, a point of the "oft-told" story Ross neglected to tell. The high honor, "King of the Sea," carried much the same meaning in the Malay world as its equivalent "Admiral of the Ocean" Columbus received from Spain's rulers. Lingard earned it less for his navigation skill, which was impressive, than for his feats as a one-man navy, being named Rajah Laut in recognition of his success in defeating the Sulu pirates who made life and trade unsafe along the Borneo shores.[14]

In an empire-building era, when European powers were ruthless in their exploitation of the Eastern lands they conquered, it was rare for a white man to win such Malay admiration. Lingard's difference in outlook, as a white man in the East, was a difference which marked him early. He was born about 1824 in Lancashire, England. The village of his birth is unknown but is thought to have been in the Clayton le Moors or Altham area where Lingards (a name derived from ling-gatherer) have lived since the sixteenth century, old English stock believed to have originated in Crofts and Keighley, Yorkshire. The first William Lingard to appear in church registers was buried at Altham on June 22, 1635; from Lancashire and Yorkshire bases, the family with its many branches spread widely throughout England and abroad.[15]

In 1843 when nineteen, young Lingard left England to begin a roving life. Somewhat like Conrad, he broke away from the land tradition of a family long settled in the dales, and chose the sea. His name first appears in print in the Singapore newspapers of 1848, where he is listed as a ship's master, a commander of twenty-four sailing ships to the East Indies. His adventures before that time remained a mystery, even in Singapore, and Conrad wrote into Tom Lingard's life aspects taken from that other of Singapore's prominent captain-traders, Captain John Dill Ross.

The fictional Tom Lingard was a "child of generations of fishermen from the coast of Devon," a Brixham trawler boy and afterward a youth in colliers. Leaving England as a young man, he traded in the Pacific with "a rotten old cutter" and arrived in Australia, where he had his first run of luck: "I was a gold digger at one time. Some of us used to come down to Melbourne with our pockets full of money." In Australia he bought the little brig *Flash* (called *Lightning* in *The Rescue*), "the instrument of Lingard's fortune. They came north together—both young —out of an Australian port, and after a very few years there was not a white man in the islands, from Palembang to Ternate, from Ombawa to Palawan, that did not know Captain Tom Lingard and his lucky craft." He traded in New Guinea and in Celebes, in Halmahera, the Philippines, in Palembang, on the west coast of Borneo, Singapore, Macassar, and finally a river on the east coast of Borneo. He was called Rajah Laut by the Malays, had fought Sulu pirates along the Borneo coast, and is an old man on "his river" in *Almayer's Folly* when he leaves for England and is not heard of again.[16]

Some of those details of Tom Lingard's life—the "rotten old cutter," the gold mining near Melbourne, the beautiful brig he bought in Australia and sailed to Singapore—were true of Captain Ross.[17] The son of a sea captain, Captain Ross was born in Batavia about 1820 and educated in Australia. Following a voyage to Holland and back in a Dutch East Indiaman, he served as the young assistant and secretary to his Scotch relative, Captain J. Clunies Ross, owner of the Cocos Islands. Leaving those islands, young Ross bought a rejected revenue cutter, the *Caroline*, in Batavia and sailed to Australia to become a gold miner. In Melbourne he acquired the *Wild Irish Girl*, a beautiful brig he sailed to Singapore, arriving there in the early 1850s. Between 1854 and 1888 he owned and traded out of Singapore with the sailing ships *Samson* and *Lizzie Webber*, and the steamships *Cleator* and *Paknam*. During one voyage of the *Lizzie Webber* he fought an eight-hour running battle with pirates, an encounter followed by another when raiders attempted to board the *Cleator*, grounded on a reef near Celebes. A "genial sailor" and "maritime celebrity" in Singapore, F. W. Burbidge described him as the owner in the late 1870s of the "mail steamer *Cleator* which runs between Singapore, Labuan, and Brunei, on the northwest Borneo coast. Captain Ross is well acquainted with the principal places in the whole Malayan Archipelago; and few residents have an equal colloquial knowledge of their languages. He has been attacked by pirates more than once in the old days, and is quite a nautical authority in every way."[18]

Ross and Lingard traded to different sections of Borneo, Ross centering his business in the northwestern part and the island off that coast, Labuan. His partner in the Labuan Trading Company, established at Sandakan in 1872, was a Singapore merchant, Carl Schomburg, a bay near Sandakan bearing his name for a time. It was presumably this trader's name Conrad adopted for the German hotelkeeper, Schomberg, in *Victory*, fashioning Schomberg's hotel and billiard rooms upon Emmerson's in Singapore. Labuan was a coal-rich anchorage and for some years was expected to have a brilliant future, to become one day a second Singapore; but the coal petered out, dreams of riches collapsed, and the jungle reclaimed the bypassed island—even as Heyst's island in *Victory* had much the same fate, the history of Labuan perhaps supplying Conrad with some of the background for his story.

Captain Lingard, taking no part in promotion schemes, was a seaman first and last, an independent trader with his own small trading posts in Berau, Bulungan and Macassar.[19] Holding an attitude similar to Conrad's, he loved sailing ships and despised steamers, criticizing his friend Ross for having "gone in for a damn steamer instead of the good old sailing-ships which made his money." Among the ships Lingard owned,[20] some wholly and some partially, were the 93-ton brig *Nina*, the 134-ton schooner *Coeran*, the 36-ton sailing ship *Fanny*, the 324-ton three-masted barque *West Indian*, the schooner-rigged steamer *Johanna Carolina*. He also at times commanded, and may have had a temporary financial interest in, the barque *Pulo Laut*[21] and the S.S. *Paknam*.

The first ship in which Singapore registers show he had any owner's interest was the *Nina*, wrecked on a reef in the same area as Tom Lingard's *Flash*. Lingard was master of the *Nina* when, registered in Singapore on February 18, 1861, she was owned by the Singapore merchant Francis James Secretan. Two years before that time Secretan had drawn up a will, dated September 20, 1859, in which he appointed two friends as executors, William Lingard and James Weir, Weir being a partner in the Singapore mercantile house of William Spottiswoode & Co. For four months after Secretan's death in 1864 Captain Lingard was in effect the owner of the *Nina* and when she was sold to Koh Eng Chuan and Dr. Wee Chy Seng—who increased the ship's size to 103 tons—he continued to be master of her off and on until she was wrecked in 1874 on the island of Lingga, south of Singapore.[22] It was partly with the *Nina* that Lingard developed the trading station he established at Berau.

In 1862, at thirty-eight, he was married, in Singapore, to Johanna Carolina Olmeyer, a niece or cousin of Charles Olmeyer—Conrad's Almayer. Having no children, his wife sailed with him on some of his voyages. Pirates were frequently met in the Celebes Sea—the Rajah Laut had guns mounted on his ships for just such encounters—and one well-remembered story in Berau concerns a day, November 25, 1875, when Captain Lingard's *West Indian*, with his wife on board, was attacked at the anchorage off the mouth of the Berau River by a pirate fleet.[23] They had watched the Rajah Laut go ashore in his steam launch and at 3 A.M. swarmed down on the ship. On board were the first and second mates, Mr. Avery and Joshua Lingard, the twenty-three-year-old nephew of the Rajah Laut who had come out from England the year before, two or three Chinese and about twenty lascars. For two hours the unequal fight went on, the officers firing with rifles and the Chinese wielding choppers, bottles, and throwing boiling water down on the raiders —Mrs. Lingard shot one in the act of jamming the rudder. At 8 A.M. the pirates renewed their attack. The Rajah Laut, fifty-one that year, was returning to his ship in the launch when he ran into the battle; opening fire on the nearest prau, he caused panic to spread through the fleet, and the *West Indian*, her sails already loosed, got away. Reporting the attack to Dutch authorities in Macassar, Captain Lingard took the occasion to praise the bravery of his officers.

This story had a strong appeal for the people of Berau, but neither they nor the historians in Singapore mentioned an incident which had brought Captain Lingard into international notice eight years earlier. It occurred in the same waters as the celebrated pirate attack and Conrad's *The Rescue* very likely had its genesis in this rescue of Lingard's.

The ship on this occasion was Lingard's schooner *Coeran* which, named for the Coeran River, a tributary of the Pantai and a boundary of Sambaliung, he had had built in Singapore in 1864, owning it at first in equal partnership with Captain Thomas Morgan Craig.[24] This Singapore pilot (sent to Aden in 1880 to take temporary charge of the *Jeddah*) Conrad referred to in Tom Lingard's words in *An Outcast of the Islands:* "I spoke to Craig in Palembang. He is getting on in years, and wanted a manager or partner. . . . Craig is an old crony of mine. Been shipmates in the forties."[25]

In 1866 Lingard bought out Captain Craig's share of the *Coeran* and traded about the East Indies, frequently to Java and the island of Lombok where his cargo was upon occasion rice and pigs. At times Captain F. O. Hanish was in command of the ship, Lingard, however, being on board.[26] In May, 1867, when he was forty-three, the Rajah Laut was sailing the *Coeran* along the east coast of Borneo when he came upon the Dutch steamship *Reteh*, run ashore and stuck fast. Without his "unwearying assistance" the steamer would have been lost, according to communications sent by Netherlands East Indies authorities to the Colonial Minister in The Hague. King William III of the Netherlands, in appreciation of Lingard's rescue of a ship which presumably had important personages on board, conferred a knighthood upon him. By a royal decree issued on February 6, 1869, Lingard, described as "a merchant living at Gunung Tabur," was made an Officer of the Order of the Netherlands Lion (*Officier in de Orde van de Nederlandsche Leeuw*).[27] The honor, granted for civil merit and founded in 1818 by William I of Holland, was rarely bestowed upon a foreigner. Lingard never wore any title before his name, seeming to be content with Rajah Laut, and the details of the rescue did not appear in published records. Assisting in refloating a ship, in itself, would not have merited a knighthood and it is quite possible that the true reason was what Conrad gave in *The Rescue*—Lingard securing the release of prominent European passengers on the ship who were held as hostages by piratical Malays of the coast. That William Lingard, the great talker and teller-of-tales, failed to circulate news of his Dutch knighthood in Singapore would have appealed to Conrad, who, from similar modesty, refused a British knighthood offered him in 1924 in recognition of his achievements as an author. It was long after Lingard's death, and Conrad's, that the Rajah Laut's knighthood was mentioned in a general publication—in Holland, not in Singapore or England—when G. Knijpenga wrote of him in a series of articles, "Archipelago Trade in the Past," appearing in the Amsterdam K.P.M. periodical *de Uitlaat* of December, 1954, and January, 1955. There Mr. Knijpenga described Lingard as his reputation had sifted down through Dutch records.

"There sprang up a settlement on the Brow river established by a certain Lingard, an Englishman, whom his Asiatic and Eastern competitors called 'Rajah Laut' and who, long afterwards, was mentioned as a pirate. He called at various stations, making trade arrangements with the chiefs. The products he secured from them he sold elsewhere, calling regularly at Singapore. What he loaded at Singapore he delivered at islets and small coastal settlements. He was too much of an adventurer to adhere strictly to import regulations, drawing the lines himself between what was lawful or unlawful. His skilled seamanship enabled him, in spite of high seas, to put his schooner (a wrecked ship one could still see in the Brow river many years later) into the estuaries of the big rivers, visiting places out of the reach of others. Lingard had his schooner armed and, if necessary, opened fire and made short work of his rivals. But he was not a sneak thief and his principles of right and wrong could have been worse. He was no stranger to good works, though in a territory without government he had no scruples.

"Circumstances made him a buccaneer but as soon as the Dutch government made itself felt in Brow Lingard conducted himself as an orderly businessman. He is mentioned, though not by name, in the Colonial Report of 1875 as an Englishman who traded at Gunung Tabur, an owner of ships."

Lingard had been trading to Gunung Tabur for ten years when, in 1870, he made a trip to England and placed his relative by marriage, Charles Olmeyer, in charge of his Berau trading station. Olmeyer was an unmarried young man then of twenty-two; he was to spend the remaining years of his life in the upriver Malay village, with the discontent Conrad wrote into *Almayer's Folly*.

In 1875 Captain Lingard had two of his nephews, Joshua and James Lingard,[28] come out from England to join him—two Lancashire brothers Conrad was to know well. They made the voyage together as apprentices on a sailing ship; Joshua was twenty-two and James thirteen. James became a trader much like Olmeyer but Joshua went on to become a master mariner, securing his mate's certificate in Singapore on August 15, 1876, and his master's certificate on September 9, 1886.[29]

In the year his nephews joined him, 1875, the Rajah Laut was not as affluent as others thought him to be. He had lost the *Nina*, run ashore and wrecked; he had lost another, unnamed ship—Berau residents believed it to have been the one which brought Olmeyer to the village— the wreck, rotting in the mud on the bank of the river, still there as late as 1896; he no longer had the *Fanny;* he had had to sell the *Coeran* —to the Dutch master mariner, Edward Ludwig Hernsheim; and for two months of 1875 he lost ownership of his mortgaged *West Indian*.[30] The barque *West Indian*, Lingard's largest sailing ship, was the one of all best remembered in Berau. The three-master, carrying the half figure of a woman as her figurehead, had been built in 1854 in England, at Pallion in Durham, and was seventeen years old when Lingard bought her from two Chinese owners in Singapore on April 4, 1871. He owned and sailed the *West Indian* for nine years, selling the ship in 1880, two years before she was broken up in Cochin China in January, 1882.[31] His special attachment for this armed, pirate-fighting vessel, which took him up Borneo streams no others could navigate, may have been partly due to the fact that she was built in England. For Lingard's feelings for England repeatedly took him home—in 1870, 1877, 1880, and his final visit in the 1890s when he died there.

It was his 1870 trip to England which caused him to settle Olmeyer in Berau, in charge of the Lingard & Co. post. Ten years later, at the time of his 1880 voyage home, he transferred his nephew James Lingard from Bulungan, where the teen-age boy had spent five years learning the trading business, to Berau. Conrad, knowing Olmeyer and Jim Lingard in the village where the Rajah Laut had placed them, was to use features of the two men in *Almayer's Folly* and *Lord Jim* and also, through their lives in that village, to envisage the fate in store for white men in the "lands of brown nations, where a stealthy Nemesis lies in wait, pursues, overtakes so many of the conquering race."[32]

One who was not overtaken was the Rajah Laut. Drawing the lines himself between what was lawful or lawless—like Dominic Cervoni— he yet lacked the conqueror's drive, his small enterprise falling apart when he ceased to conduct it. If "the fear of his heavy hand" brought internal peace to the district, the great need for that peace, in the warring sultanates of Gunung Tabur, Sambaliung and adjacent Bulungan, can be judged by the chronicle of local events in the archives of the sultan of Gunung Tabur. Written in its present form by a Dutch administrator about 1920, from Malayan records begun in the eighteenth century, the chronicle is weighted by its Dutch compiler, credit for the frequent peacemaking being assigned, not to the Englishman Lingard, but to

Netherlands officials at Samarinda. Of the local feuding and pirate menace during the years when Captain Lingard was the dominant figure
on Borneo's east coast the history gives a brief and pregnant account.

"1866: The quarrel between Bulungan and Gunung Tabur, which had
lasted several years, was settled by the Assistant Resident of Samarinda.

"1871: On the East Coast of Borneo the number of pirates increased,
the situation becoming worse day by day because the Sultan of Berau,
lacking sufficient authority, dealt with the matter at his pleasure. Eventually the [Dutch] government sent the steamship *Suriname* but with
little result, since the number of pirates, who came from the Sulu
Archipelago, was enormous.

"1872: The danger of pirates decreased, through military action, and
because Dutch ships began to frequent these regions. The Sultan of
Gunung Tabur plucked up his courage, taking steps against the criminal
wrong-doers. The quarrel between Gunung Tabur and Sambaliung
was settled by the Assistant Resident of Samarinda.

"1873: The Sultan of Bulungan died and was succeeded by the legitimate heir.

"1874: In April of this year several claimants to the throne in Bulungan nearly caused a civil war but the Assistant Resident of Samarinda,
G. G. Villeneuve, settled things in time. Datu Maulana was sworn in
as sultan in April, 1875 by the Governor-General.

"1876: The Sultan of Gunung Tabur died in October and was succeeded by his son.

"1877: Division of the properties of the late Sultan of Gunung Tabur
caused a bitter quarrel between the Sultan of Gunung Tabur and the
Sultan of Sambaliung. Each received an equal share.

"1878: A new political contract was made between the [Dutch] government, Gunung Tabur, and Sambaliung. A new, fierce quarrel broke
out between Gunung Tabur and Sambaliung, the two sides firing at
each other with guns from behind stockades. A new settlement was
arranged by the Assistant Resident of Samarinda, W. A. Seitz, both sultans required to apologize.

"1881: The Sultan of Sambaliung died, succeeded by the legitimate
heir.

"1882: The Sultan of Gunung Tabur died in October. His son being
too young to rule, a regent was appointed, Hadji Adji Kuning, a first
cousin of the late sultan.

"1883: Coal is being prospected by the [Dutch] government in Sambaliung, Gunung Tabur, and the adjoining district of Kutai."33

In that year of 1883 Captain Lingard's influence in the often-troubled state of Berau was nearing its end. Lingard & Co. still had its jetty there, Lingard's house was there, but the principal trading ship, the *Vidar*, was Arab-owned. Coal in time was to change the life of the village, partially through the attention drawn to the district by a Dutch mining engineer, J. A. Hooze, who, from his base in Berau, prospected for coal from January, 1882, to April, 1883. In his thorough and encouraging report, "Onderzoek naar kolen in de Berausche landen," published in Holland in 1886, Hooze told of Olmeyer, "the Dutch agent of the firm of Linggard & Co.," who for several years had been exploring, searching out the riches of the area.

Like Raleigh, Olmeyer was bewitched by the El Dorado dream, and in this lay some of the appeal he had for Conrad. But the reward of all such quests had also been his to an extreme degree, the "loneliness impenetrable and transparent, elusive and everlasting," the "indestructible loneliness that surrounds, envelops, clothes every human soul." Overtaken by this "stealthy Nemesis" were the white men in the jungle Conrad came to know.

XIX

Four Europeans lived in Berau when Conrad knew the village, an Englishman, a Russian, and two Dutchmen; all came into his novels. Three had arrived as young men in that wild climate of never-ending summer; two died there and two, leaving in the last weeks of fatal illness, died in the hospital at Surabaya, Java. The jungle casts an immobilizing spell upon those who stay, as these four stayed, held trancelike by the brutal heat and numbing humidity, by the corroding stillness of the forest in which hope seeps away as rapidly as time. Though wanderers, mainly, are drawn to such faraway river villages as Berau, final outposts with no beyond, the lives of these four originally purposeful men were shaped by the dream-inducing gift the jungle offers with such chilling liberality, isolation. Fed by the awesome immensity of the forest and the drowsy visual monotone of green, a state just within waking is held within waking by the jungle's other gift, expectancy. In *The Sea and the Jungle* H. M. Tomlinson quotes an Englishman living in an equatorial wilderness similar to Berau and in his blurted-out words the mesmerizing force of the jungle comes through.

"I'm half afraid of it . . . not afraid of anything I can see . . . I don't know. There's something damn strange about it. Something you can never find out. It's something that's been here since the beginning, and it's too big and strong for us. It waits its time. I can feel it now. Look at those palm trees outside. Don't they look as if they're waiting? What are they waiting for? You get that feeling here in the afternoon when you can't get air, and the rain clouds are banking up around the woods, and nothing moves."

The jungle in fact is never still, but sounds are cushioned by the dense canopy of leaves and tangled creepers, by the soft, water-heavy atmosphere, by the ground layered with centuries of vegetable decay, a mattress of mold spread over the earth. Decay keeps pace with the hurry of growth, the violent and soundless duel fostering the words so often used, "gloom" and "silence." The jungle's sounds, wrote the British naturalist Henry W. Bates, whose work Darwin so highly praised, "are of that pensive or mysterious character which intensifies the feeling of solitude."

Berau had this sense of solitude, an end-of-the-road air, in 1887—for the Europeans, not for the native people living there. What the village, and the white men harbored in it, were like when Conrad knew them was told to Mr. Haverschmidt by old-time Malay and Chinese residents who, knowing nothing of Conrad or his books, talked out of memories of their home place. Throughout 1951 and 1952 Mr. Haverschmidt drew out the rajahs and villagers he had known for years, those who remembered the old days or to whom stories had been handed down. Many contributed to this saga of Berau: the sultan of Sambaliung, who in his youth had known Olmeyer and the other three white men well; the *ratu* of Gunung Tabur, widow of Sultan Achmad; Anang Dachlan, who settled in Berau in 1896; Adji Bagian, heir to the throne of Sambaliung who, married to a Dyak girl and choosing to live with the Dyaks in the interior, refused in 1919 to become its sultan; Akay, an aged Chinese whose mother knew Captain William Lingard when he established the trading campong called "Patusan" at the base of the split hills; Pangeran Prodjo, an elderly Malay nobleman who had known Olmeyer and whose parents had told him stories of Captain Lingard's exploits; Kang Si Gok, an eighty-three-year-old Chinese who, coming to Berau as a crew member of the *Vidar* in 1888—the year Conrad gave up his berth as chief mate of that steamer—lived with the Chinese trader Po Eng Seng and through that contact came to know intimately the four Europeans in the course of thirty-three years, a span ending in 1921 when the last one died. From the accumulated memories of the villagers, and from Malay and Dutch records held in Borneo and

Holland, the life of Berau can be taken back in time to what it was when Conrad knew it at twenty-nine.

The settlement then had a single street, a long footpath running the length of the village parallel to the river, the route where Olmeyer proposed to ride his pony. Between the footpath—the jungle crowded up to it, an encroaching wall—and the swirling Segah branch of the river was the straggling village, palm-leaf huts built on rafts along the muddy banks. The two large houses erected by William Lingard and Charles Olmeyer rose conspicuously from the others. Built in the native style, palm-thatched, resting six feet above ground on high stilts and with wide verandas overlooking the river, they had once been imposing structures. In 1887 Olmeyer's especially was falling into decay.

Everything that Europeans had sought to implant here in the voluptuous wilderness gave the same appearance of decay. Olmeyer's "Folly," as his very spacious, six-year-old collapsing house was known to traders, bleakly illustrated despair. Dejection showed in the rickety jetty projecting into the river from it, the Lingard & Co. wharf where the *Vidar* loaded cargo. The trade of Berau was then dominated by the Arab trading station, on the Kelai reach where Lingard's original Patusan had been. The Arab-owned *Vidar* had been Berau's trading ship since 1882 and her owner's son, Syed Abdulla, had built a large house on the *tandjung* or point where the Segah and Kelai rivers joined. Another Arab trader, Syed Alwee, had found his way up the river, competing with Abdulla, and the old Rajah Laut's monopoly was broken.

The "Folly," begun in a grand dream, was in the backwash of village change. The dolefulness of its state of disrepair was made more drear by its surroundings. A coal dump flanked it on one side and on the other ran a broad and turbid creek in which lay a big schooner of Captain Lingard's rotting in the mud, a wreck Olmeyer used as a storehouse. The crumbling unnamed vessel that had "vanished from the seas forever" had met an end like the *Nina*, wrecked off the island of Lingga in 1874; Lingard had been more fortunate with his other known sailing ships, selling the *Fanny* in 1873, the *Coeran* in 1874, the *West Indian* in 1880.[1]

One of the four Europeans, a heavy-drinking old Russian with white hair and an enormous beard, known to the village as a sea captain, slept on the wreck but took his meals with Olmeyer.[2] Conrad based two characters upon him, in *An Outcast of the Islands* and *The Rescue*, also recalling the rotting craft in those two novels.

In *An Outcast of the Islands* the actual Russian of Berau is "a Roumanian, half naturalist, half orchid-hunter for commercial purposes, who used to declare to everybody, in the first five minutes of acquaintance, his intention of writing a scientific book about tropical countries. On his way to the interior he had quartered himself upon Almayer. He was a man of some education, but he drank his gin neat, or only, at most, would squeeze the juice of half a small lime into the raw spirit. He said it was good for his health, and, with that medicine before him, he would describe to the surprised Almayer the wonders of European capitals; while Almayer, in exchange, bored him by expounding, with gusto, his unfavourable opinions of Sambir's social and political life. They talked far into the night, across the deal table on the verandah, while, between them, clear-winged, small, and flabby insects, dissatisfied with moonlight, streamed in and perished in thousands round the smoky light of the evil-smelling lamp."[3]

The orchid-hunter, Conrad said in the novel, died "a few months afterwards, and his was the second white man's grave in Sambir." The Russian original of the character died in Berau, a very old man, shortly before 1900; his was the second white man's grave in the cemetery at Gunung Tabur. The marker on his grave disappeared with time and no one in the village could remember his name.[4]

In The Rescue the hardy, aged Russian captain appears as the "powerful skeleton," the old, gaunt Norwegian, Captain H. C. Jörgenson, once master of the barque Wild Rose, who lived on the battered, decrepit wreck of the Emma, a schooner Tom Lingard had had towed up the creek and run aground, using it as a storehouse for his ammunition and guns. "There had been at that time a great rise of waters, which retiring soon after left the old craft cradled in the mud, with her bows grounded high between the trunks of two big trees, and leaning over a little as though after a hard life she had settled wearily to an everlasting rest."[5]

The decaying hulk, a landmark in Berau for some ten years after Conrad last saw the river, became a prau in An Outcast of the Islands, the mysteriously acquired vessel of the Malay vagabond Babalatchi. "The prau hauled up on the mud-bank, at the junction of the two branches of the Pantai, rotted in the rain, warped in the sun, fell to pieces and gradually vanished into the smoke of household fires of the settlement. Only a forgotten plank and a rib or two, sticking neglected in the shiny ooze for a long time, served to remind Babalatchi during many months that he was a stranger in the land."[6]

The first of the four Europeans to arrive in Berau, and to live there for thirty years, was Charles Olmeyer. A tall, heavy man of thirty-nine when Conrad knew him, dark-complexioned and with a big black mustache, his prominent traits—moroseness, frustration, a fondness for pretentious display—were reproduced in Conrad's fictional Almayer. In essence the life of Almayer in *Almayer's Folly* and *An Outcast of the Islands* bore a strong resemblance to that of the real Olmeyer.

Olmeyer was born in Surabaya, Java, in 1848, his Dutch ancestors having settled in Java in the eighteenth century. The family vault in the Peneleh cemetery at Surabaya, where Olmeyer is buried, carries the name of his father, Carel Olmeyer; a marble slab, with a carved Dutch inscription, states that Carel Olmeyer was born in Grissee, a town northwest of Surabaya, on October 16, 1799, and died in Surabaya on November 16, 1877. The spelling of the family name, variously given as Olmeijer and Ohlmeijer, appears as Olmeyer on the Peneleh vault, as it does on the Berau headstone over the graves of Olmeyer's sons.

Charles Olmeyer was apparently one of a large and long-lived family, his father living to be seventy-eight and a sister, Mrs. Frederika Coenraad, being eighty-three at the time of her death on February 25, 1941. Five of Olmeyer's brothers and sisters were buried in the Peneleh cemetery.

In 1862, when Captain William Lingard married into the Olmeyer family, young Charles was a boy of fourteen. A few years later he went to work for the Rajah Laut, probably at first in Macassar, in Lingard's trading post there. In 1870, when he was twenty-two, Lingard placed him in charge of his station at Berau. In 1874, at twenty-six, Olmeyer married an Eurasian girl, Johanna Marie Cornelia van Lieshout, in Manado or Gorontalo, Celebes. Her father was a Dutch officer, her mother a Manadonese.[7] Mrs. Olmeyer was tall and thin, as villagers remembered her, with a fair complexion and longish face, who was seventeen at the time of her marriage. The Olmeyers in their eighteen years of marriage had eleven children, five sons and six daughters, born between 1874 and 1892. Mrs. Olmeyer died at thirty-five in Berau, in December, 1892, a few days after the birth of her eleventh child, Wilhelmina, and was buried in the Gunung Tabur cemetery beside her two infant sons.

Few of the Olmeyer children lived to adulthood but three who did were the second child, William Charles Carel (known as W.C.C. or Willy); the third child, Johanna Elizabeth, who became Mrs. Andrew Gray; the eleventh child, Wilhelmina, who died on December 3, 1921, at Sukabumi, West Java, at twenty-nine. Wilhelmina, educated at a convent in Surabaya, married twice: at twenty, to Coenraad Louis Arnold Almerood, who died five months after their marriage in 1912; at twenty-four, to Anthony Hendrik Spaan, the Dutch trade controller in Berau in 1892 and, at the time of his marriage in 1916 to Wilhelmina, the Assistant Resident in Samarinda.

Willy, born in 1875 and educated in Java, spent his life in Borneo and traded in the manner of his father. One rare distinction came to him early. Because of the great respect the forest Dyaks had for his father, Willy was adopted as a brother by the young Dyak Queen Adji Dajang and given a Dyak name.[8] In the mid-1890s Willy married a Javanese girl in Gunung Tabur named Nina[9] and for many years lived in Samarinda and the Kutai district around it. Still living there in 1933, at fifty-eight, he was described in a Dutch Forestry Department report of that year as a trader in local products who had "traveled the country in all directions as a concession hunter." One he obtained, a timber concession on the Berau River, Willy sold to an American firm, the Telok Seliman Company, for $16,000. "Nothing of these concessions remains today," the August 29, 1933, report continues, "nor is there anything left to remind us of the Olmeyer family in Berau."

Living as prosperous and as long a life as Willy was Olmeyer's eldest daughter, Johanna, born in Berau in 1876. Unlike her five sisters, who were educated in a convent in Surabaya, she was brought up as a Protestant in Macassar. With her husband Andrew Gray, a Scotsman, she lived the largest part of her life and raised her family in Samarinda, where the Grays' business enterprises included a lumber mill, lemonade works and ice factory. In their late years the Grays retired to Malang, Java, where Mrs. Gray lived well into her sixties.[10]

Education and careers for his children, even wealth to leave them, were thoughts very much on Olmeyer's mind when Conrad knew him in Berau. He then had only four children, two boys and two girls; two sons had died, infants of fourteen months and four-and-a-half months. The older children, Willy, twelve, and Johanna, eleven, were away at school. At home in Berau were a small son and a daughter of five, the little girl who became the five-year-old daughter of Almayer in *An Outcast of the Islands*—with "long black hair, that framed her olive face, in which the big black eyes looked out in childish solemnity"[11]—and the teen-age Nina of *Almayer's Folly*. Early Spanish and Portuguese conquerors of the Malay Archipelago left behind words adopted into Malay, their derivation forgotten as the centuries passed. One such word was *niña*, Spanish for "little girl," which became so thoroughly absorbed into Malayan that "quite often a girl is called 'Nina' instead of her name," wrote A. K. Suki of Johore Bahru in 1951.[12] It was undoubtedly from hearing Olmeyer use "Nina" in this way for the little girl at home in Berau that Conrad, remembering, used it as the name of the daughter his

Almayer so much adored. In *Almayer's Folly* Conrad advanced the child's age to sixteen, though in Almayer's frequent phrases—"Good-night, little girl," "my dear little girl"[13]—seemed to be hearing Olmeyer's use of "Nina."

Olmeyer had been living in Berau for seventeen years when Conrad knew him. Much of his life, before and after 1887, he spent searching for gold. In 1877, according to J. A. Hooze, Olmeyer went inland from Berau as a prospector ("his principal, Linggard, being in England") and, still a victim of gold fever, applied for his last prospector's permit on December 1, 1890. His final application, made when he was forty-two, was found in 1960 in the National Archives of Java. It "is addressed to the Governor General of the Netherlands Indies," wrote Professor G. J. Resink in the December, 1960, issue of Djakarta's *Medan Ilmu Pengetahuan*, "and requests a permit to enter into contracts with the Sultan of Sambaliung and/or his subjects for the purpose of prospecting for gold and other minerals." Conrad presented a realistic portrait when he wrote in *Almayer's Folly:* "Almayer's thoughts were often busy with gold, gold he had failed to secure; gold the others had secured—dishonestly, of course—or gold he meant to secure yet." Charles Olmeyer still had not found his elusive prize when he died in 1900.

Famous as a hunter, with numerous guns in racks along the walls of the "Folly," Olmeyer sold guns, smuggled into the country in defiance of Dutch regulations, to the Dyaks of the interior—muzzle-loaders, said Adji Bagian,[14] still in the possession of Dyaks today. Olmeyer possibly stored the illegal weapons and ammunition on the wrecked ship lying in the creek, inspiring Conrad to transfer that activity to Tom Lingard in *The Rescue*. The *Vidar* had a part in the gunrunning, reminiscent of Conrad's earlier *Tremolino* and *Saint-Antoine* experiences, and led to the favored treatment the ship was still receiving in Berau in 1892, by which time Dutch steamers had entered competition for its trade. An officer of the Dutch K.P.M. steamer *Putte*, calling at Berau for a two-day stay, July 24–26, 1892, referred in his report to the usual products shipped by the picul (136 lb.) from the upriver port and to the *Vidar's* illicit trade:

"The most important exporter is the Bugis, Captain Daing, who during the second call of the *Putte* shipped to Singapore:

> 124 picul gutta-percha @ f.3,50
> 1012 picul rattan @ f.1,80

"but nothing further after that, probably because the *Vidar* came back on schedule and the master (also part-owner) Captain Craig was an old acquaintance of his.

"During the 4 trips which the *Vidar* has made since, the outward cargo must have been insignificant; 600 picul is mentioned as a maximum.

"The import of guns and powder by the *Vidar,* as the reason for the preference, was a matter of investigation but my efforts drew a blank; it is a fact that many natives have firearms but one cannot call it smuggling since no one inspects unloaded cargo or what incoming ships carry. Nevertheless, it is forbidden to export arms from Singapore, or to import them into the Netherlands Indies."[15]

That the Dutch should seek the trade of Berau, much less acquire political control there, had not been foreseen by Olmeyer. As a partner in the English firm of Lingard & Co. he had hoped for British control of Berau when Borneo's Dutch-British frontiers were finally drawn and it was in anticipation of having his own magnificent home become British headquarters in the district that, in 1881 when a provisional settlement was under way of the centuries-old contest between the two powers, he had started to build the "Folly." But when the boundaries of the British North Borneo Company were permanently settled in London in 1882—Britain making a protectorate of the territory in 1888—the Berau River fell into the Dutch, not the British, zone. Primarily because of this miscalculation of events Olmeyer's elaborate house received its name of the "Folly." Conrad wove much of this history into *Almayer's Folly*.

"The stir made in the whole island by the establishment of the British Borneo Company affected even the sluggish flow of the Pantai life. Great changes were expected; annexation was talked of; the Arabs grew civil. Almayer began building his new house for the use of the future engineers, agents, or settlers of the new Company. He spent every available guilder on it with a confiding heart. . . .

"The deliberations conducted in London have a far-reaching importance, and so the decision issued from the fog-veiled offices of the Borneo Company darkened for Almayer the brilliant sunshine of the Tropics, and added another drop of bitterness to the cup of his disenchantments. The claim to that part of the East Coast was abandoned, leaving the Pantai River under the nominal power of Holland. The slaves were hurried out of sight into the forest and jungle, and the flags were run up to tall poles in the Rajah's compound in expectation of a visit from Dutch man-of-war boats."[16]

After the visit of the Dutch navy men "the half-finished house built for the reception of Englishmen received on that joyous night the name of "Almayer's Folly" by the unanimous vote of the lighthearted seamen."[17]

Slaves, Malays who had been captured or bought—a practice continued up to and after 1896—existed in Berau when Conrad was there. In 1896 the sultans of Gunung Tabur and Sambaliung joined in an arrangement to register slaves and to attempt a decrease in the number of them. Theoretically slavery had been outlawed in 1878 when the Dutch Resident of East Borneo, Jacobus Jozephus Meijer, persuaded the sultans of the two states to sign a contract with the Dutch government by which they agreed: that the import and export of slaves and the kidnaping of slaves was forbidden; that no torturing or mutilating of criminals would be allowed, no punishment with death or banishment permitted without the sanction of the Dutch Resident; that the sultans would fight pirates found on the sea, beaches or the river; that all ships in distress along the coast or on the river would be given assistance; that all trade-cramping practices would be abolished; that all traders who wished to trade in the two states would be protected.[18]

In regard to Berau's slavery and pirates Conrad gave a true picture of the village in his fiction. He also told, authentically, of Olmeyer's gunrunning, his personality, and his house. Mrs. Olmeyer, however—Conrad used her name of Johanna for the wife of Willems in *An Outcast of the Islands*—was not the aged, "witch-like" savage he created, for the dramatic purposes of the story, as Almayer's wife. She was Conrad's own age, nearing thirty. Old she very likely did appear, in the tropics where women age early and lives are short—in Indonesia in 1953 40 per cent of the population were under fifteen—but she was not, as in Conrad's story, a captive taken by Lingard from a pirate prau.

When she died, five years after Conrad's last contact with Berau, Olmeyer was left with a large family to raise, the oldest seventeen, the youngest a newborn baby. His own life was to end eight years later. During his later years he gave up trading and lived on his money, having made a fortune in rubber—a quickly-come fortune that was also quickly gone. Most of his funds, Kang Si Gok recalled, were sent to Java for the care and education of his children. In the last year of his life, an ill and impoverished man, he left Berau for his son Willy's home in Samarinda; following an operation for cancer, he died in the Surabaya hospital on September 2, 1900. He was then fifty-two, presumably unaware, as was his remote Borneo village, that *Almayer's Folly* had been published five years before.

The third European in Berau, like the Russian captain, came under Olmeyer's wing. He was a young Dutchman named Carel De Veer—the village knew him as Sinjo ("young gentleman") Carel—who arrived one day as the assistant of a German trader. The German departed, leaving his assistant behind, and the penniless De Veer, an alcoholic with a defective hand, quartered himself upon Olmeyer, doing odd jobs for him.[19] Later he moved into a small *warong* with a native wife, who, the ratu of Gunung Tabur remembered, earned money by selling cakes. Conrad wrote of him as Peter Willems in *An Outcast of the Islands* and in the Author's Note of that novel recalled his impressions of the abject Dutchman in Berau.

"The man who suggested Willems to me was not particularly interesting in himself. My interest was aroused by his dependent position, his strange, dubious status of a mistrusted, disliked, worn-out European living on the reluctant toleration of that Settlement hidden in the heart of the forest-land, up that sombre stream which our ship was the only white men's ship to visit. With his hollow, clean-shaved cheeks, a heavy grey moustache and eyes without any expression whatever, clad always in a spotless sleeping suit much be-frogged in front, which left his lean neck wholly uncovered, and with his bare feet in a pair of straw slippers, he wandered silently amongst the houses in daylight, almost as dumb as an animal and apparently much more homeless. I don't know what he did with himself at night. He must have had a place, a hut, a palm-leaf shed, some sort of hovel where he kept his razor and his change of sleeping suits. An air of futile mystery hung over him, something not exactly dark but obviously ugly. The only definite statement I could extract from anybody was that it was he who had 'brought the Arabs into the river.' That must have happened many years before. But how did he bring them into the river? He could hardly have done it in his arms like a lot of kittens. I knew that Almayer founded the chronology of all his misfortunes on the date of that fateful advent; and yet the very first time we dined with Almayer there was Willems sitting at table with us in the manner of the skeleton at the feast, obviously shunned by everybody, never addressed by any one, and for all recognition of his existence getting now and then from Almayer a venomous glance which I observed with great surprise. In the course of the whole evening he ventured one single remark which I didn't catch because his articulation was imperfect, as of a man who had forgotten how to speak. I was the only person who seemed aware of the sound. Willems subsided. Presently he retired, pointedly unnoticed—into the forest maybe? Its immensity was there, within three hundred yards of the verandah, ready to swallow up anything."

It was clear, Conrad continued, "that in those days Willems lived on Almayer's charity." When the *Vidar* made a later three-day call at Berau

Conrad learned that the silent Dutchman "had gone on an expedition up the river in charge of a steam-launch belonging to the Arabs, to make some discovery or other." As "a newcomer, the youngest of the company," Conrad was told little more than that, but the "faint suggestion of plots and mysteries pertaining to all matters touching Almayer's affairs amused me vastly" and, the impression of the white outcast remaining strongly with him, inspired the novel written eight years later. It was published in 1896 when De Veer, as well as Olmeyer, were living in Berau; fifteen years later, in 1911, he died there and, as Conrad had forecast in his story, was buried in the Gunung Tabur cemetery.[20]

One aspect of De Veer's life, which Conrad made the core of his novel, was his enslavement to his native wife. Pangeran Prodjo recalled that he and his friends used to see Sinjo Carel carrying heavy burdens in the rice fields, walking on all fours at the command of his wife. It was this bondage Conrad alluded to in a letter of October 29, 1894, to Mme. Poradowska, written while at work on the early chapters of *An Outcast of the Islands*, a novel he had originally intended to call *Two Vagabonds:*

"As for the idea for that book now without a title . . . First, the theme is the boundless, mad vanity of an ignorant man who has been successful but is without principles or any motive other than the satisfaction of his own vanity. Nor is he faithful even to himself. Whence the fall, the man's sudden descent into physical enslavement by an absolutely savage woman. I have seen that!"[21]

De Veer's Malay wife, who earned a living by selling cakes, became the cake-selling slave girl Taminah in *Almayer's Folly*. Carrying her tray on her head, she sold rice cakes from house to house in the village on her daily round, also finding buyers for them on the moored ship, walking "hesitantly up the slanting planks of the gangway amidst the encouraging shouts and more or less decent jokes of the men idling over the bulwarks"[22]—apparently a reference to the *Vidar*. In *An Outcast of the Islands* Conrad drew her as Aïssa, the scornfully savage girl whom Willems loved with a desperation that destroyed him.

The fourth European, the Englishman Jim Lingard, lived in Berau the longest of all—forty-one years. In the village he was called Si Jim or Tuan Jim ("the" Jim or "master" Jim). Six feet tall, and very upright, with a large, fiercely curled mustache, he had a conspicuous mannerism, a stately, dignified walk. His stately airs—"the swaggering manner he assumed, when meeting our ship," Captain Craig told Jean-Aubry[23]— caused him to be dubbed "Lord Jim" by the men of the *Vidar*. Conrad, adopting his nickname as the title of *Lord Jim*, drew upon him in his setting of Berau for the second half of that novel. Beginning it in the spring of 1898 with only the *Jeddah* incident and Augustine Podmore Williams in mind—intending it as a short story—Conrad, as he wrote in the Author's Note, felt "that the pilgrim ship episode was a good starting-point for a free and wandering tale; that it was an event, too, which could conceivably colour the whole 'sentiment of existence' in a simple and sensitive character." When *Lord Jim* was published in 1900 Jim Lingard was still a trader in Berau, continuing to live in the area until 1921. During those years Conrad's books became well known in the East, Jim's brother Joshua being among the first to recognize the author of them.

"I had a visit from a man out of the Malay Seas," Conrad wrote to his literary agent J. B. Pinker in October, 1909, referring to the visit of Captain Charles M. Marris of Penang. "It was like the raising of a lot of dead—dead to me, because most of them live out there and even read my books and wonder who the devil has been around taking notes. My visitor told me that Joshua Lingard made the guess: 'It must have been the fellow who was mate in the *Vidar* with Craig.' That's me right enough. And the best of it is that all these men of 22 years ago feel kindly to the Chronicler of their lives and adventures. They shall have some more of the stories they like."[24]

Captain Marris was a half-Maori sea captain whom Conrad met but once—in England in 1909—and to whom he dedicated *'Twixt Land and Sea*. A "soft-eyed black-bearded man married to a Patani girl of good family, with a house in Penang on the beach and a small plantation of rubber trees," was Conrad's description of him to Sir Hugh Clifford. "He came here to see his people in Durham. He wrote to me, 'I am like a crow in a strange country. May I come to see you?' "[25] At the time of his visit to Conrad's home in Kent he was master and owner of the Penang island-trader *Araby Maid*, having before that commanded the *Vidar* and steamers owned by the Koe Guan Co. of Penang. A fellow officer sailing ships out of Penang for the same firm was Captain Joshua Lingard. In 1904 Joshua Lingard was master of the *Rotorua*, a steamer trading between Malayan ports and Sumatra, and when the Koe Guan fleet was bought by the Eastern Shipping Company in 1908 he continued in the same employment. Residing in Penang with his Siamese wife, he died there in 1915 or 1916, after forty years at sea.[26] Conrad knew him in 1887, a ship's officer like himself and near his own age, sailing out of Singapore.

James Lingard, born in England, in Lancashire, on August 2, 1862,[27] was a young man of twenty-five, four years younger than himself, when Conrad knew him in Berau. A trader who had lived in Borneo for twelve years and who shipped local products via the *Vidar*, he then occupied his uncle's large house, a campong of several buildings on land next to Olmeyer's, fronting on the river. Bounded on one side by a creek, the house was set in a cleared strip 1049 feet long and 262 feet wide; at a distance behind it, inland from the river and on the edge of the forest, was Sinjo Carel's *warong*.[28]

Jim made several trips to Singapore on the *Vidar* and had spent a short time in Bangkok, where a studio photograph was taken in his early twenties, showing him a sturdy, clean-shaven, straight-backed young man with a direct, clear-eyed glance; wearing a businessman's suit, he sported a jeweled watch-chain looped through a buttonhole of his jacket.[29] He was one of the men Captain Craig talked about to his elder daughter, a "man called 'Lord Jim' or 'Gentleman Jim,'" the reason for the names," Mrs. Ivy Fairweather recalled, was that "he was always well dressed, a dapper person never without his walking stick."[30] There were no dramatic incidents in his life (he lived without any serious difficulty or trouble until his final illness, said his daughter, Mrs. C. C. Oehlers). When Conrad, in *Lord Jim*, wrote that the Malays of the jungle village called the character in his story "Tuan Jim: as one might say—Lord Jim," he not only recalled Lingard's nickname but he also employed a word familiar in the East. Used in addressing a superior, *tuan* was, as it is still, a common address; Olmeyer was equally called *tuan* in Berau.

Jim Lingard, as a young man in Berau, married an Indochinese girl of seventeen called Siti (the feminine of the Moslem title Syed), the daughter of Liang Atji and a relative of the wife of Berau's principal Chinese merchant, Po Eng Seng.[31] The Lingards had six children, born in Berau, five sons and one daughter. Two of the sons died young. The youngest child, Nellie, who married Dr. C. C. Oehlers in Singapore, was born in 1900, the year *Lord Jim* was published and, like two of her brothers, she was educated in Singapore. For many years, before moving to Australia in 1951, Mrs. Oehlers was a schoolteacher in Singapore, attached to the Municipal Health Office; her brothers, who served in the British army in World War I, also lived in Singapore; one was a ship's radio operator, the other retired in his late years to Australia. All lost contact with Berau after their mother's death there in 1941.

To Jim Lingard, however, Berau was always home. He was referred to in a K.P.M. report of 1892 as a trader in Berau making the pessimistic forecast that the raw rubber supply would be exhausted in nine months, due to the local practice of cutting down, instead of tapping, the trees.

He continued as a trader until 1904, when he sold his large house to the sultan of Gunung Tabur, Mohamad Siranoedin. In the deed of sale, dated November 29, 1904, and written in Lingard's hand, he described himself as "Tuan James Lingard, heir of Tuan William Lingard." The strongly built house survived for more than sixty years, until the 1930s, and was handsome enough to serve as the sultan's palace and later as the headquarters of the territory's Dutch government.

After selling his home Jim Lingard lived with Po Eng Seng until 1914; for most of the following seven years he resided on the inaccessible Birang River, a tributary of the Segah and a short distance upstream from Berau. His flight inland coincided with the loss of his fortune, through the collapse of the rubber market, and the beginning of World War I. For years his earnings came from loaning money to villagers, negotiations conducted through Po Eng Seng, but the greater part of his income had been sent to Singapore for the education of his children and at the end of his life he was penniless. Seriously ill, he was carried aboard a ship in Berau on January 1, 1921. A fund of $480 had been collected in the village for him, donated by Po Eng Seng and two Europeans, Mrs. V. A. Cools, the wife of a Belgian who, coming to Berau in 1904, operated coal mine concessions in the district, and a French owner of cocoanut plantations who arrived in 1912, Vicomte de Thorez. Jim Lingard reached Java, where he died in the hospital at Surabaya on April 2, 1921, at fifty-nine. His widow, remarried to a Malay, lived in Berau for another twenty years.

In Borneo, where he spent four-fifths of his life, Jim Lingard became one with the Malays, speaking Malay so well, said the sultan of Gunung Tabur, that it was impossible to tell he was a foreigner.[32] Conrad's own talents as a linguist, so evident in English, also enabled him to pick up Malay, and quickly. Malay names and terms acquired as a young man in the East, remembered throughout his writing life, were used liberally in four of his novels, *Almayer's Folly*, *An Outcast of the Islands*, *Lord Jim*, *The Rescue*.

In addition to his gift with languages, one of Conrad's many distinctions as an author was his ability to give, with Proustian detail, so many facets of the lives he wrote of, to enclose a true world within his fiction. It was both a brown and a white world in Borneo. In his stories concerned with the four Europeans and "the rest of that Pantai band,"[33] he demonstrated that the causes of men's actions, and their prejudices, varied little regardless of race. His first novel, written about Malays, "in their obscure, sun-bathed existence," was begun, he wrote in his memoirs, out of "that mysterious fellowship which unites in a community of hopes and fears all the dwellers on this earth."[34]

"After all these years, each leaving its evidence of slowly blackened pages," he said in *A Personal Record* regarding his Malayan fiction, "I can honestly say that it is a sentiment akin to pity which prompted me to render in words assembled with conscientious care the memory of things far distant and of men who had lived."[35] Among those who had lived on the Berau River—as descendents of some still do—were the "Malays, Arabs, and half-castes"[36] whom he transformed into the characters of his stories.

XX

> . . . there wasn't a week without some fight in Patusan at that
> time. . . .
>
> *Lord Jim*

"Berau has many riches," a Dutch government economic report compiled in Borneo in 1933 says of the district Conrad wrote of as "Patusan" in *Lord Jim*. "There is metal ore in the interior, coal seams only six hours upriver from the coast, forests providing a high quality of timber as well as other forest products, a sea full of wealth (fish in abundance, turtle eggs on the smaller islands, pearls on the open atoll of Maratua), but still it is a country without a future. The great drawback is its lack of a good port."[1] In the forty-six years elapsing since Conrad knew Berau the future of the country had not brightened. As he saw it in 1887 it was "one of the lost, forgotten, unknown places of the earth." Wilderness though it was, as to a large extent it has remained, Conrad saw in its "Pantai band" a segment of mankind illustrating the whole. Contests over trade, over power, over boundaries, tore apart the solemn quiet of this primitive El Dorado; race, religion, social position, were issues here as in other, more sophisticated parts of the globe.

The people and the setting of Berau stayed always in Conrad's memory. "What bothers me most is that my figures are so real. I know them so well that they fetter my imagination,"[2] he told Mme. Poradowska when writing *An Outcast of the Islands*. Working on *Almayer's Folly*, he drew a guiding plan of a compound beside a river, with a large house, a smaller house, several huts and trees, illustrating from memory Olmeyer's compound in Berau. To imagined jungle areas based on Berau he sent Jim in *Lord Jim* and Heyst in *Victory* to retreats where, seemingly, the world could not reach them. At sixty-one he was writing of it again, in *The Rescue*, drawn to the Borneo hinterland by the ironic contrasts of its life. It held, in its hush and beauty and the impregnable barrier of its river, the promise of idyllic seclusion, yet it was a land of violence; its people, primitive by European standards, held royalty in as high esteem as a Louis XIV court; in a setting of lavish natural abundance, it was the epitome of poverty. A country with a history paralleling that of the Chibchas, it had the same fault. It was a rich land.

In the seventeenth century the desired wealth of Berau, as of all Borneo, had not been gold but pepper—"the passion for pepper seemed to burn like a flame of love in the breast of Dutch and English adventurers about the time of James the First. Where wouldn't they go for pepper!"[3] By the late nineteenth century pepper had been found in areas having much easier access than Berau and European traders were braving the fevers, head-hunters and pirates for the forest products required by a more mechanized age, high among them gutta-percha, the raw rubber so much in demand as insulation in underground and undersea cables. In Conrad's time it was primarily for these that Malay, Arab, Chinese and white traders came to the district. In the scramble for them Berau knew little peace.

"Almost everywhere along the coast there was smuggling of guns and gunpowder," says the shipping history *Een Halve Eeuw Paketvaart* of the period and the place Conrad knew. Trade was at the heart of the fighting; and the river port, the village of Berau, the center of trade. The village lay within the boundaries of Gunung Tabur; its ruler governed the river. In 1887 the sultan of Gunung Tabur was a youth of twenty-one, Mohamad Siranoedin, whom his people called Si Atas.[4] He had inherited the throne upon the death of his father five years earlier but a cousin, Hadji Adji Kuning, dominated the weak youth and ruled as regent. For ten years, still maintaining Si Atas was "too young to rule" as the sultan approached thirty, the unscrupulous regent, holding power, exploited traders and subjects alike. Upon Conrad's ship, the *Vidar*, the regent levied harbor charges for each call at this settlement without a harbor and extorted 5 per cent in kind of the jungle products the steamer carried to Singapore. With the forced labor of hundreds of his subjects Hadji Adji Kuning erected a new palace, barely completed before he was deposed. Initiating a feud with the sultan of Sambaliung over a thirty-two-foot piece of land, he gave Berau its years-long warfare fought with poisoned arrows, guns and spears.

When Si Atas was twenty-six the Dutch government intervened. In

December, 1892, the "guardianship" was belatedly ended by a Dutch decree and the rightful sultan placed on the throne. Appointed sultan of Gunung Tabur "because the Regency of Hadji Adji Kuning proved to be a failure" ("*Si Atas diangkat mendjadi Sultan dari Goenoeng Taboer sehingga pemerintahan dari Regent Hadji Adji Koening jang tida begitoe menjenangkan dihapoeskan*"),[5] as the chronicle of Gunung Tabur understates the political change made in 1892, Mohamad Siranoedin was installed as ruler for a reign to continue for twenty-nine years, until 1921.

In *Lord Jim* Conrad recalled the chaotic regency of Hadji Adji Kuning, when "utter insecurity for life and property was the normal condition," and portrayed the ineffectual and helpless Si Atas: "the Sultan is an imbecile youth with two thumbs on his left hand and an uncertain and beggarly revenue extorted from a miserable population and stolen from him by his many uncles."[6] Drawing upon Hadji Adji Kuning for Rajah Allang in the novel, an old man who "swallowed an opium pill every two hours," he reflected the embattled state of Berau: "There were in Patusan antagonistic forces, and one of them was Rajah Allang, the worst of the Sultan's uncles, the governor of the river, who did the extorting and the stealing, and ground down to the point of extinction the country-born Malays, who, utterly defenceless, had not even the resource of emigrating."[7]

The traders among the Malays, the Bugis, had emigrated to Berau from Celebes in an early time and, a proud and enterprising race, formed the settlement's strongest single group. Leader of the Bugis campong, on the Kelai River adjoining the stockade of the sultan of Sambaliung, was Captain Dain (Daing), Berau's principal exporter and a friend of Captain Craig.[8] Picturing him in *Lord Jim* as Dain Waris (*waris* is the Malay word for "heir"), Conrad wrote of him as "a most distinguished youth," the son and sole heir of Doramin, an immense man of the nakhoda or merchant class who, elected as leader of the Bugis immigrants from Celebes, was the "chief of the second power in Patusan."[9] In the novel Conrad created a death by ambush for Dain Waris—Jim executed by Doramin in retribution—but Captain Dain in actual life met no such desperate fate. His heirs, said Adji Bagian, founded a settlement on the Berau River at Telok Pangkal and live there still.[10] The swallowing of opium pills was a drug habit common among the rajahs, according to this royal heir who, at twenty-one, declined the rule of Sambaliung.

As with local customs and history, Conrad was equally exact with Malay terms and names in the novels he based on Berau. In *Almayer's*

Folly and *An Outcast of the Islands* many of his characters bore the names of real life: Lakamba, Babalatchi, Syed Abdulla, Dain Maroola, Jim Eng, Patalolo, Sahamin. Babalatchi and Lakamba, natives of Celebes, were Bugis traders in Berau (a bill of lading Conrad saved showed Babalatchi shipped fifty-eight bags of dammer—a resin used for Malay torches, the jungle's form of lighting—to Sing Jimmung at Donggala, Celebes, via the *Vidar* in August, 1887).[11] Syed Abdulla, son of the *Vidar's* owner, was indirectly responsible for Tandjung Redeb, the name Berau received in about 1900 and by which it continues to be known. Beside his house, on the spit of land between the two branches of the river, the Arab trader planted an imported shade tree, a *pohon dadap*, used in Java on the coffee plantations. It was unfamiliar to the people of Berau and they named it a *pohon radap;* in time the point of land or *tandjung* became Tandjung Radap and the town Tandjung Redeb.[12]

Dain Maroola, a rajah and trader in *Almayer's Folly* and the hero of the novel, owed his name to Dain Marola, a Buginese clerk in Abdulla's godown in Berau who died some years ago in Sokkan village, a downstream settlement.[13] Two other Malay traders, Hadji Sahamin in Berau and Patalolo in Donggala, were actual men[14] Conrad knew and whose names he borrowed. A major character in two of his novels, Jim Eng, was suggested by two men, Jim Eng and Po Eng Seng. Jim Eng was a Chinese trader in Singapore who shipped goods to Berau on the *Vidar*, while Po Eng Seng, also Chinese, was a prominent merchant in Berau, a loan-business partner of Jim Lingard, to whom, through their wives, he was related. During the months of Conrad's contact with Berau it was in Po Eng Seng's shop where the four Europeans—Olmeyer, Jim Lingard, De Veer and the Russian captain—spent their time drinking. Po Eng Seng's wife was still living in Berau in 1952, said the ratu of Gunung Tabur, but his son, Po Boy Hwat, was killed in the single air attack the village suffered in World War II.[15]

Into the novels of *Lord Jim* and *The Rescue* Conrad wove parts of Berau's early history. Rajah Allang in *Lord Jim* came, in name, from Rajah Alam, founder and first sultan of Sambaliung, alike in methods to a later Rajah Alam, the "much feared pirate" who lived on the river and about whom stories, said Anang Dachlan, were handed down.[16] Rajah Alam's daughter, Pangeran Bongso ("Younger Princess"), probably suggested the name for the ruler's younger son, Mohammed Bonso, in *Lord Jim.* Names Conrad used in his fiction—Doramin, Daman, Tambi, Itam, Tengga, Dain, Karain, Taminah, Sali, Tulla,

Midah, Pata Matara—were, and are, names common among Malays, which he would have heard frequently in the East.

Creating his Malayan stories while living in England, thousands of miles from Berau and, as with *The Rescue*—which was completed more than thirty years after his last sight of it—Conrad could still see the figures, still hear the speech of that Borneo outpost. Malay titles, in a barefoot world where titles meant so much, came into his work: *datu*, signifying leader, similar to rajah; *tunku*, a corruption of *tuan aku*, "my lord," an address applied to sultans; *pangeran*, distinguishing a prince or princess; *inchi* or mister, "Inchi 'Nelyus" in *Lord Jim* being Mr. Cornelius; *sherif*, pronounced by Malays as *sherip* or *serip*, used by Arab traders claiming descent from Mohammed's grandson Husein, as Syeds claimed descent from the elder grandson Hasan. Hassim, Ali, Omar, Abdulla, Mohammed were Arab names handed down during the centuries following the adoption of the Moslem religion, names of Arabs or Malays or those of mixed ancestry Conrad took from life for characters in his fiction. In a combination of Arabic and Malay he created Darat-es-Salam, the Malay *darat* for safe, dry land joined with the Arabic greeting *Salam*, "peace be with you," to make the peaceful haven or "Shore of Refuge" of *The Rescue*.[17]

Lineage, in spite of the "utter isolation of this lost corner of the earth," had no less importance in Berau than in the most aristocracy-conscious state in Europe, with dynasties tracing back into the dim past, as S. G. In 't Veld showed in his 1884 account *Aanteekeningen omtrent het rijk van Borneo*. Here in Borneo a man's name was his passport, defining his race, religion, rank, and the pureness of his blood. The Malay *Orang* or race came into Orang Blanda for Dutchmen, into Orang Sirani (Sirani from Nazarenes) identifying descendants of the Portuguese, into the races—Bugis, Kayan, Murut, Dusun, Kenyah, Kelabit, Laut, Benua, Bajau, Solok, and others combined under the general but inaccurate term of Malay, a term the proud tribes, each with its own dialect and customs, disowned. One trader in Berau whose name Conrad drew upon—Hadji Sahamin, Orang Bandjar—told by his name that he was a Moslem who had made a pilgrimage to Mecca, thereby earning the title Hadji, and that he was of the sea gypsy, Bandjar (Bajau, Bajow) race. So was the trader Achmad Bandjar, possibly the original of the "Bajow vagabond" Mahmat Banjer in *An Outcast of the Islands*. A tribal leader on the river of mixed Arab and Malay descent, Datu Sherif Maharajah Alam, was a man remembered in Berau as a fear-inspiring pirate;[18] his troublemaking exploits very likely suggested the Arab half-breed Sherif Ali in *Lord Jim*.

Most conscious of all of their ancestry, in this world of mixed extractions, were the Bugis. No people, wrote Captain Rodney Mundy[19] of the Bugis more than a century ago, were more careful of their blood. A wellborn Bugis woman was not permitted to marry out of her class and, while men might do so, their children bore a heritage mark. The name Dain was prefixed to the names of children, both boys and girls, of mixed marriages, their fathers Bugis and their mothers Malays of less pure blood. Long before white men added the complexity of Eurasians—creating the social problem Conrad gave to Almayer and his concern over his daughter's future in *Almayer's Folly*—half-castes, outsiders by birth, held a lowly position among the Malays.

As trade, race and social status contributed to the unrest of Berau, so did religion. The forest head-hunting Dyaks were pagans; the Arabs, like the largest number of Malays and some Chinese, were Moslems; Christians included the four Europeans, of different faiths, as well as the Manadonese, Malays from Celebes converted to Christianity. In the small settlement of illiterate, superstitious people, enclosed in the jungle, brotherhood was scarce. And it was brotherhood, fractured by passionate advocates of the world's many and differing religions, that concerned Conrad, whose distrust of any dogma dated from boyhood. "It's strange how I always, from the age of fourteen, disliked the Christian religion, its doctrines, ceremonies and festivals,"[20] he wrote Edward Garnett in 1902. "Great, improving, softening, compassionate it may be," he continued his views on the same subject in a 1914 letter to Garnett, "but it has lent itself with amazing facility to cruel distortion and is the only religion which, with its impossible standards, has brought an infinity of anguish to innumerable souls—on this earth."[21] It was Bertrand Russell's essay "The Free Man's Worship," with its proposal "to worship only the God created by our own love of the good," which brought from Conrad wholehearted endorsement. "You have reduced to order the inchoate thoughts of a lifetime," he wrote Lord Russell on December 22, 1913, "and given a direction to those obscure *mouvements d'âme* which, unguided, bring only trouble to one's weary days on this earth. For the marvellous pages on the Worship of a free man the only return one can make is that of a deep admiring affection, which, if you were never to see me again and forgot my existence tomorrow, will be unalterably yours *usque ad finem.*"[22]

Exposed as a boy to his father's excessive religious zeal, Conrad encountered in the East various forms of fanaticism. Berau had its zealots, hadjis who had made the pilgrimage to Mecca on such pilgrim ships as the *Jeddah*, and each end of his *Vidar* voyages, Berau and Singapore, provided an association with the famous *Jeddah* case. In Singapore was Williams, the ship chandler's water clerk of McAlister & Co., contacting vessels in the roadstead, the shore-bound seaman in the first years of his comeback. Sympathy for Williams, who had failed to meet the "impossible standards" of his own severely religious background, led Conrad, in *Lord Jim*, to transport the water clerk of his story to the retreat of "Patusan," the ironically unsafe shelter that was, in life, Berau.

Transported himself between the two extremes, the metropolis of Singapore and the jungle of Berau, by the ship he long remembered, Conrad brought the *Vidar* and her captain into many of his stories. Captain Craig became Captain Ford in *Almayer's Folly* and *An Outcast of the Islands*, Captain Kent in *The Shadow Line;* contributed to Captain Davidson in *Victory* and "Because of the Dollars," to Captain Whalley in "The End of the Tether." In the latter story Conrad reproduced the *Vidar* and the tramping route she followed—one of many precise details being the clump of three palms, the landmark guiding the fictional *Sofala* to the entrance of the river taken from the conspicuous clump of three trees at the entrance of the Berau, a direction mark appearing on navigation charts of the 1880s. The steamers *Sofala* and *Sissie* of his fiction were Conrad's versions of the *Vidar*, trading steamers following the routes, picking up the landmarks, that he, a chief officer, had learned so well.

Trading regulations Conrad and his captain had to know and abide by in Berau were drawn up and signed, on behalf of the Dutch government in its contracts with the sultans of Gunung Tabur and Sambaliung, by Jacobus Jozephus Meijer, the Dutch Resident for South and East Borneo who noted in the contracts that he had been decorated by two governments (*"ridder der orde van den Nederlandschen Leeuw en der Luxemburgsche orde van de Eikenkroon"*).[23] It was apparently his name Conrad borrowed for the Jacobus brothers in "A Smile of Fortune." Alfred Jacobus, the "wrong Mr. Jacobus" in the story—his brother Ernest being the prominent merchant of the port—was a ship chandler who, through having his illegitimate daughter live in his home, had become a social outcast. The story was one of Conrad's many variations on the theme of the disowned.

Aligned with those who had been made into "a stranger in the land," he wrote of one after another who, because of birth, accident, weakness, crime, or mode of life—victims of a galaxy of social intolerances—had either been forced out or had chosen to leave the mainstream. Rita in *The Arrow of Gold*, Jim in *Lord Jim*, Dr. Monygham in *Nostromo*, Willems in *An Outcast of the Islands*, Falk in "Falk," Leggatt in "The

Secret Sharer," Heyst in *Victory*, were but a few of the alienated Conrad sympathetically portrayed "to make you *see*."

Heyst, the intellectually detached wanderer and foreigner everywhere, was a self-portrait of Conrad as a young man, as the understanding Marlow reflected the attitudes of his older years. Heyst, determined to drift "altogether and literally, body and soul, like a detached leaf," moved restlessly in the belief that he could pass through life without suffering, "invulnerable because elusive." Throughout his twenties Conrad, with a youth's uncertainties of where to go and "how to be," was tempted by such seclusions as a whalerman's life in the Arctic, by a trader's life in the East. Having had no stable home from the age of four, he relied on the one base he was sure of and what it offered—the "intimate, equal fellowship [of] the ship and the man, backing each other against the implacable, if sometimes dissembled, hostility of their world of waters."[24]

But the age of thirty—his thirtieth birthday was passed on the *Vidar* on the Borneo run—is a milestone, the point reached then, as he wrote in *The Shadow Line*, when "one perceives ahead a shadow-line warning one that the region of early youth, too, must be left behind."[25]

At thirty nothing indicated the fame he was to have, nor did he show interest in the career to bring it to him, though twenty months after leaving Berau he would begin his first novel, *Almayer's Folly*. The river, life on the river, brought a sharp change in his point of view. (Today young Americans in the Peace Corps, college graduates stationed in the Philippines, in tropical Panay, acquire radically new outlooks in their assigned outposts, the "culture shock" of living with Malays in isolated, impoverished hamlets bringing much the same sympathetic reaction as Conrad's to the Malays of Berau.[26]) At nineteen he had been a Royalist running guns for the Carlists and was, according to his uncle, "for the Emperor" in France. But by thirty the deep convictions had been formed—in "that part of the Eastern Seas from which I have carried away into my writing life the greatest number of suggestions"[27]—that, as a critic of imperialist exploitation and social injustice, his work was to express.

Politically, Conrad subscribed to no doctrine, though such radical socialists as R. B. Cunninghame Graham were among his closest friends, and H. G. Wells, whose work he so much admired and to whom he dedicated *The Secret Agent*, was to him "the one honest thinker of the day."[28] "My misfortune is that I can't swallow *any* formula," he told Edward Garnett. To John Galsworthy he wrote that scepticism was "the tonic of minds, the tonic of life, the agent of truth—the way of art and salvation." Choosing the hardest way to live, as he was to choose the hardest and most intricate form for his novels, he had been too often exposed to the waywardness of chance, seen its effects upon too many lives, to believe in any panacea.

An introspective idealist in his early manhood, Conrad bounced from moody contemplation to sudden, impulsive action. The lethargic pace of the East, the smothering heat and general air of somnolence, were conducive to his characteristic moods of withdrawn dreaming. Nothing struck him lightly. "Living with memories is a cruel business. I, who have a double life, one of them peopled only by shadows growing more precious as the years pass—know what that is,"[29] he told Cunninghame Graham.

Perhaps the most prominent shadow in his double life was Paula ("Every one of us, you'll admit, has been haunted by some woman," he wrote in "Karain"). News of her marriage to Trabadelo in the spring of 1887 would have reached him in the East through either of the friends from Marseilles days he corresponded with, Richard Fecht or Adolf Krieger—first Fecht, later Krieger, forwarding to him the allowance sent through them by his uncle.[30] That allowance ended on Conrad's thirtieth birthday. The breaking of this tie, following so shortly after Paula's marriage, very likely contributed to the hasty move for which, in The Shadow Line, he used the domestic term "divorce."

When the Vidar docked in Singapore after his last voyage to Borneo —a part of the world to which he would never return—Conrad, on January 5, 1888, left the ship. "For no reason on which a sensible person could put a finger I threw up my job—chucked my berth—left the ship of which the worst that could be said was that she was a steamship and therefore, perhaps, not entitled to that blind loyalty which. . . . However, it's no use trying to put a gloss on what even at the time I myself half suspected to be a caprice."[31]

He quit his job, having nothing else in view, in the "inconsequential manner in which a bird flies away from a comfortable branch. It was as though all unknowing I had heard a whisper or seen something. Well—perhaps! One day I was perfectly right and the next everything was gone —glamour, flavour, interest, contentment—everything. It was one of those moments, you know. The green sickness of late youth descended on me and carried me off. Carried me off that ship, I mean."[32]

This was not to be the last of Conrad's impulsive moves. But it ended the dreamlike round of the Borneo voyages, closed his contact with the river and the people who would become the companions of his imagination for many years, to "live again with a vividness and poignancy quite foreign to our former real intercourse"[33] as they came trooping back like phantoms to his rooms in London—"that whole company of people who have spoken in my ear, moved before my eyes, lived with me for so many years,"[34] as he told Mme. Poradowska on the day he completed *Almayer's Folly*.

So deep an impression did the East make upon Conrad that of his forty-three novels and short stories twenty, or nearly half, were placed in an Eastern setting. "Sympathetic identification," writes Albert J. Guerard, "is the central chapter of Conrad's psychology."[35] His experiences in the East between twenty-four and thirty, intermittent contacts of six vital years, laid much of the foundation for his later psychological novels.

"To survey with wonder the changes of one's own self is a fascinating pursuit for idle hours," he wrote in *A Personal Record*. "The field is so wide, the surprises so varied, the subject so full of unprofitable but curious hints as to the work of unseen forces, that one does not weary easily of it."[36] Sympathizing with those who had been, in Rimbaud's phrase, "damned by the rainbow," the "lost cause" became, as Raymond Las Vergnas says, Conrad's "*vraie patrie*," the message in his work having an "affinity with the anxieties of our times."[37]

To Conrad the world was "the abode of conflicting opinions" which, offering the wide range in points of view presented in his writing, are heard like musical variations on a theme, carried by first one voice, then another. A dominant and often called his most characteristic theme, guilt—"the desperate attempt to leave in space what always travels with him in time,"[38] as Albert J. Guerard defines it—was a property of men as old as time. Existentialist thought declares that "to be is to be guilty," no man escaping the earnest reminders of experience, but long before that philosophy found expression Conrad wrote of the inner judge establishing each man's guilt to himself, the commonly-owned "heirloom" of conscience and the intangible forces creating it.

"*J'ai vécu*, as I apprehend most of us manage to exist, missing all along the varied forms of destruction by a hair's-breadth, saving my body, that's clear, and perhaps my soul also, but not without some damage here and there to the fine edge of my conscience, that heirloom of the ages, of the race, of the group, of the family, colorable and plastic, fashioned by the words, the looks, the acts, and even by the silences and abstentions surrounding one's childhood; tinged in a complete scheme of delicate shades and crude colors by the inherited traditions, beliefs, or prejudices—unaccountable, despotic, persuasive, and often, in its texture, romantic."[39]

Leaving the *Vidar* in Singapore and the comforts of a life where he "could not have been happier" a month after turning thirty, he was soon, by sudden chance, to be in the setting used for "The Secret Sharer." That exploration of a man's conscience or other self was to grow, like his equally famous "Heart of Darkness," from the experiences of his last six years at sea.

PART FOUR
THE MEN

XXI

I wondered how far I should turn out faithful to that ideal conception of one's own personality every man sets up for himself secretly.

"The Secret Sharer"

Siam, the exotically beautiful *Muang-Thai* ("Kingdom of the Free") or Thailand as it came to be known, was to Anna Leonowens "a wonder to the senses and a mystery to the mind." In the 1860s the Englishwoman from Singapore passed five years in "the city of the beautiful and invincible angel" of Bangkok and in *The English Governess at the Siamese Court* (nearly a century later to be made into the film "Anna and the King of Siam" and the play "The King and I") described the Buddhist country of fable and legend which was to provide Conrad, as captain of a ghost-haunted and pestilence-ridden ship, with one of the major ordeals of his life. He reached Bangkok on January 24, 1888,[1] in the hot rainy season, the time of cholera. From the contagion of the shore stemmed the developments of the next five weeks.

Siam's ruler was the thirty-five-year-old King Chulalongkorn who, as the heir apparent, had been Mrs. Leonowens' pupil. As the English teacher in King Mongkut's royal harem—the quarters in the palace guarded by Amazons and served by slaves which housed the king's many wives, concubines, and sixty-seven children—she had found the boy to become King Chulalongkorn ardent, serene and gentle, "modest and affectionate, eager to learn, and easy to influence." He was to prove a progressive monarch in the nearly forty years of his reign but the ease with which he was influenced enabled the regent, Siriwong Bunnag, to exert full control of the state, and a harsh control it was, for the first eleven years of that reign. Slavery, outlawed only after the regent's death,[2] was slow in being brought to an end and slaves existed in large numbers at the time of Conrad's stay in Siam.

The epidemic-prone land, with its customary greeting "Good health to you!" held a people of "vivid fancies and fiery passions," said Mrs. Leonowens, who had the Oriental's "delight in the metaphysical and the mystic."[3] Saffron-robed Buddhist priests were everywhere—what education there was was in their hands—and, in a country where astronomy was the main science, where an accused man's guilt or innocence was determined without trial, belief in the supernatural was complete. Fatalists by instinct and upbringing, the Siamese relied on forces man could not control. Spirit houses, where friendly spirits were believed to hover, stood in the compounds of those who could afford this prime protection while the entire populace of Bangkok took part in various mystic rites. In one, the Loy Krathong festival, *krathongs* or toy banana-leaf boats, filled with food and money offerings to the water spirits, were set afloat by the thousands upon the river and canals; with each leaf boat carrying away the sins of the year, a new start in life was ensured for its owner.

Both the atmosphere of myth and the injurious climate had an impact upon Conrad, caught in Bangkok in a hallucinatory time. In "The Secret Sharer," "Falk," and *The Shadow Line* he employed the setting of Bangkok and the Gulf of Siam, drawing the eerie quality of those stories from experiences of his own. Of *The Shadow Line* he wrote Sir Sidney Colvin, "I am sorry you have received an impression of horror. I tried to keep the mere horror out. It would have been easy to pile it on. You may believe me, *J'ai vécu tout cela.*"[4]

Though he insisted that the world "in all conscience holds enough mystery and terror in itself" and disclaimed the supernatural tone critics attributed to the novel,[5] it was a story true to its background. In the Siam of its setting the supernatural was wholeheartedly accepted by a people who readily believed in the unbelievable and whose annals, wrote Mrs. Leonowens from a study of them, abounded "in fables of heroes, demigods, giants and genii." So deep was the Siamese faith in magic, in the unseen, that no new venture was undertaken without an astrologer's advice—as, in 1965, astrologers are still religiously consulted in Thailand.

The Siam Conrad saw was a country of extremes. Rich in rice and timber forests, rich in gold and precious jewels, its commerce providing the king with a personal income of ten million dollars a year, it had in its capital of Bangkok more than a million people of whom many, for want of any shelter, slept in the streets. Existing on an economy of forced labor, the government required three months of unpaid work from every man each year. Ever present reminders of the caste system were the approaches on hands and knees of those of lower rank addressing their superiors. A water city of klongs or canals teeming with boats, Bangkok was dense with beggars. Yet the river was lined with golden shrines, and the Royal Palace enclosure, a square-mile area as large as the City of London, held fantastically lavish buildings, palaces and pagodas surrounded by parks of palm trees, gardens of brilliant flowers. In this traditional land of the elephant where the white elephant was sacred, the royal white elephant stalls were adjacent to the shrines. Below the vast, walled, royal grounds that fronted on the river—the river was the main street of the city—were the foreign consulates, British, American, German, Swedish and Norwegian, Dutch, French and Danish. To Bangkok's floating wharves foreign ships were coming for timber and rice; these were not many, barely two hundred ships a year.

Only thirty-three years before Conrad's arrival in Bangkok had European traders been admitted to Siam. The sole nation in Asia never to be colonized by a foreign power, it was little touched by Western ways. With its more than eighteen thousand temples, golden, ornate pagodas shining in the beating sun, it seemed a land of fantasy. Four days by steamship took travelers from bustling Westernized Singapore, "the Liverpool of the East," to the easygoing water city of Bangkok, "the Venice of the Orient," bringing in those four days a dramatic shift of view. The contrast was accented for Conrad by the circumstance that, from being jobless in Singapore, he arrived in Bangkok to take command of a ship he had never seen—his first command. The anxious time of his sudden promotion was recaptured in *The Shadow Line* which, as he emphasized to Colvin, was a literal recollection: "The whole thing is exact autobiography. . . . The very speeches are (I won't say authentic—they are that absolutely) I believe, verbally accurate."[6]

Many features of the story are now confirmed by records discovered in Australia. Included in what Conrad called the "Otago cycle" of his work, it concerned his first voyage on the 345-ton barque *Otago*, one of the four ships to which he affectionately paid tribute in his fiction: the *Tremolino* in *The Arrow of Gold*, the *Palestine* in "Youth," the *Narcissus* in *The Nigger of the Narcissus*, the *Otago* in *The Shadow Line*.

Although the *Otago* was nineteen years old when Conrad took command in Bangkok she seemed to him "a harmonious creature . . . one of those craft that in virtue of their design and complete finish will never look old. Amongst her companions moored to the bank, and all bigger than herself, she looked like a creature of high breed—an Arab steed in a string of cart-horses."[7] Built in Glasgow in 1869,[8] the *Otago* had opened her long sea career with speedy passages about the world, on her maiden voyage sailing from England to Adelaide to Sydney to San Francisco and back to England in eighteen months. In 1871 she became Australian-owned and from then on traded chiefly to ports in the Dutch East Indies, South China Sea, Australia and Mauritius.[9] The voyage to bring her into Conrad's life began in 1887.

On July 19 of that year, under the master who was to appear in ghostly fashion in *The Shadow Line*—Captain John Snadden, a Scot of fifty, born in Kirkcaldy in 1837,[10] who shared ownership of the vessel with Henry Simpson & Sons of Port Adelaide—the *Otago* arrived at Newcastle, Australia, from the South Australian port of Wallaroo. Loading coal for Haiphong, French Indochina, she sailed with a crew of eight from Newcastle on August 8, 1887.[11] The departure of that day was the last news the ship's owners were ever to have from Captain Snadden, a married man with a family in Australia.

After a lengthy passage, spending two months on the way, the *Otago* reached Haiphong. Her cargo discharged, her captain held her at her moorings for three weeks in the oppressively hot port. Captain Snadden, a burly, bald, heavily whiskered man with the stern gaze caught in photographs of him, became ill in the unhealthy harbor. Though his ship had neither cargo, proper ballast, nor an adequate water supply, he ordered her out to sea on a reason-defying course, to beat up to Hong Kong in the face of a fierce monsoon. Sails were blown away and the crew exhausted before her commander, irrational with illness, could be persuaded to turn back. On December 8, 1887,[12] he died on board, the *Otago* then in the South China Sea approaching the mouth of the Gulf of Siam.

"It's my belief," Conrad had the chief mate say of his captain in *The Shadow Line*, "he would have tried to take the ship down with him if it had been in human power. He never meant her to see home again. He wouldn't write to his owners, he never wrote to his old wife either— he wasn't going to. He had made up his mind to cut adrift from everything. That's what it was. He didn't care for business, or freights, or for making a passage—or anything. He meant to have gone wandering about the world till he lost her with all hands."[13]

The chief mate, whom Conrad called Burns in the story, was a German of thirty-three, Charles Born.[14] Making his first voyage on the ship, having joined her in Newcastle, he had hoped, though lacking a

Master's certificate and in spite of his short six months' service on board, to be given the command after the death of Captain Snadden; in that hope he had taken the *Otago*, not to Singapore with its reservoir of officers, but to Bangkok, where trained European men were scarce. The British Consul-General in Bangkok, however, cabled Singapore for a master to replace Captain Snadden, and Conrad, idle since quitting the *Vidar* and considering a return to England, was found at the Officers' Sailors' Home; jolted out of the lethargy and indecision of his two weeks' stay there, he was selected to take charge of the ship. His promotion, coming by sheer chance, was one he very nearly missed. Had it not been for a watchful skipper in the Sailors' Home, Captain Patterson ("Captain Giles" in *The Shadow Line*) the command would have gone, through the connivance of the steward of the hostel, to a loafing, ever-out-of-work officer, "Hamilton."

On January 19, 1888, Conrad received a memorandum from the Master Attendant of Singapore, Henry Ellis, which officially confirmed his appointment as commander of the *Otago:*

"This is to inform you that you are required to proceed to-day in the S.S. *Melita* to Bangkok and you will report your arrival to the British Consul which will show that I have engaged you to be Master of the *Otago* in accordance with the Consul's telegram on a voyage from Bangkok to Melbourne, wages at fourteen pounds per month and to count from date of your arrival at Bangkok, your passage from Singapore to Bangkok to be borne by the ship. Further to receive a passage from Melbourne to Singapore if you are not kept in the ship."[15]

On that day of January 19 he sailed on the *Melita* for Bangkok. Being in the "twilight region between youth and maturity," jumpy and nervous, alternately buoyant and afraid, he watched the shores as the *Melita* crossed the bar and steamed up Siam's twisting river, the Meinam, knowing that "the time was approaching for me to behold my command and to prove my worth in the ultimate test of my profession."[16]

The Meinam (Chao Phraya or "Mother of Waters") was a lively river. Heavily-loaded keng boats, like Venetian gondolas, moved on the swift tide, mixing in the congested traffic with the common rua-pêt, boats with round basket tops looking like Western covered wagons floating on the stream. Cluttered, noisy, and colorful, the Meinam wound its way for twenty miles from the gulf to Bangkok. Nearing the capital, the shores of higher land showed, as Mrs. Leonowens described the journey, "a neater cultivation, hamlets and villages quaintly pretty, fantastic temples and pagodas dotting the plain, fine Oriental effects of form and colour, scattered Edens of fruit-trees—the mango, the mangosteen, the bread-fruit, the durian, the orange—their dark foliage contrasting boldly with the more lively and lovely green of the betel, the tamarind, and the banana. Every curve of the river is beautiful with an unexpectedness of its own—here the sugar-cane swaying gracefully, there the billow-like lights and shadows of the supple feathery bamboo, and everywhere ideal paradises of refreshment and repose."[17]

Bangkok was a city of water streets. "The front part of the town, indeed, is actually afloat on the river," said the *Illustrated London News*, "along both banks of which, for three or four miles, are moored eight or ten ranges of wooden houses, built on rafts of bamboo, fastened to piles driven into the bottom of the river. Each of these houses is usually 20 ft. or 30 ft. in length."[18] Towering above the muddy river and the bamboo homes were the spires of the king's palace and the many gilded temples, "gorgeous and dilapidated," as Conrad saw them, "crumbling under the vertical sunlight, tremendous, overpowering, almost palpable, which seemed to enter one's breast with the breath of one's nostrils and soak into one's limbs through every pore of one's skin."[19] Among them was the famous temple of the Emerald Idol, the Wat P'hra Kaeo, an astonishing structure with tapered, golden roofs, elaborately carved and adorned inside and out, so fabulous that it was commonly believed that Buddha himself, in the form of a great emerald, had alighted there and, in a magic flash of lightning, had conjured up this building as his home.

Conrad spent sixteen days in Bangkok, straining to complete the loading of the *Otago* and take her out to sea. The ship had been run bare in her wanderings from Haiphong and in the additional seven weeks following her captain's death. Supplies had to be purchased and a cargo of teak loaded for Sydney (a prominent teak merchant in Bangkok at the time was the son of Anna Leonowens, Louis, a business leader in the city until his death in 1919[20]). The ship's muddled accounts also had to be put into shape. How muddled they were was indicated by a letter from the ship's owners, James H. Simpson of Henry Simpson & Sons, Port Adelaide, which, dated April 5, 1888, was addressed to Captain Korzeniowski at Sydney "to await arrival." A letter Conrad saved to the end of his life, it thanked him for the accounts he sent from Bangkok.

"The accounts which you enclosed are no doubt at all in order but I have no means of comparing them with other documents as the late Captain never favoured me with a scratch of the pen from the time of leaving Newcastle in August last and the acting Master Mr. Burns [Born] only wrote me a brief note acquainting me with his Captain's death. Therefore, I am at a loss to know what business was done by the ship after she arrived at Haiphong, whether she earned or whether she lost money. In fact, other than your documents, I have no record whatever of receipts and expenditure. Will you, therefore, please inform me whether any freight was obtained between Haiphong and Bangkok and if so, how much and generally what business was done by the ship for the ten months previous to your assuming command?"[21]

Conrad, a brand-new captain just turned thirty, was, with the exception of an Irish seaman, the youngest man on board his ship. The crew he inherited when he took command of the *Otago* in Bangkok—and whom he brought, indirectly, into *The Shadow Line*, "The Secret Sharer" and "Falk"—are on record in the Customs Department of Newcastle, New South Wales, Australia. Captain Snadden's handwritten list of the men who sailed with him on his last voyage, in addition to the first mate Charles Born, names: J. Johnson, 38, of Halifax, the boatswain who served as second mate; F. Veilvom, 46, the cook from Amsterdam (Conrad called him "Ransome" in *The Shadow Line*); five able seaman: James Justice, 40, Scotland; Thomas Kienan, 25, Belfast; R. Firth, 31, Germany; Peter Ohlssors, 29, Sweden; Daniel Watson, 31, Edinburgh. Of the eight men only Born, Watson and Firth remained well enough to make the full voyage from Bangkok to Sydney with Conrad.

In "Falk," which he subtitled "A Reminiscence," Conrad included many of the details of his own harassed stay in Bangkok. The "I" of the story was, like Conrad, a young, untried captain of a ship moored in Bangkok who, new to his ship and crew, replaced a captain who had suddenly died. His chief mate "was not particularly pleased at my coming" and "as to the second mate, all I can say his name was Tottersen, or something like that"—the actual acting second mate of the *Otago* being Johnson.

With his officers unfriendly to him, the newcomer, and his crew, one after another, dropping ill with the infection raging along the river, Conrad went through more than a fortnight of taut days. The extent of the illness on board was confirmed by a letter written by Dr. William Willis, physician to the British Legation in Siam. Addressed to "C. Korzeniowski, Esq., Master of the sailing-ship *Otago*" and dated "Bangkok, Siam, February, 1888," it read:

"I think it is not out of place on my part that I should state, though not asked by you to do so, to prevent any misapprehension hereafter, that the crew of the sailing ship *Otago* has suffered severely whilst in Bangkok from tropical diseases, including fever, dysentery and cholera;

and I can speak of my own knowledge that you have done all in your power in the trying and responsible position of Master of the ship to hasten the departure of your vessel from this unhealthy place and at the same time to save the lives of the men under your command."[22]

Conrad, living on a ship of plague-stricken men, was occupying the quarters, sleeping in the bed, where the former captain had recently died. His ghost, according to the chief mate, haunted the ship and would continue to haunt it, dogging it with trouble until the vessel passed the latitude of 8° 20′ where the late commander had been buried at sea.

Uncanny incidents, by their very weirdness and the frequency of them, fed the inherent superstition of seamen; in no part of the world were they more readily attributed to malevolent spirits than in the East. The story of such a "wild" ship as the New Zealand steamer *Waikato*, perhaps the strangest happening of any, was written about and marveled over for months. The *Waikato* left London on May 4, 1899, for New Zealand and, halfway between the Cape of Good Hope and New Zealand, her tail shaft broke. Repairs proving impossible, the helpless ship drifted erratically for four months, the longest on record. Finally found and towed into Fremantle, Australia, on October 9, 1899, she had meandered over the ocean, taken by shifting winds and currents, for a distance of 4500 miles. Using some details of the *Waikato's* weird cruise, reminded of the near-cannibalism on board the German barque *Tiger* in 1881, setting the story in the Bangkok of his own anxious days when the *Otago* seemed to be laboring under a curse, Conrad wrote "Falk" in the early months of 1901. In that story Christian Falk—like Jim in *Lord Jim* and Williams of the *Jeddah*—brought censure upon himself for his honesty, exposing an act he alone knew: on a disabled steamer, left to drift after her tail shaft broke when midway between the Cape of Good Hope and New Zealand, the food had given out and the starving crew had existed on human flesh; Falk was the only one to survive. In telling his ghoulish secret in Bangkok Falk jeopardized the one thing he most wanted in life, marriage to the niece, a tawny-haired girl of nineteen "built on a magnificent scale," of the stiff-necked German commander of the *Diana*, Captain Hermann.

Sailing ships had to be towed down the Meinam (a situation at the heart of the action in "Falk"), through the river's maze of traffic, around the sunken wreck lying in midstream off Bangkok's drydock, down to the open sea. On Thursday, February 9, 1888,[23] Conrad began his long voyage to Australia, the *Otago* leaving Bangkok in tow that day. With the exception of the cook the whole crew had been ill in port.

Not only were his men still in shaky health but on this, his initial voyage as commander, he would need to maneuver the tricky gulf passage without the counsel of that mainstay to a captain, his chief mate: Born, emaciated with fever and delirious, was carried on board from the doctor's sanitarium almost at the moment of sailing.

Redheaded Born, a man with "a red moustache, a lean face, also red, and an uneasy eye," regained his health later on and became "of all my chief officers, the one I trusted most," as Conrad wrote in *The Mirror of the Sea*. Yet he was "one of the most uncomfortable shipmates possible for a young commander," having "a little too much of the sense of insecurity which is so invaluable in a seaman. He had an extremely disturbing air of being everlastingly ready (even when seated at table at my right hand before a plate of salt beef) to grapple with some impending calamity. I must hasten to add that he had also the other qualification necessary to make a trustworthy seaman—that of an absolute confidence in himself. What was really wrong with him was that he had these qualities in an unrestful degree. His eternally watchful demeanour, his jerky, nervous talk, even his, as it were, determined silences, seemed to imply—and, I believe, they did imply—that to his mind the ship was never safe in my hands."[24]

Born showed his distrust of Conrad's seamanship early. "On our first leaving port (I don't see why I should make a secret of the fact that it was Bangkok), a bit of manoeuvring of mine amongst the islands of the Gulf of Siam had given him an unforgettable scare. Ever since then he had nursed in secret a bitter idea of my utter recklessness."[25]

For much of the voyage from Bangkok to Singapore the one man in the crew physically able to help Conrad sail the *Otago* was Veilvom, the Dutch cook. A quiet pleasant seaman of forty-six suffering with a damaged heart, he had schooled himself to caution. With "the knowledge of that uneasy heart within his breast I could detect the restraint he put on the natural sailor-like agility of his movements," Conrad wrote of him as Ransome in *The Shadow Line*. "It was as though he had something very fragile or very explosive to carry about his person and was all the time aware of it."[26] Veilvom left the ship in Singapore, probably, like Ransome, "to go and be quiet" in the hospital after the strain of nursing seven disabled men, including the fever-crazed Born. The nightmare voyage down the Gulf of Siam was realistically given in *The Shadow Line*, though the eeriness of it, according to Conrad, came into the novel unconsciously.

"Strangely enough, you know, I never either meant or 'felt' the supernatural aspect of the story while writing it," he told Mrs. E. L. Sanderson.

"It came out somehow and my readers pointed it out to me. I must tell you that it is a piece of as strict autobiography as the form allowed,— I mean, the need of slight dramatization to make the thing actual. Very slight. For the rest, not a fact or sensation is 'invented.' What did worry me in reality was not the 'supernatural' character, but the *fact* of Mr. Burns's [Born's] craziness. For only think: my first command, a sinister, slowly developing situation from which one couldn't see any issue that one could *try for:* and the only man on board (second in command) to whom I could open my mind, not quite sane,—not to be depended on for any sort of moral support. It was very trying. I'll never forget those days."[27]

He never did forget them. During a period of fifteen years, from the beginning of 1901 to the end of 1915, he returned to those days, writing of them in "Falk" in 1901, "The Secret Sharer" in 1909, *The Shadow Line* in 1915, the latter story completed when he was fifty-eight.

The remembered events of the "sinister, slowly developing situation" of the *Otago* voyage began immediately the ship left Bangkok. Towed by tug down the winding Meinam, the *Otago* anchored outside the sandy bar blocking the river mouth, the vessel there to be made ready for the long homeward sail. This anchorage, used by ships waiting for a favorable tide to carry them over the bar, lay in fishing grounds where the Siamese trapped the *platoo,* the sardine-like fish such an important part of their diet. Within sight were the two islands off the customs port of Paknam. One island was fortified, the other, raised from the bed of the river in an early time by King P'hra Chow Phra-sat-thong, held the white brick Buddhist temple P'hra-Cha-dei ("The Lord's Delight"). This background of fishing grounds and "islets of the sea" Conrad adopted for "The Secret Sharer," the "great Paknam pagoda" being "the only thing on which the eye could rest" as the young captain of that story stood looking at "the monotonous sweep of the horizon" from his anchorage at the mouth of the Meinam. The ghostly white pagoda with its tall gilded spire, mirrored in the reddish-brown water of the river, was in actuality Conrad's last landmark.

"What I felt most," he had his young captain say in "The Secret Sharer" in that setting, "was my being a stranger to the ship; and if all the truth must be told, I was somewhat of a stranger to myself."[28] Unsureness, the self-depreciatory trait so noticeable in his writing years, afflicted Conrad always (in 1918, when he was sixty, Hugh Walpole wrote of him in his diary as "a child, nervous, excitable, affectionate, confidential, doesn't give you the idea anywhere of a strong man, but *real* genius that is absolutely *sui generis*"), and on his first voyage as commander anxiety over his ability to meet emergencies defeating more experienced men was acute. In Singapore the magic word "Command" had sent him along the streets in a daze of excitement; in Bangkok the hard reality of performing in that post made him overly conscious of the risks of failure. For even the lesser misfortune of stranding his ship a captain could be "broken," kept out of command for years, while a master's handling of his ship through gales and calms—and of the two Conrad feared calm weather more—could mean shipwreck or starvation for his crew. He would have illnesses and injuries to cope with; he could be faced with mutiny. In a crisis at sea not every action taken under stress could be classed a true failure or crime; some fell into a gray zone.

To Conrad one crime in this zone occurred on board the *Cutty Sark* in 1880. The young mate of that clipper ship was attacked at sea, with a capstan bar, by an insubordinate member of the crew; the two men struggled and the mate, gaining control of the bar, struck the seaman's head with such force that he died of the injury three days later. Though the cause differed, Cumming's death on the *Tilkhurst* resulted from such a fight and head wound. The association of the tragedy he witnessed and the crime famous in its day contributed to Conrad's interest in the sea case he drew upon for a short story.

The "young fellow" of the *Cutty Sark* who "had the misfortune to kill a man on deck" and whose "skipper had the decency to let him swim ashore on the Java coast as the ship was passing through Anjer Strait" provided him with the suggestion, he declared, for the swimmer, Leggatt, in "The Secret Sharer." Leggatt, a resolute young chief mate of twenty-five, "no homicidal ruffian," escaped confinement on board the *Sephora*, anchored near the islands off Paknam (Conrad, in the story, changing the scene from Anjer Strait to the mouth of the Meinam in the Gulf of Siam), and in the night swam to the ship where a young captain new to command was alone on deck, keeping watch. In the captain's cabin Leggatt told his story: during a severe storm badly mauling the *Sephora* he had ordered the ship's sole remaining sail to be reefed, an "anxious sort of job, that"; one seaman, "half crazed with funk," turned insolent and the mate struck him, the two grappling as an immense wave crashed on deck. When the deck cleared they were found locked together, the seaman dead, strangled. For this crime of murder Leggatt—whose father, like those of Lord Jim and Williams, was a parson in England—would be turned over to a court and tried. Rather than face "the 'brand of Cain' business" before a judge and jury, he had made up his mind to swim till he drowned. The captain, sympathizing with Leggatt—so identical to himself in appearance he thought of him as his "other self," his "secret self," his "double"—hid the hunted man in his cabin until the ship could be brought near enough to land, the island of Koh Ring, for the mate to swim ashore, "a free man, a proud swimmer, striking out for a new destiny."

In the masterly, consistently extolled story "The Secret Sharer," named as one of the most perfect of Conrad's tales, the alter ego every conscious man carries within himself was symbolized, the dark brother latent in all, the personification of fear. The many-faceted story also bore Conrad's view that, in a world where acts, successes no less than failures, were largely determined by chance, no man was a hero. Taking issue with the moral standards of the time of his *Otago* voyage, the Gladstone era of righteous absolutes, he subtly posed in this story the question he had raised in *Lord Jim:* "Do you know what *you* would have done? Do you?" It was the same question implied in his Bangkok story "Falk." In Bangkok, where Conrad encountered Buddhism for the first time, the Siamese, as Buddhists, held that on earth every act entailed its consequence, good deeds unerringly rewarded, evil ones as surely punished. To his deeply skeptical mind the shadow line hazing actions in practical life defied arbitrary moral judgments. A point underlying "The Secret Sharer," it was a suggestion carried in the very title he gave, *The Shadow Line,* to the third of his Siam stories.

Like the captain of that story, he was himself faced on his voyage from Bangkok with an emergency caused by stagnant weather, with no solution he could see to try for. His crew, wasting with fever, required the fresh reviving air of the open sea. In the placid Gulf of Siam the *Otago* moved so slowly he sought an offshore breeze, maneuvering among the islands off the Cambodian coast—Koh Chang, Koh Kut, Koh Ring—with the recklessness giving his chief mate Born "an unforgettable scare." He apparently landed at, or came close to, Chantabun, 150 miles southeast of Bangkok, the Siamese port where he later recalled that some Chinese had tried to kill him and several others.

The passage down the coast was a slow creep, the *Otago* taking twenty-one days to cover the eight hundred miles from Bangkok to Singapore. For the last seventeen days Conrad was continually on deck and for the final forty hours without sleep. Aided solely by the cook with the faulty heart, he brought the ship into Singapore. There three launches bearing naval surgeons quickly answered the *Otago's* signal for medical assistance, the crew were carried off to the hospital, bluejackets from nearby men-of-war furled his ship's sails, and Conrad went ashore.

"It is strange how on coming ashore I was struck by the springy step, the lively eyes, the strong vitality of everyone I met," says the exhausted young captain in *The Shadow Line*, the character in which Conrad drew himself.

The *Otago* reached Singapore on March 2, 1888, and, before sailing a week later, took on six new members of the crew to replace the sick men, including Veilvom, left behind in that port. Conrad's handwritten list of those who sailed with him from Singapore to Sydney still exists, in Sydney's Mitchell Library. Dated May 8, 1888, the day after the ship arrived at Sydney, it gives his *Otago* crew as: Charles Born, 1st Mate, 33, Germany; Isaac Jackson, 2nd Mate, 23, England; Daniel Watson, AB, 31, Scotland; R. Firth, AB, 31, Germany; H. Green, AB, 33, Liverpool; Thomas Smith, AB, 27, Sweden; James Jensen, AB, 22, Denmark; Richard Green, AB, 48, St. John, New Brunswick; Thomas Humphrey, AB, 22, England.

Conrad's first voyage as captain lasted three months. They were hard-testing months, in every kind of weather. Toward the end of the passage from Singapore, when off the Australian coast after rounding Cape Leeuwin, the *Otago* ran into the heavy gale Conrad recalled in *The Mirror of the Sea*. "It was a hard, long gale, grey clouds and green sea, heavy weather undoubtedly, but still what a sailor would call manageable. Under two lower topsails and a reefed foresail the barque seemed to race with a long, steady sea that did not becalm her in the troughs. The solemn thundering combers caught her up from astern, passed her with a fierce boiling up of foam level with the bulwarks, swept on ahead with a swish and a roar: and the little vessel, dipping her jib-boom into the tumbling froth, would go on running in a smooth, glassy hollow, a deep valley between two ridges of the sea, hiding the horizon ahead and astern. There was such fascination in her pluck, nimbleness, the continual exhibition of unfailing seaworthiness, in the semblance of courage and endurance, that I could not give up the delight of watching her run through the three unforgettable days of that gale which my mate also delighted to extol as 'a famous shove.'"[29]

Another gale soon raked the ship, the storm-whipped *Otago* reaching Sydney on May 7, 1888. The following day the Sydney *Morning Herald* reported the "Barque *Otago* arrived 7th Captain Conrad Konkorzentow-ski [*sic*] from Bangkok February 9th." The newspaper account, based on the lean details Conrad contributed, was a recital in customary vein, limited to the weather encountered on the passage.

"The iron barque *Otago* arrived in port yesterday from Bangkok with a full cargo of teak. Her captain reports that light winds were had down the Gulf of Siam, with light winds and airs through the China and Java Seas. Passed through Straits of Sunda on March 15th. The Southeast trades were very light, and were carried down to 26 south. Passed Cape Leeuwin on April 16th, when a heavy gale from the west was encountered. The gale continued with unabated fury for two days ere it moderated. The barque behaved herself exceedingly well, and beyond plenty of water finding its way on board, no damage was done. Cape Otway was abeam on the 28th ult. and Wilson Promontory on the 2nd. Experienced NNE winds through Bass Strait, but on Friday and Saturday last a very heavy gale from the westward, the wind going around SSW and keeping her decks full. The Hornby Lt. was sighted at 8 P.M. on Sunday, and the Heads were entered at 9 A.M. yesterday in tow of the *Irresistible*. The *Otago* anchored off Elizabeth Bay."

Conrad held command of the *Otago* for fourteen months. Eight of those months were spent on long seagoing voyages, six in trading along the Australian coast. For the first three months after reaching Sydney from Bangkok he was assigned to an unexciting run, taking the *Otago* from Sydney to Melbourne in June, carrying cargo back from there to Sydney in July. Though an excellent and painstaking commander, he was quickly bored by monotony. His restlessness grew under three months of routine coastal trading and for his second long voyage as master, sailing the *Otago* from Sydney with a mixed cargo for Port Louis, Mauritius, he proposed a radical course.

"All of a sudden, all the deep-lying historic sense of the exploring adventures in the Pacific surged to the surface of my being," he said of it later. "Almost without reflection I sat down and wrote a letter to my owners suggesting that, instead of the usual southern route, I should take the ship to Mauritius by way of Torres Strait. I ought to have received a severe rap on the knuckles, if only for wasting their time in submitting such an unheard-of proposition."[30]

His owners agreed, in spite of the higher insurance rates of this riskier route, and Conrad sailed from Sydney on August 7, 1888, northbound in the face of a fierce gale for the strait the Spanish navigator Luis Vaez de Torres had discovered in 1606. Captain James Cook had roughly mapped Torres Strait in 1770—going ashore on Possession Island, twenty miles south of Thursday Island, to establish Britain's claim—but only thirty-eight years before Conrad attempted the dangerous passage had it been accurately charted, in 1848–50 by Blackwood of the *Fly* and Owen Stanley of the *Rattlesnake*. The strait offered a daring test of his navigation skill but it also attracted Conrad for its connection with three early explorers—"Great shades! All friends of my youth!"

"The fierce south-easter caught me up on its wings," he wrote of his departure from Sydney, "and no later than the ninth day I was outside the entrance of Torres Strait, named after the undaunted and reticent Spaniard who, in the seventeenth century, first sailed that way without knowing where he was, without suspecting he had New Guinea on one side of him and the whole solid Australian continent on the other—he thought he was passing through an archipelago—the strait whose existence for a century and a half had been doubted, argued about, squabbled over by geographers, and even denied by the disreputable but skilful navigator, Abel Tasman, who thought it was a large bay, and whose true contours were first laid down on the map by James Cook, the navigator without fear and without reproach, the greatest in achievement and character of the later seamen fathers of militant geography. If the dead haunt the scenes of their earthly exploits, then I must have been attended benevolently by those three shades."[31]

Conrad was drawn by the romance of adventure to out-of-the-way parts of the world, as he had been to Borneo and would be to the Congo, and Torres Strait was one of these. Upon its many islands lived a hardy, intelligent people of Papuan origin, fishermen, extraordinary swimmers. The young men were pearl divers (pearling stations had recently been set up, the local mother-of-pearl shell bringing £250 a ton in Sydney), while the elderly family men fished near their home reefs, collecting, as in Borneo, the bêche-de-mer for Chinese markets. An unspoiled people, trusting and generous, the islanders were protected by a government official, John Douglas, a "grand old gentleman" with the fatherly devotion for them William Lingard had shown for the people of Berau. Douglas had earlier been in the Queensland cabinet and premier of that colony and was as well known in Sydney as the pearl islands he watched over.

Thursday Island, in the center of the group, was the anchorage for vessels passing through the strait and there the *Otago* lay at anchor for nine hours. As his ship left the strait Conrad took a bearing on Possession Island, picturing to himself the history-making landing of Captain Cook, "the famous seaman navigator, a lonely figure in a three-cornered hat and square-skirted laced coat, pacing to and fro slowly on the rocky shore."[32]

Fifty-four days after leaving Sydney the *Otago* arrived, on September 30, 1888, at Port Louis, Mauritius.[33] There on that Indian Ocean island, settled in turn by the Dutch, the French and the British and called by its inhabitants the "Pearl of the Ocean," Conrad came to know some of the "old French families, descendants of the old colonists; all noble, all impoverished, and living a narrow domestic life in dull, dignified decay."[34] His eight weeks' stay in Port Louis supplied material for his short story, "A Smile of Fortune," but it was also there that he made a proposal of marriage he never afterward mentioned. It was not until seven years after his death that Jean-Aubry learned of it, in 1931, and wrote of it in *Vie de Conrad*, later translated into English as *The Sea Dreamer*. Jean-Aubry's source was a writer in Mauritius, Auguste Esnouf, who used the pen name Savinien Mérédac. Mérédac published two articles, "*Joseph Conrad et Nous*" in the February 15, 1931, issue of *L'Essor*, the Port Louis Literary Circle periodical, and "*Joseph Conrad chez Nous*" in the Port Louis *Radical* of August 7, 1931. From these articles and his 1931–33 correspondence with Mérédac, Jean-Aubry[35] told all that has ever been known of Conrad's romance in Mauritius and the rejection that, at thirty-one, played a part in his return to England.

XXII

Conrad reached the professional peak of his seaman's life in his thirtieth year. Commander of a seagoing ship throughout that year, the only such command he was ever to have, he drew wages, £14 a month, he was never to equal; four years later on his last voyage he sailed as chief mate again, his pay almost halved. This year at the crest was one of the very few in his life when he was spared the ordeal of trying to get a ship, the disheartening search instilling a "sense of profound abasement" consuming nearly as many of his days as those he spent at sea; it provided in unusually large measure the life away from shore he preferred, voyages in the Eastern waters he favored. As a shipmaster of proved ability whose owners relied implicitly on his judgment he had "the finest life under the sun." But in one of those moments "when the still young are inclined to commit rash actions" he sacrificed this satisfying life, the immediate cause of his change of course being a girl.

Shy with women and keenly sensitive, he became involved in a mirage-like romance in Port Louis, offering marriage to a girl he barely knew. In "The Planter of Malata" he created a romance similar, in the hopelessness of its situation and in the feelings of its hero Renouard, to the one, hardly to be called a love affair, he experienced in Mauritius.

In Conrad's story of love unreturned Renouard, an idealistic, successful young man, owner of a schooner, leads a solitary life on his silk-raising plantation on an island in the East; at a dinner party "in a great colonial city" he meets and instantly falls in love with a society girl just arrived from London. Red-haired Felicia Moorsom, strikingly beautiful, "clever, open-minded, popular, and—well, charming," a girl in her mid-twenties, had come out to the East to find the young Londoner to whom she had once been engaged. In her single-minded search for her missing fiancé she is unaware Renouard has fallen in love with her. But "fresh from months of solitude and from days at sea," he is captivated by her, the first girl he has met with a cultured European background paralleling his own. When near her he is affected by "the most powerful emotion of his life"; he sits at her side "with fire in his breast, a humming in his ears, and in a complete disorder of his mind." From the moment of meeting her, "without ever trying to resist, he went every afternoon to the house where she lived. He went there as passively as if in a dream." He is alternately reticent and voluble, stonily silent or entertainingly recounting to the group about her the adventurous episodes of his life. The "power of fascination had torn him out of his very nature so completely that to preserve his habitual calmness from going to pieces had become a terrible effort. He used to go from her on board the schooner exhausted, broken, shaken up, as though he had been put to the most exquisite torture."[1] In the elderly group surrounding her "nobody could have guessed that his quiet deferential bearing to all these grey-heads was the supreme effort of stoicism, that the man was engaged in keeping a sinister watch on his tortures lest his strength should fail him. As before, when grappling with other forces of nature, he could find in himself all sorts of courage except the courage to run away."[2]

The girl who put Conrad through the tortures of a flash love was Eugénie Renouf, a French girl of twenty-six.[3] His introduction to her came through a chance meeting, the day after his arrival in Mauritius, with a former acquaintance, Gabriel Renouf, then a captain in the French merchant marine. Four years earlier in Bombay, when Conrad was second mate of the Narcissus, he had loaned a small sum to Renouf, "a pleasant, ineffectual young man who was rather stranded there, not knowing what to do with himself or even how to get home to his island again."[4] Renouf's elder brother Henri worked in the office of Conrad's shipping agents in Port Louis, Blyth Bros. & Co., and the appreciative Frenchmen invited Conrad to their home. Orphans of one of the socially prominent families of the island, the two brothers and two unmarried sisters, one being Eugénie, lived with their eldest sister and her husband, Louis Edward Schmidt, treasurer of Blyth Bros. The Schmidt family (the "S–– family" in "A Smile of Fortune") were descendants of colonists settling on the sugar-producing island in the eighteenth century. The routine of their provincial lives struck Conrad by its barrenness: "The men, as a rule, occupy inferior posts in Government offices or in business houses. The girls are almost always pretty, ignorant of the world, kind and agreeable and generally bilingual; they prattle innocently both in French and English. The emptiness of their existence passes belief."[5]

During the eight weeks the *Otago* was detained in Port Louis—chartered as a sugar-carrier, the ship was held up due to a shortage of sugar bags resulting from a warehouse fire—Conrad called repeatedly at the Schmidt home to be near the lively, pretty girl Eugénie. He entertained the family group gathered there with accounts of his travels; often he seemed preoccupied and on occasion took an abrupt and hasty leave. No one guessed the whirling state of his feelings, the family attributing the jerkiness of his actions to simple oddness. Two days before the *Otago* was due to sail Conrad called on Henri Renouf at his office and gravely made his proposal of marriage. So casually did he know Eugénie that he had never learned she was already engaged; in less than two months, on January 14, she would marry a local pharmacist named Loumeau. Conrad remained on board his ship for the final two days of his stay in Port Louis and, sending a farewell note to Gabriel Renouf, announced in it his decision never to return to Mauritius.

Expansive and suddenly silent, charming and suddenly brusque, Conrad was as incomprehensible a young man to the sedate Mauritians as they in their "dull, dignified decay" were to him. Nearly forty-three years after his stay in Port Louis a member of the firm of his charterers, Paul Langlois of Langlois & Co., recalled his impressions of Conrad in a February 2, 1931, letter to Savinien Mérédac. M. Langlois, a major sugar exporter in Port Louis, saw Conrad almost daily for six or seven weeks in 1888, in the shipping agents' office of *père* Krumpholtz where captains in search of cargo regularly called. He remembered Conrad for his handsome, unusual appearance.

"Slightly above medium height, he had forceful and very mobile features, his expression very quickly changing from gentleness to an excitability verging on anger; large black eyes generally melancholy and dreamy, but gentle too except for fairly frequent moments of irritation; a determined chin, a well-shaped, graceful mouth and a thick, dark brown mustache carefully trimmed—such was his appearance, certainly good-looking but so strange in expression it was difficult to forget if one had seen it once or twice.

"Aside from the distinction of his manners, the most striking thing about the captain of the *Otago*, was the contrast between him and the other shipmasters. . . . These captains, usually dressed in white ducks, wearing caps or straw hats, their faces and hands tanned by the sun and salt water, their nails black with the telltale tar of their trade, their language forceful and often coarse, were not models of elegance and refinement. In contrast to his colleagues, Captain Korzeniowski was always dressed like a dandy. I can still see him (and just because of the contrast with other sailors my memory is precise) arriving almost every day at my office dressed in a black or dark-colored coat, a vest generally light in color and 'fancy' trousers, everything well cut and stylish; he wore a black or gray derby slightly tilted to one side, always wore gloves and carried a cane with a gold knob.

"You can judge from this description that he was in contrast to the other captains, with whom, by the way, he was on strictly formal terms, limited most of the time to a greeting. Also he was not very popular with his colleagues who, in irony, called him 'the Russian Count.' So much for his physical appearance.

"As to his character: a perfect education, very varied and interesting conversation, if it happened to be a day he felt communicative. That was not true every day. He who was to acquire fame under the name of Joseph Conrad was quite often taciturn and very excitable. On such days he had a nervous tic, in the shoulder and eyes, and anything unexpected, an object falling on the floor or a door banging, made him jump. . . .

"Joseph Conrad spoke equally well, and very purely, both English and French, but he preferred the latter which he handled with elegance; our conversations were always in French."[6]

In spite of two months of daily contact all that the Mauritians came to know of Conrad was the outward man—handsome, well-dressed, urbane, courtly, a fascinating storyteller. Even when the Renouf girls induced him to write, in their confession album, a personal questionnaire then in vogue, he gave serious answers to only two questions, those concerning what gifts of nature he would most like to have and what he most detested. To the query *"Quel est le don de la nature dont vous voudriez être doué?"* his reply was "Self-confidence"; to *"Que détestez-vous le plus?"* he wrote "False pretences."[7]

Conrad's impressions of Mauritians were deeply critical, judging by the story he built from his stay in Port Louis, "A Smile of Fortune." There he drew a community centered around the activities of a port, old colonial families living by the false pretenses he so much detested.

Of the two Jacobus brothers in the story, Ernest—wealthy, hardheaded merchant, member of the Council, "an importer on a grand scale," a bachelor mistreating his mulatto son to no one's disapproval—is highly respected ("Lots of people owed him money"); Alfred—quiet, hard-working ship chandler, a widower—has flouted convention by raising his illegitimate daughter and lives under the town's taboo; he and his teen-age daughter Alice exist in their isolation like "a lonely pair of castaways on a desert island." The story was compounded from different areas of Conrad's social life in Port Louis, where his contacts were not limited to charterers or fine old families. Among his acquaintances was a stevedore, James Horatio Shaw, whose daughter, nearly seventeen, was named Alice. Conrad visited at the Shaw home, remarkable on the island for its unusual rose garden. The captain's flirtation with Alice in "A Smile of Fortune," in the setting of a magnificent garden, was apparently autobiographical—in a talk with Jean-Aubry Conrad indicated it to be so[8]—while the cargo of potatoes foisted upon the captain in the story was literally true. The few tons of potatoes Conrad was pressed into taking on the Otago proved a surprising and profitable trade, a "smile of fortune," when delivered to hungry, drought-afflicted Melbourne.

On November 22, 1888, the Otago sailed out of Port Louis and after a voyage of forty-four days arrived, on January 5, 1889,[9] at Melbourne. In February Conrad took the ship from Melbourne on a short voyage along Australia's south coast to the little port of Minlacowie, there to pick up a cargo of wheat destined for Port Adelaide. Of this voyage he later wrote: "I did go to Minlacowie. The farmers around were very nice to me and I gave their wives (on a never-to-be-forgotten day) a tea party on board the dear old Otago then lying alongside the God-forsaken jetty there."[10]

The "never-to-be-forgotten day" was to be Conrad's last festivity on board the ship, his captain's farewell. In March he reached Port Adelaide, the Otago's home port, where he urged his owners to permit him to take the ship for a year to the China Seas. He had never been to China and his insistence on going there, like his choice of Torres Strait, was undoubtedly inspired by his "deep-lying historic sense" of the exploring adventures of the past. The East of Marco Polo, the Cathay goal of Columbus, the China only newly opened to Western trade, had been his goal eight years earlier when an accident prevented his sailing on the Annie Frost. He tried every means to persuade his owners to favor a China voyage but Simpson & Sons had other plans: a repeat trading trip to Mauritius. Unable to dissuade them, he had the choice of returning to Port Louis, reopening the fresh wounds of his romantic disaster there, or of resigning his command. On March 26, offering as his excuse his need to return to Europe, he resigned. His Port Adelaide owners replied in a letter of April 2, 1889.

"Referring to your resignation of the command (which we have in another letter formally accepted) of our bark *Otago*, we now have much pleasure in stating that this early severance from our employ is entirely at your own desire, with a view to visiting Europe, and that we entertain a high opinion of your ability in the capacity you now vacate, of your attainments generally, and should be glad to learn of your future success.

"Wishing you a pleasant passage home, we are, dear Sir,

Yours faithfully,

HENRY SIMPSON & SONS

Owners of the Black Diamond Line."[11]

As before, when he had quit the *Vidar*, Conrad offered as his reason his intention of visiting Europe. One purpose of such a trip was to see his Uncle Thaddeus from whom two letters,[12] written in the course of four months, were delivered in Australia. At sixty-one, writing as "an old man who has not long to live," he urged Conrad to make arrangements to visit him in the Ukraine. He was to live another five years but, disturbed by poor health, he had revised his will; it would still provide, as it had ten years earlier, a bequest of fifteen thousand rubles for his nephew. Details of this financial topic filled his letter of January 3, 1889. Thaddeus' tone had changed somewhat over the years. As Conrad's professional standing rose his uncle became less sharply critical. His cutting remarks, certain to undermine the self-confidence of his ward, never entirely ceased, nor were the personality antagonisms of this mismatched uncle and nephew ever dissolved, but a basic family affection did exist between them. Conrad's inability to please his uncle evidently troubled him; in Renouard's attitude toward his relatives in "The Planter of Malata" he appears to have reflected his own: "Renouard did not like being asked about his people, for whom he had a profound and remorseful affection. He had not seen a single human being to whom he was related, for many years, and he was extremely different from them all."[13]

It would be a year before Conrad, interrupting his efforts to obtain another command, would visit Thaddeus. His return to Europe from Australia—leaving by steamer from Port Adelaide in April, 1889, and arriving by the Suez Canal route in London in June—was directed less by the urgency of a family reunion than by his failure to secure what he had set his heart on in Adelaide, command of a China-going ship. He never achieved such a post, nor did he reach China. But the pursuit of a command, as desperation grew, made him consider the pearl-fishing islands of Torres Strait, the West Indies again, life as a Suez Canal pilot. His gratitude to the shipowner who backed him as captain of his sole ocean-going ship, a support remembered for twenty-eight years, came out in an unpublished letter written late in his life. "If the firm of Messrs. H. Simpson & Sons still exists in Adelaide," he wrote to a former employee of the firm, "please tell them that J.C. will never forget the generosity, the courtesy, and indeed the kindness of the head of the firm in '88–'89 when he commanded their barque *Otago*."[14]

The *Otago* was to outlive Conrad by many years. After he resigned his command she continued to sail about the world until 1900. Bought then by the Australian shipowners Huddart Parker Ltd., she was rigged down to a floating coal hulk, in service first in Sydney and later in Hobart, Tasmania. In Hobart in 1931 she was sold to a wrecker, Mr. Dodge, for twenty-five dollars. Towed up the Derwent River, she was beached on the eastern side of the stream at the foot of Mount Direction, near the creek where the first settlers of what Tasman named Van Diemen's Land came ashore in 1803. In this quiet bay, her bow in an apricot orchard, the *Otago* lay for thirty years, gradually rusting into decay. Christopher Morley, who met Conrad during his 1923 visit to New York and had long been an admirer of the novelist's work, learned of the whereabouts of the *Otago;* when a friend, William Stanley Hall, visited Tasmania in 1946 Morley commissioned him to buy some memento from the ship. Mr. Hall found the vessel's teak wheel still on board, in the midst of rubbish and wreckage, rotted canvas and abandoned gear, and shipped it to Morley in New York. In 1949, on the twenty-fifth anniversary of Conrad's death, Morley took the steering wheel Conrad had once used to London, presenting it in a ceremony attended by sea captains, artists and writers, to the Honourable Company of Master Mariners. Installed in their headquarters ship *Wellington*, moored in the Thames off Temple Stairs, the famous wheel remains a relic of Conrad's seaman's life. In Hobart sightseers continued to visit the crumbling *Otago* until 1960 when she was finally broken up, her steel plates torn out that year and shipped to Japan as scrap.[15] By far the oldest of Conrad's ships, the little barque made world-famous through him and whose wheel he wrote of in *The Shadow Line* as "a symbol of mankind's claim to direct its own fate," had existed for ninety-one years.

Conrad's own future as a novelist received its first turn in that direction the year he gave up command of the *Otago*. Back in London in June, 1889, he took furnished rooms in Bessborough Gardens, near the Thames, and after a spell of loafing "began to look for a ship–I should think the hardest work on earth." June, July and August produced no results and one morning in September, "one of those London days . . . of fascinating softness," he began to write *Almayer's Folly*. "The ambition of being an author had never turned up amongst those gracious imaginary existences one creates fondly for oneself at times in the stillness and immobility of a day-dream," he wrote in *A Personal Record*, "yet it stands clear as the sun at noonday that from the moment I had done blackening over the first manuscript page of *Almayer's Folly* (it contained about two hundred words and this proportion of words to a page has remained with me through the fifteen years of my writing life), from the moment I had, in the simplicity of my heart and the amazing ignorance of my mind, written that page the die was cast."[16]

Having left Berau only twenty months before he began the novel, Conrad had Charles Olmeyer fresh in his mind ("it is possible and even likely that I was thinking of the man Almayer"[17]) but, he continued the reminiscence, the "conception of a planned book was entirely outside my mental range when I sat down to write."[18] The history of this short novel, taking nearly five years to complete, bears out Conrad's remembered first groping steps as a novelist–"I was not at all certain that I wanted to write, or that I meant to write, or that I had anything to write about."[19] Sixteen months elapsed before he completed the first seven chapters or one-half of the book; in the next three years he wrote only two chapters, seeming to have hit an impasse; the final three chapters consumed five months of fairly steady writing. He was thirty-one when he began *Almayer's Folly*, thirty-six when, as he wrote Mme. Poradowska on April 24, 1894, "It's finished! A scratch of the pen writing 'The End,' and suddenly the whole company of people who have spoken in my ear, moved before my eyes, lived with me for so many years, becomes a troop of phantoms, who are withdrawing, growing dim, and merging–indistinct and pallid–with the sunlight of this brilliant and sombre day."[20]

For the five years before this 1894 day of completing the novel ("it seems to me that I have buried a part of myself in the pages lying here before my eyes. And yet I am happy–a little"[21]) Conrad clung to the career he loved, the sea, serving on the last three ships of his mariner's life. The *Roi des Belges*, a Belgian stern-wheel steamer of fifteen tons which resembled "an enormous sardine box with a flat-roofed shed erected on it" clapping her way up and down the Congo River, was the first of these.

In the same month of September, 1889, that he began *Almayer's Folly* in London, Conrad made up his mind to go to Africa, to the Congo. A map seen in the window of a Fleet Street bookseller may have influenced his sudden interest, as it did Marlow's in "Heart of Darkness," but the chance of exploration—uncharted white spaces still existed on maps of central Africa—and personal connections also had much to do with it. His friend of Marseilles days, Adolf Krieger, in London with the shipping agency of Barr, Moering & Co., had secured for Conrad a job as supercargo with the London branch of the Antwerp shipowners, Walford & Co. Conrad had hoped this temporary job might lead to his becoming master of one of Walford's ships to the West Indies and New Orleans but, such a future seeming far away, he concentrated on getting to the Congo. Again through Krieger, a letter was sent by Barr, Moering & Co. to a ship broker in Ghent, G. de Baerdemacker, requesting inquiries to be made on Conrad's behalf about a Congo steamer command. Mr. de Baerdemacker recommended Conrad to Captain Albert Thys, aide-de-camp to King Leopold and acting manager of the Société Anonyme Belge pour le Commerce du Haut-Congo, saying of Conrad in his sponsoring letter of September 24, 1889: "This man is very warmly recommended by friends in London and holds the highest certificates; his general education is better than that of most sailors and he is a perfect gentleman."

Conrad met such requirements as fluent French and, following an exchange of letters, went to Brussels early in November for an interview with Thys, of whom he took away "an impression of pale plumpness in a frock-coat." Thys promised Conrad a river-boat command when an opening occurred. None developed in two months and, informed by Thys that there would still be a considerable delay—it was to take eight months before an appointment did come through—Conrad made the visit to his uncle in Poland he had considered when he left the *Otago*. On his way to the Ukraine he stopped off in Brussels. Arriving on February 5, 1890, he called on a distant cousin, Alexander Poradowski and his novelist wife Marguerite. It was Mme. Poradowska, a beautiful and well-connected Frenchwoman of forty-two, whose influence helped Conrad to get to the Congo and with whom he maintained an active correspondence for many years. In letters to her, written in French, Conrad was to describe more fully than to anyone else his initial years as a writer.

On his uncle's Polish estate, seeing it for the first time in twenty-three years, Conrad spent two months, from February 16 to April 18, 1890. There Thaddeus delivered to Conrad the account book he had kept since 1869, noting family gifts received on behalf of his ward and sums forwarded to him. His purpose in keeping the ledger, with its comments on such episodes as Conrad's duel in Marseilles, he explained in an introductory note.

"*Cher,* in order that you, having reached a mature age, should know all the experiences of your parents and their relations with the family, I want you to know in what way the little fund was created which is to serve as the basis of your further work and independence!! I under-take this tale, not to put forth my own merits in this matter—for your other relatives, as you will soon find out, did more for your parents than I could do with my relative means—but, chiefly, in order to let you know how we all loved your mother and, through her, also your father."[22]

Thaddeus began the document with an extract of family history: "Your parents joined in wedlock on April 28, 1856 in Oratov on the inherited property of your late grandfather, Joseph Bobrowski, in the parish church of Oratov."[23] He closed the financial account "with my cordial blessing for your life ahead" and the final notation: "Thus the progress of Master Conrad to man's estate has cost 17,454 rubles,"[24] a sum equivalent at that time to $8727.

Conrad returned to London from the Ukraine by way of Lublin, where he stayed two days with relatives, going on from there to Brussels. In Brussels on April 29 he was notified that he was to leave immediately for Africa. Word had just been received that a river-boat captain, a Dane named Freisleben, had been killed during a dispute with Africans in the Congo; Conrad would replace him. In "Heart of Dark-ness," through Marlow, Conrad told the actual circumstances leading to his departure for Africa, there slightly altering Freisleben's name.

"I got my appointment—of course; and I got it very quick. It appears the Company had received news that one of their captains had been killed in a scuffle with the natives. This was my chance, and it made me the more anxious to go. It was only months and months afterwards, when I made the attempt to recover what was left of the body, that I heard the original quarrel arose from a misunderstanding about some hens. Yes, two black hens. Fresleven—that was the fellow's name, a Dane . . .

"I flew around like mad to get ready, and before forty-eight hours I was crossing the Channel to show myself to my employers, and sign the contract. . . . I had no difficulty in finding the Company's offices. It was the biggest thing in the town, and everybody I met was full of it. They were going to run an over-sea empire, and make no end of coin by trade."[25]

On May 2, 1890, Conrad wrote from London to a cousin in Lublin, Maria Bobrowska Tyszkowa: "I could not write earlier. I was unspeakably busy and even now I have a great deal to do. I am leaving for the Congo in four days and I must get ready for a three-year stay in the middle of Africa."[26] Four days later he was on his way from London to Brussels for final instructions and a physical examination, then from Brussels to Bordeaux by train; he sailed from Bordeaux on May 12 on the *Ville de Maceio*. In a May 22 letter posted at Freetown, Sierra Leone, he described the rush of his departure to his cousin Charles Zagorski.

"If you only knew the devilish haste I had to make! From London to Brussels, and back again to London! And again to Brussels! If you had only seen all the tin boxes and revolvers, the high boots and the touching farewells; just another handshake and just another pair of trousers!—and if you knew all the bottles of medicine and all the affectionate wishes I took away with me, you would understand in what a typhoon, cyclone, hurricane, earthquake—no!—in what a universal cataclysm, in what a fantastic atmosphere of mixed shopping, business and affecting scenes, I passed two whole weeks. . . . As far as I can make out from my 'service letter' I am destined to the command of a steamboat, belonging to M. Delcommune's exploring party, which is being got ready; but I know nothing for certain as everything is supposed to be kept secret. What makes me rather uneasy is the information that 60 per cent. of our Company's employees return to Europe before they have completed even six months' service. Fever and dysentery!"[27]

His voyage to the Congo took a full month. The *Ville de Maceio* called at Tenerife in the Canary Islands on May 15; called at Dakar, at Conakry, then at Freetown on May 22; went on to stops at Grand Bassam on the Ivory Coast, anchored in the open roadstead of Cotonou in Dahomey where a wall of high breakers held ships some distance from the shore, passed close to Grand Popo and Whydah. The village of Whydah, or Ouidah, was being bombarded by the French man-of-war *Le Seignelay*, an action growing out of France's decision, in March, to annex Dahomey[28] ("Once, I remember, we came upon a man-of-war anchored off the coast," Conrad wrote of this in "Heart of Darkness." "There wasn't even a shed there, and she was shelling the bush. It appears the French had one of their wars going on thereabouts"[29]). The

Ville de Maceio reached Libreville in the French Congo on June 10 and, putting in briefly at Loango and Banana along that coast, arrived at her Belgian Congo destination of Boma on June 13. Boma was a settlement of one hundred Europeans who, with a sanitarium as their first large building, were planning an "iron" church, hotel and warehouses for what they hopefully dreamed of as a future city.[30] Weary of tinned food, they were attempting to raise vegetables in their gardens, to start banana and orange plantations. A few hours in this "delectable capital" of the Congo Free State were more than enough for Conrad and he left the day of his arrival, traveling forty miles upstream on the Congo River by a smaller boat to Matadi. There, in the ivory-shipping port one hundred miles from the Atlantic, his adventure in the heart of Africa began.

He was to write of this equatorial hothouse as a region "where the merry dance of death and trade goes on in a still and earthy atmosphere as of an overheated catacomb."[31] The very profitable trade of the Congo Free State, the territory privately owned by Belgium's Leopold II from 1885 to 1908, brought that oppressive monarch an estimated twenty million dollars during the twenty-three years of his ownership. In those years, due to the slave trade, forced labor, and ruthless treatment of a subject race, its population was reduced by half.

At the time Conrad was in the Congo the House Committee on Foreign Affairs in Washington issued a report on the African slave trade. "This evil," the September 21, 1890, report declared, "destroys over one thousand human lives every day." In the Congo the slave hunt was carried on by native chiefs, the captives being used "either for barter, servants, farm laborers, and also as food and as victims offered in their funeral rites." An estimated eighty thousand Africans a year were being brought to the principal slave markets. When to this figure were added those perishing on the way, killed in villages raided for slaves, or dying after capture from privation, "it would appear," the report went on, "that at least 400,000 human lives were thus destroyed in Central Africa every year."[32]

Conrad was thirty-two when he entered Central Africa. His sights were set on exploration of the headwaters of the Congo, the unachieved goal of David Livingstone, "the most venerated perhaps of all the objects of my early geographical enthusiasm."[33] Seventeen years after Livingstone's death in Africa Conrad reached the Congo. In the last words of Kurtz in "Heart of Darkness"—"The horror! The horror!"—he summed up what he saw.

XXIII

The conquest of the earth, which mostly means the taking it away
from those who have a different complexion or slightly flatter noses
than ourselves, is not a pretty thing when you look into it too much.

"Heart of Darkness"

The source of the great 2900-mile-long Congo River was one of geography's unsolved mysteries in the summer of 1890. This fifth-longest stream in the world, exceeded in Africa only by the Nile and with a tremendous flow only the Amazon surpasses, was then believed to have its beginnings in Lake Landje, a mysterious body of water "which no white traveler has seen," said the *New York Times* that summer.[1] In Brussels Conrad had been assigned to command the Congo River steamer which would transport the exploring party of a thirty-five-year-old Belgian, Alexandre Delcommune; it was Delcommune, on this expedition, who would trace the headwaters of the river and lay to rest the myth of the nonexistent Lake Landje. Through a disillusioning set of circumstances Conrad missed the one opportunity for exploration he was ever offered.

Africa was the least known of the continents in 1890. Though the second largest of them—comprising one-fourth of the earth's land surface, equal in size to the combined areas of the United States, China, India and Western Europe—much of its center was undiscovered country. The 1885 Congress of Berlin had laid out the ground rules European powers would follow in carving up the neglected land mass and by 1890 the race to set up colonies was on. Commercial interests instigated the rush, little as anyone knew of what the heart of the continent might hold. "Slaves have from time immemorial been the chief product," *The Universal Cyclopaedia* could still say of Africa in its 1900 edition, while the "next best known and most characteristic product is ivory." Ivory was making its way in great quantities from the depths of the interior "usually on men's backs," Europe in return sending into Africa "iron and copper wire, beads and trinkets" as well as "large amounts of spirits and other drinks." Britain, France, Germany, Belgium and Portugal were in the race, each maintaining a close silence over the movements of expeditions. Everything about the exploring party he was attached to "is supposed to be kept secret," Conrad wrote in May, 1890; less than two months later, however, the secret was out.

"The Congo Commercial Company have decided to send out a fresh expedition, consisting of seven Europeans," the *New York Times* announced on July 14. The expedition would explore the streams feeding the Congo, penetrating the reputedly mineral-rich, high, cold country of the Upper Congo which "has just been touched by one or two explorers."

"The proposed expedition," the *New York Times* continued, "will be under the command of M. Alexandre Delcommune, who has already done good work in exploring some of the Congo tributaries, and who has been seventeen years on the river. He will be accompanied by Lieut. Hackanson of the Swedish Army, formerly one of the agents of the Congo Free State; Dr. Briart; Lieut. Santschoff, formerly of the Russian Army; Baron Marcel de Roert, M. Norbert Didderich, an engineer, and M. Protsch. MM Hackanson, Briart, and Santschoff have already sailed; M. Delcommune leaves on July 6, and M. Didderich on the 3rd. The escort will consist of 150 native soldiers. The expedition will meet at Kinchassa about the middle of September, and, embarking on the steamer *Roi des Belges*, will proceed by the Upper Congo and its tributary, the Lomami, to the limit of navigation on the latter river, nearly opposite Nyangwe. Thence the expedition will proceed on foot. It will be absent from twelve to eighteen months."

The prize mineral area of Central Africa—the present-day Katanga Province in the Republic of the Congo (producing, in 1965, much of the world's copper and most of its cobalt from a copper belt stretching two hundred and fifty miles)—was to be discovered as a result of the expedition's probing. Through this, and the previous four years of his travels in the Congo, Delcommune would become known as the next most prominent figure after Henry Morton Stanley in exploration of the Congo Basin, a man who added more detail than any other to the map of the river system.

Conrad was in Kinchassa in September, 1890, in temporary command of the *Roi des Belges*. He was looking forward to accompanying Delcommune, believing the exploring party to be heading for the Kasai River rather than the route it would take, up the Lualaba. "I am very busy preparing for a new expedition on the Kasai River," he wrote his cousin Maria Tyszkowa on September 24. "In a few days I shall probably leave Kinchassa again for some months, perhaps a dozen months. So don't wonder if there is no sign of me for a long while."[2] In the end, however, he did not go. Like those 60 per cent of the company's employees invalided home within half a year, his health was damaged by the climate.

A more directly affecting cause, the hostility of Delcommune's brother Camille, reduced Conrad's stay in the Congo to six months, not the three years he had planned.

"Heart of Darkness," the story he declared was "experience pushed a little (and only very little) beyond the actual facts of the case,"[3] developed from those few months in Africa. Described early by Edward Garnett in his review of it as a "most amazing, consummate piece of artistic diablerie—an analysis of the white man's morale when let loose from European restraint, and planted down in the tropics as an 'emissary of light' armed to the teeth to make trade profits out of subject races," and in later years judged, as F. R. Leavis wrote, "by common consent, one of Conrad's best things," "Heart of Darkness" has become one of the most famous stories in English literature since its first appearance in *Blackwood's Magazine* sixty-six years ago. In contrast to what the world was being told about the Congo Free State (there the Negroes, "like the Europeans," said the Belgian Consul General in Tenerife in July, 1890, "find aid, protection, and justice attached to a wise and paternal Government: no more slaves or ill-treatment"[4]), Conrad wrote of what he saw in that part of Africa from which an estimated total of fifteen million of its people had been shipped as slaves.

He suspected what lay ahead immediately upon his arrival at Matadi. In the diary he kept of his stay in the Congo his first entry, made in Matadi, was a bleak forecast: "Feel considerably in doubt about the future. Think just now that my life amongst the people (white) around here cannot be very comfortable. Intend avoid acquaintances as much as possible."[5] Ivory was reaching Matadi in large lots from the interior and on June 24 Conrad noted, "Have been myself busy packing ivory in casks. Idiotic employment. Health good up to now."[6] On the same day he added: "Prominent characteristic of the social life here: people speaking ill of each other."

Twenty-three steamers then traversed various parts of the Congo River, river boats belonging to the Congo Free State, to France, to missions and to commercial companies. Conrad was to command one of them, the large three-year-old *Florida*, waiting at Stanley Pool, the twenty-mile-long, doughnut-shaped bulge of the river two hundred miles from Matadi. The railroad was being built which, eight years later, would connect Matadi and Stanley Pool but in 1890 the distance was covered on foot. As a first intimation of the "flabby, pretending, weak-eyed devil of a rapacious and pitiless folly" he would see in the Congo, Conrad encountered in Matadi an African chain gang working on the railroad, part of the forced labor with which the line was built.[7]

"A horn tooted to the right, and I saw the black people run. A heavy and dull detonation shook the ground, a puff of smoke came out of the cliff, and that was all. No change appeared on the face of the rock. They were building a railway. The cliff was not in the way or anything; but this objectless blasting was all the work going on.

"A slight clinking behind me made me turn my head. Six black men advanced in a file, toiling up the path. They walked erect and slow, balancing small baskets full of earth on their heads, and the clink kept time with their footsteps. Black rags were wound round their loins, and the short ends behind waggled to and fro like tails. I could see every rib, the joints of their limbs were like knots in a rope; each had an iron collar on his neck, and all were connected together with a chain whose bights swung between them, rhythmically clinking. . . . All their meagre breasts panted together, the violently dilated nostrils quivered, the eyes stared stonily uphill. They passed me within six inches, without a glance, with that complete, deathlike indifference of unhappy savages."[8]

For fifteen days Conrad waited in Matadi. This tropical settlement, on a river known to Europe before Columbus' first voyage, had its beginnings in a time that can only be guessed at: perhaps as early as 3000 B.C., the period assigned to rock paintings discovered farther north. The region around Matadi was within the Kingdom of Kongo, a loose federation of tribes dominated by the Bakongo, when the Congo River was discovered in 1482 by the Portuguese explorer Diogo Cão. Four centuries later independence ended for them, in 1885, the kingdom in that year divided up by the Portuguese, the French and the Belgians. The Bakongo, when Conrad was in Matadi, were among those he saw in chains, brought "from all the recesses of the coast in all the legality of time contracts," dying of disease and starvation "as in some picture of a massacre or a pestilence."[9] (Seventy years later, in 1960, the Bakongo, forming one of the first political parties in the Congo, contributed to that state's independence.)

Conrad left Matadi on June 28, 1890, starting his two-hundred-mile walk to Stanley Pool. With him were Prosper Harou, a corpulent Belgian official of the Free State who, after a leave spent in Europe, was returning to his station, and thirty-one African porters. The caravan walked an average of fifteen miles a day, climbing the Pataballa Range of mountains, fording streams, passing abandoned villages.

"Paths, paths, everywhere," Conrad described the trek, "a stamped-in network of paths spreading over the empty land, through long grass, through burnt grass, through thickets, down and up chilly ravines, up and down stony hills ablaze with heat; and a solitude, a solitude, nobody, not a hut."[10] Fresh meat was scarce along the deserted route ("sheep, goats and fowls of a native kind" being "very difficult to find," a Belgian official warned[11]); after five days on the march Conrad noted in his diary that the caravan secured its first chicken in a village market. Though eleven rivers were crossed during the journey there was seldom water to be found clean enough to drink. The country was one of red hills covered by dark green vegetation, of intense heat at midday, of chilly nights made sleepless by mosquitoes. "Camp, cook, sleep, strike camp, march," Conrad summed up the routine of the first twelve days. "Now and then a carrier dead in harness, at rest in the long grass near the path, with an empty water-gourd and his long staff lying by his side. A great silence around and above. Perhaps on some quiet night the tremor of far-off drums, sinking, swelling, a tremor vast, faint; a sound weird, appealing, suggestive, and wild."[12]

On July 8 the party reached Manyanga station, having covered more than half the distance to Stanley Pool. For seventeen days they rested at Manyanga, a "most comfortable and pleasant halt," taken care of by an Englishman, Reginald Heyn, director of the Transport Company of the Upper Congo, and his assistant Jaeger. The march was resumed on July 25 "with plenty of hammock carriers," Harou being lame and Conrad "not in very good form." Eight days of marching brought them on August 1 to Nselemba on Stanley Pool, the last day a walk of seventeen miles and Conrad "glad to see the end of this stupid tramp."[13] It had taken thirty-six days from Matadi.

The area above the central station at Kinchassa, at the upper end of Stanley Pool beyond Leopoldville, was temporarily in the charge of Alexandre Delcommune's younger brother Camille, a former trader of thirty-one whom Conrad called "the manager" in "Heart of Darkness," a man "commonplace in complexion, in feature, in manners, and in voice" who "inspired neither love nor fear, nor even respect." Nearby Leopold-ville (today a city of 360,000 with an airport, two radio stations, three hundred night clubs and bars) then held twenty-eight European establish-ments; the cultivation of rice, sugar cane, tobacco and coffee had begun and, to satisfy European appetites, oxen, sheep and goats were being raised.[14]

For the previous six months the Company's agent at Stanley Falls, the furthest point of navigation on the Congo River, had been a French-man, Georges Antoine Klein. Word that he was seriously ill having reached Kinchassa, Camille Delcommune ordered the *Roi des Belges* to leave immediately on an upriver rescue mission. The steamboat Conrad expected to command, the *Florida*,[15] had been wrecked on July 18 (it

was never to be repaired during his stay in the Congo), and on August 4
he left Kinchassa on the *Roi des Belges,* as chief mate, for Stanley Falls.
A Dane, Captain Koch, commanded the steamer, Conrad making the
passage "to learn the river," as he wrote Mme. Poradowska. The party
on board included Camille Delcommune, an engineer named Gossens
and three of the Company's agents, Keyaerts, Rollin and Van der Hey-
den. The wood-burner carried thirty Africans as crew. Each received a
weekly pay, according to "Heart of Darkness," of "three pieces of brass
wire, each about nine inches long; and the theory was they were to buy
their provisions with that currency in riverside villages. You can see
how *that* worked. There were either no villages, or the people were
hostile, or the director, who like the rest of us fed out of tins, with an
occasional old he-goat thrown in, didn't want to stop the steamer for
some more or less recondite reason. So, unless they swallowed the wire
itself, or made loops of it to snare the fishes with, I don't see what good
their extravagant salary could be to them."[16]

For twenty-eight days the *Roi des Belges* moved upstream through a
wilderness where cannibalism was practiced and the restraint of the half-
starved crew impressed Conrad: "Why in the name of all the gnawing
devils of hunger they didn't go for us—they were thirty to five—and
have a good tuck-in for once, amazes me now when I think of it."[17]
Though a Belgian spokesman for the Free State declared that summer
that "cannibalism has ceased to exist in proximity to the stations,"[18]
there were, in the whole length of the river, less than a dozen stations.

An average of thirty-five miles a day was covered on the winding,
snag-filled stream bordered by ebony and teak trees rising two hundred
feet in the air. Conrad recalled the river journey of a thousand miles
through the closed-in rain forest as a voyage "in the night of dark ages."

"Sometimes we came upon a station close by the bank, clinging to
the skirts of the unknown, and the white men rushing out of a tumble-
down hovel, with great gestures of joy and surprise and welcome,
seemed very strange—had the appearance of being held there captive
by a spell. The word ivory would ring in the air for a while—and on
we went again into the silence, along empty reaches, round the still
bends, between the high walls of our winding way, reverberating in
hollow claps the ponderous beat of the stern-wheel. Trees, trees, mil-
lions of trees, massive, immense, running up high; and at their foot,
hugging the bank against the stream, crept the little begrimed steamboat, like a sluggish beetle crawling on the floor of a lofty portico. . . .
The reaches opened before us and closed behind, as if the forest had
stepped leisurely across the water to bar the way for our return. We

274 THE SEA YEARS OF JOSEPH CONRAD

penetrated deeper and deeper into the heart of darkness. It was very quiet there. At night sometimes the roll of drums behind the curtain of trees would run up the river and remain sustained faintly, as if hovering in the air high over our heads, till the first break of day. Whether it meant war, peace, or prayer we could not tell. . . . But suddenly, as we struggled round a bend, there would be a glimpse of rush walls, of peaked grass-roofs, a burst of yells, a whirl of black limbs, a mass of hands clapping, of feet stamping, of bodies swaying, of eyes rolling, under the droop of heavy and motionless foliage. The steamer toiled along slowly on the edge of a black and incomprehensible frenzy. The prehistoric man was cursing us, praying to us, welcoming us—who could tell? . . . They howled and leaped, and spun, and made horrid faces; but what thrilled you was just the thought of their humanity—like yours—the thought of your remote kinship with this wild and passionate uproar."[19]

On September 1 the *Roi des Belges* arrived at Stanley Falls station, "some 1300 miles from the seashore where the post-office is," Conrad wrote Maria Tyszkowa. The persistent booming of the seven cataracts of the falls accented the isolation of the outpost; the nearest settlement of any size, three hundred miles away, was the infamous slave-trade headquarters of Nyangwe, long directed by the Arab "Bismarck of Central Africa," Tippoo Tib. At Stanley Falls a five-day attack of dysentery further undermined Conrad's health, already weakened by onslaughts of tropical fever. The steamboat's commander also fell ill there and on September 6 Conrad was appointed by Camille Delcommune to take charge of the steamer, as his official letter stated, "until the recovery of Captain Koch."[20] The station's agent Klein was carried on board at Stanley Falls; two weeks later, on September 21, he died on the *Roi des Belges*, the stern-wheeler on that day reaching Bolobo station[21] on her down-river voyage under Conrad's command, one hundred and fifty miles from her destination of Kinchassa.

Conrad brought the steamer into Kinchassa on September 24, ending seven weeks on the Congo River. Those seven weeks brought to its height the feeling he was to convey in "Heart of Darkness," the setting of Stanley Falls of the story being the scene of a true, inhuman episode all too fresh and well remembered at the time of Conrad's stay there. His first reactions to his river trip were given in a letter to Mme. Poradowska written two days after his return to Kinchassa. "My days here are dreary. Make no mistake about that! I am truly sorry to have come here. Indeed, I regret it bitterly." Explaining why, he went on: "Everything is repellent to me here. Men and things, but especially men. And I am repellent to them, too. From the manager in Africa—who has taken the trouble of telling a good many people that I displease him intensely—down to the lowest mechanic, all have a gift for getting on my nerves; and consequently I am perhaps not as pleasant to them as I might be. The manager is a common ivory-dealer with sordid instincts who considers himself a merchant though he is only a kind of African shopkeeper. His name is Delcommune. He hates the English and I am of course regarded as an Englishman here."[22]

Anti-English feeling in the Congo had grown from the sensationally demonic actions of an Englishman two years earlier. Major Edmund Musgrave Barttelot, murdered near Stanley Falls, was for months the subject of headline news in Europe and America, the *New York Times* alone devoting ten news stories to the macabre history when it first became known in 1888,[23] while a controversy raged for several years in England over what the *Illustrated London News* called the "odious charges" of his "merciless ferocity."[24] The major, like Kurtz in "Heart of Darkness" who took "a high seat amongst the devils of the land," was to personify, as the story unfolded, the white man's brutality in Africa. "He won't be forgotten," Conrad wrote of Kurtz, a statement as true of Barttelot as the many other features of his history Conrad wove into Kurtz. The why of Barttelot's moral collapse was a question repeatedly posed in the major cities of the West, Stanley himself giving one answer when he arrived in New York late in 1890, two and a half years after the major's death.

On the Upper Congo Conrad was in the setting so recently connected with Barttelot; his still-fresh grave, like that of Kurtz's in similar "primeval earth," was just within the forest from the spot where he was killed.[25] Of this clever, promising, highly connected young Englishman —"a gallant officer of the British Army, an English gentleman previously of blameless character, esteemed by all who knew him,"[26] was one description of him—who so unaccountably "went wrong" in the Congo no satisfying explanation was ever given. The enigma of Barttelot was eventually dropped but, eight years after leaving the Congo, Conrad developed from it the enigma of Kurtz. What circumstances or inner flaws brought about a man's downfall was the subject he was dealing with in *Lord Jim* when, taking time away from that novel to compose "Heart of Darkness," he explored another aspect of self-failure. In his portrayal of Kurtz as a man whose "intelligence was perfectly clear" but whose "soul was mad," he reflected the conclusion Stanley had reached—madness—to explain Barttelot's actions. The "heavy, mute spell of the wilderness" which "seemed to draw him to its pitiless breast by the awakening of forgotten and brutal instincts, by the memory of gratified and monstrous passions"—Conrad's view of the forces disintegrating Kurtz—was as sound as any offered by those attempting to analyze the reasons for Barttelot's gruesome conduct. For his history gave few clues.

Major Barttelot came of an unusually distinguished family, of English and French descent. An early ancestor arrived in England from Normandy with William the Conqueror, and the family seat in Sussex, among the oldest in England, was established some years before 1428. The second son of Sir Walter Barttelot—a well-known militia colonel and prominent as a Tory Member of Parliament for thirty-three years—and a grandson of Sir Christopher Musgrave, the major was born on March 28, 1859, at Hilliers, near Petworth, Sussex. He was educated at Rugby and Sandhurst and at nineteen became an officer in the British army. Before he had been twenty months in the army he took part in two engagements during the 1880 British campaign in Afghanistan. Two years later, in the Egyptian campaign, he won a name for courage in the battles at Kassassin and Tell el-Kebir, the British under Lord Wolseley taking those Egyptian fortifications at bayonet point. Intrepid in warfare, young Barttelot was also a striking figure. "Fair, tall, broad-shouldered, wide-chested, with capital hips and arms and legs,"[27] as the London correspondent of the New York Times described him, he had "a strong face but an ugly mouth."[28] His typical traits were an imperious manner and a fiery temper, being ever ready, it was said of him, to take out his revolver in a heated argument. "Indeed a certain brusque peremptoriness was the characteristic of this rising youth," the New York Times correspondent continued. "He would not only have things done, he would have them done in his way. Stanley recognized in him at sight the man he needed as second in command, and there seemed to be a fine future before this fusilier officer who had made himself a prime favorite with Lord Wolseley because he was not afraid of taking responsibility, and had the faculty of not hesitating in making a decision. I fear it must be added that, like most self-reliant men, he had the deuce of a temper. But he was a good and clever fellow."[29]

Favored beyond most men, by inheritance, social position, education and natural gifts (as was the English-educated "prodigy" Kurtz, also of English and French descent), Barttelot died, at twenty-eight, deeply hated. The final chapter of his life began with an appointment many coveted.

Emin Pasha, the adopted name of the German scientist Eduard Schnitzer, had been in the service of the British as an administrator in the Sudan when the 1885 rebellion culminating in the fall of Khartoum cut him off from Western contact. Nothing having been heard of him for some months, the Wales-born reporter-explorer H. M. Stanley, ever a showman, decided to cross Africa to search for Emin Pasha, thereby duplicating an earlier much-publicized exploit when, as a reporter for the New York *Herald*, he had sought out David Livingstone in Central Africa. When the news of his proposed expedition became known in 1886, Stanley later told New York reporters,[30] "hundreds of applicants sent in their names to go with me" and "we picked out about twenty of the best young gentlemen who applied." Picked out to lead the rear guard of the expedition—Stanley himself would lead the advance —was the highly recommended young Major Barttelot.

Barttelot left England on January 14, 1887,[31] for Cairo where the expedition formed. By steamer from Cairo they circled Africa en route to the Congo: down through the Suez Canal to the great slave market of Zanzibar, on to Capetown, up the west coast of Africa to Banana and Matadi. With six hundred Africans drafted to carry his supplies, Stanley led his forces along the caravan trail from Matadi to Leopoldville (the route Conrad was to follow three years later), a march Barttelot described in his diary as lasting from March 25 to April 21, 1887. As Stanley moved ahead into the interior of the continent the rear guard was left hundreds of miles behind. Three months after Stanley reached Wadelai, in April, 1888, at the end of his quest—to find Emin Pasha there, well, safe, and reluctant to move—Barttelot was still in the Congo, in his stockaded Yambuya camp on the Aruwimi River near Stanley Falls, a stronghold on a high bluff built more like a fortress than a camp, where he had been for nearly a year. In his last letter to the Emin Relief Committee in London, dated June 4, 1888, he implied that his inability to move out from the camp was due to Tippoo Tib, the Arab slave dealer furnishing the expedition's carriers, who "had promised to bring 800 men and had brought only 400."[32] But the true story was something else, pieced together as it was by later accounts.

Some one of many factors, or perhaps all—the wilderness with its savage customs and hostile climate, the heady power of being in unchallengeable command (like Kurtz, "there was nothing on earth to prevent him killing whom he jolly well pleased"), the nerve-tearing sounds of the night drums, a fiery temperament foreign to restraint—contributed to the young officer's downfall. Three young Englishmen whom Stanley had carefully selected served under Barttelot and were with him in the Yambuya camp: James S. Jamieson, the naturalist-botanist of the party, who had traveled widely in Africa and Borneo; Sergeant William

Bonney of the Army Hospital Corps; J. Rose Troup, a British general's son who had charge of provisions and stores. Troup was considered supremely levelheaded and, having spent three years with Stanley in the Congo, had been especially chosen for his calmness and experience to act as a brake upon Barttelot. All three men were blamed by Stanley for failing to hold their commander in check, it being Stanley's belief that they should have mutinied and shipped Barttelot home, as he had earlier despatched a Swedish officer gone berserk in the Congo.

Barttelot's sadistic treatment of his carriers, members of the Manyema tribe—in less than a year eighty were buried in the clearing outside his camp[33]—was recorded in detail by himself. "The original log book signed by Major Barttelot, James S. Jamieson, and William Bonney day after day is simply just one record of remorseless and implacable punishment," Stanley told New York reporters.[34] More than two hundred Manyemas died who were overworked, starved, abandoned, or subjected to the major's "remorseless flogging." Accounts reaching London, from the Congo and from Belgian officials newly returned from there, told a ghastly story.

"Young Barttelot was a very clever and energetic officer," wrote one man who knew him, "with a distinct vocation for adventures but possessed of a most arrogant manner with his inferiors and full of the notion that the natives could only be managed by shooting on the spot the first who showed signs of discontent. Stanley told me just before he started that he had a great general liking for Major Barttelot's qualities, but especially valued his intrepid resolve to have his own way, no matter at what cost."[35] A letter from an official of the Congo Free State reported that "great complaint is made against Barttelot for harshness and for his disregard of Stanley's orders to consult with the other officials, who have not had a good word to say of him, while the men undeniably hate him, and several threatened to shoot him on the march."[36] The tall young Englishman was described in another dispatch as "brutal and arrogant to the last degree. There was a mutiny among his Manyema porters even before he set out on the march, and the start was made with the most of them chained together and scarified with the floggings they had had in camp."[37]

"A hideous narrative was given me last night by a man who is in close communication with the Brussels authorities," the London correspondent of the New York Times wrote.[38] Little of that report of Barttelot's atrocities could be told in print, he went on, but "one of its features was the hiring of a body of cannibals to attack, massacre, and feast upon another company of Negroes, the purpose being that Jamieson, who is the savant of the expedition, might secure photographs of this unique and interesting scene." (Jamieson's diary bore this out, in passages saying he had watched a little girl slave being killed and eaten and had made sketches of the horrible sight; Jamieson died of fever in the Congo, at Bangala on August 17, 1888.)

Barttelot carried torture to an extreme degree, ordering three hundred lashes to be given in a single flogging. As a final touch inflaming the Africans he looked on during these bloody rites with a wide grin, the stare Conrad adopted for Kurtz—"that wide and immense stare embracing, condemning, loathing all the universe." As with Kurtz, who "lacked restraint in the gratification of his various lusts" and who placed the decapitated heads of Africans on the posts of his stockaded camp, Barttelot reached such heights of savage ferocity that he was warned of the inevitable results by a man who was himself no stranger to cruelty, Tippoo Tib. (That slave raider, in 1888, had been made governor of the Stanley Falls area, where he had ten slave-collecting camps; his much-feared headman and nephew, Reshid, occupied one of them, the old Stanley Falls station on an island in the river which he had attacked and taken from the Belgians in 1886.)

In the Congo Barttelot's murder was frequently predicted. It occurred at his Yambuya camp on July 19, 1888. On that day, the official account of the killing stated, "a shot was heard and Bonney, running out, found the camp in a state of excitement and heard shouts of 'The white man is dead!'"[39] The full details were given by Stanley in a press interview in New York on November 6, 1890, the day he arrived on the S.S. *Teutonic* from Liverpool for the first of the talks, at the Metropolitan Opera House, given during his world lecture tour.

"There had been a good deal of quarreling in camp," Stanley recounted the atmosphere at the Aruwimi station on Major Barttelot's final day. "He had just come from Stanley's Falls. His presence disturbed the men in itself. He quarreled with the owner of the station, Abdulla Karonga," and, Abdulla failing to produce the sixty carriers Barttelot demanded, beat the agent with his cypress staff. "On the morning of July 19 at dawn," Stanley continued the story, "he is disturbed from his sleep by singing and drumming. He sends a Sergeant out to find who is making the noise and to tell them to stop. The Sergeant returns and says he could not find out who was making the noise. Then he sends his little boy Soudi. Soudi comes back and says there is a woman singing and a man drumming. It is always the fashion in Africa among the Manyema tribe to celebrate the dawn with music. He said, 'I will stop this and shoot the first man who disobeys.'

"He goes out with a loaded revolver in his hand and with his cypress staff, which is sharply pointed. He finds a woman sitting on the ground. He rushes up to her and tells her to stop her singing. She keeps on singing and looks up rather defiantly, for they all hated him. He again tells her to stop and then strikes her. Finally he kicks her. The husband is cleaning his gun in a hut about five yards away. He hears his wife's screams, looks out and sees the Major kicking her. He pushes his gun out from the hut through a loophole and shoots him dead. You must understand he is not a slave. He is a Chief. He has engaged forty men to accompany the expedition of Barttelot. These men love their wives just as much as more civilized men. He takes revenge as any other man would." The death of Soudi—"he gave that little boy a kick from which he died"—and a gruesome recital of acts committed by the man whom not one European in his party defied completed Stanley's account.[40]

"His was an impenetrable darkness," Conrad wrote of Kurtz. "I looked at him as you peer down at a man who is lying at the bottom of a precipice where the sun never shines."[41] While this could justly have been said of Barttelot—whose actions, William Bonney believed, were the result of temporary insanity—it also applied to a large proportion of the whites who, in the Congo, wrote one of the blackest chapters in mankind's history. Barttelot personified that history and because of the unpalatable blackness of it his story, brought out in a spate of books in 1890,[42] created an uproar lasting in England for several years. Some of the books, including one by his brother, sought to prove Barttelot a faultless, sterling man incapable of cruelty—even as Kurtz's fiancée believed of Kurtz that it was "impossible to know him and not to admire him."[43] So painful was the memory of Barttelot that his story, wishfully forgotten, was not recalled for its connection with "Heart of Darkness." But much as Conrad drew upon him for Kurtz ("I take great pains to give a cosmopolitan origin to Kurtz," he wrote to a correspondent in 1903[44]), this English officer represented the attitudes and behavior of many others. "All Europe contributed to the making of Kurtz"[45] was Conrad's indictment of the Congo history to which all Europe contributed. The bodies of Africans Conrad saw along the caravan trail were mute evidence of Belgian rule. "Saw another dead body lying by the path in an attitude of meditative repose"[46] was one entry in his diary which followed a similar one of the day before: "A few minutes afterwards saw at a camping place the dead body of a Backongo. Shot?"[47] In every colony—French, British, German, Belgian, Portuguese—the African dead mounted (seventeen thousand dying in the French Congo in the course of laying the hundred-mile railroad to

Brazzaville) as the conquest of the continent went on. The slave trade itself continued, under Arab management, until 1894; forced labor, in Portuguese Africa and the Republic of South Africa, had not ended in 1965.

During the months Barttelot made lurid history in the Congo reports of his atrocities were sent to Europe by Belgian officials on the scene. One Belgian official in the Congo throughout that time was Camille Delcommune. His hatred of the English encompassed Conrad and shortly after the *Roi des Belges* returned to Kinchassa he gave his hostility explicit form.

Deeply as Conrad regretted having come to the Congo, and much as he wanted to leave ("I am homesick for the sea and long to look again on the plains of that salt-water which has so often cradled me, which has so many times smiled at me under the glittering sunshine of a beautiful day," he wrote Mme. Poradowska on September 26 from Kinchassa[48]), he was anxious to fulfill the purpose bringing him to Africa, exploration of the headwaters of the Congo. He was ill, having had four attacks of fever in two months, and "a little bit demoralized," but an opportunity to take part in discovery would not likely come his way again. He hung on.

Early in October, scheduled to lead his exploring party into the interior at the end of the month, Alexandre Delcommune arrived at Kinchassa. Two years older than Conrad, he had come to the Congo at eighteen as a trader and, rising in the service of the Free State as an administrator and political agent, was now a full-time explorer engaged by the Brussels commercial firm, Compagnie du Katanga. His expedition, which Conrad called "the Eldorado Exploring Expedition" in "Heart of Darkness," trickled into Kinchassa in five sections, each section equipped with supplies of tents, camp stools, boxes and bales. Their talk, as Conrad told of it, was "the talk of sordid buccaneers: it was reckless without hardihood, greedy without audacity, and cruel without courage; there was not an atom of foresight or of serious intention in the whole batch of them, and they did not seem aware these things are wanted for the work of the world. To tear treasure out of the bowels of the land was their desire, with no more moral purpose at the back of it than there is in burglars breaking into a safe."[49] The leader of the expedition, Delcommune, who "carried his fat paunch with ostentation on his short legs," made as bad an impression on Conrad as the others: "In exterior he resembled a butcher in a poor neighbourhood, and his eyes had a look of sleepy cunning."[50]

The crass motives of an exploring party—this one openly being on a

search for minerals—were far from Conrad's idealistic dreams of exploration. His disillusionment was made complete when Camille Delcommune
informed him, as Mme. Poradowska relayed the news to the head office
in Brussels, "that he cannot hope for a promotion or a raise in salary
as long as he stays in the Congo."[51] The wrecked *Florida* would require another eight months at least to repair, and Conrad, meanwhile,
would not be given the command of any other steamer. His purpose
in coming to Africa having dissolved, he decided by October 19 to return
to Europe. Leaving Kinchassa for Leopoldville, "at night in a big canoe
with only half the proper number of paddlers," he rounded a bad turn
in the Congo where he "failed in being the second white man on record
drowned at that interesting spot through the upsetting of a canoe."

"I got round the turn more or less alive," he wrote in *A Personal
Record*,[52] "though I was too sick to care whether I did or not, and,
always with *Almayer's Folly* amongst my diminishing baggage, I arrived
at that delectable capital Boma." The incomplete manuscript of *Almayer's
Folly* was with him when he reached Matadi on December 4, 1890, and,
untouched still, was in his baggage when, taking a steamer from Boma,
he arrived back in England early in January, 1891.

The illness he contracted in the Congo, permanently affecting his
health, was to cause the final disablement taking him away from the sea.
From the experiences of six bitter months in Africa he wrote two stories,
"Heart of Darkness" and "An Outpost of Progress." When he completed the latter story five and a half years after leaving Africa he described it to his publisher: "It is a story of the Congo. . . . All the
bitterness of those days, all my puzzled wonder as to the meaning of all
I saw—all my indignation at masquerading philanthropy have been with
me again while I wrote . . . I have divested myself of everything but
pity—and some scorn."[53] The shock of Africa* had been intensified for
him by the contrast between the image of the continent he had held
since boyhood and what he found there. The lasting imprint of that
contrast he recalled, at sixty-six, in "Geography and Some Explorers."

As a boy dreaming of exploration he had bragged to his schoolmates
in Poland that when he grew up he would go to "the very middle of
the then white heart of Africa," the land being explored by his
"shadowy friend" David Livingstone. At that time Stanley's newspaper
stunt—locating the famous explorer on Lake Tanganyika and greeting

---

* "He spoke of the horrors of the Congo, from the moral and physical shock of
which he said he had never recovered, the impression had been so deep that he felt
he would never lose it," Lady Ottoline Morrell wrote of her 1913 conversations with
Conrad (*Memoirs of Lady Ottoline Morrell*, pp. 232–39).

him with "Mr. Livingstone, I presume"—had turned attention to Africa. Some eighteen years later Conrad reached this area, on the *Roi des Belges*, moored in the Congo off Stanley Falls station. With the memory of it still sharp after thirty-four years he looked back to a night spent there.

"Everything was dark under the stars. Every other white man on board was asleep. I was glad to be alone on deck, smoking the pipe of peace after an anxious day. The subdued thundering mutter of the Stanley Falls hung in the heavy night air of the last navigable reach of the Upper Congo, while no more than ten miles away, in Reshid's Camp just above the Falls, the yet unbroken power of the Congo Arabs slumbered uneasily. Their day was over. Away in the middle of the stream, on a little island nestling all black in the foam of the broken water, a solitary little light glimmered feebly, and I said to myself with awe, 'This is the very spot of my boyish boast.'

"A great melancholy descended on me. Yes, this was the very spot. But there was no shadowy friend to stand by my side in the night of enormous wilderness, no great haunting memory, but only the unholy recollection of a prosaic newspaper 'stunt' and the distasteful knowledge of the vilest scramble for loot that ever disfigured the history of human conscience and geographical exploration. What an end to the idealised realities of a boy's daydreams! I wondered what I was doing there, for indeed it was only an unforeseen episode, hard to believe in now, in my seaman's life. Still, the fact remains that I have smoked a pipe of peace at midnight in the very heart of the African continent, and felt very lonely there."[54]

XXIV

For thirty-three years, the last half of his life, Conrad was rarely free of the "souvenirs of Africa," the illness he brought back from the Congo. Bedridden for the major part of seven months in 1891, at thirty-three, the swellings in his hands and legs were then diagnosed as "rheumatism in the left leg and neuralgia in the right arm," as he told Mme. Poradowska. But the swellings and sudden onsets of pain, as well as the engulfing melancholy provoking his uncle to address him as "My dear Pessimist," were what present-day science, with greater knowledge of joint and nerve afflictions, terms manifestations of the arthritic disease of gout. Excruciating pain accompanies an attack of gout and the periods of relief are short. Yet, in this state of tortured health Conrad wrote twenty-seven books. The largest proportion of his manuscript pages, totaling some fifteen thousand, were written by hand; only in later years, with his right hand too crippled for use, did he occasionally resort to dictation. Also handwritten were the several thousand letters of his voluminous correspondence. Modern medical opinion gives some indication of what such labor cost. It also defines one cause of his dark depressions.

"Intense pain is the hallmark of the onset of gout," Dr. Frederic Wood Jones, an eminent anatomist and himself a sufferer, wrote in his paper on "Classical Gout" in the March 11, 1950, issue of the *British Medical Journal*. Quoting an early dictum—"Place your joint in a vice and screw the vice up until you can endure it no longer—that represents rheumatism; then give the instrument another twist and you will obtain a notion of gout"—Dr. Jones declared that the pain, different from other pains, "is revealed in the oft-repeated descriptions of gouty patients as being 'choleric and irascible' or 'querulous and irritable,'" expressions which indicate "the strangely affective, almost psychical, quality of the pain." An attack, coming without warning, "on the sudden and at once passes from a condition of normal ease to one of acute disease by a transition which knows no light or shade, nor any stages of gradation." In essence a disease affecting the nervous system, Dr. Jones continued, its most marked feature is "a dreadful apprehension." The patient "fears lest anyone should come near him and thoughtlessly touch him, or jar him with their footfall, or cause him to move. He dreads the presence of anyone who moves hurriedly, and is terrified lest the fussy person should slip, or drop something, or give him a start of any kind. And in all this it is to be remembered that it is not the actual touch, the jar, or the change of position that causes the pain, it is the apprehension that it might happen. . . . Although there is local pain, enough and to spare, it is the psychic state of dread that characterizes an attack of gout. . . . I do not know the original source of the account of the gouty patient who, having seen a fly upon the ceiling, lay in an agony of anticipation lest it should lose its hold and drop in the neighbourhood of his gouty limb. The picture is doubtless an exaggerated one, and yet it contains a very real element of truth."

For the whole of his writing life Conrad was subjected to such attacks, struggling to put the words down as his condition worsened. "It was pretty bad," he told John Galsworthy after one siege in 1909, "the horrible depression worst of all. It is rather awful to lie helpless and think of the passing days, of the lost time. But the most cruel time is after-

wards, when I crawl out of bed to sit before the table, take up the pen,—
and have to fling it away in sheer despair of ever writing a line."[1]

"His life was heroic," said Christopher Morley of this private battle
of Conrad's, "and the quality of courage that was in it carried over to
the end. I remember being told, by one who had visited him not long
before his death, how Conrad wrote when crippled with gout. His
right hand moved slowly over the paper, his left hand holding it supported at the wrist. It is well for all of us to think of that hand."[2]

When the malady first appeared, in London in January, 1891, Conrad
discounted it to the point that, limping, he traveled to Brussels to apply
for a ship command. On his return to London he spent a few days in
bed to relieve the swelling in his legs, then made a similarly fruitless trip
to Glasgow. By the end of February he could no longer stand and his
physician, Dr. Ludwig, placed him in the German Hospital in London.
Weeks went by when he was incapable of any movement. "Do not accuse
me of indifference, or even of laziness," he apologized, in an April 15
letter to Maria Tyszkowa, for his delay in writing. He had been so
ill, "and this illness has dragged on so," that it had been impossible
to let his relatives know. "I spent two months in bed," he told his
cousin. "I got up a short time ago and for three weeks walked around
with my hands so swollen that only with the greatest difficulty could
I write a few lines."[3]

At the end of three bedridden months he had made so little improve-
ment his doctor advised him to go to Switzerland, to Champel near
Geneva, for treatment at a hydropathic sanatorium. For three weeks,
from May 21 to June 14, 1891, he took the water cure at Champel,
staying at the Hôtel-Pension de la Roseraie. There he renewed work
on *Almayer's Folly*, writing the eighth chapter of the novel. Returning
to London at the end of June, he passed a dispirited summer in slow
convalescence. Malarial attacks brought daily fever and, unfit for the
sea, he took a temporary job on August 4 in charge of Barr, Moering's
warehouse on the Thames. Fighting the depression of his illness and the
tedium of his job, he took up *Almayer's Folly* again, writing most of
the ninth chapter before the summer ended.

"The earth had nothing to hold me with for very long," he said of
that low-spirited time in *A Personal Record*, a period linked with the
erratic growth of the novel. "And then that memorable story, like a cask
of choice Madeira, got carried for three years to and fro upon the sea."[4]
In those years he made the final voyages of his seaman's life, as chief
officer of the *Torrens*, one of the fastest sailing ships of her day. The
offer to join the ship came unexpectedly, through her forty-two-year-old

commander, Captain Walker H. Cope. Conrad knew Captain Cope only slightly, in a social way. But, "on hearing from his brother that I was ashore, he sent me word that the *Torrens* wanted a chief officer, as a matter that might interest me," he wrote in 1923. "I was then recovering slowly from a bad breakdown, after a most unpleasant and persistent tropical disease which I had caught in Africa while commanding a steamer on the River Congo. Yet the temptation was great. I confessed to him my doubts of my fitness for the post, from the point of view of health. But he said that moping ashore never did anyone any good, and was very encouraging. It was clear that, as the saying goes, 'my looks did not pity me,' for he argued that, so far as appearance went, there did not seem to be anything the matter with me."[5]

Conrad joined the *Torrens* in London on November 19, 1891,[6] his wages as chief mate £8 a month. Owners of the 1334-ton ship, the last full-rigged composite passenger clipper launched in England, were A. L. Elder & Co. of London. Built for the Australian trade, in 1875 by James Laing in Sunderland, she had been named for the Australian politician Sir R. R. Torrens. For fifteen years following her launching her principal owner and master had been Captain Henry R. Angel, her figurehead being a carved likeness of Florès Angel, the captain's eldest daughter. In 1880, under Captain Angel, she had made the passage from Plymouth to Adelaide in sixty-four days, a record never afterward equaled by any other sailing ship. Carrying up to sixty passengers, she remained in the Adelaide trade from 1875 until 1903. In 1906 the beautiful ship, which had cost £27,000 when originally made ready for the sea, was sold for £1500 to Italian shipowners in Genoa, Vittorio Bozzo and Giuseppe Mortola (Mortola had also bought the *Tilkhurst*, in 1903). An unlucky vessel while under the Italian flag, the *Torrens* was soon run on the rocks, for the first time in her life, and sentenced to be wrecked. But Genoese shipbreakers, impressed by her beauty and the good condition of her hull, refloated and repaired her. Seriously damaged when grounded for a second time, the thirty-five-year-old clipper was towed into Genoa and broken up in 1910.[7]

The *Torrens* was still at sea when Conrad, in 1905, began work on *Chance*, the novel into which he wrote aspects of his *Torrens* and *Riversdale* voyages. The heroine's first name in the novel, Flora, was perhaps suggested by the Florès figurehead of the *Torrens*, the only passenger ship he served in throughout his long career.

His first voyage, from London to Adelaide, was a passage of one hundred days. Leaving London on November 20, 1891, the *Torrens* cleared Gravesend the next day and Plymouth on November 25. Her crew, largely British, included two Americans, W. Martin, thirty-five, of San Francisco, and C. Godfrey, a seaman of twenty-four from Philadelphia.[8] In addition to the ship's company of thirty-five officers and crew and five apprentices, there were butchers, bakers, and stewardesses on board to look after the needs of the passengers. A cow was carried to supply fresh milk for the children and livestock was stabled for future meat consumption. Moving under sail, the *Torrens* was a quiet ship, with roomy staterooms lighted by oil lamps and candles. Though a comfortable vessel in every way, and highly popular, land was barely out of view when a passenger on this first voyage succumbed to sea fright.

"We had not been more than ten days out from Plymouth when he took it into his head that his shattered constitution could not stand the voyage," Conrad long after wrote of the man who had a deep fear of the sea. "Note that he had not had as much as an hour of sea-sickness. He maintained, however, that a few more days at sea would certainly kill him. He was absolutely certain of it, and he pleaded day after day with a persistent agonised earnestness to be put ashore on the first convenient bit of land, which in this case would have been Teneriffe." Remaining aloof throughout the three months' passage to Adelaide, he went ashore in Australia "unreadable but unforgiving, without taking notice of anyone in the ship."[9]

The *Torrens* came into Adelaide on February 28, 1892,[10] and stayed in port five weeks. On April 8 she sailed for London, calling at Capetown on June 24–25 and at St. Helena on July 14–18. In St. Helena the boatswain, John Meakins, a Ramsgate man of forty-five, was taken to the hospital where he died of an intestinal infection on July 15.[11] Ending a passage of nearly five months, the *Torrens* arrived in London on September 2.[12]

Conrad's health had greatly improved at sea and he decided to stay with the ship. After seven weeks ashore in London he signed on, as chief mate again and at the same pay, when the *Torrens* left London on October 25[13] for Australia. Calling at Plymouth for her remaining passengers and cargo, and leaving that port on October 31,[14] she spent ninety-one days on the run to Adelaide.

Two young Englishmen were among the sixty passengers, W. G. M. Edwards, nineteen, and W. H. Jacques, a quiet Cambridge man ill with tuberculosis and traveling for his health. Edwards was to provide a rare record of Conrad's sea life—photographing the *Torrens* under sail in mid-Atlantic, Conrad aboard as chief officer on the last outward voyage of his career—and Jacques, shortly afterward, was to become the first reader of a Conrad story.

On a day early in December, with the *Torrens* a month away from England and coasting in the Doldrums north of Brazil, "the skipper, Captain Cope, allowed a boat to be lowered to enable those passengers who had cameras to photograph the ship," Mr. Edwards recalled the circumstances of his 1892 photograph. "We were 90 days from Plymouth to Adelaide, calling nowhere," he said of the voyage. "The nearest we came to land was off Pernumbuco. We were near enough to read the time through glasses on the Town Clock. Letters given to fishermen to hand to the British Consul were all delivered."[15]

Swept along by the Brazil Current, the *Torrens* sailed south and crossed the Atlantic to round the Cape of Good Hope. On an impulse one stormy evening, east of Tristan da Cunha, Conrad gave Jacques to read what he had never shown anyone before, handwritten pages of the beginning of a novel. These were the first nine chapters of *Almayer's Folly*. Jacques, a young man with the sallow face of illness and deep-set eyes, became "the very first reader I ever had," Conrad wrote in *A Personal Record*. "He put the MS. in the breast-pocket of his jacket; I remember perfectly his thin, brown fingers folding it lengthwise. 'I will read it tomorrow,' he remarked, seizing the door-handle; and then watching the roll of the ship for a propitious moment, he opened the door and was gone. In the moment of his exit I heard the sustained booming of the wind, the swish of the water on the decks of the *Torrens*, and the subdued, as if distant, roar of the rising sea. . . .

"Next day, but this time in the first dog-watch, Jacques entered my cabin. He had a thick woolen muffler round his throat, and the MS. was in his hand. He tendered it to me with a steady look, but without a word. I took it in silence. He sat down on the couch and still said nothing. . . . 'Well, what do you say?' I asked at last. 'Is it worth finishing?' This question expressed exactly the whole of my thoughts.

"'Distinctly,' he answered, in his sedate, veiled voice, and then coughed a little.

"'Were you interested?' I inquired further, almost in a whisper.

"'Very much!'"[16]

After that evening Conrad made no further reference to his unfinished novel; not for another year would he pick it up again. The *Torrens* reached Adelaide on January 30, 1893,[17] Conrad having been ill for the final two weeks of the passage. To be dogged by illness at thirty-five gave him a dim view of what lay ahead. "It is not the present illness (for I feel much better just now)," he wrote Mme. Poradowska from

Adelaide on February 3, "but the uncertainty of the future—or rather the certainty of the 'uniform grey' awaiting me—that causes this discouragement. I know very well that what I have just said, and what I feel, lacks dignity; but at least the feeling is genuine. It is not morbid, for I view the situation without any bitterness. Doubtless it would be more dignified to feel this way without breathing a word, but upon my soul one can't remain always perched on the stilts of one's principles."[18]

In Adelaide Conrad spent seven weeks, one of them in the higher hills of the country to escape the city heat. On March 23,[19] bound for London, the *Torrens* sailed from Adelaide with seventeen passengers and a cargo of wool. Two young men among the passengers, John Galsworthy and Edward Lancelot Sanderson, were to become his lifelong friends. Galsworthy, then twenty-five, had recently completed his studies at Oxford and prepared for a future in law; a dozen years later he began the career that, as novelist and dramatist, was to make him known for *The Forsyte Saga* and to bring him the Nobel Prize in 1932. At the time of meeting Conrad he and Sanderson, just down from Cambridge, were completing their travels in the Pacific, having sailed out from London with the never-realized project of calling on Robert Louis Stevenson in Samoa. Galsworthy was on the *Torrens* from Adelaide to Capetown, leaving the ship there on May 18, 1893. He "sought me out in London afterwards,"[20] Conrad said of the intimate friendship begun on this voyage.

"It was in March, 1893 that I first met Conrad on board the English sailing ship *Torrens* in Adelaide Harbour," Galsworthy wrote in "Reminiscences of Conrad." "He was superintending the stowage of cargo." The dark-haired chief mate had few easy moments at the start of that passage. "All the first night he was fighting a fire in the hold. None of us seventeen passengers knew of it till long after. It was he who had most truck with the tail of that hurricane off the Leeuwin, and later with another storm. He was a good seaman, watchful of the weather, quick in handling the ship; considerate with the apprentices—we had a long, unhappy Belgian youth among them, who took unhandily to the sea and dreaded going aloft; Conrad compassionately spared him all he could. With the crew he was popular; they were individuals to him, not a mere gang; and long after he would talk of this or that among them, especially of old Andy the sailmaker: 'I likéd that old fellow, you know.' He was friendly with the young second mate, a cheerful, capable young seaman, very English; and respectful, if faintly ironic, with his whiskered, stout old captain. . . . Many evening watches in fine weather we spent on the poop. Ever the great teller of a tale, he had already nearly twenty years of tales to tell. Tales of ships and storms, of Polish revolution, of his youthful Carlist gun-running adventure, of the Malay seas, and the Congo; and of men and men: all to a listener who had the insatiability of a twenty-five-year-old."[21]

The "long, unhappy Belgian youth" who dreaded going aloft on the *Torrens* was an apprentice of seventeen with the long name of Albert Gullamene Nicholas Marie Van Melchebeke,[22] one of five apprentices on board. The old sailmaker Conrad liked was an Irishman of fifty-six, John Farrell,[23] and the cheerful young second mate was Leonard Cotter,[24] twenty-three, of Yarmouth; he had served as second mate of the *Torrens* during Conrad's first voyage on the ship. The clipper had, as he told of her, "a fame which attracted the right kind of sailor, and when engaging her crew her chief officer had always a large and promising crowd to pick and choose from."[25] The officers and crew of the *Torrens*, twenty-four of the thirty-five in their twenties, were experienced young men, eleven having served on the ship before; with the exception of five all were British.[26]

Though Conrad's last voyage was a memorably pleasant one, it had a grim side he chose not to mention, or perhaps remember. Two passengers, William Hylands and G. T. Edmunds, died at sea, and the ship's doctor, a young Englishman of thirty who joined the *Torrens* in Adelaide, C. Granville Jackson, died when the ship was a month away from England.[27] Also on board was the ailing young Jacques. In *A Personal Record* Conrad mistakenly wrote that Jacques died "either in Australia or it may be on the passage while going home through the Suez Canal," but in a letter to an Australian correspondent written in 1917 he corrected his error: "Yes, Mr. Jacques came back with us in the *Torrens*. He was laid up all the passage and I hardly ever saw him. This will partly account for my extraordinary mistake in the *Personal Record*. Strange lapse of memory! E. L. Sanderson (also a passenger that time) pointed it out to me a long time ago."[28] Jacques, in fact, died in England in November, 1893, four months after disembarking from the *Torrens* in London.

One hundred and twenty-six days after leaving Adelaide the ship reached London, on July 27, 1893.[29] Conrad remained nominally attached to her until October 17, the day of his official discharge.[30] Of that day in London Dock and the break to take place in his life he later wrote: "I took a long look from the quay at that last of ships I ever had under my care, and, stepping round the corner of a tall warehouse, parted from her for ever, and at the same time stepped (in merciful ignorance) out of my sea life altogether."[31]

There was, however, to be one postscript to his sea life. His uncle had been importuning him to make a visit to the Ukraine—"at my age to procrastinate is really to tempt fate,"[32] Thaddeus had written as if in premonition of his death then only a few months away—and in late August, 1893, Conrad traveled to his uncle's estate near Kiev, falling seriously ill during the first days of his stay. At the end of September, anxious to be at sea, he hurried back to London.

For two months he searched for a ship, making a daily call at the offices of the London Shipmasters' Society on Fenchurch Street. "In my wanderings about London from west to east and back again (I was very idle then) the two little rooms in Fenchurch Street were a sort of resting-place where my spirit, hankering after the sea, could feel itself nearer to the ships, the men, and the life of its choice—nearer there than on any other spot of the solid earth," Conrad wrote of this time in *A Personal Record*.[33] On a murky day in November Captain Froud, secretary of the Society, talked to him of a ship in need of a French-speaking second officer. The *Adowa*, an eleven-year-old British steamer of 2097 tons owned by Fenwick & Co. of London,[34] had been chartered by the new Franco-Canadian Transport Company to carry emigrants from France to Canada. Regular sailings were expected to be made between Rouen and Montreal or Quebec, the ship to carry up to 460 passengers. Conrad had never sailed to North America and agreed to make two trips on the *Adowa*, under Captain Fred Paton. He joined the steamer in London on November 29, 1893,[35] and, crossing the Channel, arrived in Rouen on December 4.

But the Franco-Canadian Transport Company "flourished no longer than roses live, and unlike the roses it blossomed in the dead of winter, emitted a sort of faint perfume of adventure, and died before spring set in."[36] The *Adowa* never went to sea under the F.C.T.C. house flag, nor carried a single emigrant to Canada. The insolvent company, sued for breaking its chartering contract, went out of business and the ship was returned to her London owners. For more than a month of hard winter weather prior to that ending, Conrad, with the chief mate Paramor and the banjo-playing third mate, Cole, remained on board, idle, in Rouen. There he began the tenth chapter of *Almayer's Folly*. That part of his tropical story was written in a steamy cabin; beyond his porthole the ice-clogged Seine and a row of grimy houses made a dismal setting: "a wide stretch of paved quay brown with frozen mud. The coloring was somber, and the most conspicuous feature was a little café with curtained windows and a shabby front of white woodwork, corresponding with the squalor of these poorer quarters bordering the river."[37]

Making a midwinter crossing of the Channel, the *Adowa* returned to London, Conrad leaving the ship there on January 18, 1894.[38] "I am very disappointed at having had to leave the *Adowa*," he wrote Mme. Poradowska. "It was very convenient to have a job near Europe. I am afraid I shall soon have to leave on a long voyage."[39]

Three months later, never leaving London, he completed *Almayer's Folly*, on April 24, 1894.[40] Weeks were spent in revising it and on July 4 he sent a brown paper package of his manuscript, by messenger boy, to a publishing house he had picked by chance, T. Fisher Unwin. Impatient for some answer after two months had gone by, he mailed a jogging letter on September 8, requesting the return of his novel. A month later, "in the first typewritten letter I ever received in my life,"[41] he was notified, on October 4, 1894,[42] of its acceptance. So much had his mind been made up to continue as a writer that he had already begun *An Outcast of the Islands*, starting this novel of Borneo in August,[43] a month after completing the first. The encouragement of Edward Garnett, his editor at Fisher Unwin, had much to do with giving him the heart to go on writing, he declared later, but, bolstering as that support undoubtedly was, his second book was under way when he first met Garnett.

Conrad was extraordinarily well prepared for his second career. A serious, wide-ranging reader since boyhood and a gifted storyteller, he had a twenty-year fund of dramatic stories to tell. The background of his life supplied incomparable material for a novelist, the breadth of his experiences, and the use he made of them, drawing the comment of Morton Dauwen Zabel: "The stage of his fiction is one of the widest ever devised by a novelist. His imagination, like his actual travels and adventures, literally circled the earth."[44]

When *Almayer's Folly* was published on April 29, 1895, it marked the official beginning of Conrad's life as a writer. Then thirty-seven, he would follow it for twenty-nine years. A man of action, restless in mind and movement, he stepped suddenly into a sedentary life as a writer who "lives in his work." "He stands there," he said of the new role of novelist he assumed, "the only reality in an invented world, among imaginary things, happenings, and people. Writing about them, he is only writing about himself. But the disclosure is not complete. He remains, to a certain extent, a figure behind the veil; a suspected rather than a seen presence—a movement and a voice behind the draperies of fiction."[45]

To the public, in spite of the enthusiasm of critics, he remained very
much of a "figure behind the veil." "While Conrad's brilliant charm arrested our notice in those early years," Garnett said of the author he
had helped to launch, "the depth of his creative vision eluded us. In his
voice we heard the seaman and the artist speaking, but the poet, secretly
inspiring the finest subtleties of his work, remained unseen."[46]

Appreciation of Conrad mounted steadily after his death. The outflow
of studies of his work, with many countries contributing to the present
high volume, is evidence that, in one sense, history has caught up with
him. The world he knew and wrote of has been brought within reach
by air travel, as it never was in the sailing-ship era, to the point that he
is one of the few writers of an earlier period who seems to be speaking
on the issues and problems of today. Yet the England in which he wrote
was Victorian and Edwardian for more than half of his writing years.
Victoria, at seventy-five, was on the throne and Gladstone only a few
months before had resigned as prime minister when Conrad met with his
publisher for the first time.

XXV

I think that all ambitions are lawful except those which climb up-
ward on the miseries or credulities of mankind.

A Personal Record

The public's favorites, when Conrad made his appearance as a writer
in England, were young Kipling, the new author of *The Light That
Failed, The Story of the Gadsbys* and *The Naulahka,* and R. L. Stevenson, whose popularity had endured for over a decade. Readers in that
complacent day, their Victorian world made up of "us" and "the others"
and the line between sharp, were offended by social criticism, coldly
unreceptive of novels that trespassed, as Hardy found with *Jude the
Obscure,* into regions of frank, unglamorous truth. In this laissez-faire
era with its conviction of Anglo-Saxon superiority making imperial dom-
ination in Africa and Asia not only a right but a mission, that government
was judged best which interfered least—a constraint equally imposed upon
authors. In such a climate Conrad's stories of "the others," sympathetic
portrayals of the nonbelonging where superiority was always a question,
met with no warm welcome from the public. Drawing his stories from
life with the realistic approach that, as H. L. Mencken pointed out, went

"far beyond meticulous representation; it struck for the inner reality of things as well," he offered to Victorian readers uncomfortable, even incomprehensible, fare. An original when conformity was the temper of the day, he was an author out of step with his times. Where bland trivialities were the demand, the shelter of ignorance ensuring peace of mind in that white-man's-burden day, he pursued a goal of making his readers see.

His difference, the most striking feature about his personality as it was of the work he produced, made itself evident on the day in November, 1894, when he first met with his publisher, Fisher Unwin, and the young editor of that house, Edward Garnett. By Mr. Unwin's arrangement the three gathered at the National Liberal Club in London to discuss Conrad's writing future. Garnett's impressions of Conrad on that day were of a "dark-haired man, short but extremely graceful in his nervous gestures, with brilliant eyes, now narrowed and penetrating, now soft and warm, with a manner alert yet caressing, whose speech was ingratiating, guarded, or brusk turn by turn. I had never seen before a man so masculinely keen yet so femininely sensitive. The conversation between our host and Conrad for some time was halting and jerky. Mr. Unwin's efforts to interest his guest in some political personages, and in literary figures such as John Oliver Hobbes and S. R. Crockett were as successful as an attempt to thread an eyeless needle. Conrad, extremely polite, grew nervously brusk in his responses, and kept shifting his feet one over the other, so that one became fascinated in watching the flash of his pointed, patent leather shoes."[1]

Though he had the plot in mind and a number of pages written of *An Outcast of the Islands,* he brushed off Mr. Unwin's inquiry about his next book with the frosty reply "I don't expect to write again. It is likely that I shall soon be going to sea." "A silence fell," Garnett said of this awkward meeting. "With one sharp snick he had cut the rope between us, and we were left holding the loose end. I felt disappointed and cheated."[2] A few weeks later he invited Garnett to his rooms at 17 Gillingham Street and had him read the pile of manuscript of his second novel. Garnett, a big, shaggy-haired man of twenty-six, was almost as new to the field of writing as Conrad, ten years older, but was already showing the talent for "discovering" authors (D. H. Lawrence and W. H. Hudson among them) which was to bring him into prominence. His enthusiasm for *An Outcast of the Islands* was immediate and the two men entered a friendship to last thirty years.

"At that time he was experiencing all the hot and cold fits and the exultations of literary creation, often thrown back and skeptical, but also boyishly eager while perfecting his strokes as the novel grew under his hands," Garnett wrote of Conrad's fluctuating moods while working on this novel, "and I was taking this development of his genius for granted and was enthusiastic over the romantic magic of his scenes."[3]

Looking back on the new writer's ups and downs, he graded the strain and the results of Conrad's initial years: 1895 a "leisurely year"; 1896 a "strenuous, prolific" year; 1897 and 1898 "years of struggling anxiety." With "Heart of Darkness," begun in December, 1898, Garnett believed Conrad "suddenly found the channel clear and forged ahead." In fact, it was a struggle all the way.

In the "leisurely year" of 1895 Conrad not only completed *An Outcast of the Islands*, on September 16, but began *The Sisters;* with the exception of three weeks spent in Champel under treatment, he also continued his pursuit of a sea job. Although he had chosen his country at twenty-eight at the time of his naturalization, and for the final thirty-one years of his life made England his home, the free-moving group to which he felt he belonged were seamen, those whose "home is always with them —the ship; and so is their country—the sea." He was not soon reconciled to shore life. France and England both attracted him and initially he chose to reside in France, acquiring there a novelty in his life, his first house. French, learned in childhood, he used with more ease than English; French authors were his favored reading and they, notably Flaubert, had the greatest influence on his work. His ties with France, particularly the south coast of his youth, remained so strong to the end of his life that he chose this region out of the many he knew for the setting of his final novels; selected a "Frenchman of Frenchmen," not an Englishman, to write the history of his life.

Conrad's general air of a Frenchman, the polished manners and expressive gestures making him stand out conspicuously, were accompanied at times by actions derived from that country of duels. "His fine courtesy kept his Polish impetuosity in check in those early years, but he resented bad manners when addressed," Garnett wrote, recalling one Gallic explosion, "and I remember how the slighting remarks of a Mr. N—— at a National Liberal Club meeting in 1895 so chafed on him that he would have sent the speaker a challenge had the country been France."[4]

In 1895 Conrad was in France in May and June, on his way to and from Champel, and in August he made three trips to Paris. The Paris trips were undertaken to help out "a very good fellow called Rorke," an acquaintance in Johannesburg, the brother-in-law of Conrad's friend Captain G. F. W. Hope, who was on the verge of losing his South

African gold claims to a German-owned syndicate organized in Paris. For the assistance they could give in straightening out Rorke's affairs Conrad crossed over to Paris to look up influential friends of his Marseilles days—Jules Guesde, member of the Chamber of Deputies, a banker named Jullien, and Pascalis,[5] a journalist on Le Figaro. The Marquise de Trabadelo, the Paula of his Marseilles romance over whom he had fought his duel with Captain Blunt, also lived in Paris.[6] Presumably he saw her there, for shortly after his return to London he began The Sisters, the story of the girl he called "Rita," his first version of The Arrow of Gold. It aroused Garnett's disapproval but Conrad, defending it as "my cherished aspiration," nevertheless continued to work on The Sisters for five or six months. He abruptly dropped the love story, which in its final form was to be so closely patterned upon his own, on the evening before his wedding.

Conrad married at thirty-eight, on March 24, 1896.[7] His bride of twenty-three, Jessie George, was a girl he had met in London eighteen months earlier through his friends the Hopes. Her father, a bookseller, had died when she was twenty and, to help support the family of ten, she worked as a typist in the London office of Calligraph, an American firm. Immediately after their marriage, at the St. George Register Office in Hanover Square, they went to Brittany, renting a house on Île Grande, near Lannion. Conrad had intended to make his home on the Continent but illness drew him back to London at the end of five months. During those months in Brittany he produced three short stories—"The Idiots," "An Outpost of Progress," "The Lagoon"—the early part of The Rescue, the first pages of The Nigger of the Narcissus.

The Nigger of the Narcissus was completed on February 19, 1897, in the first of the eight homes he rented in England, a small villa near Stanford-le-Hope in Essex, five miles from Tilbury. Six months later he and his wife moved to Ivy Walls Farm, also near Stanford-le-Hope, renting it for £20 a year. For eighteen months of 1897 and 1898 Conrad lived in the old farmhouse with its view of the Thames, writing "Karain," "The Return," "Youth," beginning Lord Jim. He was forty when he wrote "Youth," at the end of May and early June, 1898, and the father of a small son, Borys, born on January 15 of that year. He still thought of going to sea, taking his wife and the baby with him, and three months after finishing "Youth" went to Glasgow to make the round of shipowners.

"Nothing decisive happened in Glasgow," he wrote Garnett on September 29, "my impression however is that a command will come out of it sooner or later—most likely later, when the pressing need is past and

I had found my way on shore."[8] No command came out of it. Though he was "almost frantic with the longing to get away," it was his last attempt to find a ship. He moved, instead, out of Essex and into Kent, his home county for twenty-five years. Long before his second and last child arrived, John Alexander, born on August 2, 1906—Conrad then forty-eight and writing *Chance*—he had made his way on shore.

The succession of rented homes indicated how much his restlessness continued, even as a family man. He lived in five houses in Kent, in the Hythe, Ashford, Canterbury area; rented another in Bedfordshire; made prolonged stays in France, Switzerland, Capri, and Corsica. Much of *The Mirror of the Sea*, *The Secret Agent* and *Chance* was written in France, as was his short story "The Duel," but the major part of his work was produced in two homes in Kent. The first of these was Pent Farm, near Hythe, three miles from the sea. From October, 1898, to September, 1907, with the exception of eighteen months spent on the Continent, he lived and worked here. Two months after moving into Pent Farm he described it to a Polish cousin.

"From my window I can see farm buildings and if I lean out and look to the right I see the valley of the Stour, which rises, so to speak, behind the third hedge from the farmyard. Behind the house lie the Kentish Downs which slope zigzag down to the sea, like the battlements of a fortress. . . .

"On the other side of the little garden lie quiet meadows and waste-land, crisscrossed by hedges, with here and there an oak or a cluster of young ash trees. Three little villages nestle among the hills and you can see nothing but their church steeples. The coloring of the country shows yellow and pale brown tints among which can be discerned in the distance emerald-green meadows. And you don't hear a sound except the panting and sniffing of the London-Dover express trains. We live like a family of hermits. . . ."[9]

In this quiet setting of Pent Farm, rented from Ford Hueffer (Ford Madox Ford) at £27 a year, Conrad created stories in a wide range: "Heart of Darkness" (December, 1898–January, 1899); *Lord Jim* (June, 1898–July 16, 1900); "Typhoon" (September, 1900–January 11, 1901); "Falk" (May, 1901); "Amy Foster" (June, 1901); "Tomorrow" (January, 1902); "The End of the Tether" (October, 1902); *Nostromo* (January, 1903–September 3, 1904); *The Mirror of the Sea* (January, 1904–early 1906); *The Secret Agent* (December, 1905–November, 1906); "The Informer" (December, 1905); "An Anarchist" (November–December, 1905); part of *Chance*.

In September, 1907, he moved his family to Bedfordshire, to a house called Someries, near Luton. Though he spent fifteen months in it, he never learned to like the house and at the end of 1908 moved again. While at Someries he wrote most of *Under Western Eyes*, some of *A Personal Record*. His fifth house, again in Kent as his remaining ones were to be, was a cottage in Aldington. During the eighteen months of his residence, from January, 1909, to June, 1910, he wrote "The Secret Sharer," in November-December, 1909, and completed two books, *Under Western Eyes* and *A Personal Record*.

Conrad's sixth home, Capel House, was his most successful move. His stay in it of nearly nine years, from June, 1910, to March, 1919, was the longest of any. Capel House, at Orlestone, was an isolated Kentish farmhouse in a "sylvan wilderness," five miles from the nearest railroad at Ashford. "We are surrounded by woods and the soil is clay, but the house is sympathetic," he told the friend he had met on the *Torrens*, E. L. Sanderson. "I am just beginning to pick up the threads of existence after the horrible nightmare of my long illness: seven months I may say of my declining life wiped off at one fell swoop."[10] While living in Capel House his writing output excelled that at Pent Farm: "A Smile of Fortune" (completed August 30, 1910); "The Partner" (July, 1910); "Prince Roman (fall, 1910); "Freya of the Seven Isles" (December, 1910–February, 1911); *Chance* (completed March, 1912); "The Planter of Malata" (winter, 1913); *Victory* (November, 1912–June 28, 1914); *The Shadow Line* (December, 1914–December, 1915); *The Arrow of Gold* (November, 1917–June 14, 1918); part of *The Rescue*.

For six months of 1919, from March to October, his home, his seventh, was a furnished house called Spring Grove at Wye, near Ashford. Here he finished *The Rescue*, the novel begun in 1896 and struggled with for years, bringing it to an end in May, 1919. His final home was the handsome Georgian house of Oswalds, at Bishopsbourne, near Canterbury, the dower house of a large estate with Old World gardens and a bowling green he never used. Moving into it in October, 1919, he passed the remaining five years of his life there, writing *The Rover* and beginning the novel he was at work on at the time of his death, *Suspense*.

Due to restlessness almost as much as the meagerness of his income, Conrad never owned a house. He chose to live in the country, never the city, and the landscape he sought was one of rolling hills and woods, inland, not too far from the sea. He often sailed off the coast of England on the yachts of friends, and in the early months of his marriage rented a four-ton cutter, *La Pervenche*, for days of sailing along the coast of Brittany, but he never succeeded in having a boat of his own.

The living he earned, for a famous man and a writer of such industry, was one of bare subsistence. "Last year I made just £420,"[11] he told H. G. Wells of the year, 1907, when he had already published ten books, *Lord Jim* among them. He also, for the sake for money, collaborated with Ford Madox Hueffer on *The Inheritors, Romance* and *The Nature of a Crime*, books of little merit bringing credit to neither man. Earning little and without reserves—in 1896, through the failure of a South African gold mining venture in which he had invested, he had lost the fifteen thousand rubles inherited from his Uncle Thaddeus—he was helped over the worst periods by a few friends. He received loans from Garnett, Cunninghame Graham and Hueffer among others—still owing Hueffer £100 capital and £40 interest in 1913[12]—and was carried along by advances from his agent, J. B. Pinker, for eight years, until 1910. Though he was offered Britain's highest honor, a knighthood, which he declined,[13] only four times in his life did official material assistance come his way, in the form of small grants: in July, 1902, when he received £300 from the Royal Literary Fund; in March, 1905, when William Rothenstein and Edmund Gosse secured for him a Civil List Pension of £500, approved by the Prime Minister, Balfour; in April, 1908, when the efforts of H. G. Wells and J. M. Barrie resulted in a grant of £200 from the Royal Literary Fund; in August, 1910, when a Civil List Pension of £100 came through Galsworthy's appeal.

Conrad used every avenue open to a literary man to increase his income. His stories with few exceptions were sold to magazines, and his novels often serialized, prior to book publication. While this multiplied the returns from his writing, the payments in each case were exceedingly low: £20 for *Almayer's Folly*[14]; £80 for four chapters of *A Personal Record* published in the *English Review*.[15] To add to his earnings he sold his manuscripts, from 1910 to 1918 to an American lawyer in New York, John Quinn,[16] a Conrad admirer and collector; from 1918 to 1924 to Thomas J. Wise,[17] an English collector in London. Wise bought, among other purchases, the manuscript and typescript of *The Arrow of Gold* for £70 and the manuscript of *The Rover* for £150. Quinn paid even less, acquiring the MS. of *An Outcast of the Islands* for £30, that of *Victory* for £100. (When the Quinn collection was sold at auction in New York in 1923 the *Victory* manuscript brought $8100—Quinn making far more in that one sale than Conrad ever received for all of his handwritten pages—while such sums as $5300 were paid for *Almayer's Folly*, $6600 for *Chance*, $6900 for *Under Western Eyes*, $4700 for *Nostromo*. Dr. A. S. W. Rosenbach, a Philadelphia collector, bought most of the Conrad manuscripts at the Quinn sale, paying a total of $72,000 for them.[18])

Not until 1916, when he was fifty-nine, was Conrad out of debt.[19] The popular success of *Chance*—a bestseller in England and America when it came out in 1914, its American sales spurting through the energetic promotion of Doubleday's young editor Alfred Knopf—ended nineteen years of hard times. In the struggle to manage against such odds poor health presented an almost insurmountable handicap. "You know as well as anybody that of these years a full third must be taken off for illness alone,—not speaking of other pieces of bad luck," he wrote the artist William Rothenstein in 1909. "So I don't think I've been indolent or even unduly slow, taking into consideration the nature of my work."[20] His wife's accident at thirty-one, permanently damaging both knees when she fell on the pavement in London, made her a semi-invalid for the rest of her life and added further to Conrad's already heavy burdens. The repeated operations on her legs, amputation being considered in 1917,[21] brought despair each time when recovery failed to follow. Before this family tragedy added its weight of black days, Conrad's own recurring illnesses cut deeply into the time and the ease of mind needed for his work. "I have been ill again," he told Galsworthy while writing *Nostromo*. "Just got down, shaky, weak, dispirited. No work done. No spring left to grapple with it. Everything looks black, but I suppose that will wear off, and anyhow, I am trying to keep despair under . . . it is not so much the frequency of these gout attacks, but I feel so beastly ill between, ill in body and mind. It has never been so before. Impossible to write,—while the brain riots in incoherent images. It is sometimes quite alarming."[22]

Although he had spurts when his work went well—writing 110,000 words in one twelve-month period, 100,000 in another of fourteen months[23]—Conrad's poor health, lack of money, and the meticulous care given his complex stories made for slow progress. He had as a rule several pieces of work under way at the same time, sandwiching essays, criticism, autobiography, and short stories into the protracted composition of his longer novels. In the effort to obtain the most from his mind through this literary juggling, and in the process somehow to make his writing produce a living, each single work was long in growing. The maturing point of his books show how much of time alone went into them. *Almayer's Folly* required nearly five years to write; *An Outcast of the Islands*, fourteen months; *The Nigger of the Narcissus*, ten months; *Lord Jim*, two years; *Nostromo*, twenty months; *The Secret Agent*, ten months; *Chance*, seven years; *Under Western Eyes*, two years; *Victory*, twenty months; *The Arrow of Gold*, eight months; *The Rescue*, twenty-three years; *The Rover*, ten months. His shorter stories were composed more quickly: "Youth" in three weeks; "Heart of Darkness" in a month; "Typhoon" in four and a half months; "The Secret Sharer," three weeks; *The Shadow Line*, a year. Of his two volumes of autobiography a year was spent on *A Personal Record* and two years on *The Mirror of the Sea*.

The loneliness of a writer's life, emphasized by his hermit-like existence in the country, made friends of supreme importance to Conrad. Anxiety over their fortunes was as great as over his own. "He was deeply affected by what happened to those he cared for, so deeply affected, indeed, that bad news was quite capable of bringing on an attack of gout," Richard Curle wrote of him. "He would discuss his friends by name, one after the other, summing up their chances, analysing their position; and the relief when he felt assured that they were in smooth waters was intense and obvious."[24] Proud and touchy always, still as susceptible to slights as he had earlier been in Marseilles and Mauritius, he was ready, said Curle, "on occasion, to take violent and lasting offense." If he felt himself insulted "then all was over." His relations with the conceited, bruising Hueffer ended in such a manner. Following Conrad's death Hueffer published warped reminiscences of his erstwhile friend, presenting him in two accounts, factually unreliable, as "a monstrous freak," as Jessie Conrad angrily commented.[25] Unlike Hueffer, Conrad made no public matter of his quarrels. That he had few permanent disagreements with friends is demonstrated by his letters, covering a span of nearly thirty years, which show how lasting, and how warm, his ties were with those he cared for.*

Among the first of his literary friends was H. G. Wells. A brisk, plump man who "came through a doorway as if he were the wind itself,"[26] Wells was mentally and physically vigorous; irreverent, challenging, a *gamin*, deeply concerned about mankind's progress, he hated the stultifying pomposity and artificiality of his Tory times. Wells wrote a praising, unsigned review of *An Outcast of the Islands* ("perhaps the finest piece of fiction that has been published this year, as *Almayer's Folly* was one of the finest that was published in 1895") in the *Saturday Review* of May 16, 1896. Two days later, writing from Île Grande in Brittany (in one of the letters formerly believed destroyed, now at the University of Illinois), Conrad thanked the anonymous critic for his complimentary notice, learning by return mail that the author of it was

* Many of the originals of Conrad's letters, of which some were presumed lost, exist in collections held by Harvard, Yale, Dartmouth, Duke University, the Universities of Illinois, Virginia, Texas, the New York Public Library (Berg Collection), the British Museum.

Wells. The friendship opened then continued through the years, Conrad's widow keeping up the contact through 1934 when, at the close of her own life, her letters were being sent from the house she named "Torrens" for Conrad's ship, a house at Harbledown near Canterbury. Conrad admired Wells' work enormously, finding qualities in him similar to Swift, and not only dedicated *The Secret Agent* to him in 1907 but maintained unfailing praise for the controversial work Wells produced. "I am as if silenced by the multiplicity of responsive strains within me," he told Wells on January 20, 1911,[27] of his reactions to *The New Machiavelli*.

His friendship with Henry James, like that with Wells, began in 1896. Conrad that year sent James his new book, *An Outcast of the Islands*, to which James responded with *The Spoils of Poynton* and an invitation to lunch. Neighbors when Conrad lived at Pent Farm, they saw a great deal of each other over the years. Congenial in temperament, each had a profound admiration for the other's work, *Lord Jim* drawing an especially enthusiastic response from James. By preference they spoke French when together and it was in French that their correspondence began. In the first of Conrad's letters that have survived, a short note dated November 30, 1897 (unpublished and long considered lost),[28] he addressed James, the towering literary figure fourteen years older than himself, with the respectful *"Cher Maître"* he was always to use. Sending with his letter a copy of *The Nigger of the Narcissus*, he said his new book had "the quality of being short" and in *"Il a été vécu"* emphasized his own life as the source for it.

Cunninghame Graham was also among the earliest of his literary friends. Reading the satirical story "An Outpost of Progress" in the magazine *Cosmopolis*, he wrote enthusiastically of it to Conrad in August, 1897, and from that first contact as strangers grew the close friendship to endure the remaining twenty-seven years of Conrad's life. Their experiences formed a common bond, "Don Roberto" having a life as adventurous as his own had been. In appreciation of the unquenchable spirit of the friend five years older, Conrad dedicated *Typhoon* to the radical Scot. Debating the follies and hopes of mankind—Conrad pessimistic as a rule—their tussle with ideas drew from him the finest of his letters. Much as they argued, they stood basically on similar ground. "I am so much in accord with your sentiment"[29] was Conrad's reaction, in an unpublished letter, to *Success*. After twenty-four years of knowing, and debating with, the avant-garde fighter for reforms which were one day to be realized, he would write him, in 1921, "You have been one of my moral supports through my writing life."[30] "I can assure you that I never wrote a book since," he said of the years following their first meeting, "without many mental references to you, of whom alone almost amongst my readers I always thought that *he* will understand."[31]

Stephen Crane searched out Conrad, as Cunninghame Graham had done, in the same year, 1897. *The Nigger of the Narcissus*, making its first appearance as a serial in the *New Review*, excited Crane, a young author of twenty-six whose recently published *The Red Badge of Courage* was a sensation on both sides of the Atlantic. Choosing to live in England, he asked his English publisher shortly after his arrival to arrange a meeting with Conrad. In a London restaurant in October, 1897, they "shook hands with intense gravity and a direct stare at each other, after the manner of two children told to make friends," Conrad wrote of that meeting, and, the luncheon arranged by their publisher ending, spent the afternoon and evening tramping the streets together, "forgetting to think of dinner but taking a rest here and there, till we found ourselves, standing in the middle of Piccadilly Circus, blinking at the lights like two authentic night-birds."[32] Their affectionate friendship, dating from that day, was ended by Crane's death from tuberculosis in 1900. In his portrait of the brilliant writer fourteen years his junior Conrad movingly told of the quiet, intensely earnest American, overly generous, a frail man in a hurry to live whose smile was "not like a ray but like a shadow."[33]

Other writers and critics came into Conrad's life: Edmund Gosse, W. H. Hudson, Sidney Colvin, Norman Douglas, Arthur Symons, Hugh Walpole, J. M. Barrie, Bertrand Russell, André Gide. Deeply involved in work, and in the family life of raising two sons, he was sought out by admirers, made occasional trips to London for luncheons where writers met. The more meaningful of his personal ties as the years went by were indicated by the dedications of his books. Three were to his family—his wife (*Youth*), his son Borys (*The Shadow Line*), his Uncle Thaddeus (*Almayer's Folly*); others were to old friends such as the Hopes (*Lord Jim*), Adolf Krieger (*Tales of Unrest*), E. L. Sanderson (*An Outcast of the Islands*), his mother Mrs. Katherine Sanderson (*The Mirror of the Sea*), Galsworthy (*Nostromo*); most were inscribed to friends of his literary life: Garnett, Cunninghame Graham, Wells, Hugh Clifford, Mr. and Mrs. Ralph Wedgwood, Harriet Capes, Agnes Tobin, Perceval and Maisie Gibbon, Richard Curle, G. Jean-Aubry. They came to him often in the country where, exclusively an indoors man, he offered the stimulating talk and provocative arguments leaving his guests mentally flagged at the end of the day. At the head of his table with friends around him "he seemed to grow happier in their congenial company," wrote Curle. "The clouds fell away from him, and he would emerge brighter, fresher, with all the youthfulness of his heart undimmed."[34] His "astonishingly varied gifts as a talker"[35] were as impressive to friends as the traits strangers found outstanding, his "tremendous personality and his unself-conscious modesty."[36]

But he was far from a static, or even predictable, man. With his mercurial temperament and hypersensitivity he was hard to live with, according to his wife, though J.C., as he was affectionately called by his family, attempted to adjust to the domestic routine around which her life revolved. His son Borys recalled one occasion when, attempting to hang a hammock for a tea party his wife was giving, Conrad lost his grip and fell from the tree into the cups and saucers. Unhandy about the house, he was also defeated by mechanics. Motoring appealed to him, as early as 1904 when cars were novelties, and in the course of his lifetime he owned five, the first a 10 h.p. single-cylinder Cadillac. A hopeless driver, he was content to have Borys, at fourteen, behind the steering wheel. One day Conrad—arrayed in his usual motoring costume, monocle, gray bowler, and a voluminous cape-like havelock—drove to the station to pick up his son, whirled by him at breakneck speed, waving cheerily as the runaway car raced from the town. Borys took off in pursuit, found his father standing nonchalantly by the car, off the road on the side of a hill, its brake cable unfastened. "This damned thing took charge of me," he explained, "and I was quite unable to bring it to an anchor."[37]

Conrad was an anxious, devoted father, frantically worried when either child fell ill. He sat up with them through the nights they tossed with fever, read to them by the hour, amused them with sickbed toys, wrote family news in detail to such friends as Colvin. In 1914 Borys, at sixteen, enlisted with the British forces in World War I and after four weeks of training was sent to the front lines in France. Conrad followed his movements through a secret code they had arranged. On April 4, 1918, he told Colvin "the kid is unhurt so far. He's a good child. He remembered hearing me say once that I liked a special kind of olives, saw some in a shop and is sending me a jar of them—out of the very jaws of death as it were. I feel horribly unworthy."[38] Six months later he had to tell Colvin the frightening news that Borys had been gassed, wounded and shell-shocked—a month before the armistice. He played chess with John, whose forte he had first thought, hopefully, to be geography, and endeavored to have his older son follow the sea. His wife might reveal many of his failings, in books written after his death, but Conrad never admitted to outsiders any faults she might have. It was more than loyalty. "Don't imagine, my dearest, that the delights of this country make me forget my home,—which is where you are: and indeed is nothing to me but you, you alone wherever you may be," he wrote her from New York on May 24, 1923, during the only visit he ever made to the United States. "I can't give you the slightest idea how impatient I am to get back to you. I think of nothing else. The time seems interminable and yet the visit is a success."[39]

For six weeks, from April 30 to June 2, he was a guest of his New York publisher, F. N. Doubleday. Beyond a nine-day motor trip to Boston and New England, he confined himself to New York and the Doubleday Oyster Bay home. There, a shy man of sixty-five "distinctly homesick," he thought of his family back in England, sending "tenderest love and hugs to the children,—quite as if they were still little."[40] A clamoring American public sought to lionize him, and he shrank from it. Parties were given where Paderewski and Colonel House were among the many brought to meet him; he was besieged by reporters and adoring strangers. Before an audience of two hundred in the New York home of Mrs. Curtiss James he read parts of *Victory*, beginning the only public performance of his life with "a moment of positive anguish,"[41] receiving an ovation at the end from the crowd of social and literary celebrities, "the very top of the basket," who had fought for invitations to the glamorous affair.

Too retiring to enjoy the fanfare, and the overwhelming hospitality of a country where, as he wrote in one farewell note, "the cream is excellent and the milk of human kindness apparently never ceases to flow,"[42] he grew "heartily sick of all this infinite kindness," as he confessed to his wife, and eagerly looked forward to being back in his own quiet home. But he had captured New York by a personality uniquely modest for a famous man. Reporters, with the image of greatness in their minds, were amazed when a physically slight man appeared for photographs. His unexpectedness took another form: an incomparable stylist in written English, he spoke it with an accent defined as French. Contradictions abounded in him. "Enigmatic," "mysterious," "elusive" were terms liberally applied to a man no term adequately fitted; his complex novels, human commentaries to be read on several levels, were as hard to classify. "A truly great novel is a tale to the simple, a parable to the wise, and a direct revelation of reality . . . to the man who has made it part of his being," wrote John Middleton Murry in 1924. In that sentence was summarized, Carlos Baker has suggested, "the triple power which Conrad brought to the art of the novel."[43] With the meaning in his work depending on what each reader grasped, his novels received manifold interpretations. What views he held, what make of man he was, also ran the gamut of opinion.

There was a great deal of truth in his 1919 comment to Garnett that, by his inability to swallow *any* formula, he was made to appear an "enemy to all mankind."[44] To a mankind essentially partisan he was not parochial enough, had too little bias. For a world charged with isms where each crusading sect wore its colors violently he stood outside the battle, presenting, through the convincing characters of his fiction, opposing points of view. It made him an author difficult to place in a frame. In private life his flexible viewpoint left listeners unsure in the end of what his final opinions might be. Enjoying argument, the thrust and parry of debate, he upheld the conservative side in challenging socialist friends; but those who sought to tag him a conservative for this were forced to brush aside the tenor of his work. For reasons as slight as his courtly manners and his monocle he was dubbed an aristocrat—"a silly word to apply to him,"[45] in Galsworthy's view. For he was not an aristocrat by origin nor by the company he kept, and the world he chose to write of was, socially, the opposite of the drawing-room arena of James. Class distinctions repelled him, so much so that he refused to be set apart even by honors intended as tributes. Rejecting a knighthood, he also declined, being "perfectly determined to have nothing to do with any academic distinction,"[46] the honorary degrees offered by the universities of Oxford, Edinburgh, Liverpool and Durham. Behind these and other actions like them were the antipathies Curle wrote of: "If, on the one hand, any sign of posing offended Conrad, on the other any sign of fanaticism offended him equally."[47]

Attacking both religious and political fanaticism in his novels, it was inevitable that superzealots would attack him in return. A nationalist issue flaring up in Poland more than sixty years ago gave rise to a subsidiary one of which echoes are still heard today. For what was called his "defection"—emigrating from Poland, electing to live abroad, to write in English, not Polish—he was assailed in 1899 by a woman novelist, Maria Orzeszkowa, in the Polish weekly *Kraj* published in St. Petersburg. The hysterically bitter charges there leveled against him—he being one of many talented Poles denounced for leaving the country of their birth—came out early in a controversy that raged for years in Poland on the subject of national betrayal. The heated argument, waning, cropped up in a new and later form: Conrad's exploration of the human problem of guilt, in such of his novels as *Lord Jim*, was asserted to be an outgrowth and an expression of his "guilt" over leaving Poland. The allegation, made after his death by Polish critics and for a time widely circulated, overlooked the *Jeddah* incident, his source for *Lord Jim*, narrowed the meaning of the novel and of all he wrote, cast him in the mold of an anguished émigré rather than what he was, a man formed by the borderless life of the sea concerned with human, not national, values.

"I am no slave to prejudices and formulas, and I shall never be," he wrote to Barrett H. Clark in 1918. "My attitudes to subjects and expressions, the angles of my vision, my methods of composition will, within limits, be always changing—not because I am unstable or unprincipled but because I am free."[48] No one, Curle said of him, was "less attached to the ideas of any clique,"[49] and it was his noncommitment, his objectivity and tolerance, which made him incomprehensible to extremists.

For his native country Conrad had mixed feelings. With a childhood such as his there were few cheerful times to remember, but there were some; as any man in later years looks back with affection to the land of his childhood, so did Conrad. He was also strongly loyal to that land, long occupied by foreign powers, and when its future was in question during World War I he wrote, in June, 1916, "A Note on the Polish Problem"—a paper, as he said in his March 3, 1920, letter to Thomas J. Wise, never intended for publication but written at the request of a friend, to be shown to the Foreign Office in London.[50]

What slender ties Conrad had with Poland after his uncle's death were with distant cousins of the Zagorski family, with whom he corresponded. He wrote but one story with a Polish background, "Prince Roman" (1911), for the clear reason that, all of his adult years having been spent away, he did not know Poland well. He made his sole visit there in twenty years in 1914. The journey was undertaken at the insistence of his family, his own choice of a holiday place that summer being Devon. An invitation had come for "all the tribe of us" to visit an acquaintance near Cracow, he wrote Galsworthy, and "if I had not accepted instantly, I would have been torn to pieces by my own wife and children."[51] Shortly after their arrival in Cracow World War I broke out. Troops were mobilized, civilian travel stopped. Ill himself and his wife an invalid, Conrad shepherded his family through a country in the chaos and panic of war; barely escaping internment, they succeeded in returning to England by way of Austria and Italy. For a few days in Cracow, before war tore that city like so many others out of a quiet peace, crowds had gathered about him, welcoming him, saluting him for achievements that, had he spent his life in Poland, almost certainly would never have been his.

His wandering life provided the experiences his work was drawn from, made his outlook what it was, but the statelessness of his viewpoint, one of his strengths, had been won at a cost. He ceased to "belong" in Poland; he was also an anomaly in England. There, where he stood out for the strangeness of his speech and ways, he was not regarded as an Englishman, nor did he try to be one. His ever-restless movements and eloquent gestures, which Wells termed "very Oriental indeed," marked him as a foreigner. When he called on Wells at Sandgate in the early days of their friendship he arrived in the conspicuously un-English manner Wells told of—"cracking a whip along the road, driving a little black pony carriage as though it was a droshky and encouraging a puzzled little Kentish pony with loud cries and endearments in Polish, to the dismay of all beholders."[52] Giving free rein to his volatile temper, as gallant in manner as an eighteenth-century gentleman, he was looked upon in England as a Continental. His prismatic personality was caught in Garnett's description of his "buoyant temperament and resilient moods, his uncanny insight, his skeptical faith and philosophic irony, his charming frankness and great affectionateness, his flashing wit, his humor, often playful, often fiercely sardonic."[53]

His sense of humor was vital and active—he had "an almost ferocious enjoyment of the absurd," said Galsworthy—but it was not an ordinary brand. As one who "stared life very much in the face, and distrusted those who didn't," his waggish sallies were directed at "all class and catalogues." "Writing seemed to dry or sardonise his humour," Galsworthy wrote. "But in conversation his sense of fun was much more vivid; it would leap up in the midst of gloom or worry, and take charge with a shout."[54] His delight in the bizarre brought on the "wild bouts of fun" Curle remembered. At the breakfast table his talk was "like a bubbling stream of nonsense, in which each extravagance led to another and in which the ludicrous aspect of things held complete sway."[55] There was an elfish whimsy in this nonsense. But the boisterous glee friends knew was missing in his fiction where his humor, lying beneath the surface and "not altogether English," was passed over by the critics of his day.

Conrad was amused by every quirk of men, had a zest for watching the show. He admired excellence and was unsparing of himself in his efforts to achieve it. But, believing that "the chapter of accidents . . . counts for so much in the book of success," he refused to sit in judgment of his fellow men, rejected Kipling's hard-edged "law of right and wrong." Where he could agree with Yeats, "in vacillation man runs his course," and responded with compassion for the weaknesses vacillation showed, his ethical code had a stringency of its own. Bigotry outraged him. He "could be terrible in the presence of falseness."[56] His feeling about one form of falseness was given through Marlow in "Heart of Darkness": "You know I hate, detest, and can't bear a lie, not because I am straighter than the rest of us, but simply because it appalls me. There is a taint of death, a flavour of mortality in lies—which is exactly what I hate and detest in the world—what I want to forget. It makes me miserable and sick, like biting something rotten would do."[57] Truth was the core of his creed, the goal of his work. In the knowledge that "men lie to each other to conceal their dismay and their fear,"[58] as he wrote Cunninghame Graham, he placed highest those men of integrity punished by a society made uneasy by honesty. Lord Jim and Falk were two of his heroes who rejected the easy, fallacious way out while Nostromo, acting in the reverse, lived a lie and died by it. Where falseness was a mortal flaw, understandable if not condonable, the great vice to him was cruelty, inhumanity. It stemmed in his view from the existence of a dark self in men, an edge of madness. Latent in the most stalwart, it went beyond race or creed or nationality; chance could bring it out. An evil lurking in the shadowy region beyond sanity, he symbolized it in "Heart of Darkness."

Mankind was Conrad's theme, all aspects of it, weaknesses and strengths. To cope with that large theme he had the equipment of a mind so extensive in its range that it drew from Rothenstein, his friend for twenty years, the comment "Conrad understood everything." One after another, those who knew him sought to describe his intellectual power. Bertrand Russell told of the exhilarating impact of his talk with Conrad at their first meeting in 1913: "We seemed to sink through layer after layer of what was artificial, till gradually both reached the central fire. It was an experience unlike any other that I have known . . . I came away bewildered, and hardly able to find my way among ordinary affairs."[59] More than forty years later he would write of Conrad: "His intense and passionate nobility shines in my memory like a star seen from the bottom of a well. I wish I could make his light shine for others as it shone for me."[60] To Galsworthy the "storehouse of his subconscious self was probably as interesting and comprehensive a museum as any in the world."[61] A voracious reader and trilingual, the extent of his knowledge was a source of awe to Stephen Crane, made him the "brilliant conversationalist" so "formidable in argument" Cunninghame Graham knew. To Curle, a frequent companion in his later years, he had "for great subjects a great outlook,"[62] a "philosophical detachment from the cries of the moment."[63] With friends he would talk for hours on a subject, "winding into its ramifications and letting it bear him on gradually into reminiscence and by-paths that were enthralling."[64]

A superior intellect was one factor in the comprehensiveness of Conrad's work, the versatility which has given him a special standing of his own. The uniqueness inducing the New York *World* to say of him that "he was like no predecessor and he leaves no followers behind him"[65] was to some extent due to a combination of circumstances unknown to any other writer of modern times. A man with an extraordinary mind and acute sensitivity, he was exposed to a series of dramatic experiences lasting two decades of a global wandering more extensive in time and space than the myth-producing voyages of Ulysses. His wide outlook is more attuned to the present space-dissolved age than it was to the insular period he knew. In today's shrunken world, where East and West are within a traveler's sunrise-to-sunset reach, it has become accepted truth that, regardless of what areas of the earth they inhabit, men share common traits and motives. This, plus the fact that life is more frankly discussed than in his Victorian day, has given Conrad's novels more meaning than they had for readers in his lifetime. Then he was placed in the limiting category of "writer of the sea," designated an author with a "Slav temperament," criticized as a novelist dealing with what were called the "sordid" topics of death, strife, betrayal. "There are those who reproach me," he wrote to Garnett in 1908, "with the pose of brutality, with the lack of all heart, delicacy, sympathy—sentiment—idealism. There is even one abandoned creature who says I am a neo-platonist. What on earth is that?"[66]

Often he attempted to explain that he was writing of "things human." To the charge of one critic, Arthur Symons, that he gloated "over scenes of cruelty and am obsessed by visions of spilt blood,"[67] he answered, in an effort to set the record straight, how he *did* view life: "The earth is a temple where there is going on a mystery play, childish and poignant, ridiculous and awful enough, in all conscience. Once in I've tried to behave decently. I have not degraded any quasi-religious sentiment by tears and groans; and if I have been amused or indignant, I've neither grinned nor gnashed my teeth. In other words, I've tried to write with dignity, not out of regard for myself, but for the sake of the spectacle, the play with an obscure beginning and unfathomable *dénouement*."[68]

He defined his writing purpose repeatedly: "to render the truth of a phase of life in the terms of my own temperament with all the sincerity of which I was capable"[89]; "to present an unrestful episode in the obscure lives of a few individuals out of all the disregarded multitudes of the bewildered, the simple and the voiceless"[70]; as an artist speaking "to our capacity for delight and wonder, to the sense of mystery surrounding our lives, to our sense of pity, and beauty, and pain; to the latent feeling of fellowship with all creation—and to the subtle but invincible conviction of solidarity that knits together the loneliness of innumerable hearts, to the solidarity in dreams, in joy, in sorrow, in aspirations, in illusions, in hope, in fear, which binds men to each other, which binds together all humanity—the dead to the living and the living to the unborn."[71]

No novelist ever went to such lengths to pinpoint the sources of his fiction, to make it abundantly clear that it was life he sought to portray, all the colors and shades of it he had known. But his broad experience overtaxed the imagination of armchair critics and a genuine basis existed for his frequent protests of being misunderstood. It angered him to be labeled a writer of the sea but this—among other things—he was. Some of his best passages tell of the multifaced power poets from the beginning of time have made the subject of song. "If you would know the age of the earth," he wrote in *The Mirror of the Sea*, "look upon the sea in a storm. The greyness of the whole immense surface, the wind furrows upon the faces of the waves, the great masses of foam, tossed about and waving, like matted white locks, give to the sea in a gale an appearance of hoary age, lustreless, dull, without gleams, as though it had been created before light itself."[72]

The sea was the stage he often used for his human dramas—as Hardy used the heath—but the storms and calms affecting life upon it were more than atmospheric props; frequently the sea was an actor too. It was Conrad's estimate that barely one-tenth of his work was "sea stuff." Seamen appeared in his stories to a greater extent since, knowing them best, he illustrated through them how men reveal to themselves and to others in the course of their chance-directed lives a less heroic image than the ideal one of their dreams. He told Colvin in a 1917 letter of this.

"Perhaps you won't find it presumption if, after 22 years of work, I may say that I have not been very well understood. I have been called a writer of the sea, of the tropics, a descriptive writer, a romantic writer —and also a realist. But as a matter of fact all my concern has been with the 'ideal' value of things, events and people. That and nothing else. The humorous, the pathetic, the passionate, the sentimental *aspects* came in of themselves—*mais en vérité c'est les valeurs idéales des faits et gestes humains qui se sont imposés à mon activité artistique.*

"Whatever dramatic and narrative gifts I may have are always, instinctively, used with that object—to get at, to bring forth *les valeurs idéales*."[73]

Breaking sharply with the precedent set by such nineteenth-century writers as Ibsen, Melville, Hawthorne, Balzac and Zola—whose novels were dramas of obsession—Conrad argued no thesis, made no effort to convert his readers to an implanted point of view. In his fiction people were tested by life, in the way life constantly does, their responses determined by character flaws or strengths each had acquired, imperceptibly, in the course of his growing; not all lived up to "that ideal conception of one's own personality every man sets up for himself secretly." "Normally man does not know himself," Raymond Las Vergnas writes in *Joseph Conrad: romancier de l'exil*, "He needs catastrophes. More exactly, *his* catastrophe. It is by, and in, exile that the human being enters into dialogue with himself and makes his way by introspection toward his moment of truth."[74]

Much of what Conrad initiated in fiction has been acknowledged: *Nostromo*, parent of the political novel as we know it; *Lord Jim*, parent of the psychological novel of today; *The Secret Agent*, forerunner of the intellectual mystery story. But he contributed, not only to fiction, but to a better understanding of the world that we, today, live in. The emergence of new nations in Asia and Africa has given a special timeliness, for the historical insights they provide, to his stories of the East, of the Congo. "If it has become an axiom of our time that 'no man is an ilande,' it has become even more forcibly apparent that no people, race, or nation is either,"[75] Morton Dauwen Zabel has written of the close relation between the world of Conrad's books and the world today. The interpretation given those books in 1917 was one Conrad quarreled with, and justly. In the light of the vast changes since then the writer too far ahead of his day may yet find the understanding he looked for.

His human commentary left out little, either of the outward, physical world or of the inner region of each man's private contest. He wrote of fear, greed, guilt, love, isolation, brotherhood, betrayal, death, honor, revolution, the peace of mind of the unaware, the heroism of those too bereft of imagination to know fear. He wrote above all about "the wound of life," loss of self. On his voyages he learned of men suffering that loss, tested by life beyond bearing: Williams, whose story served him for *Lord Jim;* De Veer and Olmeyer in Berau; Barttelot, disintegrating in the Congo. He wrote of fears that united men, in "Youth"; fears that divided them, in *The Nigger of the Narcissus;* the gold-seeking that corrupts those it enriches, in *Nostromo*. He wrote of the seclusion and the anguish of love, in *The Arrow of Gold;* of individual and of mass guilt; of the deep-lying wish to belong, and the impossibility.

Something of that elusive wish he attained at sea. Nationalities and accents were of all sorts on board his ships, a mixing unmatched with the same ease on shore, and his fondness for the sea had some of its origin in the companionship he knew then and lost when his roving ended. He did not relinquish his voyager's life voluntarily and, through memory, retained a hold upon it. Twenty-seven of his novels, short stories and memoirs—more than half of his work—evolved directly from the memories of his sea years. A dozen years after his last voyage he inscribed *The Mirror of the Sea* to Mrs. Sanderson, "whose warm welcome and gracious hospitality extended to the friend of her son cheered the first dark days of my parting with the sea."

On the first craft ever launched men set out to make contact with their kind. This reaching out that a ship symbolizes was at the heart of Conrad's writing. The reaching out, constant and endless as it will ever be, is teamed with a parallel reality he brought out in "Heart of Darkness": "We live, as we dream—alone. . . ." A twenty-year odyssey lay ahead when he sailed in 1874 on a westward voyage from Marseilles. His first landfall was the West Indies, that cluster of aromatic islands where "the land is smelt before it is seen," where hurricanes and revolutions warn of the fragility of dreams. Other shores, illusory paradises on the sea horizon, battlefields on contact, followed in the series of lands Conrad came to know. The bittersweet harvest of his roving is summarized in a phrase of poetry, John Hall Wheelock's

> To be conscious is to be separate.
> This is the dark joy of being.[76]

APPENDIX
CONRAD'S VOYAGES

SOURCES

RECORDS: Marine Nationale, IIIᵉ Région Maritime, Archives du Port de Toulon, France; Archives Départementales des Bouches-du-Rhône, Préfecture, Marseilles; L'Inscription Maritime, Bastia, Corsica; Ufficio Museo Navale, Comando Marina, La Spezia, Italy; Ministère d'État, Principauté de Monaco; General Register and Record Office of Shipping and Seamen, Cardiff: Agreement and Account of Crew of *Skimmer of the Sea, Duke of Sutherland, Loch Etive, Annie Frost, Palestine, Riversdale, Narcissus, Tilkhurst, Highland Forest, Torrens*; Lloyd's of London and *Lloyd's Register of Shipping* (1875–94); Bureau Veritas, Paris; American Bureau of Shipping, New York; Library of Congress and National Archives, Washington, D.C.; Conrad Collection, Yale University Library; Master Attendant, Department of Marine, Singapore; Customs Department, Newcastle, N.S.W., Australia; Mitchell Wing, Sydney Public Library, Sydney, Australia; marine disaster records, 1875–94, of Atlantic Mutual Insurance Company, New York; Swan, Hunter & Wigham Richardson Ltd., Newcastle upon Tyne, England; Aitken, Lilburn & Co. Ltd., Glasgow; *Sea Breezes*, London.

NEWSPAPERS: The London *Times* (1875–94); New York *Herald* (1876–81); *Journal du Havre*, Le Havre, France (June 12–15, 1881); Sydney *Morning Herald*, Sydney, Australia (February 1–July 7, 1879; November 25, 1880–January 12, 1881; May 8, 1888); Port Elizabeth *Telegraph*, Port Elizabeth, South Africa (December 8, 1883–February 12, 1884); *Saint Thomas Times*, *St. Thomae Tidende*, Virgin Islands (1875–76); *Daily Picayune*, New Orleans, La. (October-November, 1876); Panama *Daily Star and Herald* (1875–76); *Glasgow Herald*, Glasgow, Scotland (April-May, 1881).

THE SHIPS AND THEIR JOURNEYS

MONT-BLANC. Three-masted wood barque of 394 tons built at Saint-Brieuc, Côtes-du-Nord, France, in 1853; owned by C. Delestang et Fils, Marseilles. First voyage: Conrad, 17, a passenger; sailed from Marseilles, December 11,

1874; arrived St. Pierre, Martinique, February 16, 1875; departed St. Pierre, March 30, 1875; reached Marseilles, May 23, 1875. Captain Ournier. Outward passage 67 days; homeward passage 54 days. Five months' voyage.

Second voyage: Conrad, 17½, an apprentice; sailed from Marseilles, June 23, 1875; arrived St. Pierre, Martinique, July 31, 1875; touched at St. Thomas, September 27, 1875, sailing the same day for Cap Haitien, Haiti; at Cap Haitien, October 2, 1875; sailed from Cap Haitien with cargo of logwood for Le Havre, November 1, 1875; reached Le Havre after stormy passage, December 23, 1875. Captain Duteil. Outward passage 38 days; homeward passage 53 days. Six months' voyage.

The *Mont-Blanc* was a seagoing ship for thirty-two years, until 1885.

SAINT-ANTOINE. Three-masted wood barque of 432 tons built by Barker (Barkus or Barkas in some records) in Sunderland, England, in 1870; owned by J. M. Cairo, Nantes, France; under charter to C. Delestang et Fils, Marseilles, 1875–80. Captain C. Escarras. First mate Dominic André Cervoni, 42, Luri, Corsica; César Cervoni, 18, Luri, Corsica, nephew of Dominic Cervoni, one of three apprentices. Four officers, 13 crew, one passenger outward; 4 officers, 14 crew homeward.

Conrad, 18½, acting as junior officer though enrolled as steward, wages 35 francs a month; sailed from Marseilles, July 8, 1876; reached St. Pierre, Martinique, August 18, 1876, at end of 42-day passage; sailed a few days later for Aspinwall (Colón) and Cartagena, Colombia, with cargo of arms for General Joaquin Maria Córdova, leader of rebel forces in Colombia's revolution; on return voyage to Martinique called at, among other ports, Puerto Cabello and La Guaira, Venezuela; reached St. Pierre, September 16, 1876; left St. Pierre in ballast, September 23, for St. Thomas, Danish West Indies, via St. Lucia with two passengers, Castayune Guiann and Gabriel Ribas; arrived St. Thomas, September 27; sailed from St. Thomas, October 12, with 680 tons of coal for Port-au-Prince, Haiti; reached Port-au-Prince October 26; departed Port-au-Prince, November 25, for careening island at Miragoâne, Haiti, en route to Marseilles; arrived Marseilles, February 15, 1877, with cargo of logwood and sugar. Seven months' voyage.

The *Saint-Antoine* was sold by J. M. Cairo in 1887 to E. De Lalun of Granville, Manche, France; in 1892, when twenty-two years old, turned into a pontoon in France.

TREMOLINO. Felucca of 60 tons built in Savona, Italy, about 1870, perhaps by Francesco Calamaro. Conrad, 19, using the alias "Monsieur Georges," made several voyages between March and December, 1877, running guns from Marseilles to the Gulf of Rosas coast of Spain. The ship, posing as a fruit and corkwood trader and possibly under Italian registry, carried rifles to Carlist guerrillas in Catalonia who, until 1882, fought on behalf of the Pretender to the Spanish throne, Don Carlos, loser of the 1872–76 Carlist War in Spain. The gunrunning was financed by the Carlist committee of Marseilles; the ship was nominally owned by a syndicate of four: Conrad, involved through the girl he loved, Baroness Paula de Somoggy; Captain John M. K. Blunt, an American; Henry Grand, an Englishman; a young

Frenchman, Roger P. de la S——. Under Dominic Cervoni as captain the ship sailed on her smuggling voyages with Conrad, César Cervoni, and four others in the crew.

Pursued by a Spanish coast-guard vessel, the *Tremolino* was driven on the rocks and sank off Cape Creus in December, 1877; no lives lost. Conrad's first shipwreck.

MAVIS. Steamer of 764 tons built by Edward Withy & Co. in Hartlepool, England, in 1871; owned by J. V. Gooch, London. Captain Munnings. Conrad, 20, embarked as an ordinary seaman in Marseilles, April 24, 1878. The steamer, carrying coal, continued on to Constantinople; at Yeisk, on the Sea of Azov, loaded linseed for England. Arrived Lowestoft, England, June 18, 1878. For Conrad a voyage of eight weeks.

Two years later, on November 24, 1880, the *Mavis* struck a submerged rock off the French coast, the Cherdonnière Rocks near the Île d'Oléron, while on a voyage from Cardiff to Bordeaux; ship lost; captain and six of crew got away safely in a boat; two firemen drowned.

SKIMMER OF THE SEA. Three-masted coasting schooner of 215 tons built at Yarmouth, England, in 1855; owned by Joseph Saul of Lowestoft. A coal-carrier running between Lowestoft and Newcastle. Conrad, 20, signed on in Lowestoft, July 11, 1878, as ordinary seaman, wages one shilling a month. Officers and crew of seven included: Captain William Cook, 42, Lowestoft; Arthur Chandler, mate, 28, Pakefield; Henry Boon, a.b., 36, Corton; William Munnings, a.b., 29, Mersey, Essex; Alfred Goldspink a.b., 34, Pakefield; Conrad de Korzeniowski, o.s., 20, Poland; Alfred Barham, boy, 17, Lowestoft (replaced by Ernest George Sturgeon, boy, 16, Lowestoft). Conrad made three round-trip voyages between Lowestoft and Newcastle during his ten weeks' service; signed off in Lowestoft, September 23, 1878.

A "family" coaster whose crew seldom changed, the *Skimmer of the Sea* went down at sea a few years later; some of Conrad's shipmates were lost.

DUKE OF SUTHERLAND. Full-rigged wood sailing ship of 1047 tons built by Smith at Aberdeen, Scotland, in 1865; owned by Daniel Louttit of Wick, Scotland. A wool clipper. Captain John McKay, 42, Aberdeen. Twenty-six officers and crew, five passengers, on outward voyage. Conrad, 20, joined the ship in London, October 12, 1878, as ordinary seaman; wages one shilling a month. Sailed from London for Australia, October 15; crossed the equator, November 30; passed meridian of Cape of Good Hope, December 26; rounded southwest cape of Tasmania, January 20; arrived Sydney, January 31, 1879. Outward passage: 109 days.

The clipper remained five months in Sydney, Conrad on board. On July 6, 1879, sailed for London; ship carried mixed cargo of wool and wheat, two passengers (one being Mrs. McKay), three officers, twenty-five crew. Returning via Cape Horn, reached London, October 19, 1879. Homeward passage: 106 days. Voyage of one year, four days. Those making the London-

Sydney-London voyage with Conrad were, in addition to Captain McKay: A. G. Baker, first mate, 36, Norfolk; H. J. Bastard, second mate, 44, Halifax; Otto Andersen, steward, 42, Denmark; William Edwards, cook, 34, Halifax; Hugh Davis, a.b., 21, Newport; W. B. Palmer, o.s., 15, Bristol; E. J. Hartenstein, o.s., 15, London; J. A. Rittersen, o.s., 19, Sweden.

Three years later the *Duke of Sutherland* was wrecked in heavy seas, on May 3, 1882, while at anchor in the roadstead of Timaru, New Zealand. With one thousand sacks of wheat on board and ready to sail for England, she bumped on the bottom, started her timbers, filled with water. The crew were taken off in boats; the seventeen-year-old ship, a total wreck, was sold for £84.

EUROPA. Iron steamer of 676 tons built by Palmer Bros. of Jarrow, near Newcastle, England, in 1862; owned by London Steamship Company, London. Captain Monroe. Conrad, 22, sailed as ordinary seaman, leaving London, December 12, 1879, bound for Mediterranean ports. Passed through Deal, December 14; called at Genoa, Leghorn, Naples, the Greek port of Patras and the island of Cephalonia near Patras, the Sicilian ports of Messina and Palermo. Returned to London, January 30, 1880, Conrad signing off that day. Seven weeks' voyage.

LOCH ETIVE. Full-rigged iron sailing ship of 1287 tons built by A. and J. Inglis of Glasgow in 1877; owned by James Aitken of Glasgow. Captain William Stuart, 48, of Peterhead, Scotland; commanded *The Tweed*, one of fastest clippers known, fourteen years (1863–77), commanded *Loch Etive* eighteen years (1878–96), died on board in 1896 on vessel's eighteenth voyage out from Glasgow to Australia.

Conrad, 22, sailed on clipper's third voyage; third mate and first berth as officer, wages £3 10s. per month. Sailed for Australia via Cape of Good Hope from London, August 21, 1880, the ship carrying twenty-eight officers and crew, two passengers, four stowaways; passed The Lizard, August 24; sighted Madeira, August 31; arrived Sydney, November 24, 1880. Outward passage: 94 days.

The *Loch Etive* remained in Sydney seven weeks; sailed from Sydney, January 11, 1881, with cargo of wool; arrived London April 24, 1881, Conrad signing off that day. Homeward passage: 103 days. Eight months' voyage.

Making the London-Sydney-London voyage were: Captain Stuart; first mate William Purdu, 27, Glasgow; second mate James W. Allestan, 29, Peterhead; third mate Conrad Korzeniowski, 22, Poland; carpenter John Cumming, 31, Peterhead; boatswain James Dray, 36, Padstow; sailmaker Peter Nicol, 20, Peterhead; steward W. Radenscraft, 32, Cawnpore; cook William Millar, 26, Aberdeen; ten able seamen: Olof Nilsjan, 28, Sweden; Henry Brandt, 33, Germany; Alfred Bevins, 22, London; Harry Schwikert, 23, Germany; Charles Young, 32, Glasgow; William Taylor, 46, Edinburgh; David Coe, 35, Yarmouth; H. Buse, 27, Kent; Thomas Parish, 24, London; John Baker, 47, Plymouth. In addition to these, on the outward passage to Sydney, were eight able seamen: James Davidson, 29, Dundee; D. Grossman, 19, Germany;

Charles Smith, 25, Glasgow; Patrick McElhern, 24, Antrim, Ireland; Charles Lowenheil, 26, Sweden; C. Wanabo, 34, Norway; Charles Cotfor, 25, Prince Edward Island; Thomas Lockett, 24, Stockport; ordinary seaman Henry Gimber, 20, London; two passengers: Alfred Peel and William Roberts; four stowaways: Albert Olie, Theodore Lockyer, John Woods, Charles Catford. For the homeward passage additional crew joining the ship in Sydney were seven able seamen: Pietro Volpe, 26, Italy; Metrafan Warabon, 29, Russia; A. Sorenson, 32, Sweden; H. Gates, 33, Hants.; David Todd, 26, London; T. Hibbert, 23, Canada; William Hyde, 26, London; ordinary seaman P. Butler, 16, India.

The *Loch Etive* was at sea for thirty-seven years. In 1911 she was sold to French shipowners for £1350 and in 1914 was converted to a hulk.

ANNIE FROST. Full-rigged sailing ship of 1236 tons built by Dinning at Quebec in 1863; owned by Frost & Co. of London. Captain C. Wilburn. Having sailed from London, July 28, 1880, for Cochin China and successfully completing that passage, the ship on her return from Cochin China, bound for Le Havre, anchored in The Downs, the roadstead off Deal, England, on June 5, 1881; left The Downs on June 6 in tow of the tug *Napoleon* and arrived the same day at Le Havre. Her cargo discharged, she began her departure for London and a scheduled new voyage to Cochin China; leaving the Eure basin in Le Havre on June 11, 1881, in tow of the *Napoleon* on her way out to sea, she struck the transatlantic lock, sustaining damage to starboard quarter and rails; arrived London, June 13, to undergo repairs. Conrad, 23, joined the ship in The Downs June 5 to serve as third mate on her forthcoming voyage to Indochina; was thrown in the water and injured in the Le Havre accident; returning to London on the ship, spent several days in the hospital; served on board *Annie Frost* eight days.

The *Annie Frost* sailed from London for Cochin China, July 31, 1881; completed her passage and, on her return to London, was lost in the Atlantic on September 3, 1882.

PALESTINE. Wood barque of 427 tons built at Sunderland in 1857; owned by John Wilson of London. Captain E. Beard, 57, Colchester, Essex. Conrad, 24, signed on in London, September 19, 1881, for voyage to Bangkok; second mate, wages £4 a month. Three officers, ten in the crew. Voyage accurately recalled in *Youth*. Ship twenty-three years old; series of mishaps and final disaster occurred during eighteen months of Conrad's service.

Sailed from London, September 21, 1881; left Gravesend, September 28; reached North Shields, October 20, coming through gales; left Newcastle upon Tyne, November 29, 1881, for Bangkok with cargo of 557 tons of coal and second new crew; when three hundred miles from England lost her sails in gales, sprang a leak, December 24; put back for England, reached Falmouth, January 10, 1882; eight months in Falmouth undergoing repairs; last of four crews signed on in Falmouth day before ship sailed for Bangkok; left Falmouth, September 17, 1882; six months later, on March 14, 1883, coal gas exploded when ship in Bangka Strait off Sumatra; decks blown up, flaming vessel abandoned 11 P.M. March 14, officers and crew getting off in three boats; Conrad, burned in explosion, in command of small boat holding three of the crew; *Palestine* sank, a "mass of fire," March 15. Boats rowed and sailed to Muntok on Bangka Island, arriving 10 P.M. March 15. Officers and crew left Muntok, March 21, on British steamer *Sissie*, arriving Singapore, March 22, 1883; officially discharged April 3. Marine Court of Enquiry in Singapore, in hearings conducted by Richard Spear O'Connor, Senior Magistrate, Edward Bradberry, Deputy Master Attendant, and John Blair, Master Mariner, gave verdict, April 2, 1883, that cause of fire was spontaneous combustion, vessel not prematurely abandoned, no blame attached to master, officers or crew.

Officers and crew on board for last six months and at time of shipwreck were: Captain Beard; first mate H. Mahon, 50, Dublin; Conrad, second mate, 24–25; carpenter Joseph Hawke, 21, Falmouth; cook-steward Robert Webber, 22, Falmouth; William Jennings, a.b., 42, Penryn, Cornwall; Harry Page, a.b., 25, Plymouth; Henry Aishton, a.b., 42, Plymouth; Peter Esman, a.b., 21, Antwerp; Charles Hughes, a.b., 32, Belfast; Anders Ellfsen, a.b., 34, Porsgrunn, Norway; Thomas Walters, o.s., 28, St. Kitts; Henry Vodden, boy, 16, Devonport.

Conrad remained in Singapore a month, embarking as a passenger on a Liverpool-bound steamer early in May, 1883; called at Port Said, May 13; in London by early June, 1883.

RIVERSDALE. Full-rigged sailing ship of 1490 tons built by Andrews in Liverpool in 1865; owned by L. H. McIntyre of Liverpool. Captain L. B. McDonald, 42, Aberdeen. Twenty-three officers and crew. Conrad, 26, second mate; wages £ 5 5s. a month; signed on in London September 10, 1883, for voyage to India. Sailed from London September 13, 1883; arrived Port Elizabeth, South Africa, December 7, 1883; left Port Elizabeth February 9, 1884, for Guam; arrived Madras, India, April 8, 1884. Following a dispute with his captain Conrad left the ship in Madras April 17, 1884, ending voyage of seven months. Among officers and crew were: first mate A. Johnson, 42, Shetland; carpenter J. Brusin, 29, Finland; cook William Sampson, 47, Halifax; sailmaker Edmund Butchers, 41, Devon.

The *Riversdale*, leaving Madras, was stranded May 31, 1884, at Masulipatam, India. The first mate, Johnson, took over command; because of the wreck entire crew discharged June 5, 1884, at Madras. Refloated, the ship was bought by M. C. Malik of Calcutta and in 1885 underwent repairs; in 1887 her owner was C. E. De Wolf of Calcutta; in February, 1891, she was stranded at New Caledonia; refloated, she was sold to Brown of Newcastle, Australia, her owner until 1917 when, after years as a coal hulk in Sydney, she was broken up. She had been at sea 52 years.

NARCISSUS. Full-rigged iron sailing ship of 1336 tons built at Port Glasgow, Scotland, in 1876 by R. Duncan & Co.; owned by Robert R. Paterson & Co. of Greenock, Scotland. Captain Archibald Duncan, 40, Campbeltown, Argyllshire, Scotland. Twenty-four officers and crew. The ship had sailed from Penarth, Wales, for India on November 2, 1883, without a second mate; had crew trouble throughout her voyage; reached Capetown from

Penarth, January 18, 1884; in Capetown five new men taken on to replace those quitting the ship—one seaman, Charles Dutton, left behind in Capetown prison; left Capetown, January 28, 1884; arrived Bombay, April 28, 1884, where first mate and six of crew discharged.

In Bombay on April 28, 1884, Conrad, 26, signed on as second mate; wages £5 a month. Also taken on in Bombay were first mate, Hamilton Hart, 42, Hull, and six seamen. Ship remained in Bombay thirty-six days; sailed from Bombay for Dunkirk, France, June 3, 1884; on September 24 when the ship was in the North Atlantic and three weeks away from Dunkirk a Negro seaman in the crew, Joseph Barron, 35, from Charlton County, Georgia, died of illness; the *Narcissus* reached Dunkirk, October 16, 1884, where all officers and crew signed off the following day, the ship to be overhauled. Bombay-Dunkirk voyage via Cape of Good Hope: 136 days.

The crew who sailed with Conrad from Bombay to Dunkirk were: carpenter E. Larsen, 29, Norway; cook Alfred Harvey, 29, Gosport; boatswain John Evans, 34, Canada; sailmaker W. G. Allen, 54, Sydney; Leonard Nilsson, a.b., 23, Sweden; C. Jansson a.b., 21, Sweden; Nils Lofstedt a.b., 20, Helsingborg; L. Larsen a.b., 22, Norway; George Halvorsen, a.b., 24, Norway; John William o.s.; Edward Thomas, o.s.; Evan Morgan, a.b., 23, Cardiff; Thomas Mathew, o.s., 19, Newport; Henry Powell, o.s., 21, London; John Youlton, cook, 46, Woolwich; Joseph Barron (died at sea); John Wild, a.b., 38, London; James Craig a.b., 21, Belfast; Charles Olsen, a.b., 25, Norway; John Williams, a.b., 39, Guernsey; Arch McLean, a.b., 23, Scotland.

The final six of this list joined the ship in Bombay; four—Barron, Wild, Craig, McLean—were drawn upon for leading characters in *The Nigger of the Narcissus*.

The *Narcissus* was owned in Scotland until November, 1899, when she was bought by Captain Vittorio Bertolotto of Camogli, Italy, and registered in Genoa. Converted to a barque, she traded to Australian and Pacific ports until 1907; in 1907, condemned, she was hulked in Genoa; in 1916, after seventeen years under the Italian flag, she was sold to P. Passos of Rio de Janeiro and refitted as a sailing barque; renamed the *Isis*, she sailed as a Brazilian ship until 1925. As the *Isis* her last call at a United States port was Baltimore, Md., in October, 1921; sunk in a collision at Rio de Janeiro on January 14, 1922, refloated in August of that year and sold to E. G. Fontes & Co. of Rio de Janeiro, her final owner. Sailing under the flags of three nations, she was at sea forty-nine years, closing her long career as a hulk.

TILKHURST. Full-rigged iron sailing ship of 1527 tons built by A. Mac-Millan and Son at Dumbarton, Scotland, in 1877; owned by W. R. Price & Co. of London. Captain E. J. Blake, 47, Plymouth. Twenty-six officers and crew. First mate, Alexander Samuel, 39, Peterhead, Scotland. Conrad, 27, signed on in Hull, April 24, 1885, as second mate, wages £5 a month, for voyage to Calcutta; sailed from Hull, April 27, for Cardiff to load coal; arrived Cardiff, May 14; remained in Penarth (Cardiff docks) almost a month; sailed June 10 from Penarth for Singapore with cargo of coal; arrived Singapore, September 22, remaining twenty-seven days. On eve of sailing from Singapore, October 19, a drunken quarrel broke out on board; in the scuffle an able seaman in the crew, William Cumming, 23, of Bristol, sustained a severe blow on the head; as the ship moved up Malacca Strait Cumming became delirious; a watch was kept over him, but nine days after leaving Singapore, as the ship entered the Andaman Sea, he jumped overboard, committing suicide, on October 28, 1885. The ship was then twenty-four days from Calcutta, reached on November 21, 1885; remained in Calcutta seven weeks; sailed from Calcutta with cargo of jute, January 8, 1886, via Cape of Good Hope; arrived Dundee, Scotland, June 17, 1886, Conrad signing off that day, completing voyage of fourteen months.

Cumming's death occurred a year after Barron's on the *Narcissus* and Conrad drew upon the two tragedies for *The Nigger of the Narcissus*. The original of the character Singleton in that story was Daniel Sullivan, 54, able seaman from county Kerry, Ireland, who left the *Tilkhurst* in Calcutta.

The *Tilkhurst*, eight years old when Conrad joined, served in the merchant marine of three nations, England, France and Italy. For sixteen years, 1877–93, she was owned in England; sold in 1893 to the French shipowning firm of A. D. Bordes et Fils and renamed *Blanche* for the eldest daughter of the Bordes family; owned in France for ten years; a nitrate carrier, she was damaged in a pampero in 1901 and sold, in 1903, to an Italian shipowner, G. Mortola of Genoa. She sailed under the Italian flag for twenty years, 1903–23, first in the Australian and Chilean trade. During World War I she was equipped with an engine; her last years were spent on the Atlantic. She was broken up in Genoa in 1923 when forty-six years old.

HIGHLAND FOREST. Iron barque of 1040 tons built at Leith by Ramage & Ferguson in 1884; owned by John Scott Colvil of Glasgow. Captain John McWhir, 34, county Down, Ireland. Eighteen officers and crew, four apprentices. Conrad, 29, first mate, wages £7 a month; took charge of captainless ship moored in Amsterdam early in January, 1887; a month later and two days before sailing Captain McWhir, first mate of the ship on her previous voyage, was appointed to the command. February 16, 1887, Conrad and Captain McWhir officially registered; second mate, T. Griek, 44, Holland. Sailed from Amsterdam for Java, February 18, 1887. Three weeks away from Holland, on March 11, 1887, able seaman Jan Hulskemper, 46, Holland, died at sea. Ship reached Samarang, Java, June 20, 1887, via Cape of Good Hope; voyage of four months through heavy weather. In Southern Ocean gale Conrad received leg injury, struck by flying spar; resigned berth in Samarang, July 1, 1887; hospitalized in Singapore six weeks. His six months' voyage, and Captain McWhir, were drawn upon for *Typhoon*.

The *Highland Forest* completed her voyage, returning from Java to Greenock, Scotland; in 1888 she was sold to J. R. Cuthbertson & Co., Glasgow; regularly at sea thereafter, she left her last port, New York, on January 27, 1901, with cargo for Fremantle, Australia; nearing the end of her voyage, on April 29, 1901, she was totally wrecked on Murray Reef near Mandurah, West Australia. One of seven of Conrad's ships lost at sea.

VIDAR. Schooner-rigged iron screw steamer of 304 tons built by Wigham Richardson & Co. at Newcastle, England, in 1871; registered at Singapore,

February 19, 1872; sailed under British flag; owned by Syed Mohsin bin S. Al Jaffree Steamship Company of Singapore. Captain James Craig, 33, born in England; sailed out of Singapore, 1875–1920; part owner and master of *Vidar*, 1887–92. Chief engineer, James Allen; second engineer, John C. Niven; steamer also carried a Chinese engineer, a Malay serang or boatswain, eleven Malays in crew, eighty-two Chinese for loading and unloading cargo in up-river ports.

Conrad, 29, joined the ship as chief mate in Singapore, August 22, 1887; served for nineteen weeks on trading voyages to Borneo and Celebes. Main port of call was Malay settlement of Berau, on the Berau River (formerly the Pantai) on east coast of Borneo. Conrad spent more than three weeks alto- gether in Berau—the *Vidar* calling there on each outward and homeward pas- sage from Singapore in the course of six trading voyages—and drew upon its people and setting for *Almayer's Folly*, *An Outcast of the Islands*, *Lord Jim*, *The Rescue*, *Victory*, using its background in "Karain," "The Lagoon," "The End of the Tether," "Freya of the Seven Isles."

Conrad resigned his berth on the *Vidar* in Singapore on January 5, 1888.

The *Vidar*, under Captain Craig, continued her Singapore-Borneo voyages until October 3, 1892, when she was sold to a Dutch subject and registered in Penang. She remained in those waters into the 1920s; withdrawn from service, she gradually fell to pieces in Penang, a vessel nearly sixty years old.

OTAGO. Iron barque of 345 tons built by Alexander Stephen & Sons in Glasgow in 1869; owned by Henry Simpson & Sons of Port Adelaide, Aus- tralia. Ten officers and crew. Conrad's only command, wages £14 a month.

Conrad, 30, received appointment as master in Singapore, January 19, 1888, of ship then moored in Bangkok; replaced the commander, Captain John Snadden, born in Kirkcaldy, Scotland, and resident of Wallaroo, Australia, who died on board, on December 8, 1887, at the age of fifty, when the *Otago* was at sea off the mouth of the Gulf of Siam. Conrad took command in Bangkok, January 24, 1888; spent sixteen days in Bangkok; sailed from Bang- kok, February 9, 1888, for Australia with cargo of teak; reached Singapore, March 2, 1888, taking twenty-one days to cover eight hundred miles, all the crew ill with the exception of the cook, F. Veilvom, 46, of Amsterdam. Crew hospitalized in Singapore; six new seamen were signed on and ship sailed from Singapore on March 9 for Sydney; passed through Sunda Strait, between Java and Sumatra, March 15; arrived Sydney, May 7, 1888. On board for the Singapore-Sydney passage were: Charles Born, first mate, 33, Germany; Isaac Jackson, second mate, 23, England; Daniel Watson, a.b., 31, Scotland; R. Firth, a.b., 31, Germany; H. Green, a.b., 33, Liverpool; Thomas Smith, a.b., 27, Sweden; James Jensen, a.b., 22, Denmark; Richard Green, a.b., 48, St. John, New Brunswick; Thomas Humphrey, a.b., 22, England. Born, Watson and Firth served under Captain Snadden; were with Conrad in Bangkok and for the three months' voyage from that port to Sydney. *The Shadow Line*, "Falk," and "The Secret Sharer" grew out of this voyage.

In June-July, 1888, Conrad sailed the *Otago* on voyages between Sydney and Melbourne; on August 7, 1888, sailed from Sydney for Port Louis,

Mauritius, via Torres Strait; arrived Port Louis, September 30, 1888, ending voyage of fifty-four days. Remained in Port Louis eight weeks; sailed from Port Louis for Melbourne with cargo of sugar and potatoes, November 22, 1888; arrived Melbourne, January 5, 1889. Conrad's stay in Mauritius drawn upon for "A Smile of Fortune" and "The Planter of Malata."

In February, 1889, Conrad took the *Otago* from Melbourne to Minlacowie, Australia, loading cargo of wheat for Port Adelaide; in Port Adelaide, rather than make a new voyage to Mauritius, he resigned, March 26, 1889; in April sailed as a passenger on a steamer for London, arriving in June. He had commanded the *Otago* fourteen months.

The *Otago* outlived Conrad by many years. She sailed about the world until 1900; bought that year by the Australian shipowners Huddart Parker Ltd., rigged down to a floating coal hulk, serving in Sydney and Hobart, Tasmania; in 1931 in Hobart sold to a wrecker, Mr. Dodge, for $25; beached on the Derwent River, she rusted into decay for thirty years; finally broken up in 1960, her steel plates shipped to Japan as scrap. She had existed for ninety-one years. Her steering wheel, a Conrad relic, is installed in the *Wellington*, moored in the Thames at London.

ROI DES BELGES. Wood-burning, stern-wheel steamer of 15 tons assembled at Kinchassa, 1887, operating on Congo River above Leopoldville, Belgian Congo; owned by Société Anonyme Belge pour le Commerce du Haut-Congo, Brussels. Captain Koch, a Dane; crew of thirty Africans.

Conrad, 32, appointed in Brussels, April 29, 1890, to take part in exploring expedition as commander of large, three-year-old Congo River steamer *Florida*; sailed as passenger on *Ville de Maceio* from Bordeaux, May 12, 1890, bound for Congo; arrived Boma, June 13; left Matadi on June 28 for two-hundred-mile walk to Stanley Pool; arrived Stanley Pool on August 1. *Florida* having been wrecked, Conrad, as first mate of *Roi des Belges* under Captain Koch, left Kinchassa on August 4 for upriver passage to Stanley Falls; arrived Stanley Falls, September 1; Captain Koch falling ill, Conrad appointed master on September 6 at Stanley Falls for return passage; brought steamer into Kinchassa, September 24, ending seven weeks on Congo River. His health undermined by tropical fever, he made his way by dugout canoe back to Matadi, reached on December 4, 1890; by steamer from Boma arrived London early January, 1891. Six months in the Congo. Two stories from this experience: "Heart of Darkness," "An Outpost of Progress."

TORRENS. Full-rigged composite passenger clipper of 1334 tons (1275 net tons) built by James Laing in Sunderland in 1875; owned by A. L. Elder & Co., London. Thirty-five officers and crew, five apprentices, sixty passengers. Captain Walker H. Cope, 42, London.

First voyage: Conrad, 33, first mate, joined the ship in London, November 19, 1891; wages £8 a month. Sailed from London, November 20, 1891; cleared Gravesend on November 21, Plymouth on November 25; arrived Adelaide, Australia, February 28, 1892. Outward passage: 100 days from London.

In the largely British crew were two Americans, who left the ship in

Adelaide: W. Martin, 35, San Francisco; C. Godfrey, 24, Philadelphia. The clipper carried two stewardesses, five stewards, cook, assistant cook, two butchers, two pantrymen.

Sailed for London from Adelaide, April 8, 1892; touched at Capetown, South Africa, June 24–25; St. Helena, July 14–18; arrived London, September 2, 1892. Homeward passage: 147 days. Voyage of one year, two and a half months.

Second voyage: Conrad, 35, first mate, wages £8 a month, signed on in London, October 25, 1892. Under same owner and same captain, ship sailed from London, October 25, 1892; left Plymouth, October 31; arrived Adelaide, January 30, 1893. Outward passage: 97 days from London.

Sailed for London from Adelaide, March 23, 1893; reached Capetown, May 18; arrived London, July 27, 1893. Homeward passage: 126 days. Voyage of nine months.

During the homeward, Adelaide-London, passage there were three deaths at sea: the ship's doctor, C. Granville Jackson, 30, of England, and two passengers, William Hylands, G. T. Edmunds. Among the seventeen passengers on this voyage were John Galsworthy, Edward Lancelot Sanderson, W. H. Jacques. Jacques, a young Cambridge man ill with tuberculosis, made the round-trip voyage on the *Torrens;* on the outward passage he became Conrad's first reader, Conrad showing him the first nine chapters of manuscript of the then uncompleted novel *Almayer's Folly*.

Apprentices in Conrad's charge during the second voyage were: William Kirkwood Thyne, 16; Albert Gullamene Nicholas Marie Van Melchebeke, 17; William Jones, 16; Gilbert John Milner Fleming, 14; Herbert Alexander Brabham, 17. Last three also served during Conrad's first *Torrens* voyage.

Conrad was nominally attached to the *Torrens* until October 17, 1893, the date of his official discharge in London.

The *Torrens* remained in the Adelaide trade until 1903; in 1906 she was sold for £1500 to Vittorio Bozzo and Giuseppe Mortola, Italian shipowners in Genoa; run on the rocks, she was refloated and repaired; seriously damaged when grounded a second time, she was towed into Genoa and, in 1910, broken up. She had been at sea thirty-five years.

ADOWA. Iron steamer of 2097 tons built by Strand Slipway Co. at Sunderland in 1882; owned by Fenwick & Co., London; chartered in 1893 by newly organized Franco-Canadian Transport Company. Captain F. Paton.

Conrad, 35, second mate, joined the steamer in London, November 29, 1893. The new company proposed to carry emigrants from France to Canada, with regular sailings between Rouen and Montreal or Quebec, transporting up to 460 passengers each voyage. From London Conrad, on the *Adowa*, crossed the Channel, arriving Rouen, December 4, 1893; remained on board moored ship in Rouen for more than a month; no emigrants appeared, company failed, ship returned to her owners in London. Conrad signed off in London, January 18, 1894; he never went to sea again. His first novel, *Almayer's Folly*, completed in London, April 24, 1894; published on April 29, 1895.

NOTES

PART ONE: THE SHORE

I

1. *Times*, London, Nov. 13, 1876.
2. *Daily Star and Herald*, Panama, Sept. 19, 1876.
3. Edward Garnett, *Letters from Joseph Conrad*, p. 44.
4. Thaddeus Bobrowski, letter to Stefan Buszczynski, Mar. 24, 1879.
5. Jessie Conrad, letter to H. G. Wells, Feb. 19, 1934 (University of Illinois).
6. New York *Herald*, Sept. 18, 1880.
7. Conrad, letter to A. T. Saunders, June 14, 1917 (Archives Dept., Adelaide, South Australia).
8. *New Statesman*, Aug. 24, 1957.
9. Introduction to *Nostromo*, Modern Library edition.
10. *Nostromo*, p. 391.
11. Sir Walter Raleigh, *The Discovery of Guiana*, pp. 24 ff.
12. *Ibid.*
13. *Nostromo*, p. 427.

II

1. Vicente Restrepo, *Gold and Silver Mines of Colombia*, p. 98.
2. *Times*, London, Sept. 26, 1876.
3. *Daily Star and Herald*, Panama, Sept. 7, 1875.
4. Borys Conrad, "A Famous Father and His Son," *New York Times Book Review*, Dec. 1, 1957.
5. *New York Times*, Jan. 19, 1875.
6. *Nostromo*, p. 64.
7. Zdzislaw Najder (ed.), *Conrad's Polish Background*, p. 6.
8. G. Jean-Aubry, *Joseph Conrad: Life and Letters*, I, 248.
9. H. L. Mencken, *Prejudices*.
10. *A Personal Record*, p. 59.
11. *Nostromo*, p. 213.

III

1. *A Personal Record*, pp. 193–94.
2. *Last Essays*, p. 22.
3. Roald Amundsen, *My Life as an Explorer*.
4. *Last Essays*, p. 21.
5. *A Personal Record*, pp. 219–20.
6. Archives du Port de Toulon, IIIe Région Maritime, France.
7. G. Jean-Aubry, *The Sea Dreamer*, p. 60.
8. Bureau Veritas, Paris.
9. Record Group 36, Records of the Bureau of Customs. National Archives and Records Service, Washington, D.C.

IV

1. *Saint-Antoine* log (No. 143, 1877). Archives du Port de Toulon, IIIe Région Maritime, France.
2. *Ibid.*
3. Edmund M. Blunt, *Blunt's American Coast Pilot*, 1857 edition, p. 543.
4. *Ibid.*
5. New York *Herald*, Aug.-Sept., 1876.
6. Richard Curle, *Conrad to a Friend*, p. 154; G. Jean-Aubry, *Joseph Conrad: Life and Letters*, II, 187.
7. *A Personal Record*, p. 200.
8. *Daily Star and Herald*, Panama, Aug. 27, 1875.
9. *Ibid.*, Sept. 7, 1875.
10. Ricardo Pereira, *Les États-Unis de Colombie*, p. 53.
11. *Nostromo*, p. 29.
12. *Ibid.*, p. 3.
13. *Tales of Hearsay*, Preface.
14. *Nostromo*, pp. 144-45.
15. Vicente Restrepo, *Gold and Silver Mines of Colombia*, p. 19.
16. *Tales of Hearsay*, Preface.
17. Edward Garnett, *Letters from Joseph Conrad*, p. 216.
18. *Nostromo*, p. 412.
19. Jessie Conrad to H. G. Wells, Feb. 19, 1934 (University of Illinois).
20. Conrad to H. G. Wells, April, 1907 (University of Illinois).
21. *Joseph Conrad: Life and Letters*, I, 229.
22. *Tales of Hearsay*, Preface.
23. *Joseph Conrad: Life and Letters*, II, 296.

V

1. Richard Curle, *Conrad to a Friend*, p. 154.
2. *Ibid.*, p. 147.
3. John Neilson Conrad Collection.
4. Frank Vincent, *Around and About South America*.
5. *Saint-Antoine* log (No. 143, 1877). Archives du Port de Toulon.
6. *Ibid.* Also *St. Thomae Tidende*, Oct. 4, 1876.
7. *St. Thomas Times*, V.I., Sept. 16, 1876.
8. *Ibid.*
9. *Ibid.* Also *Times*, London, Oct. 17, 1876.
10. Sept.-Oct., 1876, marine disaster records, Marine Library of Atlantic Mutual Insurance Co., New York.
11. Conrad Collection, Yale University Library.
12. Journals of the Customs Office, St. Thomas, V.I. National Archives and Records Service, Washington, D.C.
13. *Daily Picayune*, New Orleans, La., Nov. 8, 1876.
14. New York *Herald*, Oct. 19, 1876.
15. *Letters from Joseph Conrad*, p. 12.
16. *Saint-Antoine* log (No. 143, 1877). Archives du Port de Toulon.
17. *Sailing Directions for the Gulf of Mexico*, p. 44.
18. Charles Morris, *The Volcano's Deadly Work*, pp. 55-57.
19. *A Personal Record*, pp. 160-64.
20. Prof. Hubert Herring, New York *Herald-Tribune Book Review*, Oct. 21, 1962. See also "Perpetual Motion in Latin America," p. 30, *New York Times*, Mar. 15, 1965.
21. *Frank Leslie's Illustrated Newspaper*, Aug. 19, 1876; also *New York Times*, May 4, June 13, 1878.
22. *Joseph Conrad: Life and Letters*, II, 228.
23. *Ibid.*

VI

1. Thaddeus Bobrowski to Stefan Buszczynski, Mar. 24, 1879.
2. Crew Agreements of Conrad's ships. General Register and Record Office of Shipping and Seamen, Cardiff, Wales.
3. John Galsworthy, "Reminiscences of Conrad," *Castles in Spain and Other Screeds*, p. 104.
4. *Ibid.*, p. 101.
5. Mrs. Ivy Fairweather, letter to Jerry Allen, Apr. 26, 1962.
6. Conrad, letter to Clement Shorter, Dec., 1916 (British Museum).
7. *Letters from Joseph Conrad*, p. 5-6.
8. *Ibid.*, p. 12.
9. Information from Count de Melgar.
10. *The Mirror of the Sea.* "The *Tremolino*."
11. Information from Count de Melgar.
12. *Ibid.*
13. Conrad Collection, Yale University Library.
14. Information from Mme. Sireyjol, granddaughter of Joseph du Bourg.
15. Jerry Allen, *The Thunder and the Sunshine* contains an extended history of the "Rita de Lastaola" in Conrad's life. Account based upon Carlist documents in Madrid, information from Count Francisco de Melgar, newspapers of London, Paris, Madrid, New York, for the 1876–82 period.
16. Information from Tomaso Gropallo, author of *Il Romanzo della Vela*.
17. Dominic Cervoni service record. L'Inscription Maritime, Bastia, Corsica.
18. Information from J. Amiot, Chef du S/-Quartier, L'Inscription Maritime, Bastia, Corsica.
19. César Cervoni service record. L'Inscription Maritime, Bastia, Corsica.
20. Major Ben C. Truman, *The Field of Honor*, p. 29.

VII

1. *The Arrow of Gold*, Author's Note.
2. *Ibid.*
3. *Ibid.*
4. *Joseph Conrad: Life and Letters*, II, 232.
5. *Ibid.*, II, 229.
6. Richard Curle, *The Last Twelve Years of Joseph Conrad*, p. 105.
7. John Neilson Conrad Collection.
8. *Joseph Conrad: Life and Letters*, I, 248.
9. *The Arrow of Gold*, Author's Note.
10. *The Arrow of Gold*, p. 173.
11. Records of Maryland Historical Society, Baltimore, Md. Also: *Francis Scott Key* by Francis Scott Key-Smith; *Key and Allied Families* by Mrs. Julian C. Lane, pp. 58–63.
12. Victor Weybright, *Spangled Banner*, p. 285.
13. Information from Col. Wilfrid M. Blunt.
14. Bulletin No. 2, p. 4, of Maryland Original Research Society of Baltimore, Md. Pamphlet published June, 1906.
15. William S. Drewry, *Slave Insurrections in Virginia 1830–1865*, pp. 70–72.
16. Records of Maryland Historical Society, Baltimore, Md.
17. Judith Gautier, *Le Second Rang du Collier*, chap. III.
18. *Ibid.*
19. *Joseph Conrad: Life and Letters*, I, 44–45.
20. Gautier, *Le Second Rang du Collier*, chap. III.
21. *The Arrow of Gold*, p. 186.
22. Information from Col. Arthur T. Brice.
23. *The Arrow of Gold*, p. 59.
24. Information from Col. Arthur T. Brice.

25. *The Arrow of Gold*, p. 182.
26. Information from Col. Wilfrid M. Blunt.
27. *Ibid.*
28. Captain J. Y. Mason Blunt, *An Army Officer's Philippine Studies*, Editor's Fore-word.
29. *Ibid.*
30. Histories of Capt. J. Y. M. K. Blunt and Mrs. Ellen Blunt are from the author's conversations and correspondence (1959–60) with Col. Wilfrid M. Blunt; correspondence (1959–60) with Col. Arthur T. Brice; J. R. Volz, Foreword to Captain J. Y. Mason Blunt, *An Army Officer's Philippine Studies;* Heitman's *Historical Register and Dictionary of the United States Army*, I, 226.

VIII

1. *Joseph Conrad: Life and Letters*, II, 201.
2. *Ibid.*
3. Leon Edel (ed.), *The Selected Letters of Henry James*, p. 55.
4. Henry James, *The American*, p. 103.
5. *Ibid.*, p. 235.
6. *Joseph Conrad: Life and Letters*, II, 91.
7. Baroness von Hutten zum Stolzenberg, *The Courtesan: The Life of Cora Pearl*, p. 144.
8. *The Mirror of the Sea*, p. 160.
9. Conrad Collection, Yale University Library.
10. *The Mirror of the Sea*, p. 160.
11. *The Arrow of Gold*, pp. 126–27.
12. *Ibid.*, p. 242.
13. *Ibid.*, pp. 163–64.
14. Captain J. Y. Mason Blunt, *An Army Officer's Philippine Studies*, Editor's Fore-word.
15. *The Arrow of Gold*, p. 192.
16. *Ibid.*, pp. 237, 259.
17. *New York Times*, Jan. 7, 1878.
18. *Ibid.*, Jan. 1, 1878.
19. *Ibid.*, Jan. 14, 1878.
20. *Ibid.*, Jan. 13, 1878.
21. *The Arrow of Gold*, p. 341.
22. *New York Times*, May 4, 1878.
23. *Ibid.*, June 13, 1878.
24. *Ibid.*
25. *Joseph Conrad: Life and Letters*, II, 224.
26. *The Arrow of Gold*, p. 338.
27. *Ibid.*
28. *Ibid.*, p. 344.
29. *Ibid.*, p. 346.
30. G. Jean-Aubry, *The Sea Dreamer*, p. 74.
31. Thaddeus Bobrowski, letter to Stefan Buszczynski, Mar. 24, 1879.
32. *Ibid.*
33. *Le Monde Illustré*, July 13, 1878.
34. Ford Madox Ford, *Joseph Conrad: A Personal Remembrance*, p. 80.
35. *Ibid.*
36. Thaddeus Bobrowski, letter to Stefan Buszczynski, Mar. 24, 1879.
37. "Bobrowski Document," translation made from the original Polish document by Olga Scherer-Virski.
38. Records of ship arrivals, Marseilles. Archives Départementales des Bouches-du-Rhône, Marseilles.
39. Charles Moore, "Treatise on Duelling," in *A Full Inquiry into the Subject of Suicide*.

40. *Letters of Joseph Conrad to Marguerite Poradowska.*
41. *Saturday Review,* Aug. 16, 1958.
42. *Joseph Conrad: Life and Letters,* II, 224.

IX

1. *The Mirror of the Sea,* p. 157.
2. Captain J. Y. Mason Blunt, *An Army Officer's Philippine Studies,* Editor's Fore-word.
3. Maryland Historical Society records.
4. Editor's Foreword, *An Army Officer's Philippine Studies;* Heitman's *Historical Register and Dictionary of the United States Army,* I, 226.
5. Records of U. S. Army Headquarters, Fort Leavenworth, Kansas.
6. Information from Col. Wilfrid M. Blunt.
7. *Times,* Manila, P.I., Nov. 23, 1910.
8. *The Arrow of Gold,* p. 63.
9. *The Living Age,* Sept. 27, 1919.
10. *Joseph Conrad: Life and Letters,* II, 271.
11. *New York Times,* June 6, 1880.
12. *Times,* London, Mar. 19, 1882.
13. El Conde de Melgar, *Veinte Años con Don Carlos,* pp. 55-62.
14. *Ibid.*
15. *Ibid.*
16. Records of Polloe Cemetery, San Sebastián, Spain.
17. *Joseph Conrad: Life and Letters,* II, 228.
18. *The Mirror of the Sea,* p. 154.
19. *A Personal Record,* chap. I, p. 33.
20. *Joseph Conrad: Life and Letters,* I, 47.
21. *Times,* London, Nov. 25, Dec. 2, 1880.
22. Agreement and Account of Crew of *Skimmer of the Sea.* General Register and Record Office of Shipping and Seamen, Cardiff.
23. *Ibid.*
24. Agreement and Account of Crew of *Duke of Sutherland.* General Register and Record Office of Shipping and Seamen, Cardiff.
25. *Ibid.*
26. *Ibid.*
27. *Joseph Conrad: Life and Letters,* I, 77.
28. Agreement and Account of Crew of *Duke of Sutherland.*
29. Thaddeus Bobrowski, letter to Conrad, May 26, 1882.
30. Letter in Polish Academy of Sciences, Cracow, Poland. Translation by Anna Goldschlag.
31. *Ibid.*
32. *Joseph Conrad: Life and Letters,* II, 171.
33. *Laughing Anne & One Day More,* p. 20.
34. *A Personal Record,* p. 164.
35. *Morning Herald,* Sydney, Australia, July 2, 7, 1879.
36. Agreement and Account of Crew of *Duke of Sutherland.*
37. *The Mirror of the Sea,* p. 27.
38. *Ibid.,* p. 78.
39. Johannes C. Anderson, *Jubilee History of South Canterbury,* p. 222; Charles W. N. Ingram and P. O. Wheatley, *New Zealand Shipwrecks.*
40. *The Annual Dog Watch,* 1953, Melbourne, Australia, pp. 36-37.
41. *Joseph Conrad: Life and Letters,* I, 55.
42. *Times,* London, Dec. 16, 1879.
43. *Ibid.,* Jan. 31, 1880.
44. *Joseph Conrad: Life and Letters,* I, illustration facing p. 38.
45. Thaddeus Bobrowski, letters to Conrad, May 30, June 17, 1880.
46. *A Personal Record,* p. 183.
47. *Chance,* Part I, chap. I, p. 5.

48. Edward Garnett, *Letters from Joseph Conrad*, p. 279.
49. Agreement and Account of Crew of *Loch Etive*. General Register and Record Office of Shipping and Seamen, Cardiff.
50. *Times*, London, Aug. 24, 1880.
51. Agreement and Account of Crew of *Loch Etive*.
52. Preface to *The Nigger of the Narcissus*.
53. *The Mirror of the Sea*, p. 106.

PART TWO: THE SEA

X

1. British Board of Trade report to House of Commons, Feb., 1884.
2. *The Mirror of the Sea*, "Initiation," p. 145.
3. Details of 1880 incident are in two books by Basil Lubbock: *Sail: The Romance of the Clipper Ships*, I, 99–102; *The Log of the "Cutty Sark,"* pp. 183–202.
4. T. M. Lawrie, letter to Jerry Allen, Apr. 17, 1962.
5. *Ibid.*
6. Officers and crew names, details of ship and voyage, are from Agreement and Account of Crew of *Loch Etive*.
7. *The Mirror of the Sea*, pp. 38–45, 88–96 for *Loch Etive* voyage.
8. *Ibid.*, pp. 121–128.
9. *Morning Herald*, Sydney, Jan. 13, 1881.
10. *Times*, London, Apr. 25, 1881.
11. Agreement and Account of Crew of *Loch Etive*.
12. *Last Essays*, p. 50.
13. *Ibid.*
14. On each "Sunday, the 22nd" of his early sea years Conrad was in the following places: Oct. 22, 1876—off Haiti on the *Saint-Antoine*; Dec. 22, 1878—off Cape of Good Hope on the *Duke of Sutherland*; June 22, 1879—in Sydney harbor; Feb. 22, 1880—in London; Aug. 22, 1880—at Deal on the *Loch Étive*; May 22, 1881—in London.
15. *The Mirror of the Sea*, pp. 88–91.
16. Incident reported in *Times*, London, Apr. 26, 1881.
17. *The Mirror of the Sea*, Danish brig rescue, pp. 137–45.

XI

1. "Report of a Court of Inquiry held at Aden into the cause of the abandonment of the steamship *Jeddah*," dated Aug. 20, 1880. Report No. 896, India Office Library, London.
2. *Ibid.*
3. *Lord Jim*, p. 1.
4. *Lloyd's Register of Shipping*, 1881–82.
5. Henry Ellis, report to the Colonial Secretary, Sept. 13, 1880. Straits Settlements Despatches, 1880 (C.O. 273/104), Public Record Office, London.
6. Department of Marine, Singapore.
7. Aden Court of Inquiry report No. 896.
8. Mrs. Vallory Wise, daughter of A. P. Williams, letter of Feb. 12, 1961, to Jerry Allen.
9. *Ibid.*
10. *Lord Jim*, chap. VIII, p. 89.
11. Aden Court of Inquiry report No. 896.
12. *Lord Jim*, p. 127.
13. Aden Court of Inquiry report No. 896.
14. Reported in *Straits Times Overland Journal*, Singapore, Oct. 22, 1881; also in *Kyshe's Reports*, Vol. II, Reports of Admiralty Cases, pp. 35–44.

15. *Ibid.*
16. Aden Court of Inquiry report No. 896.
17. Straits Settlements Despatches, 1880 (C.O. 273/104). Public Record Office, London.
18. *Ibid.*
19. Aden Court of Inquiry report No. 896.
20. Assessor's verdict in Aden Court of Inquiry report No. 896.
21. Aden Court of Inquiry report No. 896.
22. Charles Burton Buckley, *Anecdotal History of Singapore*, I, 65, 564-65.
23. *Times*, London, Aug. 14, 1880.
24. *Lord Jim*, chap. II, pp. 11-12.
25. *Straits Times Overland Journal*, Oct. 22, 1881.
26. *Ibid.*
27. Aden Court of Inquiry report No. 896.
28. *Straits Times Overland Journal*, Oct. 22, 1881.
29. *Ibid.*
30. Aden Court of Inquiry report No. 896.
31. *Ibid.*
32. *Ibid.*
33. *Ibid.*
34. *Ibid.* Subsequent details of abandonment of *Jeddah* are from this source; also: *Straits Times Overland Journal*, Oct. 22, 1881; *Kyshe's Reports*, II, 35-44.
35. Among newspapers publishing the cabled news were these of Sydney, Australia: *Morning Herald*, Aug. 12, 1880; *Daily Telegraph*, Aug. 13, 1880; *Town and Country Journal*, Aug. 14, 21, 1880. In other ports Conrad knew as a seaman—London, Singapore, Madras—the *Jeddah* case was fully reported by the press.
36. *Straits Times Overland Journal*, Singapore, Oct. 22, 1881.
37. *Ibid.*
38. *Ibid.*
39. *Ibid.*
40. *Ibid.*
41. Aden Court of Inquiry report No. 896.
42. *Times*, London, July 15, 1880.
43. Aden Court of Inquiry report No. 896.
44. *Ibid.*
45. *Ibid.*
46. *Ibid.*
47. Aug. 10-Oct. 21, 1880, letters to The Secretary to Government, Bombay. In the Archives of Aden, South Arabia, file No. Marine Part II, No. 836 of 1880.
48. *Ibid.*
49. *Ibid.*
50. Straits Settlements Despatches, 1880 (C.O. 273/104). Public Record Office, London.
51. *Ibid.*
52. *Ibid.*

XII

1. *Times Literary Supplement*, London, Sept. 6, 1923. For further on the *Jeddah* rescue see *Times Literary Supplement*, Oct. 11, 1923, letter from Alfred Holt & Co.; also: "Return of Wrecks and Casualties in Indian Waters for the year 1880," Calcutta, 1881, pp. 71-73, Government of India (Marine Branch), Military Department publication, State Paper Room, British Museum.
2. *Lord Jim*, p. 37.
3. Department of Marine, Singapore.
4. Thaddeus Bobrowski, letter to Conrad, June 17, 1880.
5. *Lord Jim*, p. 11.
6. *Revue Française*, Dec. 1, 1924, p. 742.

7. *The Reporter* magazine, Mar. 21, 1957, p. 43.
8. *Lord Jim*, p. 81.
9. *Ibid.*, Author's Note.

XIII

1. *Youth*, p. 16.
2. Board of Trade Blue Book on shipwrecks. *Times*, London, Sept. 9, 1880.
3. New York *Herald*, Sept. 18, 1880.
4. Movements of *Annie Frost* and accident are from records of Lloyd's, London.
5. *Times*, London, July 7, 1881.
6. *A Personal Record*, p. 121.
7. Thaddeus Bobrowski, letter to Conrad, Aug. 15, 1881.
8. Agreement and Account of Crew of *Annie Frost*. General Register and Record Office of Shipping and Seamen, Cardiff: also, records of Lloyd's, London.
9. *Youth*, Author's Note.
10. Agreement and Account of Crew of *Palestine*. General Register and Record Office of Shipping and Seamen, Cardiff.
11. *Ibid.*
12. *Ibid.*
13. *Ibid.*
14. *Youth*, p. 25.
15. *Ibid.*, pp. 34–35.
16. *Ibid.*, p. 36.
17. Richard Curle, *Conrad to a Friend*, p. 114.
18. *Youth*, p. 39.
19. Report No. 1810, attached to Agreement and Account of Crew of *Palestine*.
20. *Youth*, p. 36.
21. *Ibid.*, p. 23.

XIV

1. Original Polish letter is in the Polish Academy of Sciences (PAN) Library, Cracow, Poland. Translation by Olga Scherer-Virski.
2. Agreement and Account of Crew of *Riversdale*. General Register and Record Office of Shipping and Seamen, Cardiff.
3. *Ibid.*
4. *Telegraph*, Port Elizabeth, S.A., Dec. 8, 1883; Feb. 12, 1884.
5. *Illustrated London News*, Apr. 17, 1880.
6. Agreement and Account of Crew of *Riversdale*.
7. Certificate of Discharge. Conrad Collection, Yale University Library.
8. Agreement and Account of Crew of *Riversdale*.
9. Capt. F. Rhodes, *Pageant of the Pacific*, II, 277.
10. Information from A. D. Edwardes, Adelaide, Australia.
11. *Chance*, p. 28.
12. Agreement and Account of Crew of *Riversdale*.
13. Agreement and Account of Crew of *Narcissus*. General Register and Record Office of Shipping and Seamen, Cardiff.
14. *Ibid.*
15. *Ibid.*
16. *Ibid.* Details of crew and voyage are from this source.
17. *Joseph Conrad: Life and Letters*, I, 77–78.
18. *Ibid.*
19. Agreement and Account of Crew of *Narcissus*.
20. Agreement and Account of Crew of *Tilkhurst*.
21. Agreement and Account of Crew of *Narcissus*.
22. *New York Times Book Review*, Feb. 3, 1957.

23. Christopher Morley, "A Word About Joseph Conrad," *The Mentor*, March, 1925.
24. *Ibid.*
25. *Joseph Conrad: Life and Letters*, I, 77.
26. Agreement and Account of Crew of *Narcissus*.
27. *Ibid.*
28. *Narcissus* history from *Lloyd's Register of Shipping*, 1884–1925.
29. Information from E. G. Fontes & Co., Rio de Janeiro.
30. *Joseph Conrad: Life and Letters*, I, 82.
31. *A Personal Record*, p. 184.
32. *Ibid.*, p. 185.
33. *Ibid.*, p. 187.
34. Agreement and Account of Crew of *Tilkhurst*.
35. *Ibid.* Details of crew and voyage are from this source.
36. British Board of Trade Blue Book on shipwrecks: New York *Herald*, Sept. 18, 1880.
37. Report included in Agreement and Account of Crew of *Tilkhurst*.
38. *Ibid.*
39. Agreement and Account of Crew of *Tilkhurst*.
40. *Joseph Conrad: Life and Letters*, I, 85–86.
41. Information from Capt. J. S. Roe, Singapore.
42. *The Mirror of the Sea*, p. 58.
43. *Lloyd's Register of Shipping*, 1877–1923; ship's history under Italian ownership from Tomaso Gropallo, Genoa; other sources: Basil Lubbock, *The Nitrate Clippers*; Capt. Louis Lacroix, *Les Derniers Cap Horniers Français*.
44. *Joseph Conrad: Life and Letters*, I, 83.

XV

1. Agreement and Account of Crew of *Highland Forest*. General Register and Record Office of Shipping and Seamen, Cardiff.
2. *The Mirror of the Sea*, "The Weight of the Burden," pp. 48–49.
3. *Ibid.*
4. *Ibid.*, p. 49.
5. *Ibid.*, p. 51.
6. Agreement and Account of Crew of *Highland Forest*.
7. *Ibid.*
8. *Ibid.*
9. *Ibid.*
10. *The Mirror of the Sea*, pp. 48–56, for description of Capt. McWhir and the voyage.
11. *The Mirror of the Sea*, "Landfalls and Departures," pp. 5–6.
12. Agreement and Account of Crew of *Highland Forest*.
13. *Ibid.*
14. *The Mirror of the Sea*, p. 54.
15. Richard Curle, *The Last Twelve Years of Joseph Conrad*, p. 97.
16. Richard Curle, *Joseph Conrad: A Study*, pp. 17–18.
17. Routes shown in Crew Agreements of Conrad's ships; also newspaper accounts of voyages in ports of arrival.
18. Agreement and Account of Crew of *Highland Forest*.
19. *The Mirror of the Sea*, chap. XVII, pp. 65–67.
20. *Ibid.*, p. 54.
21. Agreement and Account of Crew of *Highland Forest*. Conrad's Certificate of Discharge, Yale University Library, is dated July 2, 1887.
22. Agreement and Account of Crew of *Highland Forest*.
23. Final voyage of *Highland Forest* is described in *Treasure Lies Buried Here* by Frank H. Goldsmith, p. 209.
24. The seven ships lost at sea: *Tremolino, Mavis, Skimmer of the Sea, Duke of Sutherland, Annie Frost, Palestine, Highland Forest*.

25. Information from Mrs. Ivy Fairweather and Capt. P. A. McDonald.
26. John Dill Ross, *Singapore and the Straits Settlements.* Also, for the Singapore of this time: *Straits Settlements Blue Book,* 1879, 1887.
27. *Lord Jim,* chap. II, p. 9.
28. Certificate of Discharge. Conrad Collection, Yale University Library.
29. Records of Department of Marine, Singapore. See also: *Singapore Registry of Shipping,* 1888; *Lloyd's Register of Shipping,* 1887–88. Jean-Aubry in *Joseph Conrad: Life and Letters,* I, 93, 95, mistakenly gives the *Vidar* as 800 tons, sailing under the Dutch flag, Conrad as second mate.
30. Records of Department of Marine, Singapore. Also, information from shipbuilders, Swan, Hunter, & Wigham Richardson Ltd.
31. Name as spelled on letterheads of *Vidar* 1887 bills of lading in Conrad Collection, Yale University Library. Name spelled in five different ways in other records.
32. *Singapore and Straits Directory,* 1888, Supp. p. 145.
33. Charles Burton Buckley, *An Anecdotal History of Old Times in Singapore,* p. 565.
34. *The Shadow Line,* pp. 4–5.
35. Information from Mrs. Ivy Fairweather, daughter of Capt. Craig.
36. Singapore registry of *Vidar* closed Oct. 3, 1892, when she was sold. Records of Department of Marine, Singapore.
37. 1951 letters of A. E. Baddeley, son-in-law of Capt. Craig, to Dr. J. G. Reed. John Neilson Conrad Collection.
38. *The Shadow Line,* p. 5.
39. *A Personal Record,* pp. 142–43.

PART THREE: THE RIVER

XVI

1. *Lord Jim,* chap. XXI, p. 205.
2. *A Personal Record,* pp. 143–45.
3. Route of *Vidar* from: *A Personal Record,* pp. 123–26; "Onderzoek naar kolen in de Berausche landen," by J. A. Hooze, p. 22, in *Jaarboek van het Mijnwezen in Nederlandsch Oost-Indië 1886;* information from Mrs. Ivy Fairweather. G. Jean-Aubry in *Joseph Conrad: Life and Letters,* I, 95, mistakenly makes the two ports of Coti (Samarinda) and Berau into a single place. After 1890, K.P.M. steamers followed this trading route of the *Vidar.*
4. R. Haverschmidt, 1951 interview in Berau with Kang Si Gok who, in 1888, sailed on the *Vidar.*
5. *Report on Berouw,* 1892. K.P.M. Archives, Amsterdam.
6. *A Personal Record,* pp. 124–25.
7. Donggala is described in *Guide Through Netherlands India,* 1903 edition.
8. *A Personal Record,* pp. 125–26.
9. *Ibid.,* p. 124.
10. Deed of sale, in Malayan, is dated Nov. 29, 1904.
11. *An Outcast of the Islands,* pp. 364–65.
12. Information about Berau from R. Haverschmidt, resident there for sixteen years, manager of K.P.M. coal mine "Parapattan."
13. R. Haverschmidt, letter of Oct. 23, 1960, to the author.
14. *The Rescue,* p. 4.

XVII

1. Letter of Aug. 18, 1894, in *Letters of Joseph Conrad to Marguerite Poradowska.*
2. Recent survey of area appears in "The Perils of Singapore and Infant Malaysia," New York *Herald-Tribune,* Nov. 3, 1963, news review section, p. 16; "Review of Economic Developments in Asia," section C, *New York Times,* Jan. 18, 1965.

3. Carl Bock, *The Head-hunters of Borneo.*
4. *Een Halve Eeuw Paketvaart*, Borneo section, p. 1.
5. R. Haverschmidt, letter of Oct. 23, 1960, to the author.
6. *Ibid.*
7. Pierre Ivanoff, *Head-Hunters of Borneo.*
8. Frank S. Marryat, *Borneo and the Indian Archipelago.*
9. Capt. Rodney Mundy, *Narrative of Events in Borneo and Celebes*, I, 70.
10. *The Rescue*, pp. 3-4.
11. Marryat, *Borneo and the Indian Archipelago*, pp. 60 ff.
12. Local history of Berau from: *Petikan dari Kroniek der Zuider-en Oosterafdeeling van Borneo*, chronicle in the archives of the Sultan of Gunung Tabur, copied and translated by R. Haverschmidt; "Aanteekeningen omtrent het rijk van Borneo," by S. G. In 't Veld in *De Indische Gids*, Jan., 1884, pp. 21-27.
13. S. Baring-Gould and C. A. Bampfylde, *A History of Sarawak under Its Two White Rajahs;* Capt. Charles Hunter, *The Adventures of a Naval Officer.*
14. *Almayer's Folly*, p. 273.
15. Information from Capt. J. A. L. Pavitt, Master Attendant, Singapore; Robert Shaplen, "The Imminence of a Nation," *New Yorker*, Apr. 6, 1963, pp. 170-71.

XVIII

1. *Singapore and Straits Directory*, Singapore, 1883, p. 175.
2. F. W. Burbidge, *The Gardens of the Sun*, p. 19.
3. E. J. Robertson, *Straits Memories*, p. 20.
4. Walter Makepeace, et al. (eds.), *One Hundred Years of Singapore*, II, 517-18.
5. *Singapore Free Press*, Feb. 16, 1888.
6. *Ibid.*
7. Ship arrivals reported in Dutch East Indies newspapers, 1882. Information from G. Knijpenga.
8. R. Haverschmidt, "Statements of Residents," interviews in Berau.
9. *An Outcast of the Islands*, pp. 200-02.
10. *Ibid.*
11. *Ibid.*, p. 202.
12. John Dill Ross, Jr., *Singapore and the Straits Settlements*, p. 49.
13. John Dill Ross, Jr., *Sixty Years: Life and Adventure in the Far East*, I, 79-80, 87, 138.
14. R. Haverschmidt, "Statements of Residents," interviews in Berau.
15. Richard Ainsworth, *The Lingards of Huncoat and Their Descendants.*
16. Tom Lingard's early history in: *The Rescue*, pp. 8-18, 261; *An Outcast of the Islands*, pp. 13, 195.
17. History of Capt. Ross in two books by his son: *Singapore and the Straits Settlements* and *Sixty Years: Life and Adventure in the Far East;* also Makepeace, *One Hundred Years of Singapore*, II, 538-42.
18. Burbidge, *The Gardens of the Sun*, p. 19.
19. Dr. Roelof Broersma, *Handel en bedrijf in Zuid-en Oost-Borneo.*
20. Records in Master Attendant's Office, Singapore.
21. *Straits Times*, Aug. 3, 1880, under Shipping Intelligence gives Singapore arrival of *Pulo Laut* under Capt. Lingard.
22. Records of *Nina* in Master Attendant's Office, Singapore.
23. "Statements of Residents," R. Haverschmidt, interviews in Berau; Capt. F. Rhodes, *Pageant of the Pacific*, II, 153; G. Knijpenga, research in 1875 Macassar newspapers.
24. Records of *Coeran* in Master Attendant's Office, Singapore.
25. *An Outcast of the Islands*, p. 189.
26. Information from G. Knijpenga.
27. G. Knijpenga, "Archipelago Trade in the Past"; additional details of knighthood from Netherlands official documents, The Hague.
28. Dr. J. G. Reed, interview with Mrs. C. C. Oehlers in Singapore, Apr. 13, 1951; Joshua Lingard's records are in Master Attendant's Office, Singapore.
29. Records in Master Attendant's Office, Singapore.

30. *West Indian* register, No. 8892, in Master Attendant's Office, Singapore.
31. *Ibid.*
32. *Youth,* pp. 41–42.
33. *Petikan dari Kroniek der Zuider-en Oosterafdeeling van Borneo.*

XIX

1. Ship registers and records in Master Attendant's Office, Singapore.
2. R. Haverschmidt, "Statements of Residents," interviews in Berau.
3. *An Outcast of the Islands,* pp. 360–61.
4. Information from R. Haverschmidt.
5. *The Rescue,* p. 100.
6. *An Outcast of the Islands,* pp. 55–56.
7. R. Haverschmidt, "Statements of Residents," interviews in Berau.
8. *Ibid.*
9. *Ibid.* Also, Dr. J. G. Reed, interview and correspondence with Mrs. C. C. Oehlers.
10. John Dozier Gordan, *Joseph Conrad, the Making of a Novelist,* chap. II; Richard D. Altick, *The Scholar Adventurers,* chap. XIII.
11. *An Outcast of the Islands,* p. 192.
12. *Straits Times,* Singapore, July 17, 1951.
13. *Almayer's Folly,* pp. 22, 20.
14. R. Haverschmidt, "Statements of Residents," interviews in Berau.
15. Report in K.P.M. archives, Amsterdam; translation by R. Haverschmidt.
16. *Almayer's Folly,* pp. 40–42.
17. *Ibid.,* p. 46.
18. Contracts No. 19, No. 20 (*Zitting 1879–1880.–86; Overeenkomst met inlandsche vorsten in den Oost-Indische Archipel.*) between the Netherlands Resident in South-and-East Borneo and the Sultans of Sambaliung and Gunung Tabur.
19. R. Haverschmidt, "Statements of Residents," interviews in Berau.
20. *Ibid.*
21. *Letters of Joseph Conrad to Marguerite Poradowska.*
22. *Almayer's Folly,* p. 147.
23. *Joseph Conrad: Life and Letters,* I, 97.
24. *Ibid.,* II, 103.
25. *Ibid.,* II, 109. Also p. 133 for another reference to Capt. Marris.
26. Capt. Marris and Joshua Lingard histories are from Dr. J. G. Reed's correspondence with Quah Beng Kee, Managing Director (1908–18), Eastern Shipping Co., Penang, and with Capt. A. G. Course. John Neilson Conrad Collection.
27. Dr. J. G. Reed, interview with Mrs. C. C. Oehlers in Singapore.
28. 1904 deed of sale of Lingard House; R. Haverschmidt, "Statements of Residents," interviews in Berau.
29. Photograph from Mrs. C. C. Oehlers. John Neilson Conrad Collection.
30. Mrs. Ivy Fairweather, letter of Apr. 26, 1962, to the author.
31. R. Haverschmidt, "Statements of Residents," interviews in Berau.
32. *Ibid.*
33. *A Personal Record,* p. 26.
34. *Ibid.,* p. 27.
35. *Ibid.*
36. *Ibid.*

XX

1. *Nota over de onderafdeeling Beraoe,* Samarinda, August 29, 1933, pp. 18–19.
2. Letter of Aug. 18, 1894, in *Letters of Joseph Conrad to Marguerite Poradowska.*
3. *Lord Jim,* chap. XXII, p. 211.
4. *Petikan dari Kroniek der Zuider-en Oosterafdeeling van Borneo.*
5. *Ibid.*
6. *Lord Jim,* p. 212.

7. *Ibid.*
8. R. Haverschmidt, "Statements of Residents," interviews in Berau; K.P.M. 1892 *Report on Berouw.*
9. *Lord Jim*, p. 240.
10. R. Haverschmidt, "Statements of Residents," interviews in Berau.
11. Conrad Collection, Yale University Library.
12. R. Haverschmidt, "Statements of Residents," interviews in Berau.
13. *Ibid.*
14. *Ibid.*
15. *Ibid.*
16. *Ibid.*
17. Malaysian and Arab names and titles from: Abraham Hale, *List of Malay Proper Names;* information from Capt. J. A. L. Pavitt, Master Attendant, Singapore; S. Baring-Gould and C. A. Bampfylde, *A History of Sarawak under Its Two White Rajahs.*
18. R. Haverschmidt, "Statements of Residents," interviews in Berau.
19. Capt. Rodney Mundy, *Narrative of Events in Borneo and Celebes*, I, chaps. III–XII.
20. Edward Garnett, *Letters from Joseph Conrad*, p. 185.
21. *Ibid.*, p. 245.
22. Copy of Conrad's Dec. 22, 1913, letter, with explanatory note, received by the author from Lord Russell.
23. Contract No. 19, *Zitting 1879–1880.–86.* Preamble.
24. *The Mirror of the Sea*, p. 137.
25. *The Shadow Line*, p. 3.
26. Shaplen, "Encounters in Barrios," *New Yorker*, Sept. 28, 1963.
27. *The Shadow Line*, Author's Note, p. ix.
28. *Joseph Conrad: Life and Letters*, II, 16.
29. *Ibid.*, II, 60.
30. Letters of Thaddeus Bobrowski to Conrad.
31. *The Shadow Line*, p. 4.
32. *Ibid.*, p. 5.
33. *A Personal Record*, p. 26.
34. Letter of Apr. 24, 1894, in *Letters of Joseph Conrad to Marguerite Poradowska.*
35. Albert J. Guerard, "The Nigger of the Narcissus," *Kenyon Review*, Spring, 1957.
36. *A Personal Record*, p. 149.
37. Raymond Las Vergnas, *Joseph Conrad: romancier de l'exil*, p. 102.
38. Guerard, *Conrad the Novelist*, p. 91.
39. *A Personal Record*, p. 154.

PART FOUR: THE MEN

XXI

1. *Joseph Conrad: Life and Letters*, I, 107.
2. R. J. Minney, *Fanny and the Regent of Siam*, p. 358.
3. Anna Leonowens, *The English Governess at the Siamese Court*, p. 21.
4. *Joseph Conrad: Life and Letters*, II, 182.
5. *The Shadow Line*, Author's Note, p. viii.
6. *Joseph Conrad: Life and Letters*, II, 182.
7. *The Shadow Line*, p. 49.
8. *Lloyd's Register of Shipping*, 1886–88.
9. Information from Capt. P. A. McDonald, taken from his records of the *Otago.* See also Capt. McDonald, "Conrad's Ships," *Sea Breezes*, March, 1953.
10. *Ibid.*

11. *Ibid.*
12. *Ibid.*
13. *The Shadow Line*, pp. 61–62.
14. List of crew of *Otago*, in Conrad's handwriting, signed "J. C. Korzeniowski" and dated May 8, 1888. In Mitchell Wing, Public Library, Sydney, Australia.
15. *Joseph Conrad: Life and Letters*, I, 103.
16. *The Shadow Line*, p. 48.
17. Anna Leonowens, *The English Governess at the Siamese Court*, p. 106.
18. *Illustrated London News*, May 25, 1867.
19. *The Shadow Line*, p. 48.
20. R. J. Minney, *Fanny and the Regent of Siam*, p. 134.
21. *Joseph Conrad: Life and Letters*, I, 106.
22. *Ibid.*, I, 109.
23. *Otago* voyage reported in Sydney *Morning Herald*, May 8, 1888.
24. *The Mirror of the Sea*, pp. 18–19.
25. *Ibid.*
26. *The Shadow Line*, p. 73.
27. *Joseph Conrad: Life and Letters*, II, 195.
28. "The Secret Sharer" in *'Twixt Land and Sea*, p. 116.
29. *The Mirror of the Sea*, p. 75.
30. *Last Essays*, p. 26.
31. *Ibid.*, p. 28.
32. *Ibid.*, pp. 30–31.
33. G. Jean-Aubry, *The Sea Dreamer*, p. 138.
34. "A Smile of Fortune" in *'Twixt Land and Sea*, p. 46.
35. Jean-Aubry, *The Sea Dreamer*, pp. 139–45, 302–03. A more complete account is in the original French version of this book, *Vie de Conrad*.

XXII

1. "The Planter of Malata" in *Within the Tides*, pp. 45–46.
2. *Ibid.*, pp. 47–48.
3. G. Jean-Aubry, *The Sea Dreamer*, pp. 139–45.
4. "A Smile of Fortune" in *'Twixt Land and Sea*, p. 46.
5. *Ibid.*
6. Extracts from letter, in French, dated Feb. 2, 1931, from Paul Langlois to Savinien Mérédac, published in Feb. 15, 1931, issue of *L'Essor*, Port Louis, Mauritius.
7. G. Jean-Aubry, *The Sea Dreamer*, pp. 143–44. Full questionnaire is in Jean-Aubry, *Vie de Conrad*.
8. *Joseph Conrad: Life and Letters*, I, 113.
9. Dates of *Otago* voyage from records of Capt. P. A. McDonald.
10. Conrad's letter of June 14, 1917, to A. T. Saunders of Adelaide, Australia.
11. *Joseph Conrad: Life and Letters*, I, 116.
12. Thaddeus Bobrowski, letters to Conrad of Sept. 24, 1888, and Jan. 3, 1889.
13. *Within the Tides*, p. 34.
14. Conrad's letter to A. T. Saunders of Jan. 26, 1917 (Archives Department, Adelaide, South Australia).
15. Last years of *Otago* from: records of Capt. P. A. McDonald; Robert Morrison, "The Last of the *Otago*," *Blackwood's Magazine*, Nov., 1961; *The Mercury*, Melbourne, Australia, April 22, 1960; *Sea Breezes*, October, 1949, March, 1953; *Manchester Guardian Weekly*, October 6, 1949.
16. *A Personal Record*, p. 115.
17. *Ibid.*, p. 123.
18. *Ibid.*, p. 115.
19. *Ibid.*, p. 117.
20. Letter of April 24, 1894, in *Letters of Joseph Conrad to Marguerite Poradowska*.
21. *Ibid.*

22. Opening page of *Dla wiadomości kochanego siostrzeńca mojego Konrada Ko-rzeniowski* (For the information of my dear nephew Konrad Korzeniowski), ledger of Thaddeus Bobrowski known as the "Bobrowski Document." Translation here and in other excerpts made from photocopy of original document now in Jagellon Library, Cracow, Poland.
23. *Ibid.*
24. *Ibid.*
25. *Youth*, pp. 53–55.
26. Letter, in Polish, published in *Ruch Literacki*, No. 5, Warsaw, 1927.
27. *Joseph Conrad: Life and Letters*, I, 126.
28. *New York Times*, May 4, 10, 1890; Conrad's letter of Dec. 16, 1903, to Kazimierz Waliszewski in *Joseph Conrad: Lettres Françaises*, pp. 63–65.
29. *Youth*, p. 61.
30. *New York Times*, July 6, 1890.
31. *Youth*, p. 62.
32. *New York Times*, Sept. 22, 1890.
33. *Last Essays*, p. 24.

XXIII

1. *New York Times*, July 14, 1890.
2. Letter, in Polish, published in *Ruch Literacki*, No. 5, Warsaw, 1927.
3. *Youth*, Author's Note, p. xi.
4. *New York Times*, July 6, 1890.
5. *Last Essays*, p. 239.
6. *Ibid.*
7. The railroad between Matadi and Stanley Pool, 235 miles long, was opened in June, 1898.
8. *Youth*, p. 64.
9. *Ibid.*, pp. 66–67.
10. *Ibid.*, p. 70.
11. *New York Times*, July 6, 1890.
12. *Youth*, p. 71.
13. *Last Essays*, p. 253.
14. *New York Times*, July 6, 1890.
15. The *Florida* is described in J. R. Werner, *River Life on the Congo*, p. 181.
16. *Youth*, p. 104.
17. *Ibid.*
18. *New York Times*, July 6, 1890.
19. *Youth*, pp. 94–96.
20. G. Jean-Aubry, *The Sea Dreamer*, p. 170.
21. *Ibid.*
22. Letter of Sept. 26, 1890, in *Letters of Joseph Conrad to Marguerite Poradowska*.
23. *New York Times*, Sept. 15–Oct. 18, 1888.
24. *Illustrated London News*, Nov. 22, 1890.
25. Walter George Barttelot (ed.), *The Life of Edmund Musgrave Barttelot*, pp. 340 ff.
26. *Illustrated London News*, Nov. 22, 1890.
27. *New York Times*, Oct. 14, 1888.
28. *Ibid.*, Sept. 15, 1888.
29. *Ibid.*, Oct. 14, 1888.
30. *Ibid.*, Nov. 7, 1890.
31. Barttelot (ed.), *The Life of Edmund Musgrave Barttelot*.
32. *New York Times*, Sept. 20, 1888.
33. Werner, *River Life on the Congo*, pp. 224 ff.
34. *New York Times*, Nov. 7, 1890.
35. *Ibid.*, Sept. 15, 1888.
36. *Ibid.*, Sept. 19, 1888.
37. *Ibid.*, Sept. 23, 1888.

38. *Ibid.*
39. *Ibid.*, Oct. 18, 1888.
40. *Ibid.*, Nov. 7, 1890.
41. *Youth*, p. 149.
42. Three of the books, by Walter George Barttelot, J. Rose Troup, Herbert Ward, are reviewed in *Illustrated London News*, Nov. 22, 1890.
43. *Youth*, p. 158.
44. Conrad's letter of Dec. 16, 1903, to Kazimierz Waliszewski in *Joseph Conrad: Lettres Françaises.*
45. *Youth*, p. 117.
46. *Last Essays*, p. 244.
47. *Ibid.*, pp. 241–42.
48. Letter of Sept. 26, 1890, in *Letters of Joseph Conrad to Marguerite Poradowska.*
49. *Youth*, p. 87.
50. *Ibid.*
51. Jean-Aubry, *The Sea Dreamer*, p. 173.
52. *A Personal Record*, pp. 33–34.
53. Letter of July 22, 1896, to Fisher Unwin (Yale University Library).
54. *Last Essays*, pp. 24–25.

XXIV

1. *Joseph Conrad: Life and Letters*, II, 98.
2. Christopher Morley, "A Word About Joseph Conrad," *The Mentor*, Mar., 1925.
3. Conrad's letter of April 15, 1891, to Maria Tyszkowa in *Ruch Literacki*, No. 5, Warsaw, 1927.
4. *A Personal Record*, p. 35.
5. *Last Essays*, pp. 40–41.
6. Agreement and Account of Crew of *Torrens*, first voyage. General Register and Record Office of Shipping and Seamen, Cardiff.
7. History of *Torrens* from: *Lloyd's Register of Shipping*, 1889–94; *Sea Breezes*, Jan., 1947, account by Capt. T. W. Pickard; *Last Essays*, pp. 33–43, 106–14; information from Tomaso Gropallo and Capt. P. A. McDonald.
8. Agreement and Account of Crew of *Torrens*, first voyage.
9. *Last Essays*, pp. 35–37.
10. Agreement and Account of Crew of *Torrens*, first voyage.
11. *Ibid.*
12. *Ibid.*
13. Agreement and Account of Crew of *Torrens*, second voyage.
14. *Ibid.*
15. Extract from W. G. M. Edwards' letter donating negative of photograph to National Maritime Museum, London.
16. *A Personal Record*, pp. 36–38.
17. Agreement and Account of Crew of *Torrens*, second voyage.
18. Letter of Feb. 3, 1893, in *Letters of Joseph Conrad to Marguerite Poradowska.*
19. Agreement and Account of Crew of *Torrens*, second voyage.
20. Conrad's letter of Jan. 26, 1917, to A. T. Saunders (Archives Department, Adelaide, South Australia).
21. John Galsworthy, "Reminiscences of Conrad," *Castles in Spain and Other Screeds*, pp. 101–03.
22. Agreement and Account of Crew of *Torrens*, second voyage.
23. *Ibid.*
24. *Ibid.*
25. *Last Essays*, p. 34.
26. Agreement and Account of Crew of *Torrens*, second voyage.
27. *Ibid.*
28. Conrad's letter of Jan. 26, 1917, to A. T. Saunders.

29. Agreement and Account of Crew of *Torrens*, second voyage.
30. Certificate of Discharge, Yale University Library.
31. *Last Essays*, p. 40.
32. Thaddeus Bobrowski, letter to Conrad of May 22, 1893.
33. *A Personal Record*, p. 24.
34. Fenwick & Co. later became Fenwick, Stobart; at present is Wm. France, Fenwick & Co. Information from Joseph L. Thompson & Sons, Sunderland, England (successors to Strand Slipway Co., Sunderland, builders of the *Adowa*).
35. Certificate of Discharge, reproduced George T. Keating, *A Conrad Memorial Library*.
36. *A Personal Record*, p. 22.
37. *Ibid.*, p. 20.
38. Certificate of Discharge.
39. Letter of Jan. 20, 1894, in *Letters of Joseph Conrad to Marguerite Poradowska*.
40. *Ibid.*, letter of April 24, 1894.
41. G. Jean-Aubry, *The Sea Dreamer*, p. 202.
42. Letter of Oct. 4, 1894, in *Letters of Joseph Conrad to Marguerite Poradowska*.
43. *Ibid.*, letter of Aug. 18, 1894.
44. Morton Dauwen Zabel, Introduction, *Joseph Conrad: Tales of the East and West*.
45. *A Personal Record*, "A Familiar Preface," p. 4.
46. Edward Garnett, Introduction, *Letters from Joseph Conrad*, p. 10.

XXV

1. Edward Garnett, *Letters from Joseph Conrad*, p. 3.
2. *Ibid.*, pp. 3–4.
3. *Ibid.*, pp. 9–10.
4. *Ibid.*, pp. 10–11.
5. *Joseph Conrad: Life and Letters*, I, 178.
6. At 4 rue Marbeuf. See *Le Figaro*, Nov. 18, 1917; *Veinte Años con Don Carlos*.
7. Jean-Aubry, *The Sea Dreamer*, pp. 214–15. Jessie Conrad describes their meeting and marriage in *Joseph Conrad as I Knew Him* and *Joseph Conrad and His Circle*.
8. *Letters from Joseph Conrad*, p. 142.
9. Jean-Aubry, *The Sea Dreamer*, pp. 235–36.
10. *Joseph Conrad: Life and Letters*, II, 115–16.
11. Conrad's letter of May 27, 1908, to H. G. Wells (University of Illinois).
12. Conrad's letter of March 27, 1913, to Ford Madox Ford (British Museum).
13. Conrad's letter of May 27, 1924, to Prime Minister Ramsay MacDonald (Berg Collection, New York Public Library).
14. Jean-Aubry, *The Sea Dreamer*, p. 204.
15. Conrad's letter of March 27, 1913, to Ford Madox Ford.
16. Conrad's letter of Oct. 31, 1922, to Thomas J. Wise (British Museum).
17. Prices paid for Conrad's manuscripts are given in the thirty-five letters, beginning Oct. 2, 1918, he wrote to Thomas J. Wise (British Museum).
18. Edwin Wolf II with John F. Fleming, *Rosenbach, A Biography*. See also: Richard Curle, *The Last Twelve Years of Joseph Conrad*, p. 162
19. Details of Conrad's income are from his letters, published and unpublished. Dates when his various stories and books were written, dates of his residence in the eight homes in England are also from these letters.
20. *Joseph Conrad: Life and Letters*, II, 104.
21. Conrad's letter of Nov. 30, 1917, to Sidney Colvin (Duke University).
22. *Joseph Conrad: Life and Letters*, I, 322.
23. Conrad's letter of Jan. 19, 1900, to Cunninghame Graham (Dartmouth College).
24. Curle, *The Last Twelve Years of Joseph Conrad*, p. 19.
25. Jessie Conrad, letter of Feb. 19, 1934, to H. G. Wells (University of Illinois).

26. Frank Swinnerton, *Background with Chorus*, p. 29. See this source also for an editor's portraits of Galsworthy, Garnett, Hugh Walpole.
27. Letter in H. G. Wells Collection, University of Illinois.
28. Letter in the Houghton Library, Harvard University.
29. Conrad's letter of Nov. 29, 1902, to Cunninghame Graham (Dartmouth College).
30. *Joseph Conrad: Life and Letters*, II, 263.
31. *Ibid.*
32. *Last Essays*, pp. 140–41, 153.
33. *Ibid.*, p. 140.
34. Curle, *The Last Twelve Years of Joseph Conrad*, p. 57.
35. *Ibid.*
36. *Ibid.*, p. 59.
37. Borys Conrad, "A Famous Father and His Son," *New York Times Book Review*, Dec. 1, 1957.
38. Letter in manuscript collection, Duke University Library.
39. *Joseph Conrad: Life and Letters*, II, 313.
40. *Ibid.*, II, 307–08.
41. *Ibid.*, II, 309–10.
42. Conrad's letter of June 2, 1923, to owners and ship's company of *Tusitala* (Conrad Memorial Library, Seaman's Institute, New York City).
43. *New York Times Book Review*, Feb. 3, 1957.
44. Garnett, *Letters from Joseph Conrad*, p. 265.
45. John Galsworthy, "Reminiscences of Conrad," *Castles in Spain and Other Screeds*, p. 112.
46. *Joseph Conrad: Life and Letters*, II, 297–98.
47. Curle, *The Last Twelve Years of Joseph Conrad*, p. 120.
48. *Joseph Conrad: Life and Letters*, II, 204.
49. Curle, *The Last Twelve Years of Joseph Conrad*, p. 49.
50. Letter to Wise in Conrad Collection, British Museum.
51. *Joseph Conrad: Life and Letters*, II, 157.
52. H. G. Wells, *Experiment in Autobiography*, II, 615–17.
53. Garnett, *Letters from Joseph Conrad*, p. 27.
54. Galsworthy, *Castles in Spain*, p. 113.
55. Curle, *The Last Twelve Years of Joseph Conrad*, pp. 52–53.
56. *Ibid.*, p. 28.
57. *Youth*, p. 82.
58. Conrad's letter of Dec. 21, 1898, to Cunninghame Graham (Dartmouth College).
59. Bertrand Russell, *Portraits from Memory*.
60. *Ibid.*
61. Galsworthy, *Castles in Spain*, p. 118.
62. Curle, *The Last Twelve Years of Joseph Conrad*, p. 66.
63. *Ibid.*
64. *Ibid.*, p. 224.
65. *Joseph Conrad: A Sketch*, p. 36.
66. *Joseph Conrad: Life and Letters*, II, 83.
67. *Ibid.*, II, 82.
68. *Ibid.*, II, 83–84.
69. *Last Essays*, p. 138.
70. *The Nigger of the Narcissus*, Preface, p. xii.
71. *Ibid.*
72. *The Mirror of the Sea*, p. 71.
73. *Joseph Conrad: Life and Letters*, II, 185.
74. Raymond Las Vergnas, *Joseph Conrad: romancier de l'exil*, p. 87.
75. Morton Dauwen Zabel, Introduction, *Joseph Conrad: Tales of the East and West*.
76. John Hall Wheelock, "Dark Joy," *The Gardener and Other Poems*.

ACKNOWLEDGMENTS

In parts of the world as widely spread as the countries Conrad knew in his sea years are those who have helped this book to grow. To them, for kindnesses abundantly given, I would like to extend my wholehearted thanks. John Neilson, of New Zealand, has been unfailingly generous with assistance and encouragement and, in making available to me the contents of his Conrad Collection (included among its documents are the papers of the late Dr. J. G. Reed), offered valuable keys to Conrad's life in the East. Captain P. A. McDonald, long a master of sailing ships, has been my stanch and exacting guide in matters of the sea. A. D. Edwardes, outstanding authority on the age of sail, selected from his thousands of photographs and, from Australia, sent the rare views appearing in these pages. R. Haverschmidt, mining engineer for sixteen years in the Berau district of Borneo, there explored its past for links with Conrad; passing on to me the fruits of his research, he has richly contributed to these chapters on Berau. For the personality of Conrad, the vivid man his intimates knew, I owe much in these pages to the thoughtfulness of his friend for many years, Richard Curle. Others, searching archives, newspaper files, family papers (and attics), have added both their knowledge and their findings to the book they have had a share in making. In the hope that their pleasure in these years of contact has equaled mine, I wish to acknowledge my gratitude to the following people and institutions for material I have used.

France: Mlle. Mireille Forget, Archives du Port de Toulon; M. J. Amiot, L'Inscription Maritime, Bastia, Corsica; Mme. Sireyjol, Mondonville; M. E. Baratier and M. André Villard, Archives des Bouches-du-Rhône, Marseilles; Prof. Marcel Clavel, Aix-en-Provence.

Great Britain: G. A. Osbon, National Maritime Museum, Greenwich; Mrs. Ivy Fairweather; Mrs. Vallory Wise, who graciously provided the photograph of her father, A. P. Williams, and information about his life; Bertrand Russell; T. M. Lawrie, chairman, Aitken, Lilburn & Co. Ltd., Glasgow; P. Denham Christie, Executive Director, and S. Stevens of Swan, Hunter & Wigham Richardson Ltd., Newcastle upon Tyne; F. A. Hawkes and R. C. E. Lander of Lloyd's, London; Registrar General of Shipping and Seamen, Cardiff; S. C. Sutton, India Office Library, London; G. H. Spinney, Superintendent, State Paper Room, British Museum; Joan C. Lancaster, Commonwealth Relations Office, London. Quotations from Crown copyright records (C.O. 273/104 and C.O. 273/111) in the Public Record Office, London, appear by permission of the Controller of Her Majesty's Stationery Office. I wish to thank, too, the British Museum, for the use of the Conrad letters it holds.

Poland: For photographs of Thaddeus Bobrowski and Apollo Korzeniowski, photocopies of letters written by them, and other family documents, and for permission to reproduce and quote from them I am indebted to: the Jagellon Library, Cracow; the Polish Academy of Sciences Library, Cracow; the Narodowa Library, Warsaw. I am also indebted to the Polish Embassy, Washington, D.C., for the survey made of Conrad material existing in Poland and to Zdzislaw Najder for his difficult part, in 1956, in assembling the some two hundred items photographed for me.

The Netherlands: G. Knijpenga, whose research of Dutch East Indian history in the period of the 1800s produced, like that of his fellow countryman, R. Haverschmidt, much that is told here about people who once lived in Berau.

Italy: Tomaso Gropallo, Genoa; Dott. Proc. Valentino Vadi, Genoa; L'Ufficio Museo Navale, Comando Marina, La Spezia.

Singapore: Captain J. A. L. Pavitt, Master Attendant, graciously supplying a wealth of information in the course of our talks and, from the records of the Marine Department, histories of ships and seamen in the Singapore Conrad knew; C. E. Williams; H. P. M. Ismail, Registrar of Births and Deaths; L. C. Hoffman, editor-in-chief, and H. R. Hunter, librarian, *Straits Times;* James A. Elliot and Charles T. Foo, USIS.

Aden, South Arabia: Brian Doe, who added vital parts to this account of the *Jeddah* case.

Australia: Captain John Miles, Sydney; the Archives Department, South Australia, with whose permission Conrad's letters to A. T. Saunders are used.

Denmark: Captain J. Malling, Hellerup; Dr. Harald Jorgensen, Rigsarkivet, Copenhagen.

Spain: Count de Melgar, whose many kindnesses included sending me information relative to Don Carlos and the photograph of Paula de Somoggy; Juan Ribot, whose dedicated research is reflected in the Marseilles chapter of the book.

South Africa: A. Porter, Port Elizabeth Public Library.

United States: Jane F. Smith and Lyle J. Holverstott, National Archives, Washington, D.C.; John H. Thaxter, Library of Congress, Washington, D.C.; Mrs. Olga Scherer-Virski; Mrs. Anna Goldschlag; Col. Wilfrid M. Blunt, so cordially assisting me with the history of his father, Capt. J. Y. M. K. Blunt; Col. Arthur T. Brice; June A. V. Lindqvist, Division of Libraries and Museums, Charlotte Amalie, St. Thomas, V.I.; Capt. F. Kent Loomis, Navy Department, Washington, D.C.; Dr. John D. Gordan; Dr. Albert J. Guerard; Anthony West; Dr. Carlos Baker; DeLancey Ferguson; Prof. Alexander Laing, Baker Library, Dartmouth College; Prof. Frederick R. Karl, City College, New York; John D. Kilbourne, Maryland Historical Society, Baltimore, Md.; American Bureau of Shipping; Marine Library, Atlantic Mutual Insurance Co., New York; the New York Public Library and the New-York Historical Society Library, without whose facilities and reference works this book could not have been written. For quotations from and the use made of their collections of Conrad's original letters I am indebted to: Yale University Library; Houghton Library, Harvard University, for letters and the page of the "Congo Diary" reproduced here by permission of the Harvard College Library; the libraries of Dartmouth College, Colgate University, Duke University, University of Illinois, University of Virginia, University of Texas, the Henry W. and Albert A. Berg Collection of the New York Public Library.

For permission to quote from the works of Conrad I am most grateful to Doubleday & Company and to J. M. Dent & Sons, London. Excerpts from Conrad's unpublished letters are given, as are the reproductions of his unpublished sketches, through the kindness of the Trustees of the Joseph Conrad Estate. In warm appreciation I would like to thank the heirs of Dr. J. G. Reed for the material I have drawn upon in his two notebooks and assorted papers.

Finally, there are the many heartening friends who sustain a writer during a book's slow growth. To each of them, and especially to Mary Squire Abbot and Gertrude R. Stein, are extended my warmest personal thanks. One to whom I am also happily and exceedingly indebted is the friend whose wealth of knowledge and understanding is always a marvel—my editor, George Shively.

BIBLIOGRAPHY

WORKS OF JOSEPH CONRAD

Almayer's Folly, An Outcast of the Islands, The Nigger of the Narcissus, Tales of Unrest, Lord Jim, Typhoon and Other Stories, Youth: A Narrative; and Two Other Stories, Nostromo, The Mirror of the Sea, A Set of Six, A Personal Record, 'Twixt Land and Sea, Chance, Victory, Within the Tides, The Shadow Line, The Arrow of Gold, The Rescue, Laughing Anne & One Day More, Notes on Life and Letters, The Rover, Tales of Hearsay, Suspense.

(Complete works published by Doubleday, Doran & Co., 26 vols. New York, 1938).

Last Essays. London: J. M. Dent & Sons, 1926.

The Sisters. New York: Crosby Gaige, 1928.

LETTERS OF JOSEPH CONRAD

Conrad's original letters written 1896–1924, many unpublished. In the libraries of Yale University, Harvard University, Dartmouth College, Colgate University, Duke University, University of Illinois, University of Virginia, University of Texas, British Museum, the Henry W. and Albert A. Berg Collection of the New York Public Library, Archives Department of South Australia, private papers of Lord Russell.

Letters of Conrad in *Joseph Conrad: Life and Letters* by G. Jean-Aubry, 2 vols. New York: Doubleday, Page & Co., 1927.

Joseph Conrad: Letters Françaises, edited by G. Jean-Aubry. Paris: Gallimard, 1930.

Letters of Joseph Conrad to Marguerite Poradowska, 1890–1920. Translated from the French and edited by John A. Gee and Paul J. Sturm. New Haven: Yale University Press, 1940.

Letters from Joseph Conrad, 1895–1924. Edited with Introduction and Notes by Edward Garnett. Indianapolis: Bobbs-Merrill Co., 1928.

Conrad to a Friend: 150 Selected Letters from Joseph Conrad to Richard Curle. Edited with Introduction and Notes by Richard Curle. New York: Doubleday, Doran & Co., 1928.

Joseph Conrad: Letters to William Blackwood and David S. Meldrum. Edited with an Introduction by William Blackburn. Durham, N.C.: Duke University Press, 1958.

Letter of Joseph Conrad, in Polish, to Stefan Buszczynski, August 14, 1883 (Original letter in the Polish Academy of Sciences (PAN) Library, Cracow, Poland. *Sygn. rkp. 2064; t. III*).

Five letters of Joseph Conrad, in Polish, to his cousin Mme. Maria Tyszkowa, written May 2, May 6, September 24, 1890; April 15, 1891; September 8, 1892. Also letter of Joseph Conrad, in Polish, to A. M. Jasienski, April 25, 1905. Published in *Ruch Literacki*, No. 5, Warsaw, Poland, 1927.

DOCUMENTS

Polish:

Dla wiadomości kochanego siostrzeńca mojego Konrada Korzeniowski (For the information of my dear nephew Konrad Korzeniowski). Twenty-two-page financial record kept by Thaddeus Bobrowski of his nephew's expenses between December 1, 1869, and February 4, 1890. Referred to as the "Bobrowski Document." (*MSS nr. 6391*.) Attached is "Information which may be useful to you," handwritten page prepared by Thaddeus Bobrowski for his nephew Joseph Conrad. Family data, including date and place of Conrad's birth.

Listy Apollona Korzeniowskiego do Kazimierza Kaszewskiego z lat 1865–1868 (Letters of Apollo Korzeniowski to Casimir Kaszewski written in the years 1865–1868). *Sygn. rkp. 3057.*

Wiersz Apollona na urodziny Konrada (Poem of Apollo Korzeniowski on the birth of his son Conrad).

(*The manuscript letters and documents above are in the Jagellon Library, Cracow, Poland.*)

Listy do Conrada, pisane w latach 1869–1893 przez jego wuja i opiekuna, Tadeusza Bobrowskiego (Letters to Conrad written in the years 1869–1893 by his uncle and guardian, Thaddeus Bobrowski). *Sygn. rkp. 2889.*

Dwa listy Kazimierza Bobrowskiego, drugiego wuja Conrada, z lat 1882–1884, do Conrada (Two letters of Casimir Bobrowski, another uncle of Conrad's, written 1882–1884, to Conrad).

(*The manuscript letters above are in the Narodowa Library, Warsaw, Poland.*)

Listy Apollona Korzeniowskiego do Stefano Buszczynskiego z lat 1868–1869 (Letters of Apollo Korzeniowski to Stefan Buszczynski written in the years 1868–1869). *Sygn. rkp. 2064.*

Dwa listy Tadeusza Bobrowskiego do Stefana Buszczynskiego z 24 III, 30 V 1879 (Two letters of Thaddeus Bobrowski to Stefan Buszczynski of March 24 and May 30, 1879). *Sygn. rkp. 2064.*

(*The manuscript letters above are in the Polish Academy of Sciences (PAN) Library, Cracow, Poland.*)

Malayan:

Petikan dari Kroniek der Zuider-en Oosterafdeeling van Borneo (Excerpts from the Chronicle of the South-and-East District of Borneo). Excerpts taken by Raden Ajub, youngest brother of the late Sultan Achmad of Gunung Tabur, Kalimantan, from the Chronicle begun in 1750 in the archives of the sultan of Gunung Tabur. Local history of South-and-East Borneo, 1800–1926 (*Document in the possession of Raden Ajub, Berau, Kalimantan, Indonesia*).

"Jang bertandah tangan dibawah ini saja toean James Lingard ahlie waris dari toean William Lingard. . . ." Deed of sale of the Lingard house in Berau, Borneo, dated November 29, 1904. The house and six acres of land around it were sold by James Lingard, heir of William Lingard, to Sultan Mohamad Siranoedin of Gunung Tabur (*Document in the possession of the ratu of Gunung Tabur, Berau, Kalimantan, Indonesia*).

Original map in color of village of Berau (Tandjung Redeb) prepared in 1951 by Raden Djaja Perwira, Indonesian district officer of Berau. Map, with Malayan markings, shows: boundaries of Gunung Tabur and Sambaliung; sites of such 1887 buildings as Olmeyer's "Folly," houses of James Lingard, Abdulla, Sinjo Carel; sultans' palaces; European cemetery (*R. Haverschmidt material in Dr. J. G. Reed papers, John Neilson Conrad Collection*).

Dutch:

Original map of Berau River (*Monden der Beraoe-Rivier*) from its mouth in the Celebes Sea upstream to Teluk Bajur; map drawn in 1951 in Berau as navigation guide for steamers (*R. Haverschmidt material in Dr. J. G. Reed papers, John Neilson Conrad Collection*).

Nota over de onderafdeeling Beraoe: Samarinda, 29 Augustus 1933. Document of nineteen pages compiled by the Forestry Department of the Dutch Residency, Samarinda, Borneo, August 29, 1933. Survey of political history, climate, population, trade, concessions, natural resources of Berau.

Gedrukte stukken van de Tweede Kamer der Staten-Generaal Zitting 1879–1880.–86: Overeenkomst met inlandsche vorsten in den Oost-Indischen Archipel.; Contract met Sambalioeng, No. 19, Contract met Goenoeng Taboer, No. 20. Contract No. 19 drawn between the Netherlands East Indies government, through Jacobus Jozephus Meijer, Resident for South and East Borneo, and Mohamad Adil Djalaloedin, sultan of Sambaliung, dated October 18, 1878; Contract No. 20 drawn between the Netherlands East Indies government, through Jacobus Jozephus Meijer, Resident for South and East Borneo, and Datoe Maharadja Denda Hassan Oedin, sultan of Gunung Tabur, dated October 18, 1878 (*Archives of the Colonial Office, The Hague*).

Report on Berouw, 1892. K.P.M. survey of Berau, Borneo: conditions and trade possibilities (*K.P.M. Archives, Amsterdam*).

English:

Agreement and Account of Crew of *Skimmer of the Sea* (Official Number 14747); *Duke of Sutherland* (O.N. 45590); *Loch Etive* (O.N. 78565); *Annie*

Frost (O.N. 46677); *Palestine* (O.N. 12684); *Riversdale* (O.N. 29953); *Narcissus* (OLB National Maritime Museum, Greenwich); *Tilkhurst* (O.N. 76974); *Highland Forest* (O.N. 89909); *Torrens* (O.N. 73595) (*General Register and Record Office of Shipping and Seamen, Cardiff, Wales*).

Records of *Annie Frost* June 11, 1881 accident in harbor of Le Havre, France (*Lloyd's, London*).

"Report of a Court of Inquiry held at Aden into the cause of the abandonment of the steamship *Jeddah*," dated August 20, 1880. Report No. 896 (*India Office Library, London*).

Straits Settlements Despatches, 1880. C.O. 273/104; C.O. 273/111 (*Public Record Office, London*).

Official letters Aug. 10–Oct. 21, 1880, concerning abandonment of the steamship *Jeddah*. Marine Part II, No. 836, of 1880 (*Archives of Aden, South Arabia*).

"Return of Wrecks and Casualties in Indian Waters for the year 1880." Calcutta, 1881. Government of India (Marine Branch) Military Department (*State Paper Room, British Museum*).

Record Group 36, Records of the Bureau of Customs (*National Archives and Records Service, Washington, D.C.*).

Journals of the Customs Office, St. Thomas, Virgin Is., 1876 (*National Archives and Records Service, Washington, D.C.*).

Marine Disaster Records, 341 volumes (*Marine Library, Atlantic Mutual Insurance Co., New York*).

"Report of a Marine Court of Enquiry held at the Police Court, in Singapore, on the 2nd day of April 1883, by order of His Excellency Sir Frederick Aloysius Weld, K.C.M.G., Governor and Commander-in-Chief of the Colony of the Straits Settlements, for the purpose of investigating into the burning of the British barque *Palestine* Official Number 12,684, of London, of 427 tons burthen, on a voyage from Falmouth to Bangkok." Report No. 1810 (*General Register and Record Office of Shipping and Seamen, Cardiff*).

Ship registration records: *Jeddah, Fanny, SS Paknam, Nina, Coeran, West Indian* (*Master Attendant's Office, Department of Marine, Singapore*).

Navigation chart No. 1263. Waters of Malay Archipelago from Singapore to Molucca Sea, from Sunda Strait to Sulu Archipelago. Engraved 1887, corrected to 1947 (*Survey Department, Federation of Malaya*).

"A List of the Crew and Passengers arrived in the Ship *Otago* of Adelaide, Snadden, Master, Burthen 346 tons, from the Port of Wallaroo to Newcastle, N.S.W., 19th July 1887." Inward listings, Newcastle, N.S.W. (*Customs Department, Newcastle, N.S.W., Australia*).

List of crew of *Otago* serving under him as Master, in Conrad's handwriting, signed "J. C. Korzeniowski" and dated May 8, 1888. In "Record Book of Customs Entry of Crew and Passengers" for 1888. Same source, year 1880, list of crew, passengers, stowaways, arriving Sydney, November 24, 1880, on the *Loch Etive*; list in handwriting of Capt. William Stuart (*Mitchell Wing, Public Library, Sydney, Australia*).

Papers of the late Dr. J. G. Reed of Sungkai, Perak, Malaya, relating to his research into the life of Joseph Conrad. Two notebooks, 1950–1951 correspondence, record of April 13, 1951, interview with Mrs. C. C. Oehlers (nee Nellie Lingard) in Singapore, two photographs of James Lingard, navigation charts and photographs (*John Neilson Conrad Collection, Oamaru, New Zealand*).

Records compiled 1951–1952 in Berau, Kalimantan, Indonesia, by R. Haverschmidt: inscriptions in Gunung Tabur cemetery (Olmeyer children, George McKenzie Morgan); interviews with residents (sultan of Sambaliung, ratu of Gunung Tabur, Anang Dachlan, Akay, Adji Bagian, Raden Ajub, Kang Si Gok) in "Statements of Residents"; copy of 1904 deed of sale of Lingard house; copy of 1800–1926 Malayan Chronicle of Berau; copies of Netherlands government documents, 1879–1933, pertaining to district of Berau (*Dr. J. G. Reed papers, John Neilson Conrad Collection; also: documents received by Jerry Allen from R. Haverschmidt*).

Conrad's Certificates of Discharge, with name of official, place and date of signing: *Palestine*, Capt. E. Beard, Singapore, April 4, 1883; *Narcissus*, Capt. Arch. Duncan, Dunkerque, October 19, 1884; *Highland Forest*, Capt. John McWhir, Samarang, July 2, 1887; S.S. *Vidar*, Capt. James Craig, Singapore, January 5, 1888; *Torrens*, Capt. Walker H. Cope, London, October 17, 1893 (*Conrad Collection, Yale University Library*).

Bills of lading for merchandise shipped on S.S. *Vidar*, 1887–1888 (*Conrad Collection, Yale University Library*).

Conrad's typescript of *The Arrow of Gold*, dated June, 1918. Attached is note in Conrad's handwriting: "The subject belongs to my early life. I was conscious of it through all the years of my writing life . . ." (*Conrad Collection, Yale University Library*).

Conrad's manuscript *The Laugh*, 94 pages, early draft of *The Arrow of Gold* (*Conrad Collection, Yale University Library*).

French:

Rôle du Saint-Antoine [No. 143, 1877] (*Archives du Port de Toulon, IIIᵉ Région Maritime, Toulon, France*).

Extrait de la Matricule, Marine Marchande, de Dominique André Cervoni. Extrait de la Matricule, Marine Marchande, de César Cervoni: No. 5454lD (*L'Inscription Maritime, Bastia, Corsica*).

Register of ship arrivals, port of Marseilles, 1877–1878 (*Archives Départementales des Bouches-du-Rhône, Marseilles*).

NEWSPAPERS AND PERIODICALS

New York Times, 1875–1890.
New York *Herald*, 1875–1880.
Times, London, 1876–1894; *Times Literary Supplement*, Sept. 6, Oct. 11, 1923; Nov. 29, 1947; Dec. 6, 1957.
Daily Star and Herald, Panama, 1875–1876.
St. Thomae Tidende, St. Thomas, V.I., 1875–1876.
Saint Thomas Times, St. Thomas, V.I., 1875–1876.
Daily Picayune, New Orleans, La., 1875–1876.
Frank Leslie's Illustrated Newspaper, 1876–1880.

Le Monde Illustré, Paris, 1876–1880.
Illustrated London News, 1876–1890.
Sea Breezes, Jan., 1947; Oct., 1949; Mar., 1953.
Journal du Havre, Le Havre, France, June 12–15, 1881.
Le Figaro, Paris, 1880–1885; Nov. 18, 1917; July 19, 1909.
The Times, Manila, Nov. 23, 1910.
Morning Herald, Sydney, Australia, 1879–1888.
Daily Telegraph, Sydney, Australia, Aug. 13, 1880.
Town and Country Journal, Sydney, Australia, Aug. 14–21, 1880.
Singapore Free Press, Feb. 16, 1888; April 20, 1916.
Straits Times Overland Journal, Singapore, Oct. 22, 1881.
Straits Times, Singapore, Aug. 3, Sept. 24, 1880; Dec. 2, 1950; July 17, 1951.
Straits Budget, Singapore, Oct. 22, 1914; April 20, 1916.
Manchester Guardian, Aug. 12–16, 1880. *Manchester Guardian Weekly*, Oct. 6, 1949.
New Zealand Times, July-Sept., 1899.
Telegraph, Port Elizabeth, South Africa, Dec. 8, 1883; Feb. 12, 1884.
Le Moniteur Universel, Paris, Sept. 21–28, 1863; Feb. 1, 22, April 4, 1864.
Revue de Marseilles, Jan. 7, 1878.
New York *Sun*, Dec., 1882.
New York *Daily Tribune*, 1877.

GENERAL REFERENCES

Aa, Robidé van der. "De aanspraken van Solok op Noordoost-Borneo," *De Indische Gids*, April, 1882.
Ainsworth, Richard. *The Lingards of Huncoat and Their Descendants*. Accrington, Lancashire: Wardlesworth Ltd., 1930.
Allen, Jerry. *The Thunder and the Sunshine, a Biography of Joseph Conrad*. New York: G. P. Putnam's Sons, 1958.
———. "Conrad's River," *Columbia University Forum*, Winter, 1962.
Allen, Walter. *The English Novel*. New York: E. P. Dutton & Co., 1954.
———. *The Modern Novel in Britain and the United States*. New York: E. P. Dutton & Co., 1964.
Altick, Richard D. *The Scholar Adventurers*. New York: The Macmillan Company, 1950.
Anderson, Johannes C. *Jubilee History of South Canterbury*. Christchurch, N.Z., 1916.
André, Edouard. "América Equinoccial," *América Pintoresca*. Barcelona: Montaner y Simon, 1884.
Annuaire-Almanach du Commerce. Paris: Didot-Bottin, 1879.
d'Ariste, Paul. *La Vie et le Monde du Boulevard*. Paris: Éditions Jules Tallandier, 1930.
Aubry, Octave. *The Second Empire*. Translated by Arthur Livingston. Philadelphia: J. B. Lippincott Co., 1940.
Baines, Jocelyn. *Joseph Conrad: A Critical Biography*. New York: McGraw-Hill Book Co., 1960.

Baker, Carlos. "A Man of Action and Contemplation," *New York Times Book Review*, Feb. 3, 1957.

Baring-Gould, S., and Bampfylde, C. A. *A History of Sarawak under Its Two White Rajahs, 1839–1908*. London: Henry Sotheran, 1909.

Barttelot, Walter George, (ed.). *The Life of Edmund Musgrave Barttelot, Captain and Brevet-Major Royal Fusiliers, Commander of the Rear Column of the Emin Pasha Relief Expedition; being an Account of his services for the relief of Kandahar, of Gordon, and of Emin*. Edited from his letters and diary by Walter George Barttelot. London: Richard Bentley & Son, 1890.

Bemmelen, J. F. Van, and Hooyer, G. B. *Guide Through Netherlands India*. Compiled by order of the Koninklijke Paketvaart Maatschappij (Royal Packet Company). Translated from the Dutch by B. J. Berrington. London: Thos. Cook & Son, 1903.

Bleakley, J. W. *The Aborigines of Australia*. Brisbane: The Jacaranda Press, 1961.

Blunt, Edmund M. *Blunt's American Coast Pilot* (18th edition). New York: Edmund and George W. Blunt, 1857.

Blunt, Mrs. Ellen Key. *Bread: To My Children*. Philadelphia: J. B. Lippincott & Co., 1856.

Blunt, J. Y. M. *Maxims for Training Remount Horses for Military Purposes*. New York: D. Appleton & Co., 1894.

Blunt, Captain J. Y. Mason, U.S.A. Retired. *An Army Officer's Philippine Studies*. Edited and posthumously published by John R. Volz. Manila, P.I.: University Press, 1912.

Board of Trade, London. *Blue Book on Shipwrecks*, 1880.

Bock, Carl. *The Head-hunters of Borneo: A Narrative of Travel up the Mahakkam and down the Barito; also Journeyings in Sumatra*. London: Sampson Low, 1882.

Bro, Marguerite Harmon. *Indonesia: Land of Challenge*. New York: Harper and Brothers, 1954.

Broersma, Dr. Roelof. *Handel en bedrijf in Zuid-en Oost-Borneo*. 's-Gravenhage: G. Naeff, 1927.

Brooking, J. H. C. "Around the World Under Sail in the Eighties," *The Annual Dog Watch*. Melbourne, Australia: Shiplovers' Society of Victoria, No. 10, 1953.

Bruce-Angier, Charles. "Some Memorable Duels," *The Argosy*, London, April, 1898.

Buckley, Charles Burton. *An Anecdotal History of Old Times in Singapore*. 2 vols. Singapore: Fraser and Neave, 1902.

Burbidge, F. W. *The Gardens of the Sun: or a Naturalist's Journal on the mountains and in the forests and swamps of Borneo and the Sulu Archipelago*. London: John Murray, 1880.

Camdessus, Alfred. *Mistral, était-il Carliste?* Bayonne, France: Courrier, 1932.

Caplow, Theodore. "La Violencia," *Columbia University Forum*, Winter, 1963.

Cecil, Lord David. *The Fine Art of Reading and Other Literary Studies*. New York: Bobbs-Merrill Co., 1957.

Clemens, Florence. "Joseph Conrad as a Geographer," *Scientific Monthly*, Nov., 1940.
——. "Conrad's Malaysia," *College English*, Jan., 1941.
Coleman, Satis N. *Volcanoes New and Old*. New York: The John Day Company, 1946.
Colvin, Sidney. Review of *The Arrow of Gold*. *The Living Age*, Sept. 27, 1919.
——. *Memories & Notes of Persons & Places, 1852–1912*. New York: Charles Scribner's Sons, 1921.
Conrad, Borys. "A Famous Father and His Son," *New York Times Book Review*, Dec. 1, 1957.
Conrad, Jessie. *Joseph Conrad as I Knew Him*. London: William Heinemann, 1926.
——. *Joseph Conrad and His Circle*. New York: E. P. Dutton & Co., 1935.
Cunninghame Graham, R. B. Preface to *Tales of Hearsay* by Joseph Conrad. New York: Doubleday, Page & Co., 1925.
——. *Cartagena and the Banks of the Sinú*. London: William Heinemann, 1920.
Curle, Richard. "Conrad in the East," *Yale Review*, April, 1923.
——. *Joseph Conrad: A Study*. New York: Doubleday, Page & Co., 1914.
——. *The Last Twelve Years of Joseph Conrad*. New York: Doubleday, Doran & Co., 1928.
Debreyne, Dr. Pierre Jean Corneille. *Du Suicide considéré aux Points de Vue Philosophique, Religieux, Moral et Médical, suivi de Quelques Réflexions sur le Duel*. Brussels, 1847.
Drewry, William S. *Slave Insurrections in Virginia, 1830–1865*. Washington, D.C.: Neale Co., 1900.
Eastern Archipelago Pilot. Vol. II (Fifth edition, 1934). H.M.S.O. for the Hydrographic Department, Admiralty.
Edel, Leon, (ed.). *The Selected Letters of Henry James*. New York: Farrar, Straus & Cudahy, 1955.
Edel, Leon, and Lind, Ilse Dusoir (eds.). *Henry James Parisian Sketches*. New York: New York University Press, 1957.
Een Halve Eeuw Paketvaart. Memorial volume issued by K.P.M. to commemorate the company's fifty years in shipping. Amsterdam: N. V. Koninklijke Paketvaart-Maatschappij, 1941.
Encyclopaedia Britannica (1910–1911 edition).
d'Eugny, Anne. *Au Temps de Baudelaire, Guys et Nadar*. Paris: Editions du Chêne, 1945.
Ford, Ford Madox. *Joseph Conrad: A Personal Remembrance*. Boston: Little, Brown & Co., 1925.
Galsworthy, John. "Reminiscences of Conrad," *Castles in Spain and Other Screeds*. London: William Heinemann, 1927.
Garnett, Edward. Introduction to *Letters from Joseph Conrad, 1895–1924*. Indianapolis: Bobbs-Merrill Co., 1928.
Gathorne-Hardy, Robert (ed.). *Memoirs of Lady Ottoline Morrell: A Study in Friendship*. New York: Alfred A. Knopf, 1964.
Gautier, Judith. *Le Second Rang du Collier*. Paris: Felix Juven, 1904.

Goldsmith, Frank H. *Treasure Lies Buried Here.* Perth, West Australia: C. H. Pitman, 1946.

Gordan, John Dozier. *Joseph Conrad, the Making of a Novelist.* Cambridge, Mass.: Harvard University Press, 1940.

Gray, F. Harold. "That Day," *Mirage,* Miri, Sarawak, June, 1938.

Gropallo, Tomaso. *Il Romanzo della Vela.* Genoa: Edizioni "Maralunga," 1963.

Guerard, Albert J. *Conrad the Novelist.* Cambridge, Mass.: Harvard University Press, 1958.

————. "The Voyages of Captain Korzeniowski," *The Reporter,* March 21, 1957.

Guide Through Netherlands India. Compiled by order of the Koninklijke Paketvaart Maatschappij (Royal Packet Steam Navigation Company). Amsterdam: J. H. de Bussy, 1911. /

Hale, Abraham. *List of Malay Proper Names.* Kuala Lumpur, Malayan Federation, 1925.

Heitman's *Historical Register and Dictionary of the United States Army.* Vol. I. Washington, D.C., 1903.

Henao y Melguizo, J. M., and Arruble, Gerardo. *History of Colombia.* Chapel Hill: University of North Carolina Press, 1938.

Hommage à Joseph Conrad. Essays on Conrad by Henry James, André Gide, G. Jean-Aubry, R. B. Cunninghame Graham, Robert Francillon, Albert Saugère, and others. *La Nouvelle Revue Française,* Dec. 1, 1924.

Hooze, J. A. "Onderzoek naar kolen in de Berausche landen ter Oostkust van Borneo," *Jaarboek van het Mijnwezen in Nederlandsch Oost-Indië,* 1886.

Hose, Charles. *Natural Man: A Record from Borneo.* London: The Macmillan Company, 1926.

Hughes, John. *The New Faces of Africa.* New York: Longmans, Green and Co., 1961.

Hunter, Capt. Charles, R.N. *The Adventures of a Naval Officer.* Edited by Sir Spenser St. John. London: Digby, Long and Company, 1905.

In 't Veld, S. G. "Aanteekeningen omtrent het rijk van Borneo," *De Indische Gids,* January, 1884.

Ingram, Charles W. N., and Wheatley, P. O. *New Zealand Shipwrecks* (3rd edition). Wellington, N.Z.: Reed, 1961.

Ivanoff, Pierre. *Head-Hunters of Borneo.* London: Jarrolds, 1960.

Jean-Aubry, G. *Joseph Conrad: Life and Letters.* 2 vols. New York: Doubleday, Page & Co., 1927.

————. *Vie de Conrad.* Paris: Gallimard, 1947. Translated by Helen Sebba as *The Sea Dreamer.* New York: Doubleday & Co., 1957.

————. "More About 'The Nigger of the Narcissus,'" *The Bookman's Journal,* Oct., 1924.

Jones, Dr. Frederic Wood. "Classical Gout," *British Medical Journal,* March 11, 1950.

Joseph Conrad: A Sketch. Booklet published by Doubleday, Page & Co., Garden City, New York, 1925.

Keating, George T. *A Conrad Memorial Library.* New York: Doubleday, Doran & Co., 1929.

Keppel, Capt. Henry, R.N. *The Expedition to Borneo of H.M.S. Dido for the Suppression of Piracy, with extracts from The Journal of James Brooke, Esq., of Sarawak.* 2 vols. London: Chapman and Hall, 1846.

——. *A Visit to the Indian Archipelago in H.M. Ship Meander, with Portions of the Private Journal of Sir James Brooke, K.C.B.* 2 vols. London: Richard Bentley, 1853.

Key-Smith, Francis Scott. *Francis Scott Key.* Washington, D.C.: Key-Smith and Company, 1911.

Knijpenga, G. "Archipelago Trade in the Past," *de Uitlaat,* K.P.M. periodical, Amsterdam, Dec. 1954–Jan. 1955.

Lacroix, Capt. Louis. *L'Âge d'Or de la Voile; Clippers et Cap Horniers.* Paris: Horizons de France, 1949.

——. *Les Derniers Grand Voiliers.* Paris: J. Peyronnet et Cie., 1937.

Laing, Alexander. *American Sail, A Pictorial History.* New York: E. P. Dutton & Co., 1961.

Lane, Mrs. Julian C. *Key and Allied Families.* Macon, Georgia: Mrs. Julian Lane, 1931.

Las Vergnas, Raymond. *Joseph Conrad: romancier de l'exil.* Lyon: Éditions Emmanuel Vitte, 1959.

——. *Joseph Conrad.* Paris: Henri Didier, 1938.

Leavis, F. R. *The Great Tradition; George Eliot, Henry James, Joseph Conrad.* New York: New York University Press, 1963.

——. "Polish Master of English Prose," *Times,* London, Dec. 3, 1957.

Leeuw, Hendrik de. *Crossroads of the Java Sea.* London: Jonathan Cape, 1931.

Leonowens, Anna. *The English Governess at the Siamese Court.* New York: Roy Publishers, n.d.

Lloyd's Register of Shipping. 1875–1923.

Lohf, Kenneth A., and Sheehy, Eugene P. *Joseph Conrad at Mid-Century: Editions and Studies, 1895–1955.* Minneapolis: University of Minnesota Press, 1957.

Lorrain, Jean. *La Ville Empoisonnée.* Paris: Éditions Jean Crès, 1936.

Lovat, Lady Alice. *The Life of Sir Frederick Weld.* London: John Murray, 1914.

Lubbock, Basil. *Sail: the Romance of the Clipper Ships.* 3 vols. London: Blue Peter Publishing Co. Ltd., 1936.

——. *The Nitrate Clippers.* Glasgow: Brown, Son & Ferguson Ltd., 1932.

——. *The Colonial Clippers.* Glasgow: James Brown, 1921.

——. *The Log of the "Cutty Sark."* Glasgow: J. Brown & Sons, 1924.

McDonald, Capt. P. A. "Conrad's Ships," *Sea Breezes,* March, 1953.

Marryat, Frank S. *Borneo and the Indian Archipelago.* London: Longman, Brown, Green, and Longmans, 1848.

Melgar, el Conde de. *Veinte Años con Don Carlos, Memorias de su Secretario el Conde de Melgar.* Madrid: Espasa-Calpe, 1940.

Mencken, H. L. "Joseph Conrad," *A Book of Prefaces.* New York: A. A. Knopf, 1918.

Millican, Albert. *Travels and Adventures of an Orchid Hunter.* London: Cassell & Co. Ltd., 1891.

Minney, R. J. *Fanny and the Regent of Siam.* New York: World Publishing Company, 1962.

Moore, Charles. *A Full Inquiry into the Subject of Suicide: To which are added (as being closely connected with the subject) Two Treatises on Duelling and Gaming.* 2 vols. London, 1790.

Morf, Gustav. *The Polish Heritage of Joseph Conrad.* London: Sampson Low, Marston & Co., 1930.

Morley, Christopher. "A Word About Joseph Conrad," *The Mentor*, March, 1925.

Morris, Charles. *The Volcano's Deadly Work.* Philadelphia: W. E. Scull, 1902.

Morrison, Robert. "The Last of the *Otago*," *Blackwood's Magazine*, Nov., 1961.

Mundy, Capt. Rodney, R.N. *Narrative of Events in Borneo and Celebes down to the Occupation of Labuan from the Journals of James Brooke, Esq., Rajah of Sarawak and Governor of Labuan, together with a narrative of the operations of H.M.S. Iris.* 2 vols. London: John Murray, 1848.

Najder, Zdzislaw (ed.). *Conrad's Polish Background: Letters to and from Polish Friends.* London: Oxford University Press, 1964.

Norton-Kyshe, James William (ed.). *Straits Settlements Reports: Supreme Court.* Vol. II: Reports of Admiralty Cases. Singapore: Singapore and Straits Printing Office, 1886.

One Hundred Years of Singapore. Edited by Walter Makepeace, Dr. Gilbert E. Brooke, Roland St. J. Braddell. London: John Murray, 1921.

Pereira, Ricardo S. *Les États-Unis de Colombie.* Paris: C. Marpon et E. Flammarion, 1883.

Pérez Triana, Santiago. *Down the Orinoco in a Canoe.* With an Introduction by R. B. Cunninghame Graham. New York: Thomas Y. Crowell & Co., 1902.

Pritchett, V. S. "The Exile," *New Statesman*, Aug. 24, 1957.

———. *The Living Novel.* New York: Reynal & Hitchcock, 1947.

———. *The Living Novel & Later Appreciations.* New York: Random House, 1964.

Raleigh, Sir Walter. *The Discovery of Guiana, and the Journal of the Second Voyage thereto.* New York: The Mershon Company, 1887.

Register of the Commissioned and Warrant Officers of the Navy of the United States (1854 edition).

Renoir, Jean. *Renoir, My Father.* Boston: Little, Brown & Co., 1962.

Resink, G. J. "Tulisan dan tanda tangan Charles Olmeyer," *Medan Ilmu Pengetahuan*, No. 4. Djakarta, Java, December, 1960.

Restrepo, Vicente. *Gold and Silver Mines of Colombia.* Translated by C. W. Fisher. New York: Colombian Consulate, 1886.

Rhodes, Capt. F. *Pageant of the Pacific, Being the Maritime History of Australasia.* 2 vols. Sydney, N.S.W.: F. J. Thwaites Ltd., 1937.

Robertson, E. J. *Straits Memories.* Singapore: Methodist Publishing House, 1910.

Ross, John Dill. *Singapore and the Straits Settlements: A Descriptive Study of a British Crown Colony in the Far East.* Singapore: Kelly & Walsh Ltd., 1898.

———. *Sixty Years: Life and Adventure in the Far East.* 2 vols. London: Hutchinson, 1911.

Rothenstein, Sir William. *Men and Memories.* 2 vols. London: Faber and Faber Ltd., 1932.

Roux, Jules Charles T. *Le Cercle Artistique de Marseille.* Paris: A. Lemerre, 1906.

Russell, Bertrand. "The Free Man's Worship," *Mysticism and Logic and Other Essays.* London: Longmans, Green & Company, 1921.

———. *Portraits from Memory and Other Essays.* New York: Simon and Schuster, 1956.

Rutter, Owen. *British North Borneo.* London: Constable, 1922.

Sailing Directions for the Gulf of Mexico (1863 edition). London: James Imray & Sons.

St. John, Horace. *The Indian Archipelago: Its History and Present State.* 2 vols. London: Longman, Brown, Green, and Longmans, 1853.

St. John, Spenser. *Life in the Forests of the Far East.* 2 vols. London: Smither, Elder, 1862.

Scruggs, William L. (U. S. Minister to Colombia and Venezuela). *The Colombian and Venezuelan Republics.* Boston: Little, Brown & Co., 1900.

Service Hydrographique: Hydrographie française. Golfe du Mexique charts and maps, 1843–1888.

Shalimar (pseud. Henry, Capt. F. C.). *From the Log-Book of Memory.* Edinburgh: William Blackwood & Sons, 1950.

Shaplen, Robert. "The Imminence of a Nation," *New Yorker,* April 6, 1963.

———. "Encounters in Barrios," *New Yorker,* Sept. 28, 1963.

Sichel, Pierre. *The Jersey Lily: The Story of the Fabulous Mrs. Langtry.* New York: Prentice-Hall, 1958.

Singapore and Straits Directory. Singapore, 1883, 1888.

Skinner, Cornelia Otis. *Elegant Wits and Grand Horizontals.* Boston: Houghton Mifflin Company, 1962.

Stolzenberg, Baroness von Hutten zum. *The Courtesan: The Life of Cora Pearl.* London: Peter Davies, 1933.

Straits Settlements Blue Book. 1879, 1883, 1887.

Swinnerton, Frank. *Background with Chorus.* London: Hutchinson & Co. Ltd., 1956.

Taborski, Roman. *Apollo Korzeniowski: Ostatni Dramatopisarz Romantyczny.* Wroclaw: Zaklad Imienia Ossolinskich Wydawnictwo Polskiej Akademii Nauk, 1957.

Troup, J. Rose. *With Stanley's Rear Column.* London: Chapman and Hall, 1890.

Truman, Major Ben C. *The Field of Honor.* New York: Fords, Howard and Hulbert, 1884.

Universal Cyclopaedia, The (1900 edition). 12 vols. New York: D. Appleton & Co.

Vincent, Frank. *Around and About South America: Twenty Months of Quest and Query*. New York: D. Appleton & Co., 1890.

Wallace, Alfred Russel. *The Malay Archipelago: The Land of the Orang-Utan and the Bird of Paradise; A Narrative of Travel with Studies of Man and Nature*. New York: The Macmillan Company, 1890.

Washburne, E. B. *Recollections of a Minister to France, 1869–1877*. 2 vols. New York: Charles Scribner's Sons, 1887.

Wells, H. G. *Experiment in Autobiography; Discoveries and Conclusions of a Very Ordinary Brain (since 1866)*. New York: The Macmillan Company, 1934.

Werner, J. R. *River Life on the Congo*. Edinburgh: William Blackwood & Sons, 1889.

Weybright, Victor. *Spangled Banner: The Story of Francis Scott Key*. New York: Farrar and Rinehart, 1935.

Wheelock, John Hall. *The Gardener and Other Poems*. New York: Charles Scribner's Sons, 1964.

Who's Who in America. 1899–1900.

Williams, Frederick Benton (pseud. Hamblen, Herbert Elliot). *On Many Seas: The Life and Exploits of a Yankee Sailor*. Edited by William Stone Booth. New York: The Macmillan Company, 1897.

Wolf, Edwin II, with Fleming, John F. *Rosenbach, a Biography*, Cleveland: World Publishing Co., 1960.

Wright, Helen, and Rapport, Samuel. *The Great Explorers*. New York: Harper & Bros., 1957.

Wyndham, Horace. *Feminine Frailty*. London: Ernest Benn Ltd., 1929.

Zabel, Morton Dauwen. *Craft and Character in Modern Fiction*. New York: The Viking Press, 1957.

———. Introduction, *Joseph Conrad: Tales of the East and West*. New York: Hanover House, 1958.

INDEX